CW01645241

The Domestic
and the Foreign
in Architecture

The Domestic and the Foreign in Architecture

Edited by Sang Lee *and* Ruth Baumeister

010 Publishers, Rotterdam 2007

PAULÃO PAULÃO

ESSAYS

PHOTO ESSAYS

CONVERSATIONS

Acknowledgements

This book has been made possible by generous joint grants of the Culture 2000 program of the General Directorate for Culture and Education, the European Commission, Brussels, and The Fund for the Improvement of Postsecondary Education, the US Department of Education, Washington DC.

From its inception, the encouragement and support of Dr. Gerd Zimmermann, the Rector of the Bauhaus University Weimar, and Richard Wesley, the Chair of the Undergraduate Architecture Program, the University of Pennsylvania, have been crucial to the preparation and execution of this book. This work would not have been possible without them.

In addition, Dr. Arie Graafland, the Antoni van Leeuwenhoek Chair of Architecture Theory, and Deborah Hauptman, Associate Professor of Architecture Theory, Faculty of Architecture, at the Delft University of Technology, have provided critical advice and suggestions for the book.

Prof. Umberto Barbieri, the Chair of Architectural Composition, Faculty of Architecture, at the Delft University of Technology, has provided us with a very productive environment, generously making available to us his chair's resources.

Mary O'Toole at the School of Design, the University of Pennsylvania, Peter Benz and Birgit Röckert, both of the Bauhaus University Weimar, have overseen the administration of the grants and guided us through many logistical and administrative hurdles along the way.

Special thanks to Steffen Ahl, Heike Sinning and Christian Topp for establishing contacts and providing valuable information.

Throughout the editing process, Susan Haynes has provided much needed editorial assistance and comments on the texts. She made this book much more than what it would have been without her contribution and efforts.

Finally, but most important of all, we would like to express our sincere gratitude to all the scholars, architects and photographers who contributed their valuable knowledge and insights to this book.

Introduction by Sang Lee and Ruth Baumeister

The questions and issues regarding architecture today cover a wide portion of the general cultural debate, because architecture is an institution responsible for both the ideas and the material expressions that circulate through a society's many cultural strata. In this sense, if we consider the discussion as one of identification and representation, it includes not only the profession-specific, traditional discourse but also the distinguishing aspects of contemporary technology and economics at a global scale. In addition, architecture as a discipline contains its own system of codification of these cultural aspects, expressing them in material terms in everyday events. Within its disciplinary framework, architecture is capable of appropriating and expressing both practical and theoretical discourses. The overall theme of this book is this appropriation and expression, examined both in terms of its history and of its current state. The latter, moreover, reveals the drastic changes occurring in the cultural codification systems.

Today, the fragments of the foreign, both material and psychological, penetrate intimately into our daily lives through the mass media and free trade. Nation-states operating under various international treaties, political perspectives clash, a new imperial superstructure is emergent, and there is the supposed loss of cultural authenticity and growth of homogenization: these are some of the main criticisms set forth in contemporary debate. How does this suspicion and criticism reveal itself in architecture and urbanism? The protests against globalization, which are extremely differentiated, are raised by various NGO's, human rights organizations, religious groups, and trade unions, as well as by revolutionary or anarchist factions from left to right, some of them militant. What unifies them are their efforts to find better alternatives, though each group has its own set of priorities.

Therefore, in architecture and urbanism, too, various *ideals* – or simply "new, improved and better" notions – have frequently emerged as a popular subject of debate, and, in this respect, the entire world is seen as a work of human art. This tendency is not about architecture solely as economic production. It is in fact central to the discipline as a source of ideas concerning the material construction of the human environment, since such ideas inevitably express the way we see our world and consider how it is represented. What are the often opposing ideas of the domestic and the foreign in architectural production today, and what are their effects? How do the counter-movements critique and, at the same time, take advantage of the specific aspects of the material complexity brought on by a global economy? The discussions that follow will cite some exemplary cases regarding the appropriation of territories and provide insight into the alternative cultures, interactions and protests that have arisen in response to the *ubiquitous generic* in contemporary architecture.

Within this volatile debate, architecture occupies a peculiar position in that it is the *intersection* of the crisscrossing dimensions of not only aesthetic, scientific and cultural, but also of socio-political, economic and ideological interests and influences. As a result, urgent questions have arisen regarding the role of architecture in the representation and identification of a society's conception of its culture, specifically with regard to the balance within it of the domestic and the foreign.

We were inspired to work with these seemingly opposing notions of the domestic and the foreign by reflecting on the German expression: "heimlich (or heimelig)" and "unheimlich."[1] These contrasting notions in German represent a concept helpful in revealing various important aspects of the exchange, mix and melding of different cultures and their representation in architecture. They are derived from the stem word, "Heim," meaning home, the domesticity of one's place of origin, which also points towards the notion of "Heimat."

The word "unheimlich" literally means "unhomely," that is, something foreign, but it also incorporates the notion of the uncanny, which, in contemporary usage, serves to describe a psychological more than a material condition. Often, it is connected to the encounter of the foreign and the unknown, and therefore arouses a feeling of uncertainty and uneasiness in us. At the same time, though, "heimelig," describing the domestic conditions that define and make our home – those with which we are most acquainted and familiar and consider our own – implies both psychological and material aspects. To go even further, "heimelig" as an adjective expresses the most comfortable and secure state of being. Yet, "heimlich" is used to mean "secretly," referring to something that may be in plain sight but yet invisible.

At the beginning of the 20th century, the "Unheimliche" became a major subject of socio-philosophical and aesthetic discourse,[2] for it served to express intellectual insecurity in the face of the foreign and unknown. This was a consequence of rapid urbanization and subsequent rise of the metropolis, which not only radically changed and sometimes threatened people's built environment, but, more importantly, altered their entire way of life.

Today, in the era of globalization, we witness a similar phenomenon in the negotiation of the domestic and the foreign within architecture and our everyday life. For example, with the opening of national borders in Europe – the European Union – and the world market in trade and finance – the WTO, the IMF and The World Bank – we can observe an increasing fear that a global tide of unprecedented scale threatens to eventually overwhelm the local domestic condition. In the specific case of architecture, dialectical oppositions such as global versus local, unique versus generic, hybrid versus homogenous, etc. have dominated discourse in recent years. This volume aims to investigate the particular characteristics of the interaction of the domestic and the foreign, and the evolution of this exchange, in specific historical and theoretical contexts, and also in the practical case of material production in architecture.

While domestic narratives in architecture provide the historical context within which one – individually and collectively – can identify one's own formation, the concept of the foreign has come to offer a measure for navigation within the multifaceted, often highly contradictory, confusing and suppressed dimensions of the interactions and exchanges that take place in the process of finding and asserting one's position relative to external references. One of the most interesting examples in this respect is a Freudian interpretation[3] of the "unheimlich," because it distinguishes between the concepts as such and the way the phenomenon is actually experienced. What is most striking in this interpretation and fruitful in our analysis, however, is the claim that the "unheimlich" itself always returns to what we have long known and are most familiar with.

In architecture, by adapting this thought to the analysis of contemporary discourse about cultural exchange, we can understand the foreign that is "unheimlich" not simply as what is unknown to us and therefore causes uneasiness, but rather as what we in fact know but in a deeper, often problematic way. In our volume this notion of heimlich vs. unheimlich is dealt with in terms of the difference between the idea of one's own domesticity and its singular nature – hence, the idea of secret, stealth or the internal condition that remains opaque to the external (geheim) – and what is outside of it. In this sense, architecture has always required the effort of defining the interior (domestic, domus, domesticus, etc.) and the exterior (foreign, externus, alienus, barbaricus, etc.).

Architecture therefore can be considered not only in the construction of threshold. The discipline is in itself the mediation between the inside world and the outside one. Given this notion of architecture as such, and given the role of architecture today as a representational commodity that has become as fluid as any other form of cultural capital, it is no longer possible to consider architecture solely in terms of its traditional role of providing the interiority where one resides within its secrecy and safety. We are compelled, in addition, to investigate architecture as a means of expansion and encroachment. In the following collection of articles, architecture is no longer considered simply as the discipline devoted to the production of space. Rather, it is seen as an ideological enterprise, capable of producing and projecting memories and identities, those which used to be considered familiar and one's own. Today architecture can indeed be the hotspot of the volatile exchanges and struggles between the domestic and the foreign. Especially given recent geopolitical events, the issues of a culture's own self-image are directly connected to debates on architecture, which are highly ideological and political.

Recent architectural mobilization on a truly grand scale, as in Dubai or in vast regions in China, could be considered a conscious attempt to enhance a country's self-image and gain broader international acceptance, as well as a means of serving domestic interests. Some efforts may take the benign form of current fashion and passing novelties while others may address the urgent needs of a group's *survival.* Some may be motivated by a sincere desire to improve the well-being of the local population, while others are driven simply by the economic bottom line and political lip service. Also, some efforts may be aimed at forging a new identity, while others may end up producing a grotesque entity, which cannot by any reasonable measure be considered an advance, progress or a clarification of the ideological conflicts.

Within this general context, the articles in this volume encompass fragments of history, socio-political and economic factors, cultural aspects, and theoretical reflections, as well as personal stories. The discussions concentrate on architecture's capacity to form the environment of our daily lives and to reflect on human society and culture. Architectural space has been the primary means by which we recognize and locate ourselves both individually and collectively within time and space; and, historically, we have attempted to project *meaning* onto the structures and surfaces of architecture, thereby making our understanding of reality more concrete and tangible.

Often in our pursuit of progress and what we desire, our own self-image comes into conflict with our sense of security and the balance between the domestic and the foreign. There is a conflict between what we have, what we need and what we want, but once we attain what we want, we also develop a certain anxiety that, after all, our desire may be excessive and therefore may need to be reined in, as when industrial development endangers the environment. Specific encounters of different cultures and their ideas about architecture often modify well established categories and codes of architecture such as cultural acceptability, political and economic representation, conventions of domesticity and negotiations with what is considered foreign. Within this dynamic system of constant feedback cycles and self-adjustments, architecture links many facets of our society and succinctly expresses the steps we take in the formation of our culture, which we try to make as coherent as possible, and capable of incorporating even its failures.

We often see the future as a "project" that needs to be completed, preferably in line with the course that history will ultimately take. Because architecture is not limited to a specific *native* context of cultural ideology, economy or politics, its practice today operates beyond the conventional borders of established disciplines and classification. It is now a set of closely interconnected issues that profoundly affects all these three fields, influencing the network of states and cultures no matter where a given state may happen to be in the stages of the current political and economic development.

Responses to this expanded disciplinary framework vary widely, most notably in the conflicts arising from the orientation of such inter-contextual flows and the problematization of such issues as hegemony and dominance. When a culture views itself as being represented by images and artifacts that it considers to be foreign, then these conflicts generate questions of hegemony and autonomy, and inevitably questions about autonomy relative to outside influences take center stage. Although there will be variations depending on where one is situated according to particular native locales within these flows – consider, for example, the expansion of the British Empire or the dominance of a particular business entity such as GE or Coca Cola – it is clear that the discussions and debates will include the dynamics between the domestic and the foreign. In this sense, perhaps it is not possible to discuss architecture without considering that it is actually an ideological *camera obscura* in itself, where the projected images in the interior often dictate the way in which the mass of our lives and cultures are framed, measured and exercised relative to what may lie outside.

Since the concept of today's global architecture has no firm disciplinary anchor or privileged context, it is difficult to discuss the legitimacy of an individual architect's or firm's oeuvre vis-à-vis architecture's own history of practice and precedents.

The exemplary practices we are familiar with do not necessarily lead to discussions about their effects – in terms of their economic and technological power – beyond the new hegemonic centers in which the projects are domesticated. In addition, how the process of identification operates under this unprecedented condition within cultural industries in general, and specifically concerning the discipline of architecture itself as a material practice, is thought to be tied uniquely to a specific local context and its interests where the projects are initiated and funded. However, the mechanism that determines that very identity may be controlled by a foreign state.

Architecture in its traditional contexts has been the labor of those who dwell within a specific locale, constructing their world step by step, balancing between the past, the present and the future, as well as the inside and the outside, the domestic and the foreign. On the other hand, in order to preserve and promote its own interests, character and values a cultural entity may be compelled to incorporate the foreign into its architecture. It seems apparent that within the current context of architectural exchanges, Western popular culture has assumed the role of the alpha culture, and its manifestation on a global scale is undeniable. Therefore the perception of it as a process of transgression or domination becomes more pronounced, whether viewed as a matter or conflict or cooperation. Culture, information and media technologies, consumerism and daily life clearly all play an important role in architecture, but the relationship between them and their influence on architectural production have yet to be clearly surveyed and investigated in terms of material practice.

Considering the position of architecture in cultural industries at this new scale, what we see today are exchanges and flows in architecture that encroach upon the traditional code, which is rooted in a domestic vocabulary. Within this flux, with its explosive technological development, namely the digital infrastructure, which exerts a profound influence on our daily life, architecture has come to include dimensions that traditionally lay outside of its conventional material practice; it now includes the intangible and the fleeting within its own material practice. Especially in architecture, it is impossible to overlook the changes that have taken place in the past few decades in many areas of practice. We can cite the political and monetary federalization of Europe, for example, and various international economic treaties, such as membership in the WTO, that facilitate and encourage inter-state trade and professional standards but also create barriers. At the same time, in a more limited way, from inside out, we have experienced fundamental changes in how architecture is conceived and produced as the result of the establishment of a de-facto digital standard that is now used worldwide for the production of architecture. In essence, the adoption of globally interchangeable systems – either internal (disciplinary) or external (political and economic) – has moved architecture to the center of the cultural flux.

Concerning one aspect of the media culture, in which we can include architecture in the sense that architecture is a form of *mediation* (or interface) as described earlier, it is debatable whether or not there yet exists any entity that dominates in architecture, in the way that Hollywood movies studios do in the entertainment industry or McDonald's rules in the fast food sector. However, recent indications of urban *image-making* through architecture at a national and corporate policy level – what is now called the "Bilbao Effect" – point toward a certain standard of practice by the dominant actors. Certainly the situation is composed of various elements and there is as yet no monopoly in architecture comparable to that enjoyed by Microsoft, for example, with its globally accepted syntactic codes; but, in fact, it is evident that a small number of internationally established architectural firms in developed nations with their efficient production of knowledge and theoretical discourses wield substantial influence beyond their geographical and ideological boundaries.

If we focus on the cultural contents of the new communications media, it seems that we will eventually be able to celebrate infinite difference and differentiation.

Internet technology has already demonstrated that there can be a *forum* for participation by an infinite number of self-supporting individual voices. Or is this, instead, an indication that the proliferation of a *mass image* – if there such an entity exists – will eventually emerge, with everyone subscribing to *sameness* in the vast scheme of consumerism? Will such sameness also come to dominate architecture?

The issues involved are not necessarily limited to the realm of specific academic analyses and historiography. They include observations and reflections by individual architects who could be seen as promoting this process in varying ways that ultimately affect the core of contemporary architectural practice. Our discussions will address these problems and provide considerations at various levels. Accordingly, this volume contains informal, fragmented and anecdotal elements; for it attempts, on the one hand, to illuminate certain segments of the current debate by framing specific issues, and, on the other, to show their ambiguity, provide arguments and positions, and open up a perspective on the proliferation of certain standards specific to architecture and urbanism in terms of not only aesthetic but also of ideological issues. This approach reminds us that architecture is a cultural institution and as such, a codification process that partly determines the degree to which foreign influences are allowed to affect our domestic identity.

We begin by observing that states and cultures have tried to assert their sovereignty by establishing their authenticity in terms of history, ideology, politics and economy. Architecture is no exception in this process of establishing the *identity* of a domestic culture. It may be that throughout history architecture has been one of the most distinguishing markers for identity, and it claims to be an authentic endeavor, or in other words, a collection of traditions, cultural artifacts, and public projects that have been groomed and refined under specific domestic circumstances, incorporating the understanding of the foreign (and therefore domesticating it), but without being overrun by it. Such a process is usually cultivated through centuries of local practice.

This idea also deals with how we cope with the domestic in our everyday life and with its identity, which is constantly mutating under the influence of our contemporary conditions in accord with what we regard as the foreign. In the process of assessing the relationship between the domestic and the foreign, we must consider the issue of *representational* value, since the currency of global exchange today cannot be assessed without taking into account what is perceived as popular, beautiful and powerful. If this is the case, how do we consider similar tendencies in architecture? How does this architectural hegemony of images and representational values manifest itself and how does it formulate its agenda? Here the question of the relationship of the domestic and the foreign in architecture suggests important consequences for architecture in our world.

In this volume, the contributing authors are grouped in terms of their concentration and subject matters: The first three articles deal with the historiographic and representational aspects of architecture and its critique. In these essays, each author chooses particular instances that problematize specific issues in architecture as indicators of domesticity and demonstrates how domesticity interacts with the penetration of foreign influences. These authors cope with the issue of architectural and design products within a particular cultural and economic context in Asia. In each case, current response to a colonial past and the interpretation of that past constitute important topics. The fourth essay leads to a discussion of the problems in architecture and urbanism arising from the issues of *the cosmopolitan.*

In his article "Architectures of Global Modernity, Colonialism and Places," **Arif Dirlik**, a historian of modern China, discusses the issue of the colonial in architecture. Taking as his example the city of Shanghai in the People's Republic of China, he points out the role architecture played in colonial China and what colonial architecture has meant in general. Dirlik defines architecture as "the conquest and shaping of space and, therefore, the environment of everyday life" and subsequently identifies the discipline as a colonial activity "par excellence." By outlining some key features in the history of Shanghai's urban development, he shows how the domestic and the foreign were initially identified, negotiated and modified and, eventually, how the city was formed within this process and largely determined by colonialism.

Dirlik identifies the apparent contradiction between the specific colonial character that at first made Shanghai suspect to nationalists and communists in the early days and the present day city's status as the most successful example of China's global march and accomplishments. He concludes that colonial modernity did not erase the foreign but *rephrased* it within a new, modern context. With this proposition, Dirlik criticizes most international architecture today as based on the assumption of working with a tabula rasa, and as driven by multinational corporations with their overriding interest in the representation of their power and wealth. He characterizes this type of architecture as that of non-places, and claims it contributes to the destruction of identity, memory and significance of place that characterizes today's global modernity.

At the same time, he points out the problem inherent in defining the local versus the global and in drawing conclusions from such definitions couched in the form of opposition. Dirlik also shows that aesthetic choices are ultimately social choices, and, given the contemporary imbalance of power, he calls for building practices that accommodate both the domestic and the foreign.

On the other hand, **Gordon Mathews**, a cultural and anthropological theorist, explores various meanings of cultural identity and examines their implications for architecture. In his discussion, Mathews employs the notion of a "cultural supermarket" where all aspects of many different cultures can be identified and consumed. According to Mathews, as Western architectural forms have swept the world, and in response to the homogenization caused by the commodification of cultural elements, two seemingly opposing views emerged in architecture. One has been postmodernism's celebration of diversity, and the other has been regionalism of various types, all calling for the local affirmation of a culture's core values.

In trying to place various architectural versions of cultural identity within a broader anthropological framework, Mathews proposes an alternative view. For him, postmodern architecture caused the excesses of the "cultural supermarket," where all cultural elements are up for sale and consumption, while regionalism insisted upon a static view of cultural purity that no longer exists. Today, he asserts, there exists an opportunity to introduce an architectural process that accommodates both a sensitivity to certain cultural elements and the dynamic state of constant flux in cultural exchanges. On one hand, there is the issue of a given locale and its position within the current competition-based economic structure, and therefore the kind of hegemonic issue of "consumption" that arises in the case of a food chain. On the other hand, the urgency lies in what is consumed, how it is consumed, and at what cost.

The core of Mathews's argument for sensitivity is related to the fact that architecture as a discipline has historically served the rich and powerful, and therefore is essentially undemocratic and insensitive to the inequities inherent in such a structure. In response to this problem, he concludes with the awareness of "power differential" and resistance to certain forms of commodification in culture, and looks toward the eventual adoption of postmodernism and regionalism as common strategies to deal with the complexities in contemporary culture.

While it may be questionable to discuss colonizing forces in terms of their *contribution* relative to their atrocities, nonetheless, by citing the cases of Japanese colonial architecture in Taiwan and Korea and the criticisms of the role of the Japanese occupation over a large part of Asia, **Hajime Yatsuka**, an architect and critic based in Tokyo, shows the different discursive approaches involved in their colonial heritage and its interpretation by posterity. In reference to Antonio Negri and Michael Hardt, he claims that the potential for former colonial states to develop lies neither in their despotic past nor in the harsh present of the occupation. In other words, the best options for the progress of these nations are situated beyond their mutation toward Western societies. Furthermore, he questions how and where the references for the measure of development should be located and argues that such references and their assumptions can and will distort the essential nature of such a discussion, resulting in completely fabricated versions of stories that may end up being convenient for those who actually interpret the situation.

Yatsuka further elaborates on the contemporary reading of historical colonial architecture in Taiwan and Korea and links the issue to modernist discussions on the topic, noting that they tend to be negative because of what they see as the impurity inherent in the transgression of regional identities committed by the hegemonic states. The postmodern perspective on the phenomenon is more positive in that it generally favors the new conditions which evolved from the impurity of transnational characters.

Yatsuka describes Japan's hegemonic policy in East Asia during World War II as an attempt to replace the system dominated by Western nations with one that was ruled by the Japanese empire, which he considers to be an early endeavor to establish a localized globalism. He defines "overcoming modernity" and a "philosophy of world history" as the key topics for architects and intellectuals of that time, and he interprets them as part of an early attempt to formulate postmodernity in the context of globalism. Subsequently, the author describes the very contrasting and ambivalent reactions towards the Japanese-built structures from both architects and critics in Taiwan and Korea and cites examples of how cultural politics in these countries are critiqued in terms of the Japanese occupation.

In her article, "A Cosmopolitan View of Thinking and Being-in-Common," **Deborah Hauptmann**, focusing primarily on the co-essence of individuals, investigates the concept of cosmopolitanism, in which architecture and urbanism are dealt with in relation to the city. An underlying thread of her research is her commentary on Ulrich Beck's recent book *The Cosmopolitan Vision*. In that work, the concept of domestic within the pairing of the *foreign and domestic* is understood in the sense of "belonging to" as opposed to being "excluded from" a society or community, and not in a "stylistic" sense as it might be in architecture, or as something "native," recognizable as being from a specific place; conversely something foreign is understood as that which "comes from" elsewhere.

Hauptmann provides a brief genealogy of the notion of cosmopolitanism, touching upon Stoic philosophy, Kant, Erasmus, and, closer to home, the contemporary discourse of notable philosophers such as Derrida, Beck, Balibar and Nancy. As a point of departure she discusses the idea of contemporary cosmopolitanism both as a transnational form of life and in its relation to globalization. Furthermore, to Beck's idea of the interconnectedness of cosmopolitan society itself, Hauptmann adds the architectural and urban practices of spatial and temporal enunciations, for she claims it is a mistake to separate concrete problems of the city from abstract theories about it.

She also suggests the utility of discussing the term "agency," drawing on Balibar's definition of the term with regard to the individual and his or her identity and considers cosmopolitan individuality to be suspended within a flux of competing identities and personalities. And it is in this connection that she addresses the problematics of the distinction between the individual and the collective, ever changing in its substance and dynamics.

Hauptmann concludes with the remark that one problem with Beck's vision of cosmopolitanism is that it ultimately relies upon the self-realization of individuals to critically reformulate their own openness to the world, and, at the same time, expects them to be capable of functioning within the "new" cosmopolitan sensibility. Here, she reminds us that any exchange of ideas brings with it an exchange of power, which is inherent in the sense of "agency," as Michel Foucault has discussed extensively. Hauptman argues that we need not only new forms of research, as Beck claims, but also that we must open the discourse in two directions, taking into account both the psycho-philosophical dimension as well as the actual design of the physical environment, which is capable of hosting the conflicts, confrontations and benefits that come with such an exchange of ideas.

The next group of authors represents a different dimension in architecture in that their discussions revolve around the way architecture becomes an interpretation and reflection of the prevailing economic and political conditions. One pole of the discussion is a survey of the characteristics that helped make the Bauhaus movement celebrated worldwide. The article examines the history of the institution from its beginnings as a very small and short-lived art and design school in Germany through its development and multifaceted influence. The other pole, in terms of scope, is the essay on the theoretical and ideological aspects of globalization as an economic proposition. It provides a wide perspective showing architecture as an inherent part of the urban economy. In between the two we find the specific concept and phenomenon called "McDonaldization," a term coined in order to describe the content of socio-economic production and consumption, which is becoming increasingly hollow and "nothing" as a sociological concept. Another, more specifically local view is on the social and economic development occurring in Palestine in its sporadic times of peace under Israeli occupation and international intervention.

Fredric Jameson's essay[4] defines globalization as an intrinsic component in a new multinational stage of capitalism, which is in general associated with post-modernity. He sees the cultural and the economic in the era of globalization as mutually connected and interrelated, and further elaborates on the changes in production and labor brought about by the shift from monopoly capitalism to late capitalism, which again is paralleled by a shift from the old technology of heavy industries to the new electronic informational systems of today. Simultaneously, he understands globalization as a concept of communication which both conveys and modifies cultural or economic meanings. It brings about an enormous expansion of both global communication and markets. The consequence of acknowledging the cultural contents in this new form of communication is, for Jameson, post-modernism's rather positive contribution to the celebration of difference and differentiation.

Looking at the phenomenon from the economic point of view, however, the perspective becomes less promising, according to Jameson. We are all familiar, he argues, with the problems that are created by the forced integration of the various countries into a new and often threatening system of late capitalism, which acts entirely and exclusively on a global scale. Instead of difference this brings about unilateral standardization and forced integration into an inescapable new world system that is generating a radical change in the relationship between time, space and information, which, in turn, has necessarily and substantially altered the role of architecture and urbanism today. The former, he contends, is moving towards an aesthetic of individual creation, and the latter, towards anarchy of forces and movements.

Referring to *Modern Architecture* by Manfredo Tafuri and Frencesco Dal Co,[5] Jameson states that the main problem is the contemporary city, which is characterized by unforeseeably rapid growth, chaos and alienation. Therefore, the conventional tools of urban planning and zoning, which were conceived, developed and employed during the early modern period, prove to be no longer appropriate. Jameson considers Rem Koolhaas's concept of the "Culture of Congestion" to be the first global approach to the chaos of the contemporary city. Instead of organizing and planning, we are asked to take the opposite approach and embrace the unpredictable chaos and derive inspiration and energy from it. In the end, he concludes that we must reconfigure the problem in order to produce a new contradiction rather than try to come up with an a priori solution to an impossible contradiction, as the early modernists did.

Following Jameson's argument concerning the larger context of issues surrounding globalization today, **George Ritzer**, a sociologist and social theorist who has written influential studies on consumption, provides, in his essay, a scathing critique of today's commercial architecture through his concepts on "McDonaldization" and "nothing." Ritzer associates the process of today's commercial architecture, often global, with an accelerated development of the generic, the distinguishing feature of which is "nothingness." He argues that the vast majority of superstores, shopping malls and franchises are actually designed and built based on centralized planning and control, and are therefore "non-architecture," given his definition of architecture as the localized and unique manifestation of a specific culture.

He maintains that we are surrounded with an abundance of the nothing – including non-architecture. The result is a pervasive, subliminal sense of loss, which is not only prevalent in American society, but is also spreading to many other parts of the globe. The proliferation of nothing has provided us with convenience, but, as Ritzer points out, we are in danger of drowning in a sea of nothingness, to which the non-architecture of material consumption contributes a significant part.

Following Ritzer's discussion, **Sylvaine Bulle**, a sociologist and Middle East scholar, discusses architectural representation in Palestine in the context of regional politics. She begins her argument with the assertion that the geographical space of the "Orient" is an invention of the West and that the spatial fabric of Palestine is an example of this. Charged with historic and religious symbolism and entangled in the geo-politics of the surrounding region, it should, she argues, be investigated from a different angle.

Among the elements of the situation in Palestine, Bulle examines its architecture in light of the complex factors of internationalization, colonialism and nationalism. Subsequently, she provides an outline of the historical development of Palestine's architecture under foreign domination, as reflected in political events during the last century. According to Bulle, the influence of the intellectual urban elite and their attempt to create a modern Palestinian nation with its own identity are clearly reflected in the architectural and urban developments of this period. Choosing an example in Ramallah, in this case a café owned by young Palestinian journalists, Bulle shows how architecture, with its material, historical and psychological dimensions, is capable of contributing to a population's imaginary and identity, and how a cosmopolitan, pacifist approach, in cooperation with the international community, and thus reflecting external influence, offered an identity before local politics created a new vision of the nation.

She analyzes how, in the construction of memory, the rehabilitation and celebration of heritage successfully created a new version of patriotism in Palestine. This results from its sense of historical legitimacy, but it is also inseparable from global culture and politics. In this specific case, both architectural production and the urban fabric are actually capable of incorporating the vernacular, universal and / or regionalist aspects simultaneously, forming news zones of contact between globalization and patriotism, creating a new built environment, and projecting new images that will eventually shape the Palestinians' self-image and conception of their land.

Ruth Baumeister begins her essay with the historic case of the Bauhaus in Germany and discusses the specific characteristics that turned what was originally a rather small state school for arts and crafts into an institution that left an enduring worldwide cultural legacy. Baumeister provides a short summary of the historical role of the movement and subsequently describes the worldwide influence of the program in terms not only of its ideas and agenda but also of the production of the familiar everyday objects with which we all come in contact.

By focusing primarily on the Bauhaus's reception in the USA, she shows how its idea has been appropriated and modified in different cultural and ideological contexts. For purposes of comparison, she also cites a lesser known example of the Bauhaus's historical transmutations, namely the *Imaginist Bauhaus,* initiated during the early 1950's by the Danish painter Asger Jorn. This example helps us to better understand and address contemporary issues of culture, such as copyright, authenticity and the cult of the star in global commodification, which we all have to face in our everyday life and practice.

The last group of four essays explores theoretical views and speculations on specific issues in architecture, its methods and its relationship to the city. These essays offer observations on contemporary architecture as fabrication (making and manufacturing) and as a form of legitimization. The first one in this group analyzes representational qualities in certain cases in the US and shows how such representations are eventually embedded in the perception of realities, and are often considered to be more authentic. Taking a wider view is a discussion on the relationship between architecture and urbanity as that between the scenarios and parameters with which architects and urbanists work. In contrast, the third essay is a reflection on the mechanism of architectural production and how it can be viewed as a process of eliminating and managing noise – undesirable elements – analogous to the case in the music and recording industry. In this essay the systematic and mechanized processes pose a serious question: will their power to "sanitize" be translated into the suppression of dissent and differences. Meanwhile, the fourth in the group presents a detailed study of a specific form of communication – in this case the telephone call centers and internet cafes in Rotterdam in the Netherlands – and its spatial and, therefore, sensory influence on the user groups and their reading of the city. He cites the case of a specific minority population to which these call centers and internet cafes cater, and uses his findings to discuss the urban street space.

In contrast to the usual positions concerning the identification and maintenance of what is considered to be domestic, **Nezar AlSayyad** presents a different perspective on the "manufacture" of traditions and identity. AlSayyad asserts that, "The 20th century may have been the first century to ever witness the rise of environments that are wholly devoted to the *other*." This is his point of departure for a discussion of the role of architecture in the definition of heritage and its role in what he calls the end of tradition in the contemporary era of globalization. By describing examples of cultural heritage and the preservation of memory in architecture, AlSayyad reveals how nations and communities, by selecting and representing the relevant information for the rewriting of their own history, have developed their own self-definition and, thus, invented their own tradition.

Citing manufactured dreamscapes such as Las Vegas and Disneyland, he explains how heritage sites are exploited by being used beyond the legitimate claim to their authentic past, and therefore create a new, fabricated vernacular which has the capacity to completely insert itself into our contemporary daily lives. AlSayyad concludes that while we have reached the end of tradition as a static concept of the past, tradition can still serve as a compass for a dynamic interpretation of the present.

In their essay, **Aldo Aymonino** and **Valerio Paolo Mosco**, who are both practicing architects and scholars, offer an analysis of architecture and urbanism rooted in their notion of "non-volumetric" architecture. Their discussion starts with a claim that architecture must be capable of transcending the single building and, simultaneously, be able to emerge from, inform and reflect the city and its surrounding territory. In current practice, though, the authors argue, city and territory are completely detached from and indifferent to each other. By describing models within the contemporary urban condition, such as the territory-city, the city-territory and the consolidated city, their analysis attempts to discover the parameters that are important today for the development of new urban scenarios. Looking at large urban projects, such as the reconstruction of Berlin after 1989, and various historical preservation efforts in Italian cities, and also at contemporary practice that attempts to follow the context laid out by such reconstruction or preservation, they discover certain key conditions that they think are responsible for the development of the urban fabric. The central question for them is whether or not our cities today can be flexible enough to embrace and shape the architecture they call for. The key to this question, according to the authors, lies in the infrastructures, which they view as the determining element of a contemporary city. They suggest that the "aesthetic design" of infrastructures is an essential area for further investigation and treatment.

In contrast to Aymonino and Mosco, **Sang Lee** speculates on architecture and its production as a codification system of a specific type that is designed and utilized in order to minimize uncertainties and undesired effects. His position centers on the fact that a work of architecture is essentially laid out in a representational form, and he discusses this form in terms of drawings, specification and models of buildings to be constructed in the future. Therefore the system of representation imposes a codifying structure which is, in essence, a product of a specific domestic condition. Lee compares this to processes found in music, especially its reproduced form, which is meant to be disseminated, observing that contemporary digital technology enables architects to work in a manner similar to music producers and editors.

Setting his discussion within the overall framework of mechanization, he observes that CD's or digital files are the primary means of experiencing music today, which is more frequently heard in its reproduced form than in actual performance in real time. Further, he hypothesizes that one could develop a process of architectural production in which the process of "sampling" would be effectively used in order to capture various and even conflicting elements of today's social and cultural flux, which is simultaneously domestic and foreign.

Diego Barajas's article starts with a multi-faceted investigation of the "belhuis[6] phenomenon" in Rotterdam. He aims to identify the parameters that define the relation of architecture to an emerging *imaginary* in a given context. In describing the belhuis, he illustrates an important component of the daily urban practice of a transnational migrant community, and he discusses how spatial experience can contribute to the constant process of reflecting and transforming each individual's identity. The author introduces the notion of "New Globalized Bodies" to characterize people who are constantly exposed to the contrast between the homogenous and the differentiated, and who are neither linked to any given geographical location nor defined by any territorial structure. With the case of a call center in the heart of Rotterdam, run by a Pakistani and mainly catering to Cape Verdean immigrants, Barajas describes how the transformation of the domestic and the foreign manifests itself in a given location.

For Barajas, the belhuis becomes heterotopic, disconnected from the surrounding urban context, which serves as an interface between "here" and "there." Apart from its presence in time and space, Barajas describes how the belhuis contributes to the creation of the mental imaginary of its users. This reveals how differently from the overall population a minority can manifest itself in space, and therefore how it contributes to the reading of a city on the "glocal" level, by making use of the most up-to-date communications technologies. Within this context, he further explores the occurrence of dispersion not only as a material and spatial but also as a mental and social condition. Arguing that dispersion is activated mainly by fiction, he focuses on the architectural techniques used to create artificial de- and re-territorialization. Barajas concludes with the question of whether or not we can conceive of any alternatives to the fabricated models of today's establishment, such as the elements of the Disney empire.

Interspersed between the texts are photo essays presenting the images of a wide range of localities and their particular domestic qualities. Each set of photographs, as an intimate and personal interpretation of the topic by the photographer, concentrates on a specific theme or caricature in which she or he reveals the artifacts that make up our environment. In the first set, we witness the intensification and concentration of voyeuristic tendencies and their effects through photographs by **Jordi Bernadó** and **Stefanie Bürkle**.

In Bernado's case, the environment we live in today, seemingly detached from its actual material context, is turned inside out, depending on the economic purpose and the scale involved. In one instance, we see a once residential street in Detroit now turned into a complex of burnt down, crumbling houses, reflecting the violence and decay accompanying the decline of the Motor City USA, while another photo in his series, a giant blue superhero figure, proudly occupies a rooftop in Tenerife, which reflects the transformation of the Spanish island into a playground for leisure and consumption. His photographs seek to represent the effects of rampant economic development and its impact on the environment, turning it into a place of harsh pleasure where the line between the comic and the tragic is blurred. Bernado, a photographer based in Barcelona, has for many years pursued images around the world that became snapshots of globalization under such headlines of "Good News" and "Very, Very Bad News."[7] In these series, he documented the scenes of landscapes and urban environments, which represent a distinctive anonymity, the prevalent generic way we live today, where objects convey, simultaneously, familiarity and alienation.

The subject of Bürkle's photographs is an amusement park in Shenzen, China, where some of the best known architectural monuments of the world are assembled in one convenient location and reduced to one-fifth scale. Here one can experience the world's architectural monuments by proxy. For Bürkle, Shenzen's amusement park is an explicit example of an architectural icon born in a specific cultural context that has turned into an abstract and superficial notion of progress. The models this park presents, within the context of China, overtly express the desire to possess and appropriate the architectural elements of world prominence. One is reminded of a taxidermist's collection of rare prized animals.

In both photographers, we see intimate critiques of the relationship between ourselves and our architectural environments, which are increasingly in conflict with the homogenous generic superstructure of the global economic and political flows.

On the other hand, we also see the remnants of the decaying architecture and environments of the past documented by **Winny Dijkstra** and **Margit Bosch**. Both photographers show us the passages in time and space in which the blend of domestic and the foreign is indeed a dynamic one, with the new sometimes interfering with the old or replacing it; and, at certain other times, we find violent intervention in the form of revision and incorporation. These two series of photographs also show how such hybrid and impure conditions convey the contemporary version of authenticity. The idea of locality and its authenticity is no longer manifested in a series of static objects but rather in the ways in which such objects are incorporated into a culture and express their life over time.

Winny Dijkstra, a photographer and psychologist based in Amsterdam, presents a decaying residential complex called Aoyama Doujunkai in Tokyo. The Aoyama Doujunkai apartments were completed in 1927 in Tokyo's Aoyama district close to the Meiji shrine, during the period of the country's rapid industrialization. They are contemporary with the Imperial Hotel designed by Frank Lloyd Wright in 1923, perhaps the most distinguished building by a foreign architect in Japan at the time. The apartment complex, one of the city's first examples of modern architecture, is part of the modernization initiatives that have resulted in the vast sprawl of modern architecture in Tokyo. Consisting of nine buildings, each three stories high, with one hundred thirty-eight apartments in total, the complex was originally built for families. The rooftop with bath facilities was surrounded by relatively high walls blocking the view down to the shrine, as a precaution for the occasions when the Emperor was on his way or nearby. One was not supposed to look down on the emperor. Today the complex has been demolished, the victim of Tokyo's voracious appetite for new architecture and of its fierce real estate speculation; it is replaced by a shopping mall combined with expensive apartments designed by Tadao Ando.[8]

The next series, photographed by Margit Bosch, an architect based in Berlin, is of a cemetery in Hue, Vietnam, also known as Thua Thien Hue, which was the capital of 17th century Vietnam, founded by the Nguyen Dynasty. The city was also a fierce battle ground during the US-Vietnam war and was severely damaged during weeks of fighting in 1968. These photographs show a sublime cultural mixture at the cemetery, where the tombs attest to an eclectic necropolis, the home of not only the living and the dead but also of the domestic and the foreign. Here we see not only the wishes of the living for the dead in the eternal reincarnation (or ascension) but also of those who believed in saints far removed in space and time; the lives of those who once lived in Hue are now simply accompanied by memorials to the Christian saints who were once the symbols of rampant European conquests not only in this but also in many other regions of the world.

The next two sets of photographs, by **Varakan Tipparapa** and **Josef S. Green**, show the reverse condition, in which the photographer is the hybrid element. The photographers simply present the elements of their personal experience – rather than pursue a specific subject matter – and themselves traverse a path between the domestic and the foreign. In their view, these conditions are interchangeable. Both photographers show elements of complex individual identity composed of collected memories from diverse sources.

Tipparapa's world is made up of his negotiations among his profession as an architect and photographer, his origin by birth, in Bangkok, Thailand, and his adopted home of Chicago. For him, the constant negotiation between his notion of the domestic and the foreign expresses a state in which he isn't necessarily compelled to make such a distinction or choice. While the architecture of his adopted home is central to his work and daily life, his memory of Bangkok occupies an important place in his own self-image. Yet, both together represent a visual critique of the often harsh living conditions caused by the process of globalization.

The photographs, by Josef S. Green, a photographer whose areas of investigation cover many parts of Eastern Europe and the US, come from his daytrip from Tucson, Arizona to Nogales, Mexico. This stretch of interstate highway with its ever-changing scenery – from a typical old adobe house interior in Tucson, to an old Spanish mission of San Xavier del Bac, to a sacred mountain range of the Tohono O'odham Nation, to the heavily patrolled border crossing that resembles a turnstile entrance to a subway, and finally into the Mexico-Arizona border town of Nogales – is one of the areas involved in the current debate in the US over illegal immigration.

In this area, while some local residents on the US side have organized their own armed "defense" against the illegal border crossings, others have set up water and food stations to help those who cross into the US from Mexico. According to a local newspaper in Tucson,[9] during the fiscal year 2005–2006 as many as one hundred ninety-eight people died of exhaustion and dehydration during their journey into the US along this desert route. In this case, the photographs are charged with the underlying struggle between those who pursue better opportunities in a foreign land and those locals who believe their interests are under threat.

The second part of the book consists of interviews and conversations with practicing architects with many international projects to their credit and who display sensitivity to multicultural issues. Among them, Robert Venturi, Denise Scott Brown, Arata Isozaki and Rem Koolhaas have exerted a profound influence on architectural discourse and practice in general, while Cecil Balmond, in the course of his work for many prominent projects, has been a key figure in shaping fundamental new thinking concerning the role of structure. The work of these architects has, in varying degrees, determined the direction of architectural debate since the 1960's, and it has confronted, at different levels, the theme of this book.

Ettore Sottsass, whose work as both an architect and a designer has spanned, for many decades, a wide spectrum of design practice from small, everyday objects to architectural projects for private and corporate clients. In industrial design, specifically, we can easily identify him with many of the seminal projects of the post-World War II period. On the other hand, even though David Chipperfield, Paolo Desideri and Fred Schwartz may not be widely considered in the vanguard of the architecture scene today, it is not very difficult to recognize that their practice consists of a complex and delicate balance between what they consider to be their own domestic identity and the foreign element in their projects.

Within the life span of the architects presented here, the scope of the profession has expanded not only in programmatic, technical and conceptual complexity but also, more than ever, in terms of what this discipline represents within a particular place or context. Therefore the prominence of such potential clashes – between the will of the *domestic* and that of an architect in such a context, the *foreign* – is the focal point of discussion surrounding the contemporary, international practice of architecture.

The conversations address projects and working methods of the architects and how their practices have emphasized the notion of architecture within the current cultural and political debate. They assess the state of their practices within the structure of the global economy and the policy decisions of the cultural and national contexts in the countries they have worked and provide *experience and observations*, often presented in a spontaneous, informal and intuitive manner.

What we have tried here is not to provide a balanced representation of various cases from different continents but rather to identify specific architects and their positions within the profession. Each individual focuses on his or her interests and discusses aspects of his or her own practice. Therefore they represent specific *cases* rather than serve as models of the profession.

Robert Venturi and **Denise Scott Brown** maintain that architecture is *representation* and propose the notion "Form accommodates function." In this statement, the most important aspect is the separation between the functional requirements that a building must satisfy and its aesthetic expression as an interface and medium for communication in the form of signs. This idea is at the same time closely linked to the consideration of functionality as "convention," which again implies the historical accumulation of knowledge of how architectural practice has evolved over the centuries.

They also connect this with issues concerning the opposition between the universal and the local, maintaining that today both aspects should be acknowledged and work together. At the same time, along with the idea of "accommodation," they argue for complexity in the patterns of movements and activities buildings should engender and support, and they hold that urban and architectural planning should create a sense of community.

In this regard, they argue that within prevailing urban development *evolution* and *re-evaluation* are preferable. This position leads to the conclusion that architecture and urbanism should be practiced *pragmatically* rather than imposed ideologically. The alternative they propose is that the universal lies in the form, which should be recessive, and that the local should be aggressively expressed through surface ornamentation using the appropriate iconography.

Therefore architecture should be seen as existing in the highly complex and often "contradictory" flux encompassing urban contexts and aesthetic expression as messages and communication. With this approach, they provide the moral ground for insisting that architecture should exceed the narrow definitions of a given period's necessities.

Arata Isozaki, who considers himself a citizen of the world with a Japanese passport, starts his conversation with Jörg Gleiter by reflecting on his personal experience. Educated in the 1950's, he was strongly influenced by the classical modernist tradition: factors such as program, function and technology were the determining parameters of design. As a critique of and in response to the dogmatic perspective in modernist architecture at that time, Isozaki's generation turned to semiotics in architecture in order to express meaning in architectural form. Retrospectively, Isozaki describes this move as a shift from the rather generalized modernist concept towards sensitivity to cultural specificity.

Within the theme of the domestic and the foreign, he elaborates on the example of the introduction of modernist ideas into the Japanese building tradition starting in the early 20th century and continuing to the present. He proposes, as an alternative, the concept of a common archive, which should be accessible to anyone anytime.

Architectural heritage is not, he thinks, categorized by style, vernacular traditions, etc.; he suggests, instead, treating it as text, meaning that images and forms could eventually be disconnected from their original contexts and implanted into new ones, leading to new expressions. He claims that this method of citation, which constitutes an important part of his work, is inherently critical of the architectural process. Later in his conversation, he goes so far as to state that identity in architecture today can only be achieved through a critical process.

Citing his project for the Florence train station, Isozaki describes how the introduction of digital technology in his firm altered the design process and the optimization of the final product. He then turns to the space and time driven culture in architecture of the late 19th and the 20th century and describes the contemporary situation as undergoing yet another drastic shift, noting the introduction of digital technologies in architecture. On the conceptual level, he observes that the image now occupies a more important part of practice than ever before. Furthermore, Isozaki states that universal technology and individual bodily experience mark two contrasting categories of today's digital age. Therefore, his own interests as an architect lie in the capability of the human body to act as a mediator relative to digital technology. The drastic changes brought about by the introduction of technology constitute, for Isozaki, a fundamental paradigm shift in architecture. He concludes that we have lost the solid foundations of the last five centuries of architectural practice, but he reminds us that many great periods in history began when the solid foundations were lost.

Paolo Desideri's position can be best described as an Italian one, or more precisely, as a *Roman* perspective on the world architecture today. He starts with an explanation of the experience of an "Italian Space," which he considers the authentic resource of his own culture, and goes on to show how this conception is understood and practically applied in his work for a housing area in Tianjin, China.

In more general terms, he reflects on the development of architecture in Italy in the second half of the 20th century, emphatically exclaiming, "Italy is a problem!" The major reason for this he sees in the irreconcilable split between the semantic depth of architectural drawings and the resulting built product, to which, in general, the architect's contribution is primarily a representational one, with little physical and material involvement. Between the 1970's and 1990's, according to him, this led to an unparalleled major and, indeed, illegal transformation of territory in Italy. As a result, with the exception of very few Italian architects, Italy plays no significant role on the global market. And even in Italy most of the major prestigious contemporary building projects are awarded to foreign architects. In order to change this situation, Desideri calls for a reform of the educational system as well as of the way projects are administrated. For the future, he pleads for the local and hopes that "the Italian way" in architecture will be recognizable again, thanks to the efforts of several firms which originated in Italy but participate in the international market at the same time.

Like Desideri, **Fred Schwartz** maintains a practice deeply rooted in his "hometown," New York, but focuses his discussion on the international aspects of his work. Even though New York is a truly global metropolis, he finds his opportunities are limited, but, at the same time, they enable him to put his practice in perspective. A key element in his firm is that it can contain works that differ greatly in scale. In this respect, finding venues for public engagement plays a crucial role in his practice.

Schwartz describes his efforts to form a collaborative environment with other architects in order not only to be able to compete for large public projects but also to facilitate the exchange of ideas and learning. He states that in New York City, especially, the role of architecture is, by and large, regarded as a part of real estate speculation, and he thinks this situation is fundamentally responsible for most of the anonymous "terrible" buildings in the city. He mentions his recent competition project in Shanghai, where he found his collaborative approach with his Chinese counterparts to be very productive. Understanding the domestic Chinese conditions was crucial, he says; and the only viable approach toward such understanding, he maintains, is exchanging ideas with and learning from his Chinese colleagues about the culture and practice of architecture in China. He also observes that China is now turning toward its domestic talents and dropping its past emphasis on hiring star architects from outside of China.

He is concerned about the role of architects in the larger context of urban development and about how often large projects are monopolized by a handful of large, established firms. He also observes the role of politics in the conception and administration of large urban projects, which are often carried out in a way that runs counter to the best interests of the city and its citizens. Schwartz cites the opportunities for competitions and notes that the competition process tends to favor the established firms or those with certain political ties. In New York, he finds that the overall system is designed and implemented to favor those firms with an established track record, prior experience, political connections and influence, as exemplified by Philip Johnson.

The conversation with **David Chipperfield** starts out with a description of the advantages and disadvantages of running an international architectural practice. Chipperfield describes the practical implications of working and building in different countries and cultures, and he elaborates on his office structure and on cooperation with local firms and authorities. As a British architect whose first large-scale commissions originated in Japan – a totally foreign context as he himself calls it – Chipperfield reveals a certain *positive* indecisiveness about the distinction between the domestic and the foreign.

He appreciates difference and complexity in a culture and tries to explore a foreign country as much as he can. Interestingly, rather than employing certain specific principles and standards in his design method, Chipperfield suggests an exploration of various cultural elements to serve as the major source of inspiration. He weighs the significance of each individual decision in the design process, always with a view towards the importance of a given cultural and material context. For example, he thinks that his own design language and his choice of structure and material are more important than the intellectual notion of a certain regionalism.

He considers the architect to be the person who provides a value to a given situation and makes it more meaningful. According to him, one of the major tasks of the architect, even now, is to create frames for the rituals of daily life. This is one of the major lessons he learned by observing life and culture in Japan.

"Structure *is* Architecture." That is how **Cecil Balmond** describes his conception of the relationship between the two. Referring to his recent projects, he discusses how he communicates with architects during the design phase through diagrams and subsequently elaborates on the structural performance of a building and on the configuration of various structural systems within a building. For Balmond, the critical aspect of architecture lies in geometry and its configuration; he now considers this central to the contemporary state of the discipline. He also remarks on the role of Euclidean and Non-Euclidean geometries, ornaments and symmetry. The rejection of boundaries – practical as much as conceptual – is very important to him, and it leads to his criticism of the modernist movement, which he considers to be largely a celebration of purity.

In his view, the failure of modernism can be identified by its efforts to strip architecture of its richness and textural qualities, restricting its conception and designs within very narrow boundaries. In reaction to this, he advocates the concept of *techne,* identifying it as an indivisible synthesis of architecture and engineering. Based on this view he proposes to "resurrect" geometry in architecture, including symmetry, which has become simply a "residue." Furthermore, he elaborates on the shift from managerial and hierarchical architecture toward an *informal* one. Informal architecture, Balmond argues, essentially represents a non-linear organization in which the seemingly chaotic, unstable medium leads to coherence and equilibrium; and by understanding this, architecture can again become dynamic and vibrant.

He also describes his experience of working for and changing Arup, a firm that solidly established the term "high-tech" architecture, and one which has branches and projects all over the world. He touches on what it means in practical terms to build in various cultural contexts. Finally, he stresses the importance of research in architecture and his own desire to engage in it.

For **Ettore Sottsass**, traveling as a means of investigation, learning and inspiration was an important factor in his becoming and being an architect and designer. His first trip to India in the 1950's was motivated by his search for a new way of life different from the one he had lived in the "Old World," because that was a life that had brought about war and destruction. This venturing into unknown cultures later became a common practice for the hippie generation in the 1960's and 1970's, in their search spiritual and bodily renewal. Sottsass vividly describes how the experience of Indian culture influenced his conception of architecture, which at this time was shaped by his rationalist education.

He elaborates on his working experience in various parts of the world and also points out the impenetrable barriers that sometimes exist between people from different cultural backgrounds. Sottsass proves to be not only an enthusiastic admirer of cultural difference; he also articulates a well-focused critique, for example, with respect to the worldwide infatuation with American pop culture. Furthermore, he relates that his first trip to the US, in 1951, allowed him to experience the all-pervasiveness of an industrial culture, and that, as a result, upon his return to Italy he completely revolutionized his way of thinking about making products.

Sottsass finally reveals that his thoughts and works are always centered on human life. He points out that this focus is what, apart from aesthetic quality, made his products so popular not only with a small intellectual circle but also with a mass audience, especially in the case of his work of the Memphis period. His theoretical writings, as well as his work as an artist and photographer, reveal his appreciation of cultural difference and his playful desire to mix, match and meld.

Rem Koolhaas starts his discussion by characterizing his work as an attempt to navigate within the given conditions of a culture and its local architecture, and to allow them to influence his projects, so that difference is generated by the encounter with that culture. He maintains that those conditions can often change, and that a close investigation must be conducted to determine what the new conditions are. He holds that the local conditions are still the driving force for architectural projects and must be carefully examined and incorporated into the process. On the global stage, he argues, local elements remain strong and resistant and it is necessary to examine how the two factors can work together. Subsequently, one can be both open to the local influence and at the same time critical of it.

Koolhaas calls for awareness of the local context and the will to operate in the field, where conditions are never pure, and he notes that ideas emerge only in discussions – with engineers, designers, anthropologists and those from other cultural domains, depending on the case. He insists that the process is never a purely architectural one; indeed, the idea of impurity is a very important part of his practice. At the same time, he discusses his efforts to produce, in every case, a narrative of the project, since that is equally important. The narratives describe how the projects are measured and explored in terms of all the relevant issues. A key element in this process is the theoretical assessment of those conditions that have changed in response to the market economy and to the way the project is financed.

This volume presents a complex scenario of the historical, socio-political and cultural conditions affecting the domestic and the foreign in architecture. The interaction between these two elements is considered here as generating both identification and representation, the issues which architects are not only exposed to but are also required to cope with in their practice. In the various articles, conversations and photo essays, we did not seek to impose any unassailable principles designed to provide a framework for the arguments and discussions. Instead, working with curiosity and patience, we tried to offer a multitude of views on this general topic, which we understand as possessing a psychological as well as a material dimension. At first sight, this approach might seem to blur the vision of the materials, especially given the shifting foci and stuttering trails of after-images that represent our new time and space. But, with this compilation we wanted, even at the risk of some possible misunderstandings, to challenge and investigate established notions in order to obtain better insight into the critical issues of the topic. These issues are often related on a horizontal rather than a vertical scale. The contents of this volume have not been developed along a linear, consecutive path, because the subject matter could not be usefully treated in that manner. We encourage our readers, to employ this book as a map to be creatively applied as they attempt to orient themselves in the present, highly dynamic, and therefore seemingly risky state of the field.

ESSAYS

Architecture of Global Modernity, Colonialism and Places

Arif Dirlik

My interest in this discussion is in the issue of the colonial in architecture, first in the halcyon days of colonialism before World War II, and now, under the regime of globalization. The part architecture played in colonialism, and what colonial architecture has meant for architecture, is not something that discussions of architecture take up very often, at least not in any sustained and serious way.[1] The omission is surprising, as architecture may be a colonial activity par excellence; it is difficult to conceive of any human activity that equals it in the conquest and shaping of space and, therefore, the environment of everyday life.

If we understand colonialism in a more restricted sense as the conquest of one society by another, we can say that architecture has been significant both materially and symbolically in the reshaping of inherited living environments globally in what we ordinarily conceive as modernity. Colonial architecture, in negotiating cultural differences, anticipated some of the developments since the 1970's that have been associated with postmodernism-historicism and also with contextualism. The "cultural turn," which has left its mark on all the disciplines since the 1980's, has infused discussions of both theory and practice in architecture as well, especially since success in the architectural marketplace increasingly has demanded sensitivity to cultural difference. The "cultural turn," however, may represent only a belated recognition of an issue that had a long history in colonial politics, including the politics of colonial architecture. The issue of globalization in architecture is incomprehensible without reference to the legacies of colonialism, of which globalization may be viewed at once as a negation and a fulfillment.

The city of Shanghai in the People's Republic of China provides an almost ideal location for looking into the relationship between colonialism and globalization. The city is a product of colonialism, which rendered it suspect to nationalists and Communists of an earlier day but now qualifies it to lead the PRC on its global march. The physical make-up itself of Shanghai demonstrates this relationship. There is a wide-angle photograph of present-day Shanghai that shows both banks of the Huangpu River, historically the eastern edge of the city, but now an artery running through its center since Pudong ("East of the Pu") has been incorporated to enlarge what had been Shanghai proper, Puxi ("West of the Pu"). On the western bank is the famous Bund, the symbol of colonial Shanghai and, for all practical purposes, the symbol of Shanghai etched on the minds of many, with its neo-classical, neo-Gothic and art deco buildings dating back to the 1920's. On the eastern bank, Lujiazui adjoining the banks of the river is the center of Shanghai's claim to global status; there lies the new financial district with its (in)famous Oriental Pearl TV Tower (468 meters), and the skyscrapers built over the last decade, with the tallest (so far), the Jin Mao Tower, standing at 421 meters. Lujiazui looks down on the buildings of the Bund, which already is dwarfed by buildings to its west. Only two decades ago, Pudong was a rural area closed to foreigners, where my wife (a fellow scholar of China) and I ventured surreptitiously to look for an old Buddhist Monastery that had served as a base in 1910–1911 for local women rebelling against the Qing Dynasty (1644–1911), at least partly because of modernizing reforms that brought about increased government intervention in their lives and greater exploitation by the local elite upon whom the government depended for the execution of the reforms.[2] The relationship of Shanghai to its former rural neighbors has been reversed. Now the skyscrapers of Lujiazui seem poised to take over the very buildings that, in symbolizing the "meeting of the East and the West," legitimize Shanghai's candidacy as a global city, "the dragon-head" that will take the Yangtze River region, and the rest of China, on its long voyage to globality. And indeed, the buildings of the Bund, symbols of Shanghai history and identity supposedly protected by historic preservation laws, are in the process of being converted into business and entertainment centers in keeping with the aspirations to globality and the voracious appetites of foreign entrepreneurs who have descended upon Shanghai as the new location for hyper-development.[3]

Lujiazui may be viewed as a vanguard location in China's globalization. It also appears, in the turn the Huangpu takes at this point where it commands the convex bank opposite the Bund on the concave bank of the river, as a launching pad (among other possible metaphors) against the interior of China.The global Lujiazui, built mostly by global architectural firms from abroad, is in the process of taking over the Bund.[4] Shanghai provides the site. In fact, Shanghai may be metonymic of the PRC as a whole; which appears increasingly as a laboratory – if not a playground – for globalization. The difference from earlier days lies in those who issue the invitations. It would be impossible to grasp the dynamics of Shanghai, architecturally or otherwise, without bringing into the picture collaboration between the "socialist" state and global capital as the driving force of China's globalization.

It is a national leadership with claims to socialism that promotes Shanghai's globalization, but the globality thus created seems even more divorced from its environment than the architecture of colonial days. Colonial and globalized architecture share one thing in common: their references lay outside their immediate locales. But it appears from a present perspective that colonial architecture felt some obligation, if only for political reasons, to legitimize itself by answering localized esthetics.[5] This is a concern for global architectures as well, as globalization also has raised the question of the local. But the local here is highly problematic, as global architectural practices (actualized in global architectural firms that are themselves transnational corporations of sorts) seem to derive their esthetic legitimation not from some commitment to the local but from their ability to represent global capitalism, and the consumer clientele it is in the process of creating. The local itself is commodified, in a dialogue not between the global and the local but between the global and the global talking about the local. That dialogue is now blessed by a national leadership committed to goals of globalization, a leadership that is much better at suppressing local opposition to globalization than the Qing government was back in 1910. Ironic as it may seem, the answer to this marginalization of the local may lie in the politics of a nationalism that distinguishes the present from the late Qing.

In 1902, when the Qing imperial government decided to send a full-fledged exhibit to the Louisiana Purchase Exhibition held in St. Louis in 1904, the architects chosen to design the Chinese pavilion (a replica of the palace in Beijing of the imperial representative to the Exhibition, Prince Pu Lun) were Atkinson and Dallas in Shanghai. According to the *World's Fair Bulletin*, they were Englishmen who went to China years before to practice civil engineering and architecture,[6] and their long experience in China qualified them to design an authentic Chinese pavilion. A few years later, in 1910, Atkinson and Dallas would be selected to design – this time within China itself – the first Chinese Exposition held in Nanjing, with buildings that were even more strongly Chinese in character.

The actual building of the pavilion in 1904 would be in the hands of St. Louis contractors, Lange & Bergstrom, who had extensive experience in exhibition design and construction.[7] The intricate wood-work that would mark the building as authentically Chinese, however, was to be completed by imperial craftsmen sent from China, who were to present a real problem, as Chinese laborers were barred from the United States under the Chinese Exclusion laws, passed in 1882 and renewed just before the arrival of the Qing contingent to the Fair in 1903. The craftsmen in the end did their job, but discrimination against them considerably cooled down Qing enthusiasm about the Fair, and the following year the Qing government refused to participate at all.

One immediate reading would underline the division of labor between design, building and decoration. But even the most narrowly professional architects would probably not stop at the technical aspects of such a division of labor, and ignore the relationships it entailed; for these cut across multiple national and cultural boundaries, and were influential not only for architectural practice but in the production of architectural form. The episode, moreover, points to the entanglement of architecture in multi-layered relationships of power: professional power relations between designers and builders, but, more significantly, relations constructed out of cultural difference, colonialism and transnationalism, as well as class and race.

Technically speaking, China at the end of the Qing was not a colony, even though it did have colonial enclaves such as the International Settlement and the French Concession in Shanghai that were home to firms like Atkinson and Dallas. In all likelihood, Atkinson and Dallas was chosen for the task by the Chinese Customs Service, which was effectively in charge of the substance of the Chinese Exhibition in St. Louis and which had been under foreign directorship ever since its establishment in 1854.[8] There were, moreover, no Chinese architects in 1904. Architecture, having emerged as a professional practice in Europe and the United States only in the mid-19th century, was a foreign import in China as elsewhere in the Third World, and the first professional Chinese architects were not trained until the 1920's.[9] Until then sophisticated native buildings were constructed by craftsmen; but they would have been unacceptable to the Fair organizers in St. Louis, given their fetishism of modernity and its technologies, which considered traditional craftsmen to be mere laborers, as witnessed by the harassment to which they were subjected when they were brought over to do the work of ornamentation that was crucial to the "Chineseness" of the Chinese pavilion.

The creation of a Chinese architecture, not surprisingly, has been of great importance to nationalists. Yet, architectural theory and history in China were imports. When Atkinson and Dallas were given the job of designing a Chinese pavilion, all they had to go on was the architecture around them, especially the privileged case of imperial architecture, which disguised the complexity of architectural traditions within China. It was the stimulus provided by political calls for Chineseness, in fact, that led to the historical investigation of architecture in China, which was to reveal the diversity of architectural traditions and, therefore, the impossibility of defining a Chinese architecture.[10] It was also the colonial desire to be domesticated in China, and, therefore, to become more acceptable to the population for the purposes of its eventual transformation, that played a seminal part in the creation of a Chinese style. Modern Chinese architecture is dominated by styles that owe little to their national location, styles created by colonialism in its efforts at domestication (especially evident in university campuses, with its hybridized pretension to Chineseness, marked most conspicuously by the curves added to their roofs), and rediscovered architectures from the past which defy any idea of Chineseness in their regional diversity. Already, even before there was such an idea, this architecture, which was a product of colonialism, presupposed globality both in the practices and organization of architectural firms, and in the inspiration it drew upon; it also presupposed a clear hierarchy of power as well as of architectural form.[11] The author of a recent history of Chinese architecture characterizes the Haipai (Shanghai group, with a suggestion of Overseas in the term *hai*, sea) style as more like "Western in substance, [and] Chinese in function"(yi Xi wei ti, yi Zhong wei yong).[12]

Some analysts have suggested that in terms of the quantity and intensity of exchanges of various kinds, the late 19th century, the context for the St. Louis Exposition, was a period of considerably greater globality than the present.[13] The Qing pavilion in St. Louis, designed by an English architectural firm in Shanghai and built by an American company in the

US with the labor of craftsmen imported from China, provides prima facie evidence that transnationality and globality are by no means novel in themselves. It is nevertheless important not to erase significant differences between the present and the past, which are not to be found in empirical data on trade and migration, or precedents for transnationality. More important are differences in the historical dynamics at work. Globalization in the late 19th century culminated in the global spread of nationalism and colonialism. Presently it nourishes, and is nourished by, postcolonial and postnationalist challenges to the world created by that earlier episode of globalization. What is most important about a historical perspective on globalization is that it affords the possibility of a critical evaluation of contemporary claims to globality as well as better informed judgments concerning differences between the present and its past.

The most important differences between the present and the world of the late 19th/early 20th centuries may be cultural and ideological. Colonialism was justified by the claims of the colonizers to possession of a higher civilization which, for all the complexities in the relationships between them and the colonized, was acknowledged by those who spoke for the latter, who by and large found in emulation of the colonizers' ways the path to their own modernity. Fundamental to the undertaking were nationalism and nation-building, which included the creation of a national culture. Globalization in the late 19th century was premised ideologically and culturally on a clear distinction between the advanced and the backward, and the civilized and the primitive, and progress would supposedly come by following those who claimed to show the way to those who, less fortunate in intelligence or cultural endowment, could not find their own way into modernity.

Compared to this world, the world of Eurocentric modernity, the world of the present is radically different. It is a world of global contemporaneity – if only because of the requirements of a global political correctness, which are not lightly ignored. Cultures condemned to extinction in an earlier period have found renewed life in the service of aspirations to "alternative modernities." Of course, not all cultures are equal even under the regime of Global Modernity. At the very origins of the ideology of globalization in the 1980's was a recognition, since forgotten, that certain other cultures might be even more conducive to the success of capitalist modernity than the original European Protestant culture that had produced it, most notably Confucianism. It is a reminder that the issue has been, all along, not just modernity but capitalist modernity. Modernity itself has lost its coherence as it has become a site of contention over different futures. This is the world of Global Modernity, when we are all modern – if less equal than ever.

Ideology and culture do not exist by themselves. Ideological transformations, which find expression in international law and global relations, have a power of their own, but they are nevertheless bound up with material changes. Whatever modernity may mean in material terms, it has become global in the course of the past century. Uneven and unequal the arrival of modernity may be, but it has arrived. Colonialism is no longer acceptable, and neither is imperialism. Nation-building has not been equally successful everywhere, but nationalism has become pervasive. Most importantly, within this particular context, is the growth in numbers and influence of a modern international elite without which neither modernity nor globalization would have any serious meaning. This elite found and still finds cultural and ideological identity in the national enterprise. But increasingly, its identification lies also in its relationship to transnational institutions – from transnational corporations to transnational political, professional and intellectual organizations. Its locations are the global cities that are the nodes of networks that increasingly define globality, as opposed to an earlier stress on national surfaces that underlined the relationship of the city to its hinterland in the countryside. What is true of the elite is also true of the population at large, as the countryside pours into the global cities, turning them, we are told, into mega-cities without hinterlands.

This reconfiguration of space is crucial to understanding the forces shaping contemporary architecture. The discourse of national styles is by no means dead, but, like pleas for alternative modernities, it is more striking for the nostalgia it expresses than for the realities that it reveals. National styles and cultures have themselves become more ambivalent as they have come under attack for replicating essentialisms invented by colonialism, on the one hand, and for the colonizing function they have served in invading places and forcing their own version of homogeneity on the heterogeneous spaces of pre-national existence. One of the fundamental features of global modernity is the ongoing confrontation of the global and the local or, as I prefer say, "places."

It is in this confrontation that we may see most clearly the persistence in global modernity of its colonial legacy. Globalization is the fulfillment of a capitalist modernity spreading over the world from Northwestern Europe and North America over the last half-millennium, but it is driven presently by the headlong rush of societies formerly called Third World to make it their own.[14] Globalization is a repudiation of colonialism, and the power relations that it articulates are likely to elude us unless we recognize that it is indeed "a coalition of the willing"– an idea which would itself have been unlikely to emerge under earlier circumstances of formal colonialism. Colonialism, rather than a failure, was quite successful in creating Third World elites who have now come forward as the vanguards of globalization in formerly colonial societies, and as candidates for membership in the newly emergent transnational capitalist class.[15] It is interestingly this same bourgeoisie that seeks in the midst of transnationalization to reassert its national or civilizational particularity by claims to continuity with a pre-colonial or pre-modern past.

The relationship between nationalism and globalization parallels that between nationalism and colonialism. Colonialism generated nationalism in opposition to it, but was instrumental for the same reason in the global spread of nationalism. Nationalism, on the other hand, has been a colonizing activity itself in erasing local differences in order to create a homogenous national culture. It has also served as an agent of modernization, bringing populations globally into the orbit of modernity, if not its center. In other words, it has played a central part in the formation of globality. As it brings the local onto the plane of the global, it also brings the global into everyday life everywhere.

As studies of Orientalism have demonstrated over the last three decades, colonialists who did not think much of the colonized and their living cultures nevertheless had great admiration for their pasts, especially when those pasts lay in ruins. The interactions of the colonizing and the colonized, especially at the level of elites, were to create a particular form of modernity, a colonial modernity, that referred above all to the arts and architectures created under circumstances of coloniality; it recognized the subjectivity of the colonized, but also the importance of colonialism in shaping not only the colonized but the colonizer as well. The whole point of the recognition, however, was not to criticize or to put an end to colonialism, but to show its beneficent aspects. Robert Rydell writes the following about what he calls "the 'coloniale moderne' sensibility" in early 20th century universal expositions:

Rooted in the exotic fascination with the "Other" cultivated at European fairs before the Great War, coloniale moderne – a conjuncture of modernistic architectural styles and representations of imperial policies that stressed the benefits of colonialism to colonizer and colonized alike – developed from the desire by European imperial authorities to decant the old wine of imperialism into new bottles bearing the modernistic designs of the interwar years. More specifically, the coloniale moderne practice-*habitus* may be a better expression; for it is crystallized around efforts by governments to make the modernistic dream worlds of mass consumption on view at fairs unthinkable apart from the maintenance and extension of empire.[16]

Colonial modernity was not about erasing difference, but the rephrasing of difference within a modern context that, as the many World's Fairs and Universal Expositions in the century after 1850 eloquently attest to, was inconceivable without reference to colonialism. The alternative modernities which now assert themselves against Euro/American paradigms of modernity are products of the interaction between particular colonialisms and pre-colonial native legacies, fashioned into localized modernities by the subjects of colonial modernity. These are now also the subjects of global modernity, asserting themselves on a global scene in the ideological spaces seemingly evacuated by a provincialized Euro/America, in a tenuous negotiation over the future of modernity that bears upon it every mark of its colonial past.

Colonialism has left behind an ambivalent legacy. It has brought with it oppressive practices, added to those that already existed, and also the promise of liberation from oppression. Likewise the esthetics of colonialism, which erased the past, but also rescued from oblivion pasts that might have gone unnoticed had it not been for colonialism. It makes a great deal of sense to recognize colonialism, in its multifaceted expressions, not as a deviation from but as a formative element of history.

It is important, however, that in understanding coloniality as owing much to globalization, we do, not overlook the specificities of different power relations. In this case we must consider power relations between classes – especially the transnational class-in-formation that emerges out of a new collaboration between states and capital, with the diverse functionaries in their employ.[17] Colonialism understood in the sense of national oppression and exploitation may not seem appropriate to understanding globalization precisely because of the participation of native elites in the processes of the latter. To be sure, native elites always participated in colonial rule; but the present situation is somewhat different from in the past both in greater reciprocity between elites of different national origin, and also in the far greater possibilities it offers to far greater numbers of escaping territorial confinements. On the other hand, globalization is also about colonialism, if we understand that term in its most fundamental sense of taking space away from those who make various uses of it, including their livelihood, and putting it in the service of non-local conceptions and goals of spatial utility. If it does not seem like colonialism because the natives collaborate in its processes, it nevertheless is premised on the marginalization, if not the erasure, of alternative uses of space that are more consonant with the needs and prerogatives of everyday existence.

Referring to various global architectural projects produced by architects of different nationalities, Rem Koolhaas writes that these projects "were all planned for areas that could be described as tabulae rasae and I think this is a very important characteristic of globalization. In other words, none of them was planned for a context that consisted of an existing city. They were all created out of nothing."[18] We may recall here that there is substantial difference between *tabulae rasae* and the favored term of an earlier colonialism, *terra nullius*[19] John Dixon refers to the urban renewal projects informed by modernism as "slash-and-burn renewal, which is echoed in a Shanghai slogan, "flattening all for a new start."[20] And what follows the flattening? I cannot resist quoting snatches of Paulina Bozek's eloquent observations on a current globalized architecture driven by "multinational corporations requiring magnificent structures to mark their presence... much of the construction and development has been driven by foreign capital with little sensitivity to concerns of cultural heritage... the superb structures, which dominate the center of a city like Manila or Shanghai, are truly celebrating the success of a place very far away. This issue has been widely discussed in the context of colonial pasts, but has been largely overlooked in today's arena of global markets and investment… creating modern, urban centers that attempt to mirror each other… [while] cultural heritage as expressed by the built environment is becoming a scarce commodity."[21] The more we talk about culture, the less culture matters in the substance of architecture – and life in general. This architecture of globalization is the embodiment of a "visual capital that is recognized globally."[22] It is also, for much the same reasons, increasingly distant from the lives of those in the midst of whom it is erected.

Globalization in this perspective is a second coming of modernism, but with a vengeance; what Hans Ibelings calls "supermodernism," an architecture of "non-places" that can be seen as typical expressions of the age of globalization.[23] Koolhaas, himself an architect in global demand, sees the architecture of globalization as one of disappearance from which "there is no escape:"

> The first time I went to Singapore, I was seven, and I arrived by boat. What I remember is the smell: equal parts rot and sweetness, the smell of the tropics. But when I went back two years ago, that smell was gone. In fact, Singapore was gone, scrapped, its architecture a Petri dish of Chinese Stalinist modernism followed by Chinese postmodernism. Now the city was trying to fill the few holes left after the reconstruction with masterpieces by James Stirling, Mario Botta, and other contextualists. It was a spectacle, one that was completely and frightening plausible.

He concludes: "We all inhabit conceptual Singapores."[24] Similarly pessimistic, Richard Marshall writes that, … the most successful global project lacks any idea of the city… Lujiazui represents a modern crisis in urbanism, the ultimate aspiration of globalization and a project whose functionality, as a piece of Shanghai's global infrastructure, is without dispute, yet one that lacks any possibility to articulate or support an urbanity appropriate to Shanghai. If Lujiazui is a model for how China and the rest of the world should proceed then there is little hope for architecture and urban design…"[25]

Ironically, architects and analysts of architecture such as Koolhaas and Ibelings readily recognize the destruction that attends the emergence of a global modernity, but are not beyond contributing to it themselves.[26]

There is widespread agreement presently among both the critics and the cheerleaders of globalization that it exacts a heavy price in the disappearance of place and, with it, of history and memory. On the other hand, globalization, like postmodernism before it, does not represent the totality of architecture but coexists presently with other approaches, including postmodernism, contextualism, and regionalism, themselves responses to modernist universalism of an earlier day that are still very much alive. These critical practices offer alternatives to the new universalism of architectural globalization that is driven by the globalization of capital.

Most important among these alternatives may be "critical regionalism," which reaffirms the importance of place, while recognizing that places themselves are historical. As Kenneth Frampton explains it, the term "Critical Regionalism" is not intended to denote the vernacular as this was once spontaneously produced by the combined interaction of climate, culture, myth and craft, but rather to identify those recent regional *schools* who reflect and serve the limited constituencies in which they are grounded.[27] But, the local that is set against the global is, in many cases, quite ambiguous, ranging from the place-based and intra-national regional to the national and supra-national regional. Especially in postcolonial societies, the national is the product of a previous, colonial, globality. It serves presently as the medium for the localization of the global. The confounding of the local and the national is likely to distract critical regionalism from achieving its more democratic goals, by opening it up to service to the nation-state, which may seem anti-colonial in its contrast with the global but appears in its own coloniality when viewed from place-based perspectives.[28] It is also important to recognize that critical regionalism has its own contradictions; like globalization, its practitioners are celebrity architects whose own projects are quite global in scope.[29] This may be unavoidable, as globality has become a defining feature of the local, and colonialism an ineradicable constituent of history everywhere. Where people are headed politically should be much more important presently than where they are from culturally or ethnically.

Ultimately, the contradictions between the global and the local in architecture are integral parts of social and political contradictions that attend contemporary transformations as modernity goes global. The resolutions of these contradictions, likewise, will be part of broader political projects, which still are subject to circumstances of place and time. Manfredo Tafuri concluded nearly three decades ago that, "the crisis of modern architecture is not the result of 'tiredness' or 'dissipation.' It is rather a crisis of the ideological function of architecture... For this reason, it is useless to propose purely architectural alternatives. The search for an alternative within the structures that condition the very character of architectural design is indeed an obvious contradiction of terms."[30]

Insurgent architects have much to contribute by designing spaces that affirm life and livelihood against the abstractions of a placeless architecture driven by the fetishism of development. What makes architecture insurgent in the first place is recognition that esthetic choices are ultimately social choices as well. The problem with the architecture of globalization ultimately is that it is a negation of the social as such. It may make sense under contemporary imbalances of power to let globalization have its spaces, as in Pudong, and the many Pudongs of Global Capital, and to rebuild architectures of sociability in locations that have not completely lost memories of the social. Let us not forget that, despite all the talk about globalization, many, many of those places still exist.

Cultural Identity in the Age of Globalization: Implications on Architecture

Gordon Mathews

Cultural identity has become a significant topic in architecture.[1] However, it is not fully theorized in recently published explorations. In this article I explore the meanings of cultural identity from an anthropological perspective, and then examine their implications for architecture. The purpose of this exercise is not necessarily to teach architects something that they do not already know, but rather to place architectural versions of cultural identity within a broader anthropological framework, in a way that may perhaps shed light upon both disciplines. Let me begin by discussing cultural identity from an anthropological point of view, and then attempt to apply these views to architecture.

Cultural Identity in Anthropological Perspective

Culture, throughout most of the history of anthropology, was seen as more or less unproblematic: most often simply as "the way of life of a people." Anthropology was largely based on the study of traditional societies, and generally assumed the constancy and homogeneity of those societies: one was born within a cultural tradition and lived more or less within its guidance, in terms of beliefs and behavior, and in terms of religion, food, dance, and housing.

However, many anthropologists in recent decades have become skeptical about the idea of bounded, fixed, largely unchanging culture. Insight into how states invent culture and mask it as tradition in order to propagandize their citizens[2] is one reason for this: governments often invoke "culture" as a means of bolstering their own legitimacy. A second is globalization. Cultural borders have become porous, with people, goods, and ideas ceaselessly moving across societal boundaries, as many anthropologists have recently noted.[3] This movement is not new, but it has greatly accelerated in recent decades. Increasingly we live within a global "cultural supermarket," in which the world's cultural forms, in areas from food to religion to music to architecture, are to some extent available for appropriation by everyone.[4]

Globalization and its effects should not, however, be exaggerated; we may live within the global cultural supermarket, but we are nonetheless born into a social world that shapes us through distinct patterns of childrearing and language. Culture has a double aspect today: it is both fixed by national and ethnic bounds and fluid globally. Cultural identity, which we may define as how people, on the basis of their cultural shaping, define themselves, similarly has this double aspect, with some people defining themselves more through their involvement in global forms ("I'm a rock musician/football player/architect; the fact that I'm Japanese/French/Malaysian doesn't matter much") and others more through their adherence to a particular cultural or national identity.

Some anthropologists today proclaim that culture in its traditional sense is dead,[5] while others devote themselves to preserving traditional cultures.[6] Some analysts, particularly those of a postmodernist persuasion, write of identity as always in flux, while others continue to discuss cultural identity as enduring and substantial. Both views have validity in some contexts, but it seems clear that, generally speaking, the reality of our situation lies in the middle. Most people continue to have a cultural identity based on their membership in a particular society, as defined by language and shared history and other features; but at the same time, many of us live within the cultural supermarket, which offers us at least the illusion of global free choice. Cultural identity today is in this state of flux, neither culturally "pure" nor culturally "free," but somewhere in the middle.

To better understand this situation, let us more fully examine "the cultural supermarket," and the assertions of essential cultural identity that often serve as a response to it. The cultural supermarket is very much conditioned by national and global structures of power, through which rich countries generally dominate poorer ones thanks to the prevalence of their cultural products. It is no coincidence that global icons such as Disneyland, McDonald's, and Walkman are products of the United States and Japan rather than of Congo and Bangladesh; and this is true in the cultural as well as the material realm: why are the world's best-selling movies and books so often American?[7] Indeed, to a large extent, the cultural supermarket signifies less globalization than Westernization (with Japan as a sort of honorary member of the West), given the dominant power of its cultural forms. Cultural appropriation works in reverse as well: consider John Walker Lindh, the so-called American Taliban, transformed from California teenager to Islamic radical through ideas available on the internet. But clearly the shelves of the cultural supermarket are skewed, with the products and ideas of wealthy Western societies generally dominating those of other societies in the world.

It is in large part in response to the ubiquity of the Western-dominated cultural supermarket that cultural identity has come to be so prominently asserted throughout the world in recent decades. Sometimes this is a matter of states asserting the sacredness of their cultural identity against the power of the global market: trade protectionism, in societies from Korea to France, is often cloaked in these terms. Sometimes this is a matter of ethnic groups asserting the sanctity of their cultural identity as against the power of the state to assimilate them: we see this among groups from the Ainu to the Quebecois.

It seems that as "culture" in a traditional sense becomes attenuated, it is often all the more strongly asserted. People seek to reclaim their roots, despite the fact that in many cases these supposed roots have largely eroded. Roots, to be phenomenologically real, must have been experienced as an organic part of one's life. Thus, in terms of actual experience in their lives, the roots of many Japanese today are less kimono and koto music than McDonald's hamburgers and rock and roll, and this is true of members of developed societies across the globe. It is as if roots are asserted to the extent that they are no longer there.

And yet, as discussed above, apart from the cultural supermarket, distinct cultures do remain. The aforementioned Japanese may be more comfortable in jeans or suits than in kimono and may know rock and roll better than koto, but, nonetheless, they still speak Japanese as their native language, and in this sense, at least, are clearly rooted in a Japanese cultural context. How they sense their cultural identity depends largely on where they locate themselves between the culturally particular and the culturally universal within the spectrum of different cultural attributes in their lives.

Cultural identity can be asserted in terms of a number of specific attributes. These include ethnicity, language, literature, history, religion, food, and architecture, all of which have varying degrees of fluidity. Cultural identity as "race" may be a biological fiction but it is a clear sociological fact, if those who identify themselves as belonging to a certain ethnic group bear a physical appearance distinct from other groups: cultural identity in this sense is generally enduring. Language is also a largely fixed form of identity from the individual standpoint, in that one's native language is given virtually from birth – although states everywhere, from China to the United States, attempt to melt ethnic difference into cultural commonality through a common language of education. History is somewhat more malleable as a marker of cultural identity, as is apparent from the way states mold school curricula, reshaping the past to fit the perceived needs of the present; but for many today, a given national past may seem less real than global mass media. Food, too, is relatively malleable as a marker of cultural identity, in an era in which chicken tikka masala has been proclaimed as "a true British national dish."[8] And the same holds true for architecture. In an era in which skyscrapers and apartment blocks everywhere look more or less alike, it has become increasingly difficult in many regions of the world for a distinct cultural identity in architecture to be convincingly asserted—although from tourist boards to architects extolling traditional architecture, many try.

I have thus far emphasized cultural identity's double character today, as described by anthropologists, as based in both one's upbringing in a particular society and one's consumption patterns within the "global cultural supermarket." With this in mind, let us now consider cultural identity in architecture.

Cultural Identity and Architecture

My tracing of anthropological views of cultural identity can easily be applied to architecture. From the earthen roundhouses of West Africa to the open, airy structures of the Malaysian kampong to the communal cliff dwellings of Mesa Verde to the imperial street-grid design of Beijing and its Forbidden City to the different kinds of castle towns in Europe, Japan, and India, architecture reflecting different social structures and cultural forms, as well as different natural environments. First the social structures and cultural norms establish standards of human activities in response to the environmental variables and resources, and then architecture provides the mediation by accommodating and reinforcing such standards.

In recent centuries, there has been a massive "Westernization" of architecture, in tandem with European political colonization and, later, American economic neo-colonization of much of the globe, as wells as with universal technological developments arising first in the United States and Western Europe. From Japanese wood and paper houses to the Mongolian ger, local housing styles have given way to apartment blocks that are largely the same. Government buildings at various points across the globe may feature the same neo-classical architecture based on Roman or Greek models of the Western tradition; and the high-rise housing projects tend to look largely the same everywhere. Just as clothing has generally come to follow standard, universalized patterns, so too has architecture. This uniformity of architecture in the contemporary world has come under substantial criticism, not least because modernist architectural projects have often been so ill-suited to the needs of their inhabitants. To take an extreme example, it is hard to imagine a city less constructed with the needs of its residents in mind than La Corbusier's Chandigarh: the architect drew his grand plans with no knowledge whatsoever about the complex patterns of Indian life, leading to an absurd disconnection between the buildings and the social lives of their inhabitants.[9] The Pruitt-Igoe housing project, in the US city of St. Louis, is one more example, in this case of a construction so out of touch with the needs of its residents that it was eventually left largely unoccupied and had to be dynamited just two decades after it was built.[10] These are examples of the follies of universal modern Western architecture, which has often ignored how people actually live their lives.

Yet while the extremes of such architecture may be criticized, universal modern architecture has had its merits: in some areas of the world, it is Western-style apartment blocks that first provided their residents with electricity and indoor plumbing. In any case, a universal architecture based on Western patterns seems inevitable, both because of Western technology's influence on mass housing design, and because of the ongoing dominance of Western cultural and social forms, shaping what gets built on the world's economic peripheries. Within such essentially Western architecture, the regionally distinctive may be allowed in as a matter of minor ornamentation, a "traditional 'hat' placed atop standard... [modern] forms."[11] This can be seen, for example, in the Chinese-style parks that surround many of the massive high-rises that make up Hong Kong public housing, signifying that such habitations, for all their Western design, are indeed "Chinese." Standard Western architectural forms, often with very small variations representing "culture," have become a worldwide norm.

Increasingly, however, architects have rebelled against this universalism. There has been, on the one hand, the idea that one can appropriate from all the world's architectural forms as one chooses, regardless of what culture they may happen to come from; this view has most recently been given the label of postmodernism in architecture. On the other hand, there has been the idea that those of different cultural backgrounds have full and largely exclusive possession of their own architectural forms; this idea has been expressed in various schools of architecture, including regionalism, critical regionalism, and, most recently, new traditionalism. Both these ideas are problematic. Neither "the cultural supermarket" nor "cultural purity" is sufficient for comprehending cultural identity today, and this is as true in architecture as in any other field. But let us examine each of these ideas in turn.

As discussed previously, some cultural attributes are fixed, while others are more fluid; some are more easily appropriable than others. Unlike, for example, full understanding of a foreign country's poetry, which is extraordinarily difficult to acquire when one is not a native speaker of the language, architectural forms may readily cross cultural boundaries and be appropriated by those of a different cultural background. To take one historical example, Chris Abel describes how British architects in Malaysia combined Islamic and Italian Renaissance forms in colonial government buildings, creating a religiously-sensitive assertion of imperial authority, and a new cultural hybrid.[12] Architecture throughout history has had this fluidity, but I suspect that it has become considerably greater this past century, reaching a pinnacle with postmodernism in its capricious borrowings of architectural forms from all cultures and ages. Postmodern architecture, as Kenneth Frampton describes it, epitomizes the values of the cultural supermarket:

> It is the conscious ruination of style and the cannibalization of architectural form, as though no value either traditional or otherwise can withstand for long the tendency of the production / consumption cycle to reduce every civic institution to some kind of consumerism and to undermine every traditional quality.[13]

Despite this criticism, there is something to be said for the freedom to utilize the world's heritage of architectural forms: why not make all the world's architectural forms the world's creative legacy, to be used as one desires? Certainly this can make architecture more variegated and interesting. But the problem, as Frampton implies, is that it is the rich and powerful who are able to do the appropriating. Architectural elements are ripped from their cultural moorings to become the decorations of the affluent, in the capitalization as well as Disneyfication of the world. Consider, to take just one example, the Buddhist statue hustled out of Burma to lend an air of exoticism to a garden in New York. This represents the freedom of "the cultural supermarket," but even more, the hegemony of the rich, in appropriating the world's cultural traditions as personal "lifestyle signifiers." We see today the world's artistic and architectural forms stripped of their complex cultural, historical, and spiritual meanings, to be made items of conspicuous display purchased through disembodied capital in a globalized world. This might not be a bad thing, if all the globe were equally detached from history and culture, equally uprooted in a world of common affluence. But this is not the case, and thus much postmodern design may represent the uprooted rich plundering and playing with the rest of the world's more or less rooted cultural treasures.

Moreover, such roots, in architecture in particular, now seem globally endangered. Local architecture has more or less given way to the standard Western models, making cities everywhere look increasingly alike. Architectural schools from regionalism to critical regionalism to new traditionalism offer as one of their key tenets the celebration of regional culture, and resistance against the universal homogeneity of modernization / Westernization. As Frampton writes, "Critical Regionalism tends to flourish in those cultural interstices which in one way or another are able to escape the optimizing thrust of universal civilization."[14] His words apply to all these schools.

There is much that is valuable in this new emphasis on the regional. As Udo Kultermann has noted, "There is an inexcusable gap between the research devoted to European architectural tradition and the traditions of India, Africa, China, Southeast Asia, and Latin America. And, as if the old architectural monuments in the Southern Hemisphere are of no value, much of its architectural heritage… has been and continues to be destroyed."[15]

Through such architectural movements as regionalism, critical regionalism, and new traditionalism, the traditional architecture of non-Western societies has become more fully valued, cherished, and preserved. However, in today's world there are not many examples of traditional architecture left, and far fewer examples of areas within Frampton's "cultural interstices" untouched by the global cultural supermarket. In examining the multitude of websites to be found on the topic of "traditional architecture," one finds the largest proportion of these sites to be set forth by tourist boards and by architectural faculties in the countries concerned, reaching out to a global audience. Traditional architecture is thus a means of attracting cosmopolitan attention, and in particular, tourists and their dollars, euros, or yen. While this architecture may escape the homogenizing "thrust of universal civilization," it certainly does not escape the "global cultural supermarket." In this sense, traditional architecture seems in large part to be a marketing device – this is the inevitable consequence of globalization.

Indeed, in the non-Western world, people on occasion seek to architecturally preserve their culture, only to find that which they were protecting is already gone. Consider, for example, the wealthy young Japanese who builds a traditional Japanese house only to find that he cannot live kneeling on tatami mats, having been brought up in a world of

Western chairs; he can no longer return to his culture. As the Japanese architect Arata Isozaki has stated, "Japan... has no clear form anymore and no character of its own... How is one to represent something that no longer has a clear-cut definition?"[16] It may be that in less developed areas of the world, there is somewhat more room to explore one's own cultural tradition's architectural alternatives, since globalization and universal Western architectural forms have made less headway; but everywhere, these cultural roots are being eroded. In a globalized world, no one can claim exclusive rights to one's own cultural tradition, for almost inevitably it is no longer one's own, or at least no longer only one's own. Movements such as critical regionalism and new traditionalism may thus involve less the preservation of traditional local architecture than the intellectual and architectural "invention of tradition" in order to define one's roots and identity in a globalized world.

Towards Cultural Complexity

In this essay, I first traced out the difficulties of formulating cultural identity in an anthropological sense, between culture as "the way of life of a people" and culture as "the global cultural supermarket." I then examined cultural identity as it applies to architecture. Western architectural forms have swept the world – and just as in many other fields of cultural contestation,[17] responses to the Westernized, more or less homogenized world of modernist architecture, have been two-fold. One response has been postmodernism, celebrating the diversity of world architectural forms that may be chosen from. Another, opposite response has been regionalism, critical regionalism, and new traditionalism, all at least in implication proclaiming the local and affirming the cultural possession of roots.

These two responses typify two logically opposing strategies in a world becoming increasingly culturally interlinked: cultural identity can be asserted as the inalienable possession of the members of a given group, or it may be proclaimed as no one's possession and available to all if they have the means to possess it. Both responses are understandable and justifiable, given the flood of homogenization with which the world has been culturally faced; but both are also problematic. If all the world's cultural traditions are held to be available for global appropriation, as postmodernism implies, then it is the rich and powerful who in arenas such as architecture are most able to engage in that appropriation, leaving out everyone else. If, on the other hand, the world's cultural traditions are held to be available only to those who "belong" to such traditions, as regionalism, critical regionalism, and new traditionalism imply, then the cultural hybridity of the world today is denied in favor of a cultural purity that no longer exists. Those who believe they possess their culture are perhaps possessing no more than a mirage.

These problems may, however, be transcended. One can imagine a democratic and culturally sensitive postmodernism: all the world's information available to anyone with an internet connection and access to a library (a qualification which, however, still excludes some 90 percent of the world's people). Architects and builders have tended to serve the rich and powerful, by the nature of their discipline; but to the extent that architects are aware of the power differentials in their societies that their work serves, and seek, in whatever ways they are able, to democratize what they do, as has been already happening in much architecture of late, this problem can be mitigated.[18] At the same time, to the extent that architects can remain sensitive to cultural boundaries and avoid appropriating the culturally sacrosanct in their work, the excesses of postmodernism may also be mitigated: "the cultural supermarket" should not mean that all cultural elements in the world are for sale. One can also envision a hybrid regionalism, one not tied to vanished cultural tradition but to culture's contemporary state of flux. As Abel has written of contemporary architectural forms, "To my mind, the proper and most useful definition of cultural identity will arise out of a fuller understanding and appreciation of the creative processes of cultural interaction, not out of some kind of pre-selection of the supposedly more pure elements of regional or national culture."[19]

If culture is defined not as static and pure but as dynamic and hybrid, then regionalism can be not a matter of the dead cultural past but of the dynamic cultural present.

Thus, postmodernism and regionalism may become not opposites but rather common strategies for creating a contemporary architecture that reflects contemporary cultural complexities. But this process transcends architecture, and could be said to describe our world at large. Between cultural frozenness and freedom, cultural purity and promiscuity, lies an uncomfortable yet potentially liberating middle zone. This is the world we live in: maybe it's time to fully embrace it.

Fragmented Subjects in Former Colonial Cities

Hajime Yatsuka

In today's colonial studies, there seems to exist odd differences in the basic ideas underlying certain types of discourse about the problem of colonial domination. While modernist discourses on the colonies adopt a negative stance towards the transgression of regional identities committed by ex-suzerain states, the postmodern view tends rather to accept the ultimately hybrid nature resulting from violent occupation in the colonial past as allowing the establishment of transnational conditions.

At issue here is a problem of modernization. The type of argument, often called historical revisionism, that claims colonization successfully modernized colonies which would not otherwise enjoy the standards found in the civilization of their suzerains (i.e. Western countries) is surely to be rejected, in that it is an attempt to evaluate process without referring to the subjects under colonial rule. This argument implies that the colonies were devoid of such capability (or, more bluntly, that they had been stagnant for so long they were unable to modernize by themselves). Anti-revisionism has been, and still is, rejecting this type of discourse as politically incorrect, but the polemic is reversed in postmodern discussions; the difference evaluated negatively by modernists becomes regarded here as advantage or even a privilege to be affirmed. A previous understanding of progress is now radically revised, from a single-track operation to multi-track processes in which we cannot fix the sole outcome of modernization. Revisionists might make a new claim, that intercultural colonization should be welcomed inasmuch as it generated such desirable modernization in the former colonies. But the revisionists have been too fixated on the assumptions of their own culture's supremacy to evaluate these new types as both transnational and trans-territorial. On the other hand, arguments that respect the nationalist sentiments of the ruled could be criticized as not consistent with the objective application of postmodernist thought. Also rare is any attempt to interrogate postcolonial discourses that condemn suzerain nationalism while defending similar stances in the (ex-)colonies, arguments which are highly dependent on the very notion of identity – identity being the most essential prerequisite of the notion of modernism.

Michael Hardt and Antonio Negri, in their much discussed book *Empire*, claimed that "subaltern nationalism" is progressive only when it serves a defense against external forces. They criticize Karl Marx for his lack of understanding regarding other potentialities in India, for example, that belonged to neither the despotic past, nor the savage present (of the era under British governance). Hardt and Negri's criticism implies that for Marx the only possibility of progress lay in mutation to a Westernized society. Their criticism seems to be relevant, but their argument is still eclectic, inasmuch as they also never presented other potentialities (for India) in concrete form, either. Indeed, this is a very difficult question to address, unless we properly formulate the problem of the theme. The first part of this essay will discuss such issues, using as a case study the problem of architecture and urbanism in Taipei under the domination of Japan and afterwards.

Hsia Chu-Joe, a Taiwanese critic, in his article "Building Colonial: Rewriting Histories of Architecture and Urbanism in the Colonial Taiwan,"[1] offered the very same proposition as Hardt and Negri (presumably by chance): he proposed another potentiality for Taiwan (differing from occupation by Japan), and then analyzed "the notion of colonial modernity as modernity devoid of the process of building up the subject." Among the various topics he discussed, from the period preceding Japanese domination, when Taiwan was part of the continental Chinese Empire, through the period after World War II, I shall focus especially on the colonial Government-General building (GG), designed and built by the Japanese, in Taipei. This is one of the two Japanese colonial Government-General buildings from the pre-war era (the GGT, Government-General Taiwan and the GGK, or Government-General Korea, built in Seoul). In spite of the fact that both structures were built without regard for the historical and cultural context of their sites, in the city center of colonial capitals, the Korean counterpart was more scandalous from its inception; for the Japanese government demolished Kwanghwa Gate, one of the ancient city gates, and built the huge GGK building there, completely blocking views of Kyungbok Palace (identified with the Korean royal dynasty), neglecting strong opposition not only from local people, but also from leading Japanese intellectuals of the time. The building, designed by a Tokyo-based German architect, Georg de Lalande, in the neo-Renaissance style and completed in 1926, became a constant reminder of the hated Japanese colonialism.

Its counterpart, the GGT building in Taipei, was initially designed by U-hei-ji Nagano, the winner of a competition in 1909. The designs of both GG buildings were modified from their original states, because there was no definitive idea of architectural authorship or copyright protection at that time. Ichiro Nomura was eventually placed in charge of completing the two buildings, as a chief architect of the building department for the two GG buildings. Nagano, who was well informed about Western architectural practices, protested that these modifications destroyed the original character of his design. (This problem is not without interest within Japanese architectural history.) However, the critic Hsia was concerned not with the problems of Japanese architects, but with the context for the building as it relates to the people in Taiwan, and this will be the focus of our concern here.

Hsia took notice of the difference in how these two former GG buildings were viewed by local people during the post-war period. Both buildings, by the very fact of their construction, erased memories tied to the historical features of the sites. However, while the former GGK building, converted to a national museum after the war, was eventually demolished (and the event celebrated) in 1996, the GGT building experienced a mutation of its meaning, in light of the even harsher domination of Taiwan by the Nationalist party. It had massacred many local people in 1947, and, after the Nationalist defeat on the Chinese mainland led the Nationalists to flee to Taiwan in 1949, they placed the country under martial law until 1987. This caused strong antagonism between the native Taiwanese and Nationalist settlers, and modernization under Japanese domination was seen favorably in comparison. Thus the GGT building, converted to the headquarters of the Nationalist government, became, rather than a symbol of tyrannical Japanese colonialism, a source of nostalgia for those "good old days."

Hsia observed with some irritation that an active distortion of history became more complicated and annoying when this building became established as part of society's memory. Not only the GGT buildings, but also other facilities built by the Japanese were preserved; some of these buildings even came to be used, after 1987, as museums to commemorate positively Japanese modernization of the country in such key areas as social welfare systems and infrastructure (which I shall discuss further below). These, for Hsia, introduce prejudice in the name of objectivity, and this prejudice is devoid of the intellectual basis that actually measures the perspective of this "reflective modernity." However, he was honest enough to admit that the Japanese GG buildings offered sophistication in their architectural treatment and care in their technique and materials, reaching a level of quality generally lacking in post-colonial buildings by local architects. Hsia was faced with the dilemma of aesthetic degeneration in the indigenous culture, the result of the fact that the native culture fails to activate its own cultural identity in modern forms, because it is not equipped with the proper knowledge or discipline. He calls this condition "colonization from within."

Hsia's dilemma is similar to that of the Japanese intellectuals during the period immediately after World War II: they could not be so optimistic as to believe that the disappearance of previous constraints (militarism and the Imperial system in the case of Japanese, and colonial domination in the case of Taiwan and Korea) would automatically introduce the right way of governing society. The Japanese Communist Party was the only organization to have resisted militarism during the war, but in the immediate post-war period it quickly lost the trust of most citizens by self-righteously attacking other parties, and ultimately it was ineffective in preventing dictatorship by the army. Accordingly, it was argued that the establishing of an autonomous self, the modern subject, was the most essential task, and that this was preferable to depending on the Marxist notion of class and party, or on more abstract ideas. The controversy related to the subject among leftist (and non-communist) philosophers was extended to that over cultural issues, such as national literature and architectural tradition. The basis of these polemics was a critical awareness by intellectuals of the danger of "colonization from within" due to the overwhelming American influence on everything from politics to culture and art at that time. Japanese intellectuals were seeking a way to revitalize a damaged national identity by establishing a solid foundation to carry out this task, namely a proper conception of the subject. They emphasized the significance of the subject because of their observation that they should be sensitive of the ambivalent fact that tradition and nationality themselves were already discussed by intellectuals in wartime and had eventually led to a justification for Japanese supremacy in the Greater East Asian Co-prosperity Sphere. However, the postwar debate may not have actually succeeded in repudiating the old ideology represented by prewar polemics of "overcoming of modernity" or "the philosophy of world history" (proposed by philosophers of Kyoto University), as both foreshadowed contemporary postmodernist views to a certain extent.

The main protagonist in the debate over architectural tradition in the 1950's, Kenzo Tange, made a dramatic debut by winning the 1941 competition for the Monument to the Greater East Asian Co-prosperity Sphere, which was an architectural expression of the "overcoming of modernity." The Greater East Asian Co-prosperity Sphere was advocated by Japan, albeit to disguise her imperialist ambitions, as a challenge to a system of global politics monopolistically dominated by the West. It was an attempt to establish an alternative type of localized globalism under the hegemony of Japan. Tange's competition project provided a prototype for his postwar Hiroshima Peace Park, which served politically opposite ideals from its predecessor, and it also was a prototype for his 1960 Tokyo Bay Project. His dramatically successful career as a post-war Japanese architect supports recent politico-sociological discussions in Japan that emphasize similarity and continuity of the warfare state before 1945 with the post-war, welfare sate in social institutions and infrastructure, and provides an interesting topic concerning the problem of reconciling the significance of Tange's extremely opportunistic political position with his great accomplishments.

This seems all the more ironic, when we, who are Japanese, read the recent remarks by Lee Hyun-Ju, a young Korean student, concerning Korea's delayed controversy on the topic of tradition. This arose in connection with the design of the National Museum of Puyo by the leading architect of the post-war period in Korea, Kim Su-Gun, who studied architecture in Tange's studio in Tokyo. Kim's design for a museum gate was criticized for its association with Japanese Shinto shrine gates, a symbol of Japanese despotism before and during the war. (Koreans demolished the Korean Shrine in Seoul – designed by the Japanese architect Chuta Ito – immediately after the war for this reason.) For opponents, this association with Japan was absolutely unacceptable, especially in a project for the National Museum. Lee observed that the weakness of the Korean polemics lay in the fact of its emergence under a despotic government; the opponents lacked the autonomous and modern consciousness that, by contrast, was firmly possessed by these contemporary Japanese architects. It is not without interest to compare this observation with the argument by Hsia Chu-Joe.

Edward Said, having defined Orientalism[1] as a concept of the Orient (Asia) as perceived by others, namely from the Occident, argued that the Orient had no means to represent itself. Achieving indigenous representation is impossible without establishing the subject. The abovementioned polemics by critics in Taiwan and Korea relate to this problem. In this respect, it may seem possible to summarize this kind of argument in the absence of the modern subject as derived from the consciousness of the deferred state of culture in occupied nations, delayed relative to Japan, in the case of Taiwan and Korea, and delayed relative to the West in the case of Japan. However, to claim that Taiwan and Korea are still obsessed by an old problem that Japan has already overcome would not be justified; rather, the real problem lies not in whether they (or we Japanese) have already caught up with the West or not, but on whether to see catching up with the West as an ideal achievement. The evidence of the downfall of modernity demonstrates that this idealized notion of modernization (Westernization) is nothing but an illusion. If a postmodern polemic is valid at all, it should be based on an acknowledgement of this point.

To turn away from "Orientalism," however, and to advocate an Asian (and modern) notion of the subaltern subject assumes a different problem. Shin Muramatsu, an activist and a historian of modern architecture in East Asia, recently noted that modern buildings in these countries (especially in Taiwan), built in colonial eras and representing the distorted culture of the time, are now being discussed as objects appropriate for historical preservation. By modern buildings, Muramatsu, like most other Japanese historians, means buildings constructed from the mid-19th century onward, regardless of style – most, therefore, are actually historicist and eclectic. Muramatsu insists that one must first respect existing built environments as they are. For this purpose, he maintains, we should be free from the Eurocentrism that privileges products of the West's modern movement as the only significant buildings. With this premise, he tries to analyze how individual styles and buildings were introduced in colonial countries, depending on categories such as "transplantation/enforcement," "copying/learning," "nutrition/application," and "reaction/opposition." However, while terms like transplantation and copying may be straightforward, categories such as enforcement (by occupiers) and learning (by those under occupation) are too ambiguous and represent how the classifier sees and evaluates the process in advance – they even demonstrate the intervention of stereotypical judgment on the part of the colonial dominators with respect to how they characterize their role in the occupied territories.

But then what is the reason colonialism often induces this kind of stereotyped judgment? Modernization in the colonies, as a typical project of the Enlightenment, had both its lighter and darker sides. Modernization has been characterized by a strange combination of the progressive and the oppressive. In the case of Taiwan, the colonizing government, under the initiative of Shinpei Goto, an enlightened director in charge of civil affairs between 1898 and 1906, was based upon extensive investigation of Taiwanese customs and regulations. These were gradually revised to fit a modern system totally alien to the Taiwanese people. Goto introduced the modern notion of land ownership and property taxes; sanitary regulations, along with the establishment of a modern medical system (Goto himself was a doctor); and modern infrastructure (roads, railways, dams, water service, electricity, etc.), as well as other aspects of modernization. But these efforts were accompanied by the violent suppression of rebellion by the native (and sometimes non-Chinese) people. The enlightened positions that became the justification for contemporary nostalgia towards this period, irritating Hsia, can never compensate for the dark side, but it is also unfair to negate the enlightened efforts, as is done by Muramatsu, who insists that these achievements by the occupiers meant only harsh exploitation of the wealth and labor of most indigenous people, excepting those who allied with the occupiers and, accordingly, enjoyed some of the surplus profits. Inspired by contemporary polemics like French Regulation Theory, which demonstrate a more dynamic way of understanding social economy (beyond classic schemes based on the dualism of exploiting capitalists and exploited laborers), recent analysis of the warfare state of Japan rediscovered what was called Productivity Theory at the time – Productivity Theory even anticipated contemporary French polemics. In this light, the above-mentioned argument regarding the question of who the buildings and structures were built for in the colonies seems too simplistic. This is not to justify colonial modernism, but to show that complicated issues require a complicated approach, and colonialism and globalization are such issues. As Michel Foucault once noted in an interview on power and space, it is impossible that one specific entity belongs to the realm of (absolute) "liberation," while another entity belongs to that of (absolute) "oppression." I completely agree with Foucault's remark that such situations are always more complicated than they appear.

Accordingly, concerning the distortion of history at the basis of Hsia's arguments, we should note that any history is, in principle, a post-facto reflection (or "any history is a contemporary history," according to Benedetto Croce), and the discrimination between a "correct" image and a distorted one is only relative. The validity of this argument depends upon the context. Peter Gay, discussing the possibility of introducing psychoanalytic methods to historical science, noted that what Freud understood and what most social scientists do not is that dilemma is normal (e.g., the dilemma of rationality and irrationality, or the two faces of the enlightenment). This holds true particularly in the case of analyzing the problem of colonialism (or its offspring, contemporary globalization); we need to keep in mind the position of the therapist or analyst as a subject in considering the problem.

Concerning this problem, it is interesting to see the criticism by Tetsushi Maruoka, a Derridian deconstructionist, of the nostalgia towards the colonial period that is unmistakably present in some New Taiwanese Cinema currently enjoying an international success. Maruoka notes that if Japanese audiences share this nostalgia without critical awareness, this could nullify the geopolitical asymmetry between the ex-suzerain Japan and the ex-colonial Taiwan. Maruoka's view is similar to Muramatsu's noted earlier: in their arguments, the subject of the nostalgic Taiwanese is invalidated. Alternatively, do they, like Hsia, dare to criticize the Taiwanese? It seems unlikely. Muramatsu's proposition is to respect what is present, be it buildings or the city, a proposition based on an interest in the presence of architecture regardless of the historical context, which might eventually undermine some of his own categories for assessment, such as "enforcement." Here, the view of the colonies is extremely convoluted.

In recent cultural-anthropology practices, an acknowledged problem is that researchers from ex-suzerain countries isolate and emphasize what they perceive (favorably) as traditional characteristics in the topic of the study, but this problem generates an argument that eventually results in a fabricated tradition. This is often suggested and criticized by local (neo-)-nationalists to be a neo-colonial type of intervention. Both oppressive memory and nostalgia are none other than parts of the micro-political dynamics of semantic space-time fields; public buildings built for non-specific citizens survive a very long time and are exposed to these differing fields. This process is inherently part of modern architectural practice, regardless of the intentions of those who originally did the buildings. This raises a different problem from that of whether we are trying to justify colonization. That argument is impossible to make without framing the position of the subject properly, and that position is certainly distorted, whether in the colonial cities or in the developed (and often suzerain) countries. To understand this, it suffices to consider the conditions in the "reactionary" era of Fascism and Stalinism, for instance. Our problem is not so simple as to allow us to make a proper balance-sheet regarding the achievements of a modernization project; it does not seem possible to achieve an objective judgment in this regard. Here lies a fundamental and paradoxical aporia of modernity and colonialism.

The problem appears not only in a modern framework, but also in the postmodern context. However, unlike in modernity, where the subject is a central assumption, in postmodernity the subject is considered a construction, an illusion to be dissolved. And yet, this is not simply an issue related to individuals; the subject as nation-state has also been seriously put into question. Most arguments on post-colonialism and globalization have focused on this point. However, it was the subject of the occupier that was criticized and condemned. This tendency also produced, as a reaction, an attempt to recover the refuted and dishonored subject of the occupier – that is now called revisionism. One cannot call it postmodern, since it tries to appeal to the notion of identity and is totally unaware of the impossibility of the traditional notion of the subject; much of the opposing argument tries to refute revisionism as actually being modern in this regard, inasmuch as revisionists never doubt the existence of the subject. This takes us again to the problem we see in the discussion above. If we are simply to adopt the politically correct formulation in order to negate the proposition that Taiwanese and Korean critics' arguments are based on delayed societal development and are still occupied by the problem of modernity, which has already been overcome in Japan, we might lose the sight of the central core of the problem of contemporary globalization. As a matter of course, I do not intend to attribute the difference only to societal (and inevitable) delay; that is none other than the old (and now ill-reputed) Hegelian/Marxian progressivist view of non-Western societies. We should go further to analyze the possible significance of this "difference" in the context of the contemporary globalization.

This difference is always possible for an individual person to overcome. Architectural design is now borderless; whether you are Egyptian or Iraqi won't offer any obstacle for acquiring international celebrity. However, I would like to claim that we cannot reverse the proposition and say that whether you are European or American won't make any difference. This is because the first proposition is valid almost only in the case of individuals whose practices are based in the West. Global politics is still asymmetrical and the basic condition, that the West is still setting global standards, remains as yet unchallenged. The argument by Muramatsu, who tried to refute Euro-centric privilege, focuses on this condition.

Successful Asian people (or South Americans or Africans) are no longer excluded, whether in art or philosophy. But the majority of these protagonists are based in the US, and thus reinforce American supremacy in globalization. It is quite ironic, considering the anti-American (or Western) tendency in many of these intellectuals. (We should keep in mind – unlike most star architects – that the problem of post-colonialism is not often discussed in architecture, when compared to other fields.) These new post-colonial heroes are demonstrating the very notion formulated by Western intellectuals (e.g., the nomadism or deterritorialization formulated by Deleuze and Guattarri), but on an even more genuinely global and de-nationalized scale than most Western professionals. These new subjects of the contemporary diaspora seem to acquire post-modern subjectivity, regardless of the "obsolete" requirement proposed by critics like Hsia, to establish the modern subject. If these intellectuals have really succeeded, it is decidedly welcome, but the situation is not so simple because they run on the border's edge and not the secured area beyond the border. We should further investigate the position of these blade-runners.

Shih Shu-mei, a typical intellectual in this situation, a Chinese critic born and raised in Korea, educated in Taiwan and now working in the US, made an interesting observation on the danger accompanying the blade-runner's position. Referring to discourses that commend transnationalism, she dismisses the idea that Asian plurality and its discourses can potentially compete with the American hegemony, calling them both utopian and dystopian. What is at issue here is not the fact that national borders are transgressed by individual subjects, but the capital flow, or in Hardt and Negri's "Empire"[1] what we could also call the reality of globalization today, where transnationalism through new approaches to the division of international labor, for instance, can actually support and even reinforce the oppressive nation-state, instead of negating it. Against this danger, the transnationalistic argument advocates the possibility of transnational subjects that resist global hegemony and try to overturn the oppressive view of immigrants and minorities, who are otherwise always regarded as suffering. According to Shih, one may introduce a non-resistant vision for constituting an individual as a transnational entity that does not need to be governed by oppressive nation-states. This proposition contains nothing negative. But this new transnational individual does not thus turn his/her nation itself transnational as well. Shih admits the possibility of the rhetoric that transnationalism could make the Third World contemporary to the Western counterparts by circumventing the natural evolutionary stages of progress, such as the Chinese are doing today in our field of contemporary architecture, and by introducing star architects from the West. However, she is ultimately skeptical of regarding this as a postmodern blessing; it is potentially dangerous in that it could ignore the difference derived from history and power; it might, ironically, repeat the same universalism that underlies the modernization of the past.

In the same text, Shih then goes on to analyze the works of Taiwanese film director Ang Lee, by examining the reality of a Taiwan pervaded by American culture (rather than Japanese culture, as was true in the recent past); Lee himself characterized today's Taiwanese as psychological immigrants to the US, even when not physical immigrants; three stages of colonialization – by China, Japan and then by the US – were overlapped as if Taiwan had been a palimpsest. This seems to coincide with what Husia Chu-Joe called "colonization from within." Meanwhile, in the US, Taiwanese culture is obviously marginalized (modified and condensed through film) and remains unchallenging, according to Shih, but merely satisfying American audiences' voyeuristic tastes, – the trans-modern subjects becoming the objects of novel exoticism in our postmodern age.

Dai Jin-Hua,[4] a Chinese feminist film critic of recent Chinese films that have been well received in the West, attributes their success to several factors. First, they are imbued with the characterization of otherness, presenting heterogeneous and unique imagery, because Occidentals do not want merely a copy of their culture, although, on the other hand, they do not want any kind of contemporary self-portrait of an autonomous culture indigenous to Asia, either; a self-contained expression of the Orient is not what the West wants to see; and, in some cases, the West cannot see such an expression as a self-expression, because it is too alien. Thus, Shih points out that the later works of Ang Lee, produced in the US following his move to Hollywood, respond to the expectations of American audiences just as Dai outlined above. In order to develop a reputation in the West, most Asian artists, not only cinematographers, necessarily accept stylistic modification leading to a stereotypical condensation of their culture of their origin.

Dai's analysis exactly coincides with my argument regarding how the early Japanese modernist architects Sutemi Horiguchi, Isoya Yoshida and Kenzo Tange were received in the West, which is discussed in my essay for the catalogue accompanying the End of the Century exhibition curated by the Museum of Contemporary Art in Los Angeles.[5] There, I remarked critically on Kojin Karatani's essay "Japan as a Museum," written for another exhibition on the Japanese avant-garde held at the Guggenheim Museum in New York.[6] I found Karatani's assertion, that the Japanese artists well acknowledged in the West had been actually regarded in Japan itself not as Westernized in their work, to be depending much too uncritically on Western standards. But rather, the traditionalists (those deeply engaged in the tradition or who returned to tradition after their engagement with modernism) and their followers had simply ignored those who were regarded as Westernized. This kind of standards underpins the present acknowledgement in the West of the early phase of modern Japanese architecture, for which only Tange enjoys an international reputation. If we are to adopt Dai's assessment, Horiguchi's works would have seemed too much like copies of Western modernism when viewed from the West, and Yoshida as too alien to the West and too internal an expression of the Orient (both evaluations less likely to be the case for Asian observers), while Tange was lauded because he reflected clichés of Western appreciation, integrating Western logic into the presentation of a heterogeneous and yet unique Asian imagery. This formulation remains valid, I believe, ten years after my original essay – as in the case of appreciation for Tadao Ando's stout and existential walls, altered by the movement of natural light entering from above. Both these devices, in fact, are alien to the Japanese architectural tradition but have been treated by critics as uniquely Japanese: one sees only what one wants to.

The problem of the subject in the age of globalization, from the colonial past to the postmodern present, is folded in quite a complex manner. These folds are multi-dimensional, and are not the same in Japan as they are in ex-colonial cities. The task of unfolding is certainly much more significant than the superfluous computer-generated forms, which are now so haughtily celebrated but do not take into account external politico-social conditions or material construction techniques.

Bad News
Jordi Bernadó

GOLF CLUB
LINKS KOHNOSU

PAULÃO
PAULÃO
PAULÃO

PAULÃO PAULÃO

แฟลต ศักดิ์สิทธิ์
(038) 425567-8
โทนี่
TONY'S
ENTERTAINMENT COMPLEX
THE BEST DISCOTHEQU
WALKING STREET
SOUTH PATTAYA
LIVE BANDS NIGHTLY
Tel.(038)425-79

วัดธรรมสามัคคี
เมืองพัทยา ต.หนองปรือ อ.บางละมุง จ.ชลบุรี พ.ศ.๒๕๓๒
มอเตอร์ไซค์
รับจ้างทั่วไป

Panasonic
DVD
桌球俱乐部
silent café
专卖
XION

商場保健品总汇
淮海中路344号
热线电话:63363567
XIONG
专卖
雄
银联

A Cosmopolitan View on Thinking and Being-in-Common

Deborah Hauptmann

> The founding duality of the national outlook – foreigner – native – no longer adequately reflects reality. All methods of enquiry that operate with statistical concepts such as "foreigner" and "native" are unprepared for the realities of life in a world that is becoming increasingly transnational and involves plural attachments that transcend the boundaries of countries and nationality.[1]

This paper takes up as its primary task a commentary on Ulrich Beck's recent book *The Cosmopolitan Vision*. It will also seek to extend, or at least to address, one small problematic which arises within cosmopolitan discourses, namely that of the co-essence of individuals as expressed in Jean-Luc Nancy's construction: *Ego Sum = Ego Cum*. Architecture and urbanism will be briefly addressed in relation to the problem of the city. In other words, notions of the *Domestic and Foreign* will not be developed based on the view which sees in architectural "style" (in the sense of a vernacular vs. an international style for instance) a recourse to, say, the domestic understood as "native" and natural or recognizable as a place, and the foreign understood as that which "comes from" elsewhere (thus belonging to someone/where else). Simply put, the ideas of inclusion and exclusion (which haunt the notions of the domestic and the foreign) will not be seen solely as the "formally" invisible or illegible. Rather, they will encompass as well the manner in which an actor or agent is able to articulate his or her aspirations within the space of the city – in the sense of "belonging to" as opposed to being "excluded from" a society or community. This is the occasion to note that the (cosmopolitan) city, as it will be discussed here, has nothing to do with a discourse on the city that focuses on the scale or size, the extension, or the scope of the city as "metropolis" (capitol city, global city etc); the (cosmopolitan) city, that I seek to address, will be about intensities and a disposition towards living in common; or, calling upon the title of a work that will be cited below, it will display an inclination towards the *Being Singular Plural* of individuals and collectives as they form and transform the world.

Cosmos-Polis

The ancient notion of the cosmopolitan (*kosmopolitês*) – "citizen of the world" – appears historically in various, and often diverse, forms.[2] The shifts in formulations have acted upon the very concepts of what constitutes the city (*cite*) in religious doctrine, political philosophy and, more recently, the social sciences. The Stoic philosophers were perhaps the first to offer a definitive philosophy of cosmopolitanism; this was followed by, among others, Roman, Judaic and Christian interpretations. The Dutch philosopher Erasmus drew on ancient interpretations specifically in a plea for national and religious tolerance. Further, Kant's writing on cosmopolitanism still acts as a fundamental source for contemporary interpretations.[3] It is arguable that the modern vision of the city is rooted in the Enlightenment belief in a "good society," i.e., one founded in accord with Kantian (or neo-Kantian) cosmopolitanism. At its core, the principle of cosmopolitanism, which asserts that all human beings have the right to belong to a single community, continues to endure (of course, with various caveats and limitations). It is necessary, however, to point out that any view of cosmopolitanism must accept the fact that it not only contains emancipatory principles, but establishes restrictions as well. Regarding cosmopolitanism as it is formulated in Enlightenment thinking, Derrida contends that the laws of cosmopolitanism are not restricted to "the conditions of universal hospitality" only; for with Kant we can identify two limitations: first, the exclusion of hospitality from a "*right of residence*" in favor of the more limited "*right of visitation;*" secondly, by defining hospitality under the rule of the law, it is consigned to a condition dependent on state sovereignty.[4] In contemporary discourse on this notion of a "citizen of the world," Derrida, for instance, asks whether it is still possible to make an accurate distinction between the City and the State as the generally accepted forms of the metropolis. That leads us to one of the primary characteristics of cosmopolitanism, namely the possibility that the city should provide a place of refuge to anyone seeking asylum and that the cosmopolitan city, as such, has the obligation to provide "hospitality" (offering hospitality to the foreigner, the immigrant, the exiled, the deported, the stateless or the displaced).[5]

At the beginning of his book *The Cosmopolitan Vision*, Beck quickly draws a distinction between the terms "globalization" and "cosmopolitanization." He defines globalization as primarily a "one-dimensional" *economic* condition in which the global market and its defense of neo-liberal economic growth is understood in terms of the free-flow of capital, commodities and labor across national (or other such defined) boarders. In contrast, he considers cosmopolitanization to be "multi-dimensional," seeing it as a process that has "irreversibly changed the historical 'nature' of social worlds and the standing of states in these worlds."[6] Suggesting that cosmopolitanization "comprises the development of multiple loyalties as well as the increase in diverse transnational forms of life, he points to the emergence of non-state political actors (from Amnesty International to the World Trade Organization), and the development of global protest movements against (neo-liberal) globalism and in support of a different kind of (cosmopolitan) globalization…"[7] What were earlier conceived as the primary oppositions upon which socio-political discourses were based (democracy vs. communism, capitalism vs. socialism etc.), primarily denoted ideological differences in terms of political and economic position and policy; while, contemporary conflicts include major cultural antagonisms and clashes of values between civilizations… "culture, identity and religious faith, which used to be subordinate to strategic political and military imperatives, now set the priorities on the international political agenda." Culture, in this sense is invading politics. In other words, the aestheticization of politics has become the rule for all political practice.[8] We will return to this point shortly in discussing matters commonly considered under the the rubric of "postmodern."

Offering a view of what a contemporary "cosmopolitan vision" might entail, Beck first distinguishes between what he calls the "philosophical" (normative) and "social scientific" (analytical-empirical); subsequently, he proceeds to outline several existing models, or "social modalities," which deal with the notion of cosmopolitanism.[9] We will very quickly reiterate a few of these modalities.

Nationalism (or "methodological nationalism") has traditionally been based on the assertion that the nation-state is what defines a national society; as such it imposes a territorial model, or a self-containment model, by which, among other things, the nation-state both creates and grants both human and civil rights. Issues of morality, the area of human rights, for instance, have been taken as universal presuppositions. Yet, whether or not the nation-state generated and sustained the rights *of* the people, or the demands for rights *by* the people forced the foundation of the republic, both individual and collective rights were held (relatively) under the sovereignty of the nation-state. However, today it can be argued that human rights (universally) cross all national boundaries. Additionally, we would add that a moral ("just" or "good") society does not develop merely on the basis of rights; it develops equally on the basis of obligation. Furthermore, that obligation addresses itself immediately to community, while rights address directly to the individual. Today it appears that we are witnessing a disconnection taking place between the nation, the state, and society, which in previous times were held to be inextricable. Thus, to Derrida's question as cited above, the problem arises as to how it is now possible to distinguish – within a concrete social context – between foreigners and nationals, between citizens and non-citizens, between human rights and civil rights. A "national outlook" under these conditions must be sustained, as Beck argues, within a "territorial social ontology" that goes to the heart of everyday life in domains (that were once) as diverse as politics and mass media.[10] Beck further claims that "realistic" cosmopolitanism begs the question: "how do 'societies' deal with 'difference' and 'borders' under conditions of global interdependence crises?"[11] A question we will return to shortly.

Universalism as a social modality presumes equality between all men. Yet, in its aspirations towards pure equality it levels differences by assuming a form of human and social similitude as well as applying a form of cultural homogeneity. Such a disposition can limit curiosity about what makes others different, and, by extension, can thwart deference to another's individual or community values. According to Beck, moreover, "the particularity of others is sacrificed to an assumed universal equality which denies its own origins and interests;" universalism thereby becomes duplicitous, leading to an excess of "respect and hegemony, rationality and terror." Continuing with this critique, he argues that such a view is dependent on the presumption of "a" national and "an" international territorial distinction – which, in principle, does not take into account the fact that the two are so interdependent that the first actually presupposes the second. In other words, there exists an internal fallacy within the universalist position in that it applies a particular set of (social) principles to the general (universal) society. Significant problems thus arise when we attempt to transfer (correlate or contrast) "our own" (nationalistic) understanding to an "other's" model. This leads, according to Beck, to a conflation of internal and external structures which can, respectively, be isolated in terms of spatial perspectives.

Relativism, for very similar reasons, stands no better to resisting hegemonic forces than does universalism. Its aspirations towards the recognition and subsequent acknowledgement of contextual (geographic, biological or cultural) difference, are conceptually plausible, but, in practice, it reverts to an incommensurability of perspectives which only furthers our ignorance. Beck, for his part, offers the notion of a "realistic cosmopolitanism," one which is practiced "not in an exclusive manner but in an *inclusive* relation to universalism, contextualism, nationalism, transnationalism, etc." He argues that it is precisely "this particular combination of semantic elements which the cosmopolitan outlook shares with the universalistic, relativistic and national outlooks and which by the same token distinguishes it form these other approaches."[12] Beck summarizes this in the following way: "the unintentional irony of the relativist incommensurability thesis is that it is almost indistinguishable from an essentialist world view;" on the other hand, contextualist universalism, in assuming the historical norm of cultural intermingling, presupposes that various forms of interventionism are inevitable.[13] And this is also what is meant when we refer to our contemporary era as exhibiting the "crisis of global interdependence." The crisis, as such, issues from what we might refer to as an ethics of tolerance (inclusionary in principle) which is confronted by an incommensurable practice of integration (exclusionary in actuality).[14]

Beck further includes *multiculturalism* as a social modality. To my mind, however, multiculturalism as a mode of thinking has become all but irrelevant when it is utilized only to indicate diversity and as a strategy for dealing with difference. Yet, for the purposes of this paper, it remains worth noting that under the terms of Beck's "non-integrationist supposition," that multiculturalism (when conceived using the model of the nation) does not recognize the individual as such, but only that of multiple nations.[15] Similarly, Étienne Balibar suggests that political violence often leads us to the problems of multiculturalism, since it is based on the fact that certain linguistic, religious, geographical, and historical identities are not officially sanctioned as "legitimate mediations" of (secondary) national identity. He writes: "(w)e speak of *exclusion* in this case because the logic of hegemony ought to be able to use *all primary identities* in order to integrate them into the national community, or to construct a 'fictive ethnicity.'"[16] This same line of thinking leads to misunderstandings of pluralism, or *cultural plurality*, which rely on either universal homogenization (the generic) or incommensurability of perspectives (particularism). The main point is that when culture is conceived as "territorially circumscribed," then the question of plurality leads to a sterile and false alternative: either universal sameness (McDonaldization) or relativistic perspectives that resist comparison (incommensurability). Many of the claims made by so-called postmodernism seem to fall easily under similar modalities. In architecture, these two modalities were perhaps seen in the shift away from the immutable and the pure, towards plasticity and plurality. Here we might simply recall Robert Venturi's famous pronouncement "less is a bore" in response to Ludwig Mies van der Rohe's canonical statement, "less is more." This is, of course, something other and something more than merely a shift in style from what we often think of as the "international" to the "postmodern." Beck discusses the relation between postmodernism and postnationalism using terms such as "playful," "satirical" and "ambivalent." Here we might add the term irony, since it has been so widely discussed in architecture. He notes the use of "various styles, symbols, and concepts stemming from older historical cultures:"

> this shallow cosmopolitanism of quotation and montage can indeed exploit the past to renew itself continually and try to pass it off as a fashionable invention. But is it widely thought that it cannot locate itself in history or dispel the basic fact that cultures and cultural imagination are historically specific and rooted, and hence territorial, phenomena.[17]

In this sense the question points to the importance of memory, specifically cultural memory. Yet, anyone who has studied objects of cultural production would no doubt agree that within this now almost axiomatic critique of postmodernism lies at least one misconception: that there is actually something new about eclecticism. Even in Western architecture's earliest treatise we know that Vitruvius privileged both Roman exemplars and precedents from Greek architecture, primarily Hellenistic, extending his references to all of Asia Minor. Despite the existence of imbedded vernacular or indigenous examples of cultural and social expression found in relatively isolated situations, any socio-cultural formation that took place in the city (*cite*) incorporated a multiplicity of various influences and streams, thereby simultaneously incorporating and producing "cultural memory." In fact, one might suggest that the "purity" of the modern vision provides the exception and certainly not the historical rule. Modern art and architecture aspired to pass from the material to the non-material, progressing from abstract expressionism and minimalism on its way to its own purification, its own erasure through self-effacement and self-actualization in conceptual art.[18] What Beck identifies as the problem of post-nationalism's non-signification was already present in the modernist turn towards abstraction (in art, architecture, literature and theater), which equally sought a "universalist" view of humanity. In this sense, "historical dislocatedness," so often attributed to postmodernism, took on its contemporary form long ago when, in philosophy's "gray on gray," as Nietzsche so expressed it, the Owl of Minerva took flight.

Of course this observation sits dangerously close to what Beck identifies as "contextualist universalism" (and from a "social scientific" view point this may well be the case).[19] Nevertheless, while many social scientists, geographers, economists, and others, offer profound discourses on "space," rarely do they discuss "what is above the surface of the globe." And whatever potential dangers of failure (or incommensurability) lurk within the manner in which different disciplines approach their understanding of cultural production, in my view, the point remains that if we are going to extend analysis to practice, then we must seek to grasp not only the methodological instants, but the movements that fluctuate and thereby elude our most rigorous analytic filters. Thus, going against the common logic which sees architecture and urbanism as a fixed and immutable field (on which "the social" is simultaneously enacted and indifferent), I therefore suggest that we keep our minds open to the "spacings," the "intervals" and the "betweeness" of which the city *is* a living and breathing participant.[20] Furthermore, the crisis, mentioned just above – i.e. the conflict between inclusionary principles (tolerance) and exclusionary practice (incommensurability) – is being enacted not only through reflexive but also through recapitulative productions of socio-political *and* spatio-temporal knowledge and practice.[21]

Furthermore, the socio-political implications of the postmodern (post-national) view of cosmopolitanism require, for Beck, a "realistic cosmopolitanism" that can include the recognition of differences "beyond the misunderstandings of territoriality and homogenization."[22] In this respect, he reiterates that any thinking about difference that is theorized through boundary confirming categories such as "internationalism" will find itself unduly restricted. The cosmopolitan view, by contrast, has the potential to transform international relations by "opening and redrawing boundaries, by transcending or reversing the polarity of the *relations between us and them*, and not least by rewriting the relation between the state, politics and the nation in cosmopolitan terms [my emphasis]."[23] In other words, unlike the international outlook, the cosmopolitan outlook is capable of grasping the changes taking place within what Beck refers to as a "social and political grammar." Moreover, and this is particularly important, he adds that through the process of integration "the cosmopolitan outlook determines multiple spatial, temporal and practical both/and realities to which the national perspective remains blind."[24]

At this point we can turn to what may be thought of as the temporal dimension of cosmopolitanism as opposed to the spatial dimension of globalization.[25] With respect to identity, it has been suggested that cosmopolitanization accepts multiple (plural) loyalties and nationalities. It is perhaps no accident that Beck here moves from the question or the challenge of the "temporal" (read here as memory), directly to that of identity. It is worth noting, for instance, his commentary on "patriotic identity," while recalling the above reference to Balibar. When patriotic identity is seen as the only legitimate form of identity, there is generally a tendency to see "ethnic" conflicts as nothing more than "tribal feuds."[26] Suggesting that inhabitants of cosmopolitan modernity, by contrast, seek to overturn such categorical limitations, he states that they do not seek to avoid the conflicts that may arise out of conflicting identities. In fact, Beck contends, they know that it is precisely through this "overlapping and conflict with other identities" that "individuality" itself becomes productive, arguing that each individual makes his/her own contribution to this process. At the same time he adds that there are certain forms of "indifference" and "social distance" which can also "make a positive contribution to social integration." This leads to the idea that cosmopolitan society arises to the extent that national societies are split and "disintegrate."[27] Thus, cosmopolitanism derives great benefit from "transnationalism," which offers a completely different view of borders and frontiers. For, as Beck observes, the cosmopolitan outlook "has its home in amazement, in the expanding in between, in which seemingly eternal certainties, borders and differentiations become blurred and effaced."[28] Here we find transecting identities, something we might think of in terms of multiplicities (rather than "multitudes"). But what becomes important here is not merely the complexity suggested within the individual (as the construction of "self"), as if incorporated and multiple experiences and perspectives will, in and of themselves, constitute cosmopolitanism. It is equally important to stress that the individual, or the trans-identity of self, is not restricted to, nor constructed within, multiple national identities alone (we will return to this below with Balibar's reference to the "transindividual").

Balibar offers another position regarding identity, arguing that "ethnicity" as a model of identification, though powerful thanks to the fact that it can combine cultural characteristics, always produces fictive elaborations founded on the basis of "genealogies and religious or linguistic affinities." He further suggests that every individual must be understood as a "multiplicity of competing identities;" and every individual must confront the same problem: "how to proceed in order to orient oneself – to 'find oneself' – among one's multiple personalities, with the help of others (who can be *abstract or ideal others*: memories, stories, symbols or institutional emblems, 'maps' in the most general sense of the term)."[29] We might return here to Beck's notions concerning the interconnection between space and society; for the temporal dimension must be considered along with the spatial if we are not to be led to some form of "ahistorical reification," or one-dimensional view. Such a simplistic, entirely spatial view "exhausts itself in its concentration on the pluralization and interpenetration of identities and boundary-constructions." What Beck will then refer to as a "*deeper* real-cosmopolitanism" is one which "alerts us to the empirical-analytical and the normative questions produced by the cosmopolitanization of society and politics, of history and memory in the temporal dimension."[30]

Yet, here, too, we find a distinct overtone with regard to the political dimension of memory. For instance, he asks, "how does globality get refracted historically in the non-simultaneity of concurrent cultural situations and self-definitions?" In this sense the "global" has no memory, or as he writes: "the present is colonizing the future *and* the past. The polis that is extended *only* in the spatial dimension is conceived as the expansion of loyalties, identities, obligations and rights. The cosmopolitan outlook trapped in the metaphysics of the eternal, turbulent, catastrophic present remains restricted..."[31] Beck is here introducing us to the problem of the "instant;" that which in other terms can be understood as the sptatialization of time, which replaces the flow of the continuous (belonging to human experience) with the frozen frame of the discrete (belonging to socio-political analysis). To get at the problem of the individual (beyond the frame of trans-national constructions of identity) it may be helpful to turn to the ideas of Jean-Luc Nancy in order to address the relation between the individual and the collective, or what was referred to above, citing Beck, as the "relations between us and them." For behind the "I," indeed perhaps in front of it, as Nancy has argued convincingly, is the "we:"

> The one/the other is neither "by," nor "for," nor "in," nor "despite," but rather "with." This "with" is at once both more and less than "relation" or "bond," especially if such relation or bond presupposes the preexistence of the terms upon which it relies... "With" is the sharing of time-space; it is the at-the-same-time-in-the-same-place as itself, in itself, shattered. It is the instant scaling back of the principle of identity: Being is at the same time in the same place only on the condition of the spacing of an indefinite plurality of singularities.[32]

Being "together," in this sense goes to the heart of simultaneity, to the sharing of time and space without the reduction to the instant, or the instantaneity of *pure succession*.[33] To quote Nancy: "'Same time / same place' assumes that 'subjects,' to call them that, share the space-time, but not in the extrinsic sense of 'sharing'; they must share it between *themselves*; they must themselves 'symbolize' it as the 'same space-time' without which there would not be time or space." This position not only treats time and space as philosophical abstractions but also as concrete practices that include the "distinctness of place;" continuing with the previous citation, we note that "the passage from one place to another *needs time* [*du lieu à l'autre,* il faut le temps]. And moving in place [*du lieu à lui-même*] as such also needs time: the time for the place to open itself as place, the time to space itself."[34] I would like to suggest that it is also the notion of a "we" that has falsely generated the idea of the "other" (found in Enlightenment, post-colonial and psychological theories of self, the self-same, and the other, which includes Erasmus' concept of tolerance). In other words, concepts of both individualism and collectivism, which utilize denotations (and dualities) such as *the* foreign and *the* domestic, are simply inadequate to reflect our daily realities.

Now, returning to the above challenge to memory, and against the absence of a collective memory, Beck argues that the global might well be in the process of producing a "collective" future. Or it would be if we take seriously the "world-threat" and the "self-endangerment" of civilization together with the possibility of imagining a "transnationally shared past which takes on concrete form in the dialectic of memory and forgiveness." It should be argued, as well, that this concrete form is acted in place, in community itself, and that we must be willing to examine the *concrete* as signifying what Nancy refers to as "the real object of a thinking of being-in-common."[35] To proceed further in this vein we must also be able to distinguish between our *consciousness* of and *practice* of cosmopolitanism. In this connection, Beck argues that while we may be witnessing a shared "global awareness" of a collective future, there is, in fact, no current set of practices which corresponds to this awareness. Of course, many might take issue with this, for instance environmental awareness (our systematic destruction of "the globe," has for some decades now been on the agenda of architects and urbanists). However, here Beck is attempting to open up a perspective that, even in his view, does not yet surpass theoretical constructs.[36] Nevertheless, Beck continues to provide illumination, models of thought that allow us gain a deeper understanding of cosmopolitanism. For instance, he argues that a *monological imaginary* is found at the core of the nation-state's nationalistically centered image of self (domestic) and other (foreign); and that this can only result in the manifestation of exclusionary practices. He offers a counter-position in the form of what calls a *dialogical imaginary of the internalized other*. Introducing Nietzsche's observation that modernity was engaged in an "age of comparison," Beck subsequently interprets Nietzsche within the framework of the cosmopolitan, writing that what was important was the latter's recognition that cultures had begun to "interpenetrate," producing a changing of perspectives whereby "the cosmopolitan worldview becomes an imagining of *alternative* paths within and between different cultures and modernities."[37]

Following Dominique Schnapper, Balibar offers a similar distinction between "substantialism" and "formalism." The former is based in the citizen's participation in "a single traditional culture, a single language, or ethnic heritage, inaccessible to all those who have not inherited them by birth or been entirely assimilated into them;" and, in the latter case, "citizenship would stem entirely from individual adherence to certain moral values (the rights of man), from the respect of certain juridical (constitutional) rules, and from the 'contract' implicit in republican institutions."[38] Balibar further suggests that the nation must escape from forms of exclusionary (nationalistic) practice while simultaneously creating what amounts to a "singular identity." In other words, the nation must work both to integrate and welcome the non-national (foreigner) and to "bring forth a belonging that is *experienced in common* and transmitted from generation to generation... [my emphasis]."[39] Yet this bringing forth of belonging occurs both at the level of thought and at that of action, as mentioned at the beginning of this essay. With rights come obligations. Obligations and rights become acted and enacted not only in our minds, our homes, and our neighborhoods (our institutions); they are transcribed within the very dynamics of our cities as well. The city is not simply the passive frame, the background upon which our interconnected lives play out. Nor, as Nancy argues, is the city primarily community; nor is it simply public space:

> The city is at least as much the bringing to light of being-in-common as the disposition (dispersal and disparity) of the community represented as founded in interiority or transcendence. It is "community" without common origin. That being the case, and as long as philosophy is an appeal to the origin, the city, far from being philosophy's subject or space, is its problem. Or else, it is its subject or space in the mode of being its problem, its aporia... philosophy is the problem of the city; philosophy covers over the subject that is expected as "community."[40]

One might simply say, as well, that the problem of the city includes our aspirations towards an "open society," one in which the "cosmopolitan view" can live. To realize such a dis-position it will be necessary to think through the question of who, in fact, might be the "we" within a complex society (of domestic *and* foreign inhabitants). In other words, the "us" and "them" of the "domestic" and the "foreign" as a category of distinction which aligns oppositional fields of interest in the form of both knowledge and practice must be abandoned in order to make way for inclusionary as opposed to exclusionary practices. Accordingly, we must discuss relations of people to people and not only those of states to states. Simply put, issues of identity (as shared articulations) are not, so to speak, represented, but practiced – inclusion/exclusion at the levels that are the most subtle and most difficult to discern; they generate urban patterns of practice and habits of movement and encounters that remain unarticulated in most urban or architectural analysis. With Nancy, we might simply add that the task is to "understand how history – as a singular, Western accident – 'became' what one might call 'global' or 'planetary' without, at the same time, engendering itself as 'universal.'"[41] But here we must accomodate, as already discussed above, a different sense of the "universal" – not as it is applied to society *as such* but as it speaks to the nature of the individual and, even more importantly, of the individual in community with other individuals.[42]

Using the framework outlined above, Beck deepens his analysis of the "cosmopolitan real" by developing a concept, or modality, of "interconnectedness," understood, of course, from a social-scientific point of view.[43] Here he utilizes the metaphor of liquidity, arguing that cosmo-olitanism should examine and explore "the boundary-transcending and boundary-effacing multiperspectivalism" of social actors and political agents through new theoretical and analytical filters.[44] The cosmopolitanization approach, Beck writes:

> distinguishes systematically between the perspective of social actors and that of social scientific observers; (b) it replaces the opposition between national either/or "streams," "networks" and "scapes" with a both/and typology (transnational, translocal, global-local, global-national, etc.); and (c) it inquires into the congruence or lack of congruence between actor and observer perspectives, and thereby highlights discrepancies among the options open to social and political actors and institutions, on the one hand, and social scientific approaches and perspectives, on the other, and traces their implications for concepts and theories in the social sciences (e.g., of conflict and integration, domination, inequality, the state).[45]

Of course I take this to include architectural and urban practices of both the actors (the designers, planners etc.) and the agents (the performers, transformers, interpreters, transcribers, etc.) of spatial and temporal enunciations ("expression," perhaps in Beck's terms). In fact, to my mind, nothing is to be gained by continuing to separate the (concrete) problems of the city as seen from the perspective of urban researchers from the conditions formulated in (abstract) theories propounded in numerous "spatial"/and or/"spatio-temporal" discourses – a separation rooted in long held antagonisms. Nevertheless, Beck also poses a similar set of problems, asking such questions as, "does public space emerge in which seemingly sharp oppositions between 'us and them' become blurred and a conflictual and cooperative culture of transnational openness and reconfiguration of the local arises?"[46]

Perhaps we can get at this further by returning to the notion of "agency." Let us provisionally accept the theory that the "global" or the "local" do not exist as such, but, instead, are made at every moment within language and through various (social-political-economic-spatial/temporal) practices. And let us also agree for now that it is impossible to address such concerns independently of a position on the status of the "individual" and the "collective." (We can interpret this term "collective" in a broad sense also as community or citizenship, as long as we understand by this that which provides a sense of "belonging.") On this point Balibar offers the following assessment with regard to the individual: "*every identity as such is transindividual...* Nothing like the predeterminate models of *collective* identity that *Völkerpsychology* and more generally 'organicist' or 'culturalist' theories of social psychology use to represent national characters and group identities... but neither does anything allow us to think that the individual 'self' constitutes an autonomous and self-sufficient reality whose identity could be formed independently of social processes and a collective imaginary."[47]

And with regard to a "collective identity," Balibar argues that such an identity is not "a given, a metaphysical prerequisite of agency, and it is certainly not a mythical image that could be forcefully imposed upon reality by inventing this or that historical criterion... It is a *quality* of collective agency, which changes form and content in time, as new agents come into play and new solidarities are built among those who, not long ago, were ignoring or fighting each other."[48]

Thus we must question if it is even possible to think any "generic notion of the common." Balibar asks, "*can difference and sharing, conflict and the general interest be thought together?*"[49] Of course on this point Beck appears to remain clear with regard to what he calls the "cosmopolitan sensibility," writing that "what characterizes a domain of experience or horizon of expectations" as cosmopolitan, is that the "cosmopolitan sensibility and competence arise from the clash within one's own life" as it encounters what amounts to cultural collisions at the heart of everyday experience. "The cosmopolitan constellation *qua* domain of experience and horizon of expectations means the *internalization* of difference, the co-presence and coexistence of rival lifestyles, contradictory certainties in the experiential space of individuals and societies." Here he situates the "*dialogical imagination*" in both quotidian and scientific experience. "This involves two things: on the one hand, situating and relativizing one's own form of life within other horizons of possibility; on the other, the capacity to see oneself from the perspective of cultural others and to give this practical effect in one's own experience through the exercise of boundary-transcending imagination."[50] This very idea of transcending boundaries through the faculty of imagination is, in fact, precisely what we are currently witnessing in both the analytic and intuitive thinking about architecture and urban theories and practices today.[51]

One problem with Beck's "cosmopolitan vision," it might be suggested, is that, in the end, it relies upon the self-realization of individuals to both critically reframe their own openness to the world and willingly act within a "new" cosmopolitan sensibility. Thus, we must be willing to take a leap of faith with Beck, the leap to the belief in the individual's ability to place his/herself in an open disposition towards "others." Yet, this disposition *towards* must be also a positioning of the *with*, which, in fact, seeks to obliterate the potential negativity of difference in favor of its positivity. Yet it would be naïve to ignore the fact that within any exchange of ideas – the "clash of cultures," even "within" one's own life perspective – there is also an exchange of power; "power acting upon power" (as Michel Foucault would remind us) which remains inherent in any form of socio-political and spatio-temporal practice.[52] Thus, to turn the idea of cosmopolitanism into that of an active disposition, a practice, we will not only need new forms of research and thinking (as Beck argues); it will also be necessary to open this discourse in two extreme directions. On the one hand, we must establish a philosophical (and, for some, a psychological) problematic that is receptive to discourse on the self and the other. And, on the other hand, it will be necessary to invent, to design, modalities for conceiving this perspective in a way that takes into account the physical environment within which both "conflicts" and "confrontations" and "being-in-common" take place.

I won't now try to summarize my theory of postmodernity – which goes back to the early 1980's – except to say what it tried to do: to correlate a set of psychic and cultural symptoms, if I may put it that way, with an underlying socio-economic periodizing hypothesis. The cultural and psychic symptoms included a growing predominance of the spatial over temporal (which had been the dominant of an older high modernism); a reorganization of the hierarchy of the arts in such a way that the visual image became the central aesthetic phenomenon (a place hitherto reserved for language, and in particular for poetic language); and finally a reduction of experience to the present instant and to the body. These features redefine art and culture just as they reorganize the psychic subject.

The socio-economic hypothesis, meanwhile, posited a shift from that older moment of monopoly capitalism which Lenin called the "imperialist stage" to a new postimperalist and postcolonial stage, which, following the German usage, I called "late capitalism." This stage is characterized by a shift from the older technology of heavy industrial capitalism to the newer cybernetic and informational electronic systems, which has resulted in a conclusive transformation of production and labor. As far as business is concerned, the transformation meant an increasing predominance of finance capital and financial speculation (not least in currency and in land values), and a lightning-like rapidity of money flows all over the globe. These economic effects are, I believe, primarily what is meant by globalization, and I regret not having been prophetic enough to insist on that aspect of things in my first accounts of postmodernity. Postmodernity and globalization are identical, and to insist on the identity between them probably goes a long way towards ensuring a serious social content for a concept – postmodernity – which is often thought to be frivolous and merely cultural. Indeed, one of the originalities of postmodernity itself is to have secured a kind of identity between the economic and the cultural: in the world of global (or as some call it, postmodern) marketing, there is no economic product which is not a cultural object of some kind; while culture today has almost universally become a commodity, sometimes a commodity with a good deal of investment value and profitable returns. Meanwhile, and as a consequence, all the older, traditional, classic ideas of the autonomy of the aesthetic have vanished like the snow and glaciers of the ice age. Still, the economic and the cultural perspectives on globalization are rather different from each other, and I want now – after offering a brief "definition" – to outline what I take to be the four essential or logically possible positions on the matter.

The concept of globalization reflects the sense of an immense enlargement of world communication, as well as of the horizon of a world market, both of which seem far more tangible and immediate than in earlier stages of modernity. Roland Robertson, surely one of the most ambitious theorists of the matter, has formulated the dynamic of globalization as "the twofold process of the particularization of the universal and the universalization of the particular." This is a valuable lead, even though Robertson is intent on offering something like a Utopian vision of "globality," of some new global ethnic and consciousness in the world today, rather than a structural account of the forms that globalization takes in the various realms of the political, the economic and the cultural. I believe that it is necessary to add a dose of negativity to his formula, and to insist on the relations of antagonism and tension between these two poles. I thus propose to "define" globalization as an untotalizable totality which intensifies binary relations between its parts – mostly nations, but also regions and groups, which, however, continue to articulate themselves on the model of "national identities" (rather than in terms of social classes, for example). But what we now need to add to the other qualifications implicit in the formulation – binary or point-to-point relations already being rather different than some plural constellation of localities and particulars – is that such relations are first and foremost ones of tension or antagonism, when not of outright exclusion. In them each term struggles to define itself against the binary other. We must therefore, now add that such relationships (between a state claiming universality, for example, such as the US or the West, and another claiming local particularity, or between particulars, or betweeen universals) are necessarily symbolic ones, which express themselves in a range of collective imaginaries. This does not of course mean that they are somehow merely cultural, let alone unreal. For such symbolic transmission requires the preexistence of economic and communicational channels and pre-established circuits. What emerges world-wide are, then, patterns of negative and positive exchanges which resemble those of class relations and struggles within the nation-state, even though, as I have insisted, they do not (yet) define themselves in that way and currently remain fixed and thematized at the level of the spatial and the geopolitical. I should add that, even on this provisional "definition," the status of the older nation-state under globalization remains a topic for heated debate: it will be more productive to keep this matter open, and in particular to insist that the definition does not imply any transcendence of the older form of the nation-state, nor even a form which might be thought eventually to replace it (world government, world culture, or whatever).

Four positions on our topic seem logically available. The first affirms the opinion that there is no such thing as globalization (there are still the nation states and the national situations; nothing is new under the sun). The second affirms that globalization is nothing new, that there has always been globalization and that it suffices to leaf through the history books to see that as far back as the neolithic trade routes have been global in their scope, with Polynesian artifacts deposited in Africa, and Asian potsherds as far afield as the New World.

Then I suppose one should add two more. One affirms the relationship between globalization and the world market, which is the ultimate horizon of capitalism. One need only to add that the current world networks are simply different in degree and not in kind. While a fourth affirmation (which I have found more interesting than the other three) posits some new or third, multinational stage of capitalism, of which globalization is an intrinsic feature and which we now largely tend, whether we like it or not, to associate with that thing called postmodernity.

Meanwhile, above and beyond all this, there are the judgments: one can deplore globalization or celebrate it, just as one welcomes the new freedoms of the postmodern era and the postmodern outlook, and in particular the new technological revolutions, or on the other hand elegiacally laments the passing of the splendors of the modern: the glories and possibilities of modernism in the arts, the disappearance of history as the fundamental element in which human beings exist, and not least, the end of an essentially modernist field of political struggle in which the great ideologies still had the force and the authority of the great religions of the earlier times. But I do think we have an interest in at least provisionally separating this now familiar postmodern debate from the matter of globalization, all the while understanding only too well that the two issues are deeply intertwined and that positions on the postmodern debate are bound to make their way back in eventually.

Let's start from the principle that we already somehow know what globalization is, and try rather to focus on the concept of globalization, on its ideological structure, if you like (it being understood in advance that this word ideology is unprejorative, and that a concept can be ideological and also correct and true all at once). I believe that globalization is a communicational concept, which alternately masks and transmits cultural or economic meanings. We have a sense that there are both denser and more extensive communicational networks all over the world today, networks that are, on the one hand, the result of remarkable innovations in communicational technologies of all kinds, and, on the other, have as their foundations the tendentially greater degree of modernization in all the countries of the world, or at least in their big cities, which includes the implantation of such technologies.

But the communicational focus of the concept of globalization is essentially incomplete: I defy anyone to try to think it in exclusively media or communicational terms; and we can find a point of contrast and distinctions in the images of the media in the earlier 20th century, that is to say in the modernist period. There did then seem to be a certain semi-autonomy about the development of the media: radio did seem to penetrate for the first time into remote areas (both at home and abroad); the progress of film around the world was both a swift and a startling one, which seemed to bring some new kind of mass consciousness with it; journalism and reporting, meanwhile, were somehow at their outer reaches heroic acts, which shed new light and brought back new information. No one can feel that the cybernetic revolution is like that, if only because it builds on

to be continued on page 113

Windows to the World

Stefanie Bürkle

those first, already established, networks. The communicational development today no longer projects the image in all its connotations, but rather simply that of new technologies.

This is why, along with the communicational concept of globalization, one always finds other dimensions smuggled in. Thus, the newer phenomenon essentially distinguishes itself from the older modern one by technology rather than by information (even though this term is then itself reappropriated and ideologically developed today on a grand scale). What happens is that the technology and what the computer people call information begins to slip insensibly in the direction of advertisements and publicity, of postmodern marketing, and finally of the export of TV programs, rather than the return of startling reports from remote places. But this is to say that the surface concept, the communicational one, has suddenly acquired a whole cultural dimension: the communicational signifier has been endowed with a more properly cultural signified or signification. Now the positing of an enlargement of communicational nets has secretly been transformed into some kind of message about a new world culture.

But the slippage can also take another direction: the economic. Thus, in our attempt to think this new, still purely communicational concept, we begin to fill the empty signifier in with visions of financial transfers and investments all over the world, and the new networks begin to swell with the commerce of some new and allegedly more flexible capitalism. (I have to confess that I have always found this a ludicrous expression.) We begin by remembering that the newly flexible production was made possible by computerization precisely a loop back to the technological again. And we also remember that computers and their programs and the like are themselves among the most hotly exchanged forms of goods among the nations today. In this variant, then, the ostensibly communicational concept has secretly been transformed into a vision of the world market and its newfound interdependence, a global division of labor on an extraordinary scale, new electronic trade routes tirelessly plied by commerce and finance alike.

Now I think we are better equipped to understand the flows of debate and ideology around the slippery concept, whose twin and not altogether commensurable faces now seem to produce two distinct types of position, which are, however, themselves reversible. Thus, if you insist on the cultural contents of this new communicational form, I think you will slowly emerge into a postmodern celebration of difference and differentation: suddenly all the cultures around the world are placed in tolerant contact with each other in a kind of immense cultural pluralism which it would be very difficult not to welcome. Beyond that, beyond the dawning celebration of cultural difference, and often very closely linked to it, is a celebration of the emergence of a whole immense range of groups, races, genders, ethnicities, into the speech of the public sphere, a falling away of those structures that condemned whole segments of the population to silence and to subalternity. A world-wide growth of popular democratization – why not? –

which seems to have some relationship to the evolution of the media, but which is immediately expressed by a new richness and variety of cultures in the new world space.

If, on the other hand, your thoughts turn economic, and the concept of globalization becomes colored by those codes and meanings, I think you will find the concept darkening and growing more opaque. Now what comes to the fore is increasing identity (rather than difference): the rapid assimilation of hitherto autonomous national markets and productive zones into a single sphere, the disappearance of national subsistence (in food for example), the forced integration of countries all over the globe into precisely that new global division of labor I mentioned before. Here what begins to infuse our thinking of globalization is a picture of standardization on an unparalleled new scale, of forced integration as well, into a world system from which "delinking" (to use Samir Amin's term) is henceforce impossible and even inconceivable. This is obviously a far more baleful prospect than the preceding joyous vision of heterogeneity and difference, but I'm not sure that these visions are logically incompatible; indeed they seem somehow to be dialectically related, at least in the mode of the unresolvable antinomy.

But now, having achieved these first twin positions, having in some first moment rotated the concept in such a way that it takes on these distinct kinds of content, its surface now glittering in light, and then obscured again by darkness and gloom – now it is important to add that the transfers can begin. Now, after having secured these first initial structural possibilities, you can project their axes upon each other. Now, in a second moment, the baleful vision of identity can be transfered onto the cultural realm: in what will be affirmed, in some gloomy Frankfurt School fashion, in the world-wideAmericanization or standardization of culture, the destruction of local differences, the massification of all the people on the planet.

But you are equally free to do the inverse, and to transfer the joyous and celebratory difference und multiple heterogeneities of the first, cultural dimensions, onto the economic sphere. Where, as you may well imagine, the rhetoricians of the market pop up and feverishly reassure us as to the richness and excitement of the new free market all over the world, and the increase in sheer productivity which the open market will lead to, the transcendental satisfaction that human beings have finally begun to grasp exchange, the market and capitalism, as their most fundamental human possibilities and the surest sources of freedom.

Now I want to offer a few reflections and speculations about the impact on architecture of this new situation. Actually, as far as postmodernity itself is concerned, I have the feeling that it was architecture which offered the first signals and symptoms of the great transformation. It was in architecture that the end of aesthetic modernism, and presumably even of social modernity itself, and also prophetic thoughts such as Frampton's critical regionalism began to become visible. Indeed, we may speculate that the new emergence of a far more thorough going globality than anything hitherto known in human history was registered somehow in the convulsive transformations of spatiality itself. Time is eclipsed in the instant transfers of capital all around the globe, while space becomes a strange new type of living matter, throwing up grotesque new forms which are neither living nor inorganic and imposing hitherto unknown categories and mental forms on a present time that has shed the reassuring familiarities of an everyday life now rendered obsolescent, if not extinct.

What new kinds of relations can or will emerge from this metamorphosis? This is the central political question, commanding all the others.

It is difficult to think, not merely because of the multiplicity of fields to be interrogated, but above all because postmodernity has become the place of antinomies; in this instance, a sense of increasing, omnipresent standardization and homogeneity, accompanied by an almost equal universal celebration of heterogeneities. In such a situation, the experience and diagnosis of contradiction, which seemed to be the fundamental figure of the modernist period, has seemingly become less serviceable as an instrument of analysis. A contradiction may be unresolvable but it is at least thinkable: an antinomy is however defined in advance as what cannot be properly conceptualized or articulated in thought. I want to follow this process now in the area of architecture by confronting one of the great histories of high modernist architecture, *L'Architettura Contemporoneo* (*Modern Architecture*) by Manfredo Tafuri and Francesco Dal Co, with some rather different postcontemporary problems.

Uniquely among architecture historians, however, the opposition is not one between stylistic features – around which Tafuri and Dal Co organize their narrative – such as rationalism and expressionism, or technology versus aesthetics, or baroque extravagance versus ascetic minimalsim – although these are all real oppositions which must be subsumed in the scheme somewhere. Rather, it is between two realities, the building over against the city, and it is in particular this urgency of the city and the dilemmas with which it confronts architecture which marks out the central contradiction of this work and also the most interesting area in which to confront it with present-day realities and concerns. From a philosophical standpoint, the opposition between the city and the individual buildings replays the ancient and perennial problems of the universal and the particular and also of the totality and the individual. But from a concrete standpoint it admits of many meanings. Thus the city is for these authors the context in which the central theme of planning appears, so that its more purely architectural opposite would then be the anarchy of the individual commision, or even the fluctuation in the value of land and site.

At the same time, the city sets in place the question of political power, in which case its opposite is surely the pure aestheticism of architecture as style, as aestheticism or paper architecture. In the light, however, of other canonical descriptions – for the authors, as for many of us, the central text will still be Simmel's *Die Großstadt und das Geisterleben* – the city is also chaos and anxiety, so that its aesthetic opposite is one or another form of order or at least of allaying or coming to terms with that anxiety. Yet if the new industrial city is a more standardized form of chaos or alienation, its opposite number might just as plausibly be the regional or the national, as in Holland, Scandinavia and Catalonia. But if the city is degeneracy and a flood of degraded messages and images, including new dead architectural styles – remember that for Loos the riot of ornament and ornamentation in Vienna made it a "tattooed city" – then its opposite could be the purism and the purity of a Loos or even of a Corbusier. But perhaps the city also means sheer industry and engineering, and in that case – as for the very history of the emergent Bauhaus itself – its opposite can be, not only mysticism, but another form of mystique art. And this is the place to observe that for Tafuri and Dal Co the contradiction is concretized in social life and even more specifically in the role of intellectuals, so we have engineers versus artists, and eventually, as the artistic pole gathers moment and begins to fight back, we have the emergence of avant-gardes, as opposed the politicans and planners, or to engineers.

Now there is no time to read this immense and complex narrative in detail: I will merely characterize its perspective as one in which no real solution, no genuine synthesis, no concrete overcoming or transcendence of this basic contradiction, is possible. The history of modern architecture is the history of so many failed attempts to resolve it, or if you prefer, so many purely symbolic gestures of resolution. Yet this otherwise depressing series of failures does according to the authors enjoy certain luminous climaxes, which correspond, not merely to the two poles of the opposition – the building and the city – but also to its negative and positive valences respectively.

The exemplary "symbolic solution" which corresponds to the pole of the individual building is the work of Mies van der Rohe, which also, for the authors, embodies absolute negativity: the zero degree of building, an icy Mallarmean silence, a void at the very center of the city, on whose glass surface all the trash and detritus of the real city is collected as in a Schwitters Merzbild (their comparison). What is exemplary about Mies is thus not his attempt to resolve the contradiction, but rather his implacable espousal of it: he cleaves to the contradiction itself and keeps it alive: this is the sense in which he is the purest of architects.

The other pole – the city itself – is for the authors occupied by what seems to be a positive realization, namely the great *Siedlungen*, of the 1920's and 30's, and in particular, in Vienna, the *Karl-Marx-Hof* of 1927, which constitutes for Tafuri and Dal Co "a most complete 'Magic Mountain' of Austrian Marxism." But this success is only apparent, and if about Mies, we could deploy the Sartrean Paradox, "Loser wins!", to Karl Ehn's immense working-class monument, we could sound its correlative and its inverse: Winner loses! For to the degree to which the *Siedlungen* are successful as projects, in other words to that very degree to which they marry affordable housing of real architectural quality with the whole panoply of urban services (including proximity to the work place) – to that very degree they become attractive to middle-class dwellers as well, their prices go up along with the value of the land and the rate of taxation, and the *Siedlungen* in question cease, by virtue of their very success, to offer a solution to the problem of workers' or low-cost housing. The *Siedlungen* attempted to solve the dilemma of the city, but in an enclave inside the larger totality: just as the city is an enclave within the nation, so the *Siedlungen* are one within the city. The *Siedlungen* are thus merely allegorical of a radical transformation which would have to be realized concretely throughout the social totality first in the surrounding city, then in the nation itself: it cannot persist within the hostile context of a surrounding capitalism and is quickly reabsorbed within it.

Now it is time to turn from the modern to the postmodern period. I hope I've made it clear that the contradiction around which Tafuri and Dal Co organize their history – that between the individual building as an aesthetic creation and the city as an anarchy of forces and styles – was an intractable one. None of their architects or planners were able to solve it; nor in a certain sense could it ever be solved, for all kinds of different reasons – philosophical, empirical, political ones. Now I want to suggest that in the postmodern epoch, the period of nascent globalization, this contradiction no longer exists as such. But it no longer exists, not because in the intervening break it has somehow miraculously been solved, but rather because the two terms which made it up, in their very opposition – those two terms have been modified beyond recognition. In other words, the city in the form it took in the modernist period, with all its impending crises of various kinds, no longer exists, and the building as a locus of artistic and functional possibilities no longer exists either.

This does not mean that the "crisis" no longer exists: I'm sure everyone will agree that things are far worse today than in the period in which Le Corbusier reflected on the future and the destiny of the city, only it may not be right to use the word "crisis" for this new state of things. Perhaps I can put all this in a different way by suggesting that the logic of the crisis presupposes an order which has been thrown into instability for a longer or shorter period of time, if not indefinitely. But supposing one confronts a permanent instability, a permanent chaos, from which briefly, from time to time, a kind of order emerges, only to vanish again. Can that still be called a crisis? As for the notion of contradiction, it presupposes that you can articulate a troubled or conflictual situation, that you can posit oppositions and force fields within it such that its tensions become thinkable, even if you are unable to resolve them. I'm suggesting that we have to do today with something closer to an antinomy than a contradiction, since within it even those conflictual oppositions our historians posited for the modern period are no longer detectable in that form. And what I want to suggest is that the notion of the contradiction offered the hope of a solution even when it might have seemed Utopian or fantastic; and this is owing to the very structure of the contradiction itself – for when you have two opposing terms, it becomes irresistible to speculate on possible mediations or synthesis between them. (On some level, of course, I am repeating current doxa about the disappearance of Utopias and the waning of the political itself in our time.) Still, the narrative of Tafuri and Dal Co reminds us that the modernist situation did not only provide the space for the elaboration of Utopias alongside this or that pragmatic but nondialectical program; it also suggested that another form of dialectical authenticity lay, as in the case of Mies, with a lucid and implacable commitment to the contradiction itself, beyond any hope of solution or resolution. In Adorno's words, "Gleich ihrem Gegenstand bleibt die Erkenntnis an den bestimmten Widerspruch gefesselt." This possibility also, I believe, disappeared from the scene in postmodern times.

But let me now outline the reasons for the disappearance both of the classical building and the classical city. Those reasons lie deeply embedded in the logic of globalization itself. In the Third World, one of the poisoned gifts of the new late stage of capitalism has been the Green Revolution, which destroyed the self sufficiency of the older peasant mode of agricultural with hybbids and chemical fertilizers (not to speak of current genetic experimentation), and set those peasant countries on the path to the ratios of the advanced countries in which, on the whole, no more that seven percent of the population is still engaged in agricultural pursuits. The mass of unemployed peasants then moved in desperation to the cities, where staggering demographies now defy every political solution or form of urban planning. Oddly, there is a structural resemblance of these enormous agglomerations with the equally desperate structures of the First World, whose problems are in effect caused from the other end of the social spectrum, and in particular by the upper-class strategies of gentrification and land speculation which have driven the poor and the unemloyed out of the cities into peripheral areas.

The fiscal crisis of the Western cities – as it is so often described – merely underscores the fundamental point I want to make here, namely, that in our time the city's problem cannot be solved by means of the city form, by any purely urban mechanisms; and that therefore older modernist visions of planning, zoning, and immanent urban solutions of all kinds, are no longer thinkable. This does not mean that the dilemmas of the postmodern city can be solved by extra-urban means, or by the state itself: probably they cannot be solved at all. But the older modernist urbanisms are no longer on the cards – which is to say that even the concept and image of the city that used to be available in the modernist period is not longer present. There is no such thing any longer as what used to be designated by that word "city:" true postmodernity would probably mean being able to invent a new one. In any case, I trust the relationship between this dissolution of the urban and globalitation has also become clear: the Green Revolution as a world-wide capitalist development, on the one hand, the land speculation which has accompanied the new global finance industry, on the other. Meanwhile, as globalization is generally celebrated under the rubric of some new contradiction of the local and the global, or some conflict between the old-fashioned state and the decentralization on a political as well as a social basis, I want to dispel that thought as well. Saskia Sassen has discredited the new celebrations of decentralization, pointing out, in her latest book, that the finance industry must very definitely occupy crucial centers, even if the relationship of those world centers to the individual cities in which they are housed is problematic, at least for the categories of the modern. As for the local and the regional, what was meant by that once upon a time had to do with nature, that is to say, with older agricultural modes: the local in the older sense has disappeared along with them, leaving in its place so many tourist images for the delectation of a new world-wide society of the spectacle. To oppose non-Western to Western values is to be taken in by old culturalist ideologies and the propaganda of contemporary religious (which is to say, fundamentalist) movements. The world today is standardized and at least tendentially postmodernized. What were formerly "non-Western cultures" are merely the ingredients of an immense image hybridity, it being understood that there is no "Western" culture either and that global modernity – better to call it global postmodernity – is neither Western nor non-Western.

About the survival today, of the other pole of the former contradiction – the individual building – I want for the moment only to quote a remark made by Peter Eisenman in private conversation: "You could build the most remarkable building in the middle of Tokyo and no one would pay any attention." I don't know whether architects build private homes any longer today (they would need, like Koolhaas' Bordeaux villa, to have unique specifications in order to generate some kind of symbolic value), but one has the impression that innovation in office buildings – if any are still needed – is today simply a matter of greater and greater height. So only museums are left, which already have some purely lateral or marginal relationship to the city fabric: black holes of the past into which the new urban crowds eagerly implode, as Baudrillard remarked a number of years ago. I will come back to the individual buildings in a moment.

First, I want to see whether we can find any equivalent today for the purity of the Miesian contradiction. Such an equivalent would then necessarily have to be radically impure, and welcoming of chaos as enthusiastically as Mies' glass repels it. I believe that alone of the architects who have come after modernism, Rem Koolhaas has succeeded in providing a program for what Venturi, Brown and Rauch only descibed as a situation: and I want to add at this point that Rem offers the image of the first truly global architect, the first true architect of globalization: not because he builds buildings all over the world – lots of great architects do that, but because – as in his Pearl River Delta Project – he eagerly seeks out urban and architectural difference, not for culturalist or pluralist-humanist reasons, but because such fresh collisions "cause epidemics... Globalization destabilizes and redefines both the way architecture is produced and that which architecture produces."[1] For Koolhaas, whose experience thus ranges from Japan to Los Angeles, from China to the former Berlin Wall, from Singapore to Atlanta, globalization brings "the return of Babel," whose exhilarating program established "an infrastructural project to change the world, its aim a montage of maximum possibility collected from any point, lifted from any context, pilfered from any ideology. It promises the final installment of the Promethean soap opera."[2]

Rem's Culture of Congestion, then, to return to that – illustrated in *Delirious New York* – marks a first articulation of a new postmodern, truly globalized approach to chaos and demography. It asks us to revel in the new situation and to affirm it in such a way as to derive enthusiasm and energy from it. I quote – but now from that labyrinth which is *S, M, L, XL* (an extraordinary spatial book which would have gone a long way towards helping print culture overcome the CD-ROM had it not compromised itself by agreeing to number its pages) – from *S, M, L, XL* I quote a characteristic passage, this time about the Forum des Halles in Paris: "Here an entire urban region is now a seamless, almost Babylonian amalgam of destruction, kitsch resurrection, authentic historical particles, a delirium of infrastructures, a mass grave of both good and bad intentions that crawl out of the pit like the rejected species of an alternative evolution... What about the culmination at La Defense, where all the geometric rigor of a city collapses in a maelstrom of randomness and incoherence, made more pathetic by a profusion of roads, ramps and other 'connections' that resemble a wind-tunnel test accidentally executed in concrete? Yet it mysteriously works or, at least, is full of people."[3]

"Full of people:" this is the crux of the Koolhaas aestethic, and his immense megastructures are planned, not to channel or to organize city crowds, but to augment and magnify them, to increase the chaos: to let it happen, if one can imagine reading this expression as the sign of an active rather than a passive operation. So it is clear that what used to be negative in the older modernist era has now become positive in the era of globalization, and marks the place of a first affirmation on Koolhaas' part. Yet so far there does not seem to be any opposition at work here, even allowing for the obsolescence of contradiction; an antinomy also demands some kind of binary tension: with what kind of term does Congestion seem incompatible and somehow irreconcilable?

I believe that it is to be found in the image of the act of levelling, bulldozing, clearing away, flattening out: the true gestural equivalent of the end of nature in which the "Tabula Rasa" of late capitalism and its speculators and developers finds its active embodiment. The razing of all the qualities of a former "site" offers all the exhiaration of an new kind of reduction: something one senses in Koolhaas' celebration of the American "typical plan" (the "plan without qualities"), and in his manifesto for an abstract "generic city" as the emergent form of the new globalized world. But his evocation of Singapore is more vivid, and so I will quote from it. Singapore is unique in being a one-time only combination of late capitalist anarchy and communist planning and regimentation; as Koolhaas puts it, it produces a condition of permanent instability, not unlike the "permanent revolution" proclaimed by the students of May 1968."[4]

"Its motto, the new republic's blueprint, its dystopian program (becomes): displace, destroy, replace. In a delirium of transformation the island is turned into a petri dish: gigantic clearances, levelings, extensions, expropriations create laboratory conditions for the importation of social and architectural cultures that can be grown under experimental protocols, without the presence of anterior substance. Singapore is turned into a test bed of tabula rasa. The transformation of the entire island in the name of an apocalyptic demographic hypothesis is in apparent contrast to its smallness and its permanent land shortage… a regime like the one in power in Singapore is a radical movement: it has transformed the term urban renewal into the moral equivalent of war…"[5]

I have no more time to explore the extraordinary ways in which the work of Koolhaas and OMA project and develop this persistent and virulent antinomy between Congestion and Tabula Rasa. But as I've suggested, I must feel myself this productivity is somehow dependent on positing these two terms, which others might still relate dialectically, as an antinomy or as what de Man called an aporia.

Now I want to turn to the status of the individual building in our newly globalized and postmodernized era, and for this I turn to the work of Peter Eisenman and in particular to his Aronoff Center (at the University of Cincinnatti), surely one of the most extraordinary buildings of the last decade. I want to think about it in terms of a phenomenon that has lately been a matter of fascination for me: namely the way in which a building which does not and cannot fit into the city fabric is capable, not merely of separating itself out and turning away from that fabric altogether, but at one and the same time of replicating that entire city fabric within itself, becoming itself a miniature city and a microcosm of its external context. Remember that Mies' buildings remained events within the city: even if they constituted black holes or an icy void at its center. Nonetheless, they did something to it. For Tafuri, in much the same fashion the skyscraper is considered a kind of unique event within the metropolis: a strike, an interruption, a sudden touch-down, which is necessarily made to comment on the city and to emit a message about it.

The kind of building I am thinking of will no longer be an event inside the city; it will no longer comment, its exterior will neither allude nor repel: something paradoxical enough to say about a very large form disposed across a hill on the order of Duchamp's Nude Descending a

Staircase, or better still (Eisenmans own image, and the alleged inspiration of Aronoff in the first place) the interlocking of those conveyor-belt plates that move your baggage out along the airport display ramp. But perhaps Aronoffs parasitic relationship to the remnants of the two older already existing structures it so unexpectedly "completes" and incorporates can be thought of as some kind of protective concealment from the logic of the urban fabric outside it.

What I want to stress here, however, is the way in which the interior of the building, through which hundreds of students stream every day, offers a unique and somehow self-contained experience: this is the way in which it substitutes for the city, which in its disaggregation today can no longer offer the classical spatial-urban pleasures. It is useful to contrast this temporal experience with the one Le Corbusier so carefully planned out in advance for his visitors: – Villa de Roche – "This house... will be rather like an architectural promenade. One enters and the architectural vista presents itself immediately to view; one follows a set route, and a great variety of perspectives present themselves: there is a play of light, highlighting the walls or casting shadows. Bays open onto perspectives of exterior, and one rediscovers architectural unity..."[6]

"One follows a set route:" what intervenes between this dictate of the modernist demiurgic act and the aleatory pathways of the Eisenmann center is not only the aesthetic of chance, but above all the computer. Eisenmann delights in those computer-generated variants of space in his building which he himself could not consciously have planned or predicted. Far from a new or neo-classical sense of order, it is a chaos, indeed a Koolhaas "culture of congestion," which is simulated within this miniature city – this mimesis, not of a traditional city center, but of an underground post-World-War-III warren of corridors and ancillary spaces of all shapes and kinds. Pedestrian bridges and misplaced monumental staircases trace out a kind of miniature indoor Venice, whose campus surges without warning out of artifical alleyways and stairwells, down upon which the windows of offices gaze. The equally aleatory multiplication of vistas and points of view, persperctives and gazes, projects some new role for sight in these spaces of the urban future, a free-floating sight and visibility abstracted from the familiar humanist supports. If the skyscraper remains the emblem of a heroic modernism, perhaps just such underground cities can lend their image and their concept to the styles and production of a globalized future.

But the two "poles" of our present opposition – congestion on the tabula rasa of a bulldozed surface, congestion in movement underground – do not seem to add up to a contradiction in the modernist sense. So their problem, whatever it is, cannot really be articulated. Perhaps the Utopian approach today is not the older modernist one of projecting a possible solution to an impossible contradiction; but rather reconstructing the problem and producing the new contradiction itself in the first place.

Can Globalized Commercial Architecture be Anything but Highly McDonaldized?

George Ritzer

This essay examines contemporary commercialized[1] architecture from the point of view of two sets of theoretical ideas developed in my work on McDonaldization[2] and "nothing."[3] These ideas are related, but they are distinct and, as the reader will see, can be usefully applied separately to architecture.[4]

I will offer a far more detailed definition of both concepts, but for the moment let us connect McDonaldization and nothing with the term "generica."[5] The vast majority of commercial architecture, e.g. superstores, shopping malls, franchises, is generic, repeated endlessly in more or less the same form. The architecture of contrast is something unique, but relatively little commercial architecture is of this type.

The process of globalization is more associated with the generic than the unique. Generica is more easily and profitably globalized than that which is unique. What is unique, including unique architecture, cannot be mass produced; its costs are therefore necessarily comparatively high, and the demand for the truly distinctive that is characteristic of such unique architecture is almost by definition limited to the relatively small number of people who can understand, appreciate and afford it. Within the realm of commercial architecture, the main focus here is on what I have called the "means," or "cathedrals," of consumption.[6] While some of them are certainly distinctive architectural creations, in the main they are generic. They are often very basic and functional structures (e.g., those that house chains like McDonald's, Old Navy, and even Gucci) that are repeated, cookie-cutter fashion, from one geographic locale to another, increasingly throughout a large portion of the globe, and mostly following well-defined patterns (e.g. shopping malls with department stores on either end of a row of shops).

While commercial architecture has long been impelled in the direction of generica, a number of recent social changes have greatly accelerated the development and proliferation of this type. Among them are globalization, the development of large, international architectural firms, technological changes including AutoCAD, the increasing need for diverse subspecialties for each large-scale project, and a large organization to oversee them.[7]

McDonaldization

The essence of McDonaldization involves its proliferation from its roots in the fast food industry to many other settings and from its source in the United States to many other parts of the world. More specifically, what is involved is the spread of its underlying principles.

Efficiency involves the search for the best possible means to an objective, whatever it may be. The emphasis is clearly on the means far more than the end, indeed the means often become ends in themselves. As in much else about McDonaldization, quality, in this case of the end-product, is subordinated to the efficiency of the process and delivery by which it is produced or attained.

It would be hard, to put it mildly, to think of great architecture that is produced efficiently, let alone architecture that is produced – and consumed – as efficiently as, say, Chicken McNuggets. Architectural creations that have the character of Chicken McNuggets – mass-produced and virtually identical to every other one – would be thought of by few, if any, as great architecture.

Calculability is an emphasis on quantity rather than quality, on that which can be counted and numbered. Thus, at McDonald's the emphasis is on the size of products, the Big Mac, for example, and the numbers sold – "billions served." This often has an adverse effect on their quality. Big Macs are large in size, but few would think of them as being nutritious and therefore high in quality.

Significant architecture is, of course, defined by qualitative characteristics. As we know, a great architectural work would be more likely to be significant in not only the discipline itself but also in a larger social or cultural context as if it is produced slowly and carefully and there it is only one a kind. Architects who turn out similar – or worse, identical – work in a mass-production assembly-line manner rarely, if ever, achieve prominence as great architects.

Predictability involves the production and consumption of essentially the same, or very similar, products or services from one time or place to another. Thus, a Burger King Whopper is pretty much the same today as it was yesterday and as it will be tomorrow, and the same in New York, London, Tokyo and everywhere else.

Predictability, of course, just about precludes the possibility of a work of architecture being considered great. If all of one's work is pretty much the same, if one repeats one's self endlessly, one is apt to be regarded as a hack. The degree to which an architect's work becomes predictable in these and other ways is the degree to which it is not likely to be considered significant architecture.

On the surface, style would seem to represent a problem, in that having a style appears to imply doing something consistently, or predictably. Yet, developing a distinctive style does *not* mean doing the same thing over and over. Indeed, great architects are more likely to bring their distinctive style to bear on diverse subjects in very different ways.

Finally, McDonaldization is characterized by *control* over various unpredictabilities, especially the use of non-human technology to control the unpredictable things and events caused by human beings. This often involves a "de-skilling" whereby skills are extracted from humans and built into technologies that then exercise control over them.

Clearly, architects, at least those who hope to be considered significant, cannot afford to be "deskilled" or controlled by non-human technologies. Great architecture is associated with great skills, especially great technical and creative skills. Architects are supposed to be creative and creativity is greatly reduced, if not totally eliminated, if there is external control, especially by non-human technologies that, by definition, lack creativity.

Among the *irrationalities of rationality* spawned by McDonaldization are dehumanization and disenchantment. McDonaldized systems are not conducive to human capabilities and human relationships among those who work in and are served by such systems. It is likely that the work involved in much commercial architecture, especially the kind mass-produced in large commercial architectural firms, is equally dehumanized and alienating.

McDonaldized systems are also by definition disenchanted systems since the latter is simply another way of saying that they are rationalized (a near-synonym for being McDonaldized). It is highly unlikely that much magic is involved in the creation of most commericalized architecture.

Thus, it is very difficult to associate great architecture and a high degree of McDonaldization. However, more mundane commercial architecture has clearly been affected, and to a great degree, by the process of McDonaldization.

Nothing

Little escapes the globalization of "nothing," including architecture, especially commercial architecture. The term "nothing" has a negative connotation and it is difficult, especially for architects, to associate it with their field. However, there are exceptions such as the "blur building" that was part of Swiss Expo 2002.[8] It was a steel structure built in a lake and swathed in a cloud created by atomizing the water. At times the steel structure disappeared leaving nothing visible but the cloud. However, it is the antithesis of nothing – something – that is far more likely to be associated with great architecture.

Nothing is a social form that is in general centrally conceived and controlled, and comparatively devoid of distinctive substantive content. This leads to a definition of *something* as a social form that is in general indigenously conceived and controlled, and comparatively rich in distinctive substantive content. This makes it clear that neither nothing nor something exists independently of the other, each makes sense only when paired with, and contrasted to, the other. While presented as a dichotomy, this implies a *continuum* from something to nothing and that *all* phenomena manifest degrees of nothing-ness and something-ness.

For example, in the realm of consumption in general, and of the cathedrals of consumption in particular, the superstore, both in general and in its architecture, meets our definition of nothing. Indeed, it is often quite revealingly called a "big box" store and this reflects the idea that all that is needed architecturally is a large rectangular structure into which many different sets of products can be placed and through which many consumers can flow. Thus architectural structures built for any given Bed Bath and Beyond, Crate and Barrel, or Best Buy is likely to have little, if any, distinctive content. Not only are they architecturally nothing because they are lacking distinctive content, but they also are likely to be centrally conceived and controlled. That is, the central headquarters for these chains of big box stores are likely to dictate in great detail what any given superstore should look like and how it should function. Of course, there are variations over time, due to the demands of local geography and culture, but, in the main, all superstores of a given chain are going to look and function pretty much the same way, apart from insignificant differences which stem from the nature of specific contents and, more importantly, from the countless ways in which customers use superstores, many of which may not have been anticipated by the architects and owners.

Within the confines of this analysis, if the superstore is an example of nothing, then we can think of most concert halls and opera houses as something. The architecture of virtually every one is locally conceived and controlled, and many are rich in distinctive content (the Sydney Opera House is arguably the most distinctive of these structures; Gehry's Walt Disney Concert Hall is a new candidate for that distinguished group).

After all, concert halls and opera houses are often signature local creations, and great time, effort and money are invested in them. Is the creation of an architectural structure that is "something" merely a matter of investing more money in it? The answer is a resounding no! For example, small local shops everywhere in the world, while they would not be distinguished from an architectural point of view, are "something" in that they are locally conceived and controlled with small revenue in comparison, but rich in distinctive elements.

Types of Nothing and Something

Of great relevance to this discussion as it relates to architecture is anthropologist Marc Auge's work on the concept of *non-places*.[9] Non-places are clearly geographic locales that meet the definition of nothing: centrally conceived and controlled, and lacking in distinctive content. In contrast, *places* would meet the definition of something: locally conceived and controlled, and rich in distinctive content. Furthermore, the nature of the architecture involved is crucial to defining non-place/place. That is, a setting characterized by architecture that is locally conceived and controlled, and rich in distinctive content would be highly likely to be considered a place. Indeed, architecture that is something would almost necessarily mean that its locale would be considered a place. In contrast, a locale with architecture that is centrally conceived and controlled, and lacking in distinctive content would likely be a non-place.

However, this is not a hard-and-fast rule and it is possible for non-places to have architecture that is something, while places can have architecture that lies toward the nothing end of the continuum. In terms of the former, McDonald's has been criticized for its architectural uniformity and, as a reaction against this, has taken up residence in historic buildings throughout the world that would be considered close to the something end of the continuum. Take the relatively new McDonald's restaurant housed in a landmark building (the Candler) on Times Square in New York City. It has a unique theater marquee and interior design devised to fit in with the New York Theatre District of which it is part. Furthermore, "interior designer Charles Morris Mount [note the fact that it *had* an interior designer] created a 'backstage' ambiance for the restaurant's decor by exposing the building's original brickwork and using authentic theatrical lighting fixtures to illuminate the space in dramatic style."[10] Whatever one may think of the architectural merits of Mount's creation, it is close to the something end of the continuum since it has at least some unique characteristics and there was considerable local (Manhattan) conception and control (by the entrepreneur involved in its building). Nonetheless, in spite of the somethingness of its architectural structure, it remains part of the McDonald's chain and, as a result, can also be thought of as a non-place, i.e. nothing.

Similarly, places can be marked by non-architecture. For example, while there is great controversy concerning this, it is possible to see I. M. Pei's glass pyramid and its associated entranceway (and shop; yet another cathedral of consumption) as being out of context with the structure and nature of the classic Louvre Museum in Paris and trivial in comparison to its classic architecture. Nonetheless, in spite of the presence of the generic pyramid and its associated elements, which may be seen as derived from the typology of nothingarchitecture, hardly anyone would consider that the Louvre has become a non-place because of this intervention.

Part of the reason for this disconnect is that there is far more to the nothing-something continuum than whether a setting is a place / non-place or is characterized by architecture / non-architecture. To deal with this, I have extended the idea of non-places to *non-things, non-people,* and *non-services* and, following the logic used above, none of these make sense without their polar opposites – *places, things, people* and *services.* On the one hand, this means that a non-place is still a non-place, even with architecture that is something, because it continues to house non-things, non-persons, and / or non-services. Thus, even with the something-ness of its architecture, the Times Square McDonald's remains close to the nothing end of the continuum because it continues to offer non-things (Big Macs, Egg McMuffins, etc.), to employ non-persons (the counterpeople who follow the same procedures and scripts as McDonald's workers everywhere), and to offer non-services (customers must still line up at the counter for their food and clear away their own debris). Thus, architecture alone does not make a place: it does not make "something."

Further Specifying Nothing and Something

A variety of continua is necessary to better distinguish something from nothing and, more specifically, architecture from non-architecture (The Something-Nothing Continuum and Its Five Sub-Continua):

SOMETHING	NOTHING
Unique (One-of-a-Kind)	Generic (Interchangeable)
Local Geographic Ties	Lack of Local Ties
Specific to the Times	Time-less (Due to disconnection from time)
Humanized	Dehumanized
Enchanted	Disenchanted

First, the *unique, one-of-a-kind – generic, interchangeable* sub-continuum is premised on the idea that that which is unique is highly likely to be indigenously created and controlled, and to be rich in distinctive substance, while that which is generic is likely to be centrally created and controlled, and to be lacking in much, or even any, distinctive substance. Thus, architecture that is something tends to be unique and one-of a kind, while non-architecture is likely to generic and interchangeable.

The second sub-continuum, *local geographic ties – lack of local ties*, is based on the view that phenomena with local ties are more likely to internalize the rich complexity and the distinctive substance of the local environment while those without such ties are likely to be lacking in such complexity and distinctive substance.[11] Thus, architecture that is something tends to reflect and be tied to a specific geographic area, e.g. Frank Lloyd Wright's Fallingwater, while non-architecture tends to lack such relationships to the local (much of the *International Style* and its derivative modern architecture [Mies van der Rohe, Gropius, et al.], the nondescript high-rises that used to be built as part of low-income housing projects, most tract houses, and even "McMansions," which are built to largely the same specifications wherever they are constructed).

However, non-architecture is often not totally without local ties. Over time, McDonald's has had to adapt to the local environment to some degree both in cuisine and architecture. However, these concessions have always been in the form of minor additions to the basic menu (a pseudo-local item or two) and structure (a few minor architectural embellishments that reflect the local culture), not fundamental changes in either.

The *specific to the times – relatively time-less*[12] sub-continuum posits that what is specific to a time period would tend to have distinctive content while that which is more time-less would tend to lack such distinctiveness. Thus, architectural products that reflect the time in which they were built, and/or the period in the history of architecture during which they were created, would be something. Non-architecture would have few ties to either time period; it would be time-less in both world and architectural history. Non-architecture might also be tied to many different time periods; it might offer a pastiche of styles from many different time

to be continued on page 145

Chicago – Bangkok

Varakan Tipparapa

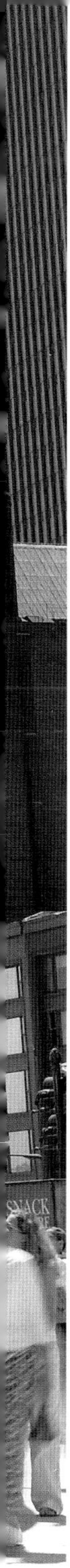
SNACK

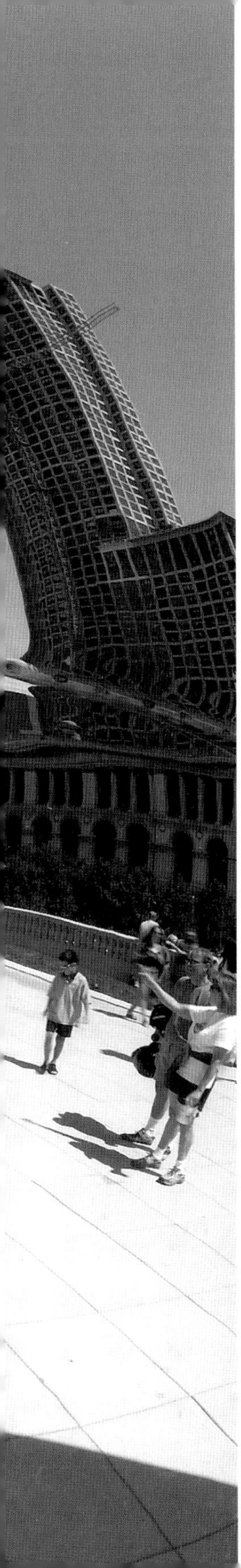

HOTEL
Hotel
Mozart
PLANET

periods. A good example of the latter is Disney World, where many different real and imaginary time periods are represented in its structures.

For purposes of the *humanized – dehumanized* sub-continuum, what is enmeshed in strong human relations islikely to manifest a great deal that is substantively distinctive about such relationships while dehumanized phenomena are far less likely to reflect any personal relationships among those involved. Non-architecture is likely to be dictated by corporate policies and directives and is more likely to be produced by committee and / or computer.

Finally, the *enchanted – disenchanted* sub-continuum is based on the idea that that which is something tends to have an enchanted, magical quality, while that which is nothing is more likely to be disenchanted, to lack mystery or magic. Staying with the example of McDonald's in Times Square, that outlet seeks to associate itself with the magic of Broadway and the theater, while virtually all other McDonald's restaurants have few, if any, such associations and are therefore highly disenchanted. Indeed, their effort to be highly rationalized and functional is another way of saying they are disenchanted.

Conclusion

Perhaps the key intent of this essay is to argue that the concepts of McDonaldization and nothing not only extend to contemporary commercialized architecture, but also enable us to cast new and interesting light on it. Thus, we can see such architecture as part of the overall process of McDonaldization; they involve increased efficiency, calculability, predictability and control, as well as various irrationalities of rationality.

Furthermore, this analysis adds the idea of "non-architecture" to the nomenclature associated with nothing – non-places, non-things, non-people and non-service.

The problem is not non-architecture, or more generally nothing, per se, but rather what I have termed "loss amidst monumental abundance." That is, we live in an era in which nothing – including non-architecture – is very abundant and offers us many advantages. However, there is a pervasive, if largely subliminal, sense that even with this monumental abundance, there has also been loss. Most generally, that loss is of something, but more specifically it is the loss of architecture (that is something) in a steadily swelling wave of non-architecture, which, in turn, is only a small part of the tidal wave of nothing that is overrunning much of American society and many other parts of the globe. While there are many reasons to welcome this tidal wave and feel that it will serve to elevate all of us, there are also reasons to fear drowning in a sea of nothingness in which only one of the many rip currents is non-architecture.

Production of Locality, Architecture, Nationalism and Globalization in Palestine, 1995–2004

Sylvaine Bulle

In Palestine, the urban and territorial question has always been inextricably connected to geopolitics and caught up in the conflict over the competing claims of legitimacy put forward by both Israelis and Palestinians, and previously by Jews and Arabs. The continuous conflict has resulted in a century of wars, destruction, occupation and disciplinary systems; the space has become militarized and protective fences are being erected. The production of space in Palestine still remains to be analyzed in accordance with a specific geography of power, the dark remnants of a colonial military power that governed the Palestinian territories for a century, particularly during the time it was occupied by Israel (1967–1994). I wish to approach the making of architecture from a different point of view, notably that of the interaction between internationalization, colonialism and nationalism.

Edward Said in *Orientalism*[1] developed a substantial part of his notion of imaginary geography in discussing the conquest and mapping of the Orient. Orientalism as the "invention" of a geographical space by Western Civilization is, however, physically present in Palestine, as a part of the Holy Land with its landscape, buildings and streets of great symbolism. An international dimension (the *world time*[2]) is also present in Palestine, which bears the traces of several forms of foreign presence, as well as of the convergence of internationalism, capitalism and imperialism in a colonialism that emerged over a century ago. The country has never freed itself from its colonization or occupation, and it has always constituted a part of the world economy. There was a large opening towards the Occident with the first capitalists and financial institutions at the turn of the 20th century, under the auspices of British imperialism in the form of the British Mandate (1917 to 1948). It was also strongly influenced by Christianity and Western countries throughout the century, including during the very transitory period of peace between Israel and Palestine (1994 to 2002).

The period of "return to the world" for the Palestinian community during this short period of peace also corresponded to a phase of internationalization and globalization of its territorial identity, on to which the national imaginary was transplanted. Political and economic modernization was expressed in the city, in the spheres of culture and real estate, which were characterized by cosmopolitanism, and by political and urban entrepreneurship. The framework of urban production and its architectural styles was also created by the astonishing development of nationalism, which intersected with an emerging capitalism. Paradoxically, the Palestinians' troubled attempt to build an autonomous state leads us to propose a double bond linking universalism and a national imaginary, a bond that manifests itself in urban form. Behind the walls drawn up by international geopolitics, the world economy left its mark – an intrusion of globalization combined with the local identities that were beginning to be expressed in urban activities.

The "Open City" and the Symptom of Cosmopolitanism

In 1993, Israelis and Palestinians reached a peace accord[3] by which the Palestinian territories became the human and material basis for the establishment of a kind of "post" colonial, autonomous nation. In the following five-year interim period, leading to the creation of the Palestinian state[4], the end of the Israeli military occupation led to an uprising of an emotional or symbolic movement for "liberation" in the newly autonomous Palestinian territories. With the promise of the formation of a Palestinian State, the exiled population and especially the elite members of the diaspora turned towards the dream of a nation, an idea of modernity, and the production of new places and identities. The new urban space[5] symbolized the end of occupation, a symbolic liberation from a material tradition as well, that of liberalism. Ramallah and Gaza, the cities that embody new territorial and economic functions, are where the new decision makers and their new national and regional administrations are established. It is in these cities that the 150 000 Palestinians who returned from exile in Europe or the Gulf Countries have settled. They have effectively become the homeland, a symbolic meeting place for the Palestinian community scattered between the Arab countries and the Occident, between the Diaspora and the refugee camps.

If the pre-foundation of the nation has symbolic and imaginary dimensions,[6] it does not remain any less dependent on economic materials and contingencies, such as the concern for exchange values, the circulation of capital and the execution of diplomatic and domestic strategic agendas. Nationalism itself is not a monolithic entity. In Palestine, the construction of the nation necessarily relies on an external logic, such as the internationalization process in which foreign influences, namely the European states and the UN, structured the local scene a century ago; but the role of the Palestinian Diaspora[7] should not be forgotten. There are cosmopolitan influences on the discourses of nation-building as well as on the material forms of the private and public urban spaces and environments.

From Liberation to Urbanization of Capital

A local-global elite was born in the wake of national construction; it was related to a cosmopolitan political system,[8] defending certain universal values (peace, democracy, good governance, freedom of movement of the capital and modernism) or "moral universalism" From this cosmopolitanism there emerged a new form of local "government" directly linked to the values of pacification, democracy and the welfare state. Thus, more than two thousand NGO's or social entrepreneurs have been involved since 1994 in the "governance of the city," helping to construct a democratic and liberal space of political action in the background. Liberalism and entrepreneurship succeeded the national movement of liberation (1987–1992). Economically oriented and politically active Palestinian entrepreneurs turned towards the perspective of the accumulation of capital and access to the symbolic resources offered by the construction of a viable nation and its infrastructure. They occupy all the spheres of the economy, real estate and communication, and have created new ways of thinking about both their patriotic duties, on the one hand, and the market economy, on the other.

The field of architecture and the city itself express this "new spirit of capitalism." The attempt to construct a Palestinian nation has revealed, in particular, the cycle of accumulation of capital, which remains in the hands of the transnational investors of the diaspora or the returnees, generally from the countries of the Gulf. And this has taken place without any public intervention. The great movement of "return to the world" (1995–2001) was submerged by emergent capitalism. The *urbanization of capital*[9] had imposed its law on physical and social space. It is the private sector of construction or the transnational economy, which has the greatest impact on the appearance of Palestinian Territories;[10] for when returning to the Palestinian homeland, the returnees, the urban and

A new shopping mall in Ramallah

intellectual elite abandoned their revolutionary values and began to occupy themselves with new domains such as communications, heritage, or culture, which in turn intersected with real estate and trade. They settled mostly at this intersection of political entrepreneurship, trade and culture, and they recreated places of consumption, and modes of habitat according to their own (often transnational) cultural references at certain local places they chose to patronize. Fast food, bars, café concerts, luxury malls, new models of *hammam* and other signs of globalized consumption appeared. The universal references drawn from the Western world but also from nearby Israel were transposed in a new culture of urban places, and in objects reflecting an increasing desire to follow international trends in taste.

In cities open to cosmopolitanism and the influx of capital new urban attitudes are visible; this is where the elite expresses its desires or need for expression in the public and urban sphere. The transnational class and intellectual elite turned naturally to the central city of Ramallah,[11] which is more easily accessible than Jerusalem.[12] It is in Ramallah, far indeed from the traditional life styles of the Arab Palestinian villages nearby that one could be free from certain dress codes, and from traditional codes of moral conduct. The upper class residences in the district of Masioun, a

New hammam in Ramallah

residential district at the entry to Ramallah, are inhabited by the elite or members of the Diaspora coming from Chicago, Paris, Abu Dhabi, New York or Frankfurt. A wide variety of café restaurants in Gaza and Ramallah have also replaced the traditional ones, once the places of male socialization attended by intellectuals and a transnational clientele. Luxury hotels were also created on the shore of Gaza, catering to foreigners, reproducing the cosmopolitan myth of the travellers at the King David and the American Colony, two prestigious hotels created in Jerusalem around 1920 by the British rulers.

These kinds of local capitalism or productive nationalism had relevant uses and urban forms that are longer popular. Now, traditional and vernacular elements are reformulated in a globalized local style. Here one finds the theme of *hybrid* identities or of a certain *locality* created by contact with an internationalized culture re-interpreted on a local scale and in a native context. The transplantation of international culture is most evident in the imaginary and in its social practices, which have created life styles and architectural images that produce modes of subjectivization[13] in both private and public spaces. New urban forms could be seen as the individual and subjective expression of trans-nationalism, post colonialism or globalization.[14] But in Palestine one must not forget that the local context in which the internationalization of the built city and urbanization operates is that of a national sentiment which is expressed collectively and individually.

Vernacular Capitalism or Productive Nationalism

The *Café Stone* is located in Ramallah's old center. Its owners, young journalists, preferred the English word *Stone* as a name for the cafe to the

Arab word *Hajjar*. Stone in Palestine is the object of much attention with its multiple metaphorical dimensions. First of all it, it exalts Jerusalem as a symbol of the Palestinian community, a place from which Palestinians are "cut" off.[15] *Hajjar is also* the material symbol of the national uprising (*Intifada*), the instrument of the struggle used for more than twenty years against their Israeli occupier. The *Café Stone* is situated in a traditional residence. Only half built in rather precarious conditions, the café evokes the repertory of the ambivalent – in part unconsolidated shelter and in part reconsolidated ruin. The original stone structure is preserved; the new part contains contemporary and technological references like concrete, glass, and wood. Obviously *Café Stone* is the meeting place of an international culture (academics and international press), which can identify with this new object and with the intensity of national feeling it represents, yet without neglecting the economic interests involved.

During the "golden age" of the Oslo Accords, heritage and architecture became a privileged sector of investment for the Palestinian diaspora and the elite. Urban objects emerged on the shore of Gaza, the entrance to

A new residence in Nablus

Ramallah, borrowing a repertory of heterogeneous signs. They juxtapose international references (concrete, glass, sloping roofs in vague reference to the Californian villa that could be also those of Israeli settlements), but they also reactivate images of local architecture. The sentimental and nationalist aspects appear with the respect accorded the stone symbolizing Jerusalem, and these are intensified with references to traditional or rural architecture, to the image of the village hidden under the *Nakba*.[16] The following examples particularly reveal these emerging models at the point of contact between vernacular capitalism and a nationalism that is beginning to be profitable.

The first is the condominium of Tal el Safa, not far from Ramallah, built on one of the most beautiful hills in the area, free of any construction and open to the wild horizons of Jaffa and the Dead Sea. Its promoter, Zaki Khouri, a rich Palestinian born in Jaffa, but living in Manhattan, is an American citizen who wants to invest in land in Palestine. His building in Palestine goes beyond a personal policy of return. It proceeds from a nostalgic attempt to rediscover the old village, possibly Jaffa: a village lost after the Israeli-Arab war of 1948, which has become a point of reference, an imagined world. The residence does more than suggest traditional architecture. The plans are based on the appearance of the

Café Stone in Ramallah

village, which had terraces, with staircases, patios and spaces of transition. The residence adopts the rules of the gated community: private access, common services, private security, and tennis courts for the international occupants. The allegorical presence of architecture is thus combined with the economic system of production, converging on the new model of gated communities, far from the popular districts of Ramallah and the "bazaar" of the city[17] – in a certain way distant from the living and local community.

The second example is the gigantic business complex at the entry of Hebron, built opposite the pools of Solomon, an ancestral irrigation site attributed to Solomon or Herod representing a long stretch of Palestinian history. The project was carried out by one of the most powerful real estate companies of the Palestinian diaspora, PADICO, with the support of Yasser Arafat. It includes a hotel, shops, a business and conference center and an amphitheatre. It was designed as a private center for foreign customers and, in particular, businessmen from the Gulf. The complex combines functionality with generous spaces, destroying the existing landscape and leaving only the memory of the place, ancient Palestine. In the name of that memory, and in order to legitimize the long history of Palestinian places and memory, the site has been sacrificed to a universal and commercial destiny: a luxury condominium complex reserved for transnational Arab citizens. The commercial gesture has to be monumental here; it includes some traditional architecture of white stone and marble drawn from the quarries of Hebron and worked by the masons into plazas and vast patios. The project also integrates the ruins of the old buildings. The vast commercial operation was halted in 2001, however, with the blow the investors received from the second wave of *intifada*.

The project was not completed, but the skeleton was easily re-appropriated by armed groups from Hamas.

In Palestine, the intensity of the territorial representation and the imagined geography unfolds in a mythological way in its cultural and urban practices and architecture. The Palestinians' attempts to rehabilitate or to preserve the remaining physical traces are the reaction to a century of destruction. Historical signs such as the arch of a house, the Ottoman or Mameluk dome, and especially the shape of the white stone of Jerusalem answer to the duty of memory, which is re-actualized in local architecture with varying degrees of sophistication. Landscape and architecture serve nationalist feelings and activate the imagined community, exiled or alive inside its territories. New architecture, urban models and their aesthetics, in order to create new built environments, modify the perception of the landscape and its architecture, *stimulating* the national imaginary to authenticate each sign of the Palestine's presence and history. This contemporary architecture built on the field of this memory does not turn back toward the past. In being reconstituted and reinforced as a part of these cultural and commercial objects, it invents a tradition and a new national imaginary.

Connecting with the World:[18] International Celebration of Heritage

Collective memory or national discourse is not inert. In *Imagined Communities,* Benedict Anderson has shown the kind of political materials and figures within the media and culture that are capable of generating nationalism in such communities. The conservation of heritage and of architecture can also be read through the filter of the national imaginary, using the notions of the circulation of ideas and capital. The attention paid by the Palestinian elite and decision makers to the historical centers threatened by destruction or natural degradation[19] shows not only the patriotic character of the conservation effort but also its "cosmo-political" dimension.

The gigantic operation *Bethlehem 2000*, undertaken for the rehabilitation of the old city on the occasion of its millennium commemoration, could be seen as this kind of contemporaneous enterprise located at the point of contact between world culture and the national imaginary. *Bethlehem 2000*'s activities, held between 1997 and 2001, included all sectors of urban life and cost more than 200 million dollars. It was the first nationally directed technical project for the conservation of heritage and was the first under the presidential mandate of Yasser Arafat. For the Palestinian decision-makers, Bethlehem's heritage, rehabilitated under the initiative of the Palestinian Authority, was viewed as no longer exclusively Christian, or Moslem, but rather Palestinian and national. But the operation remains tributary to the strong international presence in the Holy Land. European nations with a claim to authority over certain holy places – for example, the Nativity Church or Milk Grotto – wished to control the operation, just as they have guaranteed stability for a century, and are keen to put their stamp on the restored buildings and consolidate their diplomatic presence in the Holy Land.

We are thus speaking about a local and international project where local constraints and interests meet those of the international community. The Palestinian Authority entrusted the direction and execution of the projects in architecture, tourism and communication to a group of Palestinian professionals (architects, engineers or administrators) trained abroad; these members of the elite regularly submitted the schedule of the program to the international consultants and donors. When it came time to actually restore the old city, the powerful transnational investment company called CCC (Consolidated Contractors Company), which was controlled by the entrepreneurs of the Palestinian Diaspora, was charged with supervising the whole operation; but it had to take into account the requirements of each donor nation and its embassy or affiliates.

Here we have evidence of the strong influence of "techno-cosmopolitanism," lying halfway between the acceptance of Western standards and the customs of the local entrepreneurs. On the one hand, the projects' Palestinian managers have assimilated the sophistication of Western standards and the requirements of foreign experts, such as organizing international competitions and conveying the image of a sophisticated operation and the appearance of transparency. But they are also confronted by particular local and the interests of the residents involved: the Greek Patriarch owner of the holy places, and the peasants and tradesmen dislodged from the *souk* of the old city.

After the preservation of cultural heritage, the second domain of symbolic investment of *Bethlehem 2000* was the domain of communications. It consisted of a vast number of cultural events to promote Bethlehem as the first pacified city of Palestine of the third millennium. The artistic events for the millennium were not so much addressed to Christians, Orthodox local communities or to the residents of Bethlehem, but rather to certain Arab populations or the international public in general. This returns us to the methods of the diffusion of the imaginary by an emergent public sphere, that of the transnational bourgeoisie involved in the communications sector. The organized spectacles of *Bethlehem 2000* drew from Mediterranean, Palestinian, European and other international traditions in order to appeal to Christian pilgrims coming from the whole world. Folklore groups of Gaza and Ramallah celebrated the homeland, and their concerts were broadcast via satellite. Each cultural event was initiated at the symbolically important Manger Square, which within a few seasons became the expression of a public space, desacralizing the space by submitting it to plural influences.

Appadurai[20] had emphasized the idea of a new public culture in the post-colonial or the global world context, formed by the sectors of tourism, media, and museums, conjoining private and public interests. One must understand the *Bethlehem 2000* operation in the context of this new form of public culture, localized at a meeting place between different interests. The inclusion of cultural heritage and the city as a political and social good within an internationalized national project led to the emergence of the communication and management spheres, shared or appropriated by a part of the cosmopolitan elite. Beyond its devotional side, the Holy Land can be considered an economic resource, which makes it possible to

A squatter interior in East Jerusalem

mobilize, as well, the real estate, construction, tourism and communications sectors. Wouldn't *Bethlehem 2000* represent a type of synthesis of the idea of locality? A modern notion of heritage was deployed by Palestinian technical experts and politicians under the auspices of the local middle class, in order to make Bethlehem a national cultural *good.* But this was also made possible by entrepreneurs, along with the tourist guides, and local owners of shops and restaurants, including in the bazaars. During the last few years of festivities, Manger Square has functioned not so much as a place of coexistence between the Christian and Moslem communities or as a place of pacification, but rather more as an icon, a mediatized space.

Belonging to the World?

For a short time during the period of the Oslo Accords, the Palestinian cities joined the rest of the world until the resumption of the conflict. A large range of knowledge, practices, and styles of life, including the most international, served the symbolic reunification of the community; this sometimes included participation in the emerging global economy. The political and economic ruin acquired for a short time a global and universal destiny. The national rebuilding produced "locality." Urban and architectural *objects* appeared halfway between vernacular capitalism, transnational financial exchange and public culture, following the example of *Bethlehem 2000.* All these intervened in the construction of a nation, but they cannot be dissociated from the inevitable influences of transnational communication and capital.

While the nationalist activities created universal modes of existence and circulation, and even some modes of subjectivization in private or public space, it did not make the cities more livable. It has also sharpened the disparities between natives and returnees, refugees and the bourgeoisie. While the elite and the Diaspora built their local capitalism, Palestinian natives of Jerusalem, as well as refugees of the camps, who lacked both citizenship[21] and economic means, remained excluded from the resources of the "rebuilding and pacification," deprived of symbolic access to the global city (for instance Jerusalem) and its possibilities of income and resources. Today in Palestine, gated communities and other high-class buildings are closed off from the refugee camps, whose residents have been constantly pushed back by the wars and who remain without identities. In Jerusalem, abandoned buildings occupied by squatters or Beduins remain closed off from the cosmopolitan American Colony Hotel. Since the resumption of the conflict in September 2002 (Intifada al-Aqsa), new walls have appeared, erected by the Israeli military, with newly designated categories of the Palestinian population enclosed behind new barriers and frontiers.

The Palestinian case shows how necessary it is to nuance the theory of hybridity and of globalization and its spread.[22] The Palestinian natives, even though they are in contact with a multiplicity of global markets and influences, are far from *belonging to the world*,[23] far from crossing borders. They are far from being included in these transnational identities.

In Bethlehem, at the end of 2002, one year after the end of the diplomatic festivities of the Millennium that included visits by the Russian President and the Secretary General of the United Nations, among others, the city closed in on itself under the reoccupation by the Israeli Defence Force. Manger Square, this icon of global communication, once again became the space of a highly mediatized combat between soldiers and activists when the Church of the Nativity was occupied by the Palestinian resistance, and then bombarded in turn by the Israeli military.

All photographs by the author

The Worldwide Proliferation of Bauhaus and Its Cultural Legacy

Ruth Baumeister

> Just as we acquainted ourselves with materials and just as we must understand the nature of our goals, we must also learn about the spiritual position in which we stand. No cultural activity is possible otherwise; for also in these matters we must know what is, because we are dependent on the spirit of our time. Therefore, we must come to understand the carrying and driving forces of our time. We must analyze their structure from the points of view of the material, the functional and the spiritual. We must make clear in what respects our epoch is similar to earlier ones and in what respect it differs.[1]
> Mies van der Rohe
>
> FOREIGN: "Everything's foreign." Rem Koolhaas

Today, the Bauhaus has become an icon not only in architecture and the arts, but even more significantly in graphics and product design. Who does not know of Walter Gropius's famous Bauhaus building in Dessau, Marcel Breuer's chairs or the legendary Wagenfeld lamp, which has made its way into so many sophisticated living rooms around the world?

Therefore, the Bauhaus, more than any other movement in modern architecture, can serve as an example par excellence of the negotiation, the dissemination and the modification of the domestic and the foreign in culture. One might well ask how this rather small school, founded in the provincial town of Weimar – which for seven out of its fifteen years' life span did not even offer an independent, self-standing architecture education – gained such great international recognition. Furthermore, how can one explain why even today its ideas, pedagogy and products, get distributed and seemingly easily incorporated into so many various cultural contexts?

As we know today from almost a century of reception history, the Bauhaus is impossible to describe as a homogeneous, consistent movement; it is multi-facetted, interdisciplinary and contradictory in character. In its time, it reached far beyond the conventional aesthetic and scientific categories of art and architecture education, for it also had a strong socio-political, economic and ideological dimension. The teachers were some of the most outstanding artistic personalities from all over Europe, yet often with mutual opposing views. That, along with the strong promotion of the school by Walter Gropius and its suppression by the Nazis contributed greatly to its future fame. But how can this historical example inform us about the contemporary situation, where techno-economic dynamics seem to be the determining factor in the various areas of cultural production.

The purpose of this essay is neither to write yet another Bauhaus genealogy nor to assert that the worldwide dissemination of Bauhaus ideas, education and products has led to a homogenization and universalization in culture, which it obviously has not. Instead, the quote from the former Bauhaus director Mies van der Rohe, which alerts us to the determining forces of our time so that we can understand the spiritual position in which we find ourselves, will guide this analysis. I would like to start by describing the intrinsic features that led to the broad success of the movement itself, and subsequently show how the original movement was transported and integrated into various different socio-political and cultural contexts and how it was altered and finally transformed by this. The negotiation between the domestic and the foreign will thus provide the underlying theme of the analysis.

Founded in 1919 by Walter Gropius as a school of fine and applied arts in Weimar, the Bauhaus went through many different changes in staff, program, curriculum, visions and ideology. Gropius's initial goal was the reunification of art and craft in order to eliminate the conventional separation of artist and craftsperson. He claimed that artists and architects should first of all be educated as craftspersons, and therefore study at the Bauhaus began with the famous six-month-long "Vorkurs," a preliminary course originally conceived and taught by the Swiss pedagogue and artist Johannes Itten. In it, each student had to perform various exercises with

Bauhaus Building in Dessau by Walter Gropius, 1925

different materials, e.g. stone, wood, metal, glass, textile, which were combined with an elementary formal education: the combination was expected to reveal his or her artistic and practical leanings and talents that would later provide direction for further specialization.

In Gropius's opinion, a building should be the result of the cooperation of the architect, the artist and the craftsperson. Thus, he considered teamwork, rather than the celebration of individual artistic achievement, to be an integral part not only of the education of students, but also of the design and building process.

Soon after the Bauhaus's inception, industrial production was integrated into the curriculum and its pedagogical focus shifted from the manual production of arts and crafts objects to prototypes for large-scale industrial production. Due to the rising specter of the Nazi regime's cultural policy in Weimar, the Bauhaus was forced to move to Dessau in 1925. There Gropius built the famous Bauhaus building, one of the first curtain wall buildings, which later served as a model for innumerable office build-

Wassily Chair
by Marcel Breuer, 1925

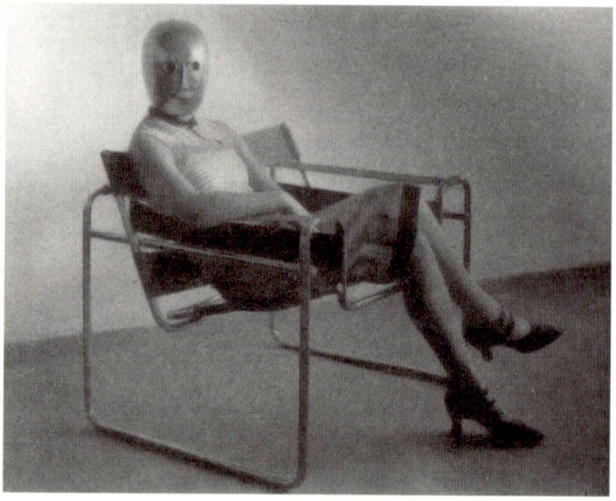

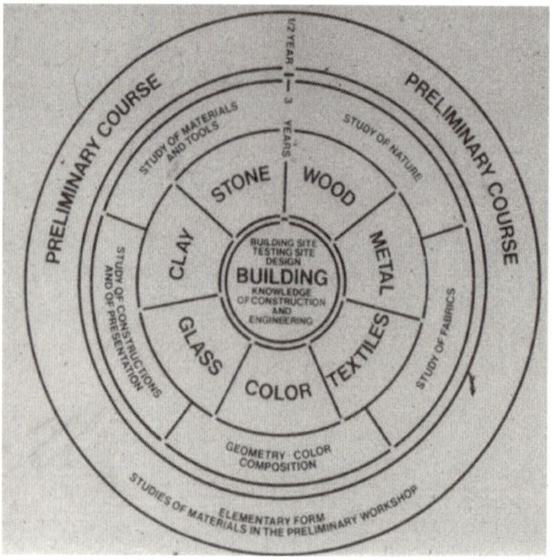

Diagram of
Bauhaus Curriculum,
1922

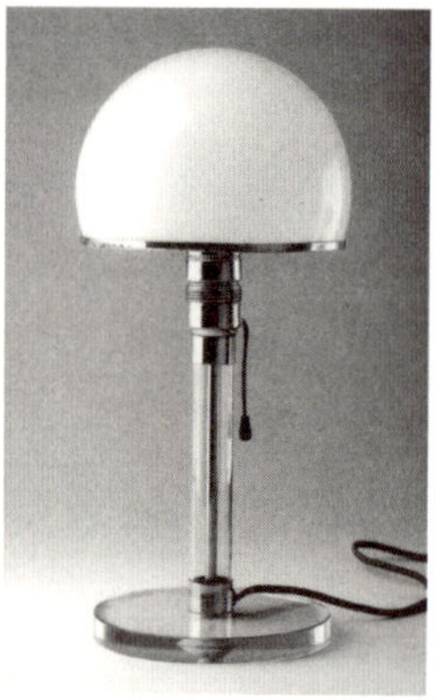

Table Lamp
by Wilhelm
Wagenfeld,
1924

ings in the US, Asia and Europe. The change of location was accompanied by a change in curriculum, and the focus shifted even further to a more scientific education in arts and architecture, supported, in addition, by the change in directorship from Walter Gropius to Hannes Meyer in 1928. From then on the students were taught to experiment with sociological, biological and scientific studies as a basis for their design. Because of political problems between Meyer, a convinced communist, and the local authorities in Dessau, Meyer was forced to resign only two years later. He was followed by Mies van der Rohe, who implemented an education focused more on the quality and virtuosic manipulation of material and technique in architectural design than on its socio-political aspects. Despite his efforts to de-politicize the school, and despite its move from Dessau to Berlin in 1932, the school was finally shut down by the Nazi regime in 1933.

Given the rather short life span of the Bauhaus in Germany, its inconsistencies in terms of program, pedagogy and ideology, as well as its rather small actual output in architecture, one must ask how this movement gained such broad recognition and influence. But before elaborating on the movement's reception, I would like to focus explicitly on those characteristics of the Bauhaus which were significantly different from other art and architecture schools of the period and which thereby contributed greatly to Bauhaus culture and to the notoriety it gained beyond the borders of Germany.

Integration of various Cultures and Disciplines

Gropius's initial goal was to unify the arts and crafts under the primacy of architecture. The early phase in Weimar was characterized in large part by the spiritualism of artists such as Paul Klee, Wassily Kandinsky and Johannes Itten. In Dessau, under Hannes Meyer, natural and social

Johannes Itten

sciences, including subjects like physics, mathematics, chemistry, biology, psychology and sociology, began to play a more important role in the education of young artists and architects. We are all aware of the problems and frictions that were created among the staff and students because of the coexistence of such contrasting temperaments ranging from the emotional, esoteric and spiritual, to the rational and scientific. But Gropius's aim was to combine and integrate all of this into a holistic pedagogy.

In this respect, the education at the Bauhaus had much to offer. One of the rather extravagant examples was Johannes Itten's belief in the Mazdaznan movement, a mystic philosophy that originated in the United States but incorporated various elements of Hinduism and other Eastern religions. Itten expressed his beliefs in his physical appearance and clothing, which remind us of a Buddhist monk.

Mazdaznan followers believe that the means to perfection in the material world lies in the power of breath, and therefore the movement teaches a discipline of breath control, rhythmic prayer and chanting. The physical exercises are further supplemented by a vegetarian diet. Itten's belief in this not only greatly affected his own life, but as the "master" he also imposed it on his students in the preliminary course at Weimar. Looking

Bauhaus' International Students

at pictures of Itten and his students one is reminded of a religious sect or hippie movement. His instructions for leading a healthy life and the dress code he established were ritualistic in character, and during the early years they had a strong impact on the community life and spirit of Bauhaus students. His spiritual beliefs also affected his understanding and teaching of aesthetics. Itten believed in an aesthetics which emphasized the individual's creativity and his or her subjective experience. Moreover, one of the less popular, early cases from the curriculum of 1920 was Gertrud Grunow's basic "Harmony Theory,"[2] which can be understood as an attempt to introduce and combine music, physical education and meditation into the arts. Within meditative exercises the students were instructed to connect 12-tone music to a 12-tone color range and to transpose this into expressionist movements. This shows clearly how early Bauhaus pedagogy was not only addressing the rational mind but was meant to be a holistic concept, focusing on both the mind *and* the body.

At the other end of the spectrum were Hannes Meyer's efforts to develop a systematic and scientifically based design method during his years in Dessau. Rational analysis performed in a scientific laboratory environment became the key for both understanding and creating architecture. For example, diagrams of daily, monthly and annual cycles, as well as investigations of natural sunlight, became the decisive parameters for design decisions in Meyer's classroom.[3] On the whole, the pedagogical concept was characterized by an experimental transdisciplinary and transcultural approach which in general favored diversity and integration over separation and exclusion.

to be continued on page 169

Cemetery in Hue, Vietnam
Margit Bosch

PHẦN MỘ
MARIA
ĐÀO THỊ TOÀN
SINH 1929
TỪ TRẦN 9.6 1998
(15.5) MẬU DẦN
THỌ 70 TUỔI
HỒ CẦN
PHỤNG LẬP
1998

ANNA MARIA
CÔNG TẰNG TÔN NỮ THỊ MAI
GIOAN BAOTIXITA
NGÔ VĂN THƯỞNG
1939

TÂM LÀNH SANH TỊNH ĐỘ

福

Internationalism, Public Relations and Marketing

Even though the initial conception and the rise of the Bauhaus is strongly related to the specific domestic cultural-political context of its time, the school itself held no claims to "national rights," and "authentic cultural traditions" were of secondary or no importance. A quick glance at the roster of Bauhaus students[4] shows the international make-up of the student body.

The Bauhaus had a significantly higher share of non-German students than did other contemporary German art schools.[5] Students came to the Bauhaus not only from many European countries, but also from as far as Russia, the United States and Japan, in order to experiment with and produce within the different disciplines of "Gestaltung" beyond any national boundaries and barriers. This, among other facts, later contributed greatly to the Bauhaus's influence abroad.

> The solutions which the Bauhaus has developed up to this day are a result of the common work of the best artistic forces in Europe. And rightly so; the Bauhaus has always absorbed, examined and processed anything which was achieved in the spirit of innovation anywhere, and in the excellent series of its Bauhaus Books... it itself contributes to the growth of the comradely community of this European work.[6]

Adolf Behne, an architecture critic of the period, pointed out the key features of the Bauhaus's success and future fame: star cult and international marketing, both outstandingly nurtured and promoted by Walter Gropius. As is widely known, one of the director's most successful marketing tools was to intentionally attract some of the most outstanding avant-garde artists from across Europe to teach at the Bauhaus, such as the Russian-born Wassily Kandinsky, Johannes Itten and Paul Klee, both of Swiss nationality, and the Hungarian Laszlo Moholy-Nagy. The fact that such artistic personalities came to the provincial town of Weimar provided a reason for a large number of students from all over the world to follow them. Undoubtedly, Gropius's strategy of recruiting international celebrities in his advertising and thus attracting students has become a well established practice for major architecture institutions all over the world today.

This, combined with a very effective marketing strategy, gained the small school some exceptional attention not only far beyond the domestic borders of Germany but also far beyond the professional circles of the discipline. Apart from his own propagandistic writings, Gropius, with a series of Bauhaus books, established a forum for the publication and distribution of the theoretical ideas of the Bauhaus teachers. Advertising among the general public and for students was also a rather innovative strategy, which is still rather uncommon among the majority of German universities today. As early as 1923, in the first Bauhaus exhibition, its pedagogy, products, and visions of architecture were presented to the local authorities and general public as well as to specialists in the field from Germany and abroad. In Dessau, Hannes Meyer developed an advertising department based on Gropius's model from 1927. „Junge Menschen kommt ans Bauhaus"[7] was a brochure he printed in the summer of 1929 in an edition of 500, in order to attract young students to come and study at the Bauhaus.

Radicalism and Life Style

The Bauhaus was neither an architecture nor a design philosophy, nor only a place for education and production in those domains. Instead, Gropius wanted to provide content and shape for the life of modern man, and his strategy for doing this was to address many different levels of human life and consumption. As the picture of his living room indicates, he promoted this idea by showing himself in an environment that conveyed a modern life style. Originally the Bauhaus was intended to function as a community. Walter Determann's rather expressionist design for the campus "Am Horn," in Weimar in 1920, reminds us more of a pattern for a tapestry than a plan for an urban community.

Walter Gropius with Lucia Moholy in his living room

But what is most striking about it is that it was planned without any connection to the outside world. It was a self-contained entity, with space for housing, administration, culture and education, production, sports and leisure, etc. In this environment, entirely designed by members of the Bauhaus, the same people were to perform their work, grow their own food and live together, autonomously. Even though this vision of the artists' commune never materialized, it reveals the ambitious intention to create an ideal environment for modern man. But the aspirations did not stop there. Far more influential were some of the Bauhaus product designs meant to express the life style of a future generation. Later examples of this are the Wagenfeld lamp, Marcel Breuer's metal chairs and tables, Marianne Brandt's ash tray, etc., which were subsequently produced on an industrial scale and continue to be sold worldwide today.

Worldwide Dissemination

What was the reason for the wide-ranging dissemination of both the Bauhaus idea and Bauhaus architecture? The biographies of various Bauhaus students and teachers show how enormously they were impacted by the politics of their time. Ironically, the emigration, exile and exodus that resulted from the Nazi policies in Germany in 1930's contributed greatly to the worldwide spread of the Bauhaus ideas, rather than to their repression, as intended.

Hannes Meyer, for example, traveled with the famous student group, "Bauhaus Brigade," to the Soviet Union and later to Mexico, hoping to be able to transform into architecture his socio-political visions, which he conceived and nurtured during his years at the Bauhaus in Dessau.

Because of the rather favorable cultural-political context for the Bauhaus, some years saw as many as 30 former Bauhaus members emigrate to and work in the US. The fact that these émigrés managed to continue and to further develop what was originally conceived during the Weimar Republic and doomed by the Nazi government in Germany made the

Bauhaus Community "Am Horn," Weimar, by Walter Determann, 1920

United States appear to be the land of freedom and unlimited opportunities. Events like the large 1938 exhibition at the Museum of Modern Art in New York, "Bauhaus 1919–1928," prepared the way for many former Bauhaus teachers and students. Various "Bauhouses" were established in the US, most of them run by Gropius's former collaborators. Moholy-Nagy took over the New Bauhaus in Chicago, Josef Albers and Xanti Schawinsky introduced Bauhaus pedagogy at Black Mountain College in North Carolina, Ludwig Mies van der Rohe went to the Armour Institute in Chicago, and Ludwig Hilberseimer to the School of Industrial Design in New York. But this only shows the influence of the main protagonists; there were innumerable smaller and less well-known schools throughout the United States that introduced some modified form of Bauhaus pedagogy.

Among the former Bauhaus students were many less famous figures who ventured to foreign lands and thus contributed greatly to the worldwide spread not only of Bauhaus ideas but also of its ideology and architecture. Rene Mensch went as far as Persia and Konrad Püschel lived in North Korea working to contribute what he learned at the Bauhaus to the building of a New Republic. Pius Pahl built extensively around Stellenbosch, South Africa, and many of his single-family houses would easily pass the criteria for what is nowadays commonly called the "Bauhaus Style." Not to be overlooked are also Arie Sharon, Edgar Hecht, Shlomo Bernstein and Shmuel Mestechkin, convinced socialists who, after the exodus from Germany, went to Palestine, where, under more benevolent conditions, they were able to further develop and execute what they had originally conceived during their studies at the Bauhaus in Germany in the 1920's.[8] It is interesting to note that at the time of their arrival there, buildings from many different time periods and cultures formed the domestic architectural context. The Bauhaus language, which was seemingly disconnected from any cultural or historical reference or style, appeared to be the most appropriate one to use in formulating a new beginning for themselves and Israel. With this architecture the young generation hoped to break radically with any national, ethnic or religious heritage in order to establish an identity in built form and thus help create a new nation in their adopted country.

At the same time, the reception of the Bauhaus in the US is particularly interesting because, on the one hand, the US was the main focal point of attention of both the movement's ideas and its protagonists, and, on the other hand, it showed the strong impact of the political dimension of the new context within the transformation of the Bauhaus' heritage.

The Bauhaus in the Cultural, Social and Economic Context of the New World

Walter Gropius left Germany in 1934 and came to the United States in 1937 after a short stay in England. His adopted country at that time offered an excellent environment and many possibilities for the adoption of both his vision and methods. The pedagogical principles he conceived of and developed during his years at the Bauhaus matched well with those of the period's American Pragmatists such as John Dewey. Dewey's socio-biological pedagogy was based on the belief that acting is a precondition *and* goal of understanding and knowing, and required a connection to the arts, science and the society. In this case, the dynamic, activist ideal of European collectivism blended well with the Anglo-Saxon concept of social harmony.

Apart from his pedagogical efforts, Gropius founded TAC,[9] a teamwork-based collaborative of architects, thus realizing his early idea of an architectural practice based on teamwork. In collaboration with Konrad Wachsmann, he developed the famous "packaged house system" and thus contributed to the development of the US building industry. This building system for single-family houses was based on the idea of a building kit, and its goal was the development and design of a variety of single-family houses constructed entirely of standardized, machine-made parts. This can of course be read as a continuation of Gropius's early efforts to introduce industrial production into the building process.[10] It is important to notice, however, that his European projects[11] were all designed for mass housing, and in the US – due to the demands of the market – he applied his idea of the prefabricated building system exclusively to the suburban free-standing single and two-family house. Unlike the case in Europe, it was then and continues today to be the prevalent form of housing in the US.[12]

Mies van der Rohe and Lazlo Moholy-Nagy also found a fruitful climate when they arrived in Chicago. Large and rather influential corporations, like the Association of Arts & Industries and the Container Corporation of America, were very much interested in the Bauhaus name and subsequently founded the "New Bauhaus." Here, at last, the conditions existed that would make it possible to develop the connection between the worlds of architecture and industry that was once called for by the Deutsche Werkbund in Germany. More than any other Bauhaus protagonist, Mies succeeded in contributing to the worldwide proliferation of the Bauhaus and its cultural legacy with his built architecture.

His design for the IIT campus in brick and steel frame architecture can be read as a continuation of his visions and experiments with industrial architecture during his early years in Germany.

> And I said, man, just make the shed big enough so that you can walk back and forth in it and not only move in one prescribed manner, and not only be used in the way you envisioned it, or how you wanted it to be used. We do not know whether or not people will use it the way we would like them to do. First of all, functions are not entirely clear, and second, they are not constant. They change much faster than our building. Our buildings last for a couple of hundred years.[13]

Mies' words date back to Germany in the 1920's. On one hand, he criticizes here Hugo Häring's tribute to functionalism; on the other hand, he envisions an architecture that is multi-functional and places no restrictions on the user. It took him almost thirty years to finally see these thoughts take on material form. He reached this goal when he built Crown Hall (1950–56), which was the first realized open plan, a space with hardly any functional or spatial restrictions. In addition to his buildings for the IIT campus, his early ideas for high-rise buildings, e.g. the famous glass skyscraper for the Friedrichstrasse competition (Berlin, 1921) finally took shape in his apartment buildings at Lake Shore Drive, Commonwealth Promenade and the Seagram Building. Chicago, as a growing city after 1945, with a high demand for new housing and infrastructure and an adequately developed building industry, created the ideal economic context for what he has already envisioned in Germany during the 1910's and 1920's.[14]

With the New Bauhaus[15] Moholy-Nagy wanted to transfer and integrate the European Bauhaus into American mass society. Taking the original Bauhaus program as a point of departure, he modified it and developed it into a new pedagogical concept centered around the human capacity to perceive and experience. Compared to the original Bauhaus curriculum, scientific education was enlarged, and film, photography, music and poetry were introduced into the education of artists, designers and photographers. His theory of the senses proved to be a good match with Anglo-Saxon socio-biological theories of aesthetics, such as those of Susanne Langer and Rudolf Arnheim, which at that time were widely discussed in the US.

Simultaneously, Moholy-Nagy experimented with "space modulators," moving sculptures of curved planes and lines made from plexiglas. Through movement and proper lighting these sculptures produced a rhythmic interaction of lines and planes in which he found a correspondence with his biological design theories. He transformed both his theoretical and experimental work into a new formal language, which proved to match well with "streamlining," a dominant design language in the US of the 1950's. Streamlining meshed well with analogies of the "organic," which at that time was commonly associated with the "democratic."[16] Thus, Moholy-Nagy's new design language proved, on the one hand, to fit easily into the political and ideological context, while, on the other hand, it was well suited to create the emotional incentive for buying products which were produced industrially and on a large scale. Both characteristics were ideal preconditions for integration with the existing cultural context of the *New World* and the further development and success of his own artistic work.

Reception History

The success of the Bauhaus in the US is due to the fact that it was heavily promoted by both the US government and industry. At the same time, though, the Bauhaus managed to develop an aesthetic language that was attractive to a large number of people beyond ethnic, linguistic and cultural differences. Looking back, we can see how the Bauhaus often served as a pattern for an ideal creative society and was seen as offering a radically new and benevolent philosophy which opposed established, Old World conventions. Furthermore, the fact that the institution was shut down by the Nazis in 1933 contributed greatly to this perception. Its typical student was retrospectively pictured as a politically interested, socially and creatively engaged individual whose personal history was free of aggression or discrimination based on race, nationality or gender. Thus the student became the role model for a future, better world. However, a glance at the memoirs of two former female Bauhaus students, Anni Albers and Marianne Brandt, proves that this is more a subject of mythologizing, glorification and again promotion of the Bauhaus than its true reality. Certainly, the number of women inscribed at the Bauhaus in the 1920's was fairly high compared to their numbers at other contemporary institutions.

But, at the same time, men, after successfully passing the preliminary course for example, could choose which studio they wanted to work in. Women, in contrast, were doomed to a „typically female" discipline, the weaving studio.[17] In cases where they chose differently, they were subject to prejudice and discrimination.[18]

To take another example, the extensive "Bauhaus Exhibition" at the Museum of Modern Art in New York in 1937–8, was based on a dynamic but one-sided view of the movement, whereby differences, contradictions and conflicts were ignored in favor of a representation that suggested and harmony and continuity were stressed. It was intended to function as a propaganda instrument in order to open doors and make way for Gropius and his followers. A similar case in this respect was the famous "International Style" exhibition by H.R. Hitchcock and Philip Johnson held at,the same museum in 1932. This presentation removed the European architecture of the 1920's from its ideological context and reduced it to aesthetic and formal categories, making possible the promotion of the

Bauhaus Students

various European modern movements and their protagonists in the New World. I could cite more examples like these, but what is important to notice is how, on the one hand, discourse about the Bauhaus during the 1920's, as well as after World War II in the US, differed from the actual facts, and, on the other hand, how the original ideas and ideology became subject to interpretation, modification and transformation. In general, the Bauhaus in the US was very much defined by a cult of personality and by the existing socio-political and economic context. Consequently, the radical communist ideology of the early period was denied, and those who were not willing to accept this approach, for example Hannes Meyer, Konrad Püschel, Rene Mensch, among others, had to venture to other, ideologically more favorable grounds.

Prospects for the future

In surveying the reception of the Bauhaus in the US, we have seen how the movement, after being removed from its original background, was transported and integrated into a new, different socio-political and cultural context and how it was altered and subsequently transformed by the latter. What were the implications of this for the relationship of the domestic and the foreign, and what can this case possibly teach us about the current process of cultural transformations which we have to face every day?

One rather negative but simplistic interpretation of the case would be that Bauhaus was manipulated and eventually even used as an instrument of US imperial cultural policy, which resulted in the movement being stripped of all its original benevolent socio-political intentions and visions. Some might even argue that the Bauhaus in the US became a crucible of good intentions and design ideas, nothing more than a brand label, since, as already shown, in the end, the major marketing goal was to create an image which a large number of people would recognize and identify with.[19] Another, more positive and seemingly less critical interpretation would be to say that the case of the Bauhaus proved how the European vision of modern architecture and culture was actively and consciously modified and converted into something different and new.

To provide an interesting perspective on this discussion today, I would like to glance back once again at the Bauhaus reception after 1945 and show a lesser known example, the Danish artist of CoBrA group, Asger Jorn's: "*International Movement for an Imaginist Bauhaus*,"[20] because with this little episode Jorn touches on some of the most crucial issues involved in any process of cultural transformation today. During the early 1950's, the Swiss artist and architect, and former Bauhaus student, Max Bill was put in charge of establishing the "official" successor to the original Bauhaus movement, the "Hochschule für Gestaltung," (HfG) in the then West German city of Ulm. Jorn, completely unknown, broke and without much success in his professional and personal life at that time, addressed Bill in various letters, asking to collaborate in the new Bauhaus. This resulted in an argument between the two artists about the importance of the historical dimension and the future of the new Bauhaus. After Jorn's request was rejected by Bill, he decided to found his own "Imaginist Bauhaus."

Jorn told Bill that his movement at HfG was basically just a convenient address, and the members in Ulm did little other than allow Jorn the use of their names on the letterhead. Without any clear didactic program or fixed location, the Imaginist Bauhaus was clearly far from being a serious competition to Bill's HfG in Ulm. On the whole, as the name indicated, Jorn wanted it to be an idea, an experiment, or an imaginative representation of something that could happen in the future, rather than a preconceived project.

Yet Bill seemed to be seriously threatened by it and claimed copyrights to the Bauhaus name, stating that only he himself knew how to continue working in the manner of Kandinsky, Klee and Moholy-Nagy.[21] Jorn's undiplomatic answer to Bill's claim for abstract originality and authenticity was to say that he did not give a damn whether Gropius had sold, given or contracted the Bauhaus name to him. Instead, what he believed really important was whether Bill had morally earned the name, which meant for him whether or not he was capable of creating the same inspiring effect and whether he could attract personalities of the same calibre as the original Bauhaus had.[22] Jorn further stated that this was not a question of originality and claimed that he as an artist was certainly more interested in "creating culture" than in being original, which he also humorously proved many years later in his self-portrait.

Self-Portrait by Asger Jorn

In this dispute, Jorn touches on ideas such as *copyright, authenticity, morality, personality, inspiration and imagination*, which in my opinion are the relevant factors not only in the specific case of the reception and the influence of the Bauhaus but also in general for any cultural transformation today.

As I have tried to show with the case of the Bauhaus, developed cultures have in their history a record of change, exchange and transformation of ideas, materials and people. Consequently, we must realize that dislocation, world-wide distribution and the introduction of the foreign are not the end of a culture. As the quote from Rem Koolhaas at the beginning suggests, being foreign or alienated is an intrinsic condition of modernity, and we have to accept and embrace this fact in order to see the stimulating potential that lies in it. Countless discussions focus on the question of whether globalization today results in a homogenization or in a differentiation of culture; for architecture and urbanism, specifically, the topics center around the dialectics of the local versus the global or, as the title of this book suggests, the domestic and the foreign. The fact is that the multifaceted processes of conception, development and evolution of culture evoke contradictions, uncertainties and threats. Therefore issues such as "cultural identity," "authentic culture," "places vs. non-places," and other numerous determining categories for architectural production become the seemingly secure points of reference within the discussion. But the idea of an authentic culture, which suggests some form of original authorship devoid of external references, is a pure fiction, because cultures are never pure. The same holds true for our individual identities, which are characterized by fragmentation, mixture and alienation. Architecture and urbanism in particular are products of the overlay, exchange and transformation of relationships and, therefore, can only develop in contact and in confrontation with the other, the foreign, which is a process inherent in any development and progression in culture and one which is certainly not, as some might argue, an invention of modernism. For instance, the eternal city of Rome is an excellent example of a mixed, sampled and cross-cultured product, and who is not to be fascinated by its beauty, richness and diversity?

Unfortunately, dualisms like copy and original, domestic and foreign, global and local are commonly used to either propose a concept of cultures in their "pure" form and content or to describe the alienation of one culture by the introduction of another. This inevitably ignores the potential of creating something new by absorbing, mingling, copying, etc. Most obviously, technologies not only change how we do things, but also how we perceive and conceive the world. Roaming and trawling have become common practices of collecting and appropriating information, especially in architecture, where the introduction of digital technology, procedures like "copy and paste," and "slicing and sampling," have become common, everyday production techniques.

With the technologies we have at hand today, there is a greater possibility than ever to share and exchange information and knowledge. This has, on one hand, changed the traditional mechanisms of selection and distribution of information and, on the other hand, created new forms of organization, practice and actions. As the case of the Bauhaus demonstrates, the real issue is not about the original and the copy, nor the domestic and the foreign, but about whether or not the individual can find connections to his or her own experience and needs in order to inspire the continuation of culture. This depends on every one of us, his or her personality and the capability to imagine, conceive and create. Can we find things that connect and excite, that encourage reflection? Or, as Jorn put it in his argument with Bill, creating culture is more important than preserving it!

The following institutions and persons
kindly gave permission for the use of the images:
Bauhaus-Archive Berlin, The Bauhaus Museum
Weimar, Stephan Consemüller and Jaqueline de Jong

Consuming Heritage or the End of Tradition

Nezar AlSayyad

The 20th century may have been the first century ever to witness the rise of environments that are wholly devoted to the *other*. Many nations and communities have resorted to heritage preservation, the invention of tradition, and the rewriting of history as forms of self-definition. In an attempt to understand the impact of globalization on the built environment, I will expand upon an earlier typology of manufactured heritage environments elaborated in my book, *Consuming Tradition/Manufacturing Heritage*. There, in an attempt to understand how built environments are often packaged and sold in an economy of global image consumption, I employed the lens of tourism to problematize many assumptions regarding heritage and tradition, showing that a new vernacular decoupled from place has now emerged. Drawing upon new theoretical developments regarding the notion of *endings*, I argued that we have always been fascinated by *ends*: the end of the world, the end of our lives, the end of our youth, etc.

We have reached the end of tradition, too. By this I do not imply the death of tradition, but instead the end of our *conception* of tradition, in the disciplines of architecture and urban history, as a repository of authentic and hence valuable ideas that have been handed down from one generation to another. The notion that a tradition must be associated with a specific place and a certain group of people has been significantly modified by the scholarship on globalization in fields such as anthropology, geography and cultural studies. The implication of isolation and rootedness fostered by earlier work on tradition has also been significantly overturned.

An issue of *Time* magazine in July 2002 with a cover of a cross engulfed in flames and the title "The Bible and the Apocalypse" reported that 59% of Americans believed the events depicted in *Revelations* are coming true.[1] This popular and often evangelical anxiety about "the end" gained new import in a post 9/11 world. One noted scholarly discussion about this subject was Daniel Bell's *The End of Ideology*,[2] written in the late 1950's, which chronicled the great catastrophes of the 20th century and concluded with the necessity of accepting the failure of the intellectual left to bring about an era of social harmony through its "social engineering" projects.[3] The next major proposition was Francis Fukuyama's *The End of History and the Last Man,* written in the 1980's,[4] in which he identified a similar "end" and heralded the international consensus on Liberal Democracy as the "endpoint of mankind's ideological evolution."[5] The book became very important in the late 1990's, but 9/11 of course made it abundantly clear that serious challenges to liberal democracy remain. In the 1990's, with *The End of the Nation State*, Kenichi Ohmae picked up where the others left off.[6] Curiously, Ohmae proposed the end of the very institution Fukuyama claims had reached ubiquity. In his book, he described the dissolution of that particular political unit in the new global economy. Russell Jacoby's *The End of Utopia* takes these arguments a little further.[7] Jacoby makes the claim that the notion of a future that can transcend the present is dead. He engages in a calculated assault on the "left" and sees "Cultural Studies" as a contributor to this situation because, for him, it was founded on the utopian notion of the preservation of difference. He believes that "It is the rootless, not the rooted, who fetishize their roots."[8] In this light, the concern with heritage and tradition can be seen as a preoccupation with defining and redefining one's position in an ever-changing world; and, at present, it may also be seen as a product of the unequal relationship between the First and Third worlds. To understand this, one must frame the heritage discourse within its proper historical context.

We can distinguish three relevant phases in attitudes towards heritage and tradition in the last two centuries.[9] First, in a colonial phase, there was initial interest in indigenous people and practices but a distant association with it. During the second phase, following the success of the independence struggles, nations invoked nationalism and resorted to heritage preservation as a form of resistance against the homogenizing forces of modernity. Finally in this third phase, which we call globalization, nations compete in an ever-tightening global economy, as they find themselves needing to exploit their natural resources and built vernacular heritage to attract international investment. Touristic development has consequently intensified, producing entire communities that cater almost wholly to, or are even occupied year-round, by the *other*. The new norm appears to be the outright *manufacture* of heritage coupled with the active consumption of tradition in the built environment. Kenichi Ohmae contends that: "If given the choice, people will not choose nationalism or soil, but satellites and Sony."[10] Recent events may have shown him wrong.

But while cultural heritage attractions offer income-producing opportunities to some of the poorest – as well as the richest – communities in the world, mass tourism has often resulted in the irreversible destruction of traditional places and historic sites. This in turn has inflamed local and international passion and caused anxieties about "the end." Understanding the connection between heritage preservation and tourism development requires grounding in both history and political economy. It is important to try to understand how global consumers today seek "difference" and "hospitality" as economic goods, and how producers and suppliers make their living catering to this demand.

In the heritage discourse of the First and Third Worlds, one may notice that, while both possibly possess an equal desire to explore the heritage and culture of the "other," they have fundamentally different motivations for wanting to do so.[11] These differences may be attributed to or explained by earlier relationships of colonialism, political nationalism, and economic dependency. Today, as a result of such historical and economic forces, Third World countries often wish to emulate the "progress" of the First World and adopt its developmental practices — but only if they can do it without risking the destabilization of their local cultures. This is clearly a situation of wanting to have one's cake and eat it, too.

As Benjamin Barber points out in his appropriately titled book *Jihad vs. McWorld*, such nations want the veil, but they also want the World Wide Web and Coca-Cola.[12] Timothy Mitchell, on the other hand, argues that Jihad is not antithetical to the development of McWorld, and that McWorld is really McJihad, a necessary combination of a variety of social logics and forces.[13] Thus, Third World countries evolve their own local appropriations of many First World practices. Meanwhile, for its part, even though the First World appears more interested in consuming the Third World's cultures and environments, they are often the main advocates for and financial patrons of the preservation of Third World's built environments as part of what they define as "universal" heritage, even when those countries' "natives" and their political leaders fail to recognize its historic value. The case of the two Buddhas in Bamian, Afghanistan under the Taliban and the outcry about their destruction is a good example. Despite much international condemnation, the repressive Taliban regime, and the resulting apathy induced in much of the Afghan people, destroyed these two major monuments without any local opposition.

The First World with its wealth and power, and often acting with a sense of guilt and responsibility toward its former colonies, has tried at times to maintain or assist in preserving the dying or disappearing lifestyles and traditions of undeveloped peoples and places. Yet First World organizations, foundations and governments also have often condemned or rejected much of the social and political practices of the societies whose traditions they claim to want to preserve — especially when they diverge from Western standards of human rights, gender equality, and environmental sustainability. For example, women in traditional dresses performing traditional functions that were meant to sustain the curiosity of visiting tourists illustrate these conflicting sentiments and desires, and highlight this developmental paradox.

One may distinguish today three types of physical environments produced under conditions of globalization with the intent of making places of representation of the other's cultural tradition: dream landscapes which replicate historical settings; heritage sites which use history beyond their legitimate claim to an authentic past; and nostalgic places which exploit cultural heritage and normalize it for everyday life.[14] The first type, dream landscapes, is based on using history to create a variation of "The Wizard of Oz," where all conflicts within a given culture are resolved and all cultural aspects are reduced to their basic representations. In such a vision, all icons of a culture, such as architectural styles, building typologies, and spatial configurations, simply *become* the cultures that they are meant to represent. Here authenticity is desired and achieved though the manipulation of images and experiences. The ultimate example is, of course, Disneyland, which was the first to recognize the permanent, continuing commercial potential of such installations, though the 19th century "World's Fairs" pioneered the idea of replicating places of the "other." This process of the manufacture of global cultural products has been developing long enough that a certain convergence of consumer preferences and behaviors has already taken place, as evident in the worldwide appeal of many places like Disneyland.[15] Obviously, such places prove that, even if distorted, history and heritage sell.

Another type in this same category exploits cultural heritage but with no claim to history, and this is where the loosening ties between the signs of a culture and their referents may be most apparent. Quite simply, to optimize the desire of the producers to manufacture cultural heritage and the tourists to consume it, it becomes common for both groups to simply agree to dispense with any pretension to reality altogether. Las Vegas is of course the best place to see this; for there the sophisticated themed casino complexes do not pretend to authenticity. Here the real Dodge's Palace does not sit directly on the Piazza San Marco, but the Venetian, a 120,000 sq. ft. gambling casino, creates an easy adjustment. Likewise, the Rialto Bridge in Las Vegas connects two powerful gambling institutions, and over the Bridge of Sighs, originally the name used by prisoners in Venice en route to their execution, the only "sighs" are likely to come from gamblers losing money at the casino. Unlike real cities and nations, which often resort to the manufacture of heritage for political purposes or have willfully allowed the consumption of their traditions by others out of economic necessity, Las Vegas is the ultimate site for the consumption of the heritage of the "other." Yet before rushing to dismiss such a project as kitsch, one must consider that in Las Vegas no hidden agenda exists. Las Vegas presents a blatantly manufactured heritage, based on the concept of copying traditional forms found everywhere for the consumption of everyone. In Las Vegas, the domestic and the foreign are torn out of place and time and repackaged for the world bazaar. Time and distance no longer mediate the encounter with the "other."[16]

Heritage sites with a legitimate claim to an authentic past are the second category of environments, where the difference is in the process of objectification; these places were once sites of important historic events but over time became marginalized. An attempt to resuscitate such environments – which may often be entire cities – by remaking them in their former image may serve one or both of two primary motives: to attract tourists for financial gain and/or to serve as *banks* of national memory and pride to help ward off the subversive effects of historical change. Colonial Williamsburg is a good example of such an environment. A replica of the capital of Revolutionary-era Virginia, it is arguably America's premier public historic entertainment site, with its legitimacy dependent on its claim to be rooted in "real" history, as embodied in real historic buildings and artifacts. But Colonial Williamsburg has long been criticized by historians for many of the same reasons as any other theme parks. As one author asserts: it is little more than "an airbrushed, consumer-oriented, patriotic shrine celebrating an upscale idyll loosely based on the life style of Virginia's Colonial elite."[17]

Such criticisms have not gone unnoticed. Cultural administrators have sought to keep Colonial Williamsburg at the cutting edge of historical knowledge, and in the late 1970's they hired a new group of historians in an attempt to refashion the site by, among other things, bringing greater prominence to African-American history both in the ranks of its employees and in its narrative of nationhood. Yet the influence of these historians has ultimately remained limited, even though the historians made serious efforts to manufacture an imaginable history and were not reluctant to contribute to the consumption of heritage. Instead, this happened because management was concerned that visitors would not come, or return, unless their visits were pleasant and enjoyable.[18] Thus, depicting the harshness of slavery or any other aspect of early America's undesirable past would create a level of discomfort that might ultimately cut into Colonial Williamsburg's popularity or profit. A deep irony here is that although tourists generally long to visit "authentic" places, the authenticity they seek is primarily visual: their encounter with "real" history remains marked by distance. While they may wish to meet the world of the "other," they also take great pains to limit its influence on them.[19]

Santa Fe provides a slightly different version of this second category. Here, while the built heritage may convey the meaning of a real place, and although the town's distinctive indigenous adobe forms may be historically inspired, they have long been diluted and dissociated from their original cultural and historic context. Dependent almost entirely on purely commercial consumption, many of Santa Fe's authentic-looking "adobe" structures are in fact cement-plastered, wood-frame buildings that only provide the "look." A group of critics labeled the town's particular architectural style "Santa Fake." In this regard, one might contrast the "fake" authenticity of Santa Fe to the "authentic" fakes of Las Vegas. One might even say that places such as Santa Fe represent consumed tradition but not manufactured heritage.

The island of Bali provides another example. Here, however, the First World has played the role of the guardian of Third World traditions, but only in order to allow would-be First World visitors to appreciate and consume them. In this environment, the tourists' expectations fundamentally condition the behavior of the local people. Even though the locals are supposed to "be themselves," they end up being conditioned to *perform* their presumably still genuine culture in a manner that blurs the line between the stage in a fictitious theater and the realities of their way of living.[20]

The third type, produced by globalization, consists of nostalgic places which exploit cultural heritage in an attempt to normalize it for everyday life. This is, for example, what architects and planners who proclaim themselves New Urbanists (originally known as neo-traditionalists), have been producing in the US The towns of Seaside and Celebration, Florida are perhaps their best-known icons. Developed according to strict zoning and design codes known as Traditional Neighborhood Development (TND), Seaside has been a great success in real estate terms. But like much of New Urbanism's output, it has also been dismissed as a fake, little more than selling nostalgia.[21] Both Seaside and Celebration have also been criticized for their exclusionary aesthetics and lack of social diversity. But perhaps the most severe criticism has been directed at their particular form of physical determinism, best represented by the belief that "community" can be created by simply copying historical urban forms. Perhaps the most serious critique of Seaside was its use as the set for the film *The Truman Show* which captured the voyeurism in a society of fakery. Here the main character, sarcastically named "Truman," is, unbeknownst to himself, the performer in a reality television show about his ordinary life in a totally fake studio set that resembles a traditional American small town.

Another example in this category comes from Britain, namely the town of Poundbury. It originates from Prince Charles' fight with the British architecture establishment. Designed by Leon Krier and built as a traditional English village on land owned by the prince, it has attempted to create the feeling of a community that has grown up over time. Of course, the desired effect also includes a long stopover in the golden age of the 18th and 19th centuries before the advent of architectural modernism. Thus, all services – telephone, electricity, gas and drainage – are buried in channels behind the housing, and the one large satellite dish that serves the entire community is hidden behind a high masonry wall. All that is visible protruding from the roof of a Poundbury house are stately brick chimneys or a polished weather vane. When its plans first emerged in 1989, Poundbury, like Seaside, was derided as the product of a kitschy time warp. Yet despite its sentimental pastiche of outmoded styles and small-town nostalgia, it has increasingly gained favor with its residents as well as writers and back-packers – as one commentator pointed out, "the effect is polite, elegant and as English as a vicar's tea party."[22]

The village of New Gurna near Luxor, Egypt provides a counterpoint to Poundbury's story of grudging critical acclaim. New Gurna was planned by Egyptian architect Hassan Fathy in the 1950's as the new home for people whom the Egyptian government wanted to evict from their houses in a settlement located among the archaeological sites of the ancient Theban necropolis. Fathy designed the village using elaborate mud-brick structures that he imagined represented indigenous traditions. However, in his search for an ideal vernacular, he turned to the geometries and proportions of Islamic styles which had flourished in Cairo several centuries earlier. Among other things, this resulted in the use of unfamiliar forms for the project – domes and vaults – which the local people associated with the tombs and shrines of the dead. New Gurna was an elegant depiction

to be continued on page 201

Aoyama Doujunkai

Winny Dijkstra

エメワールド(株)

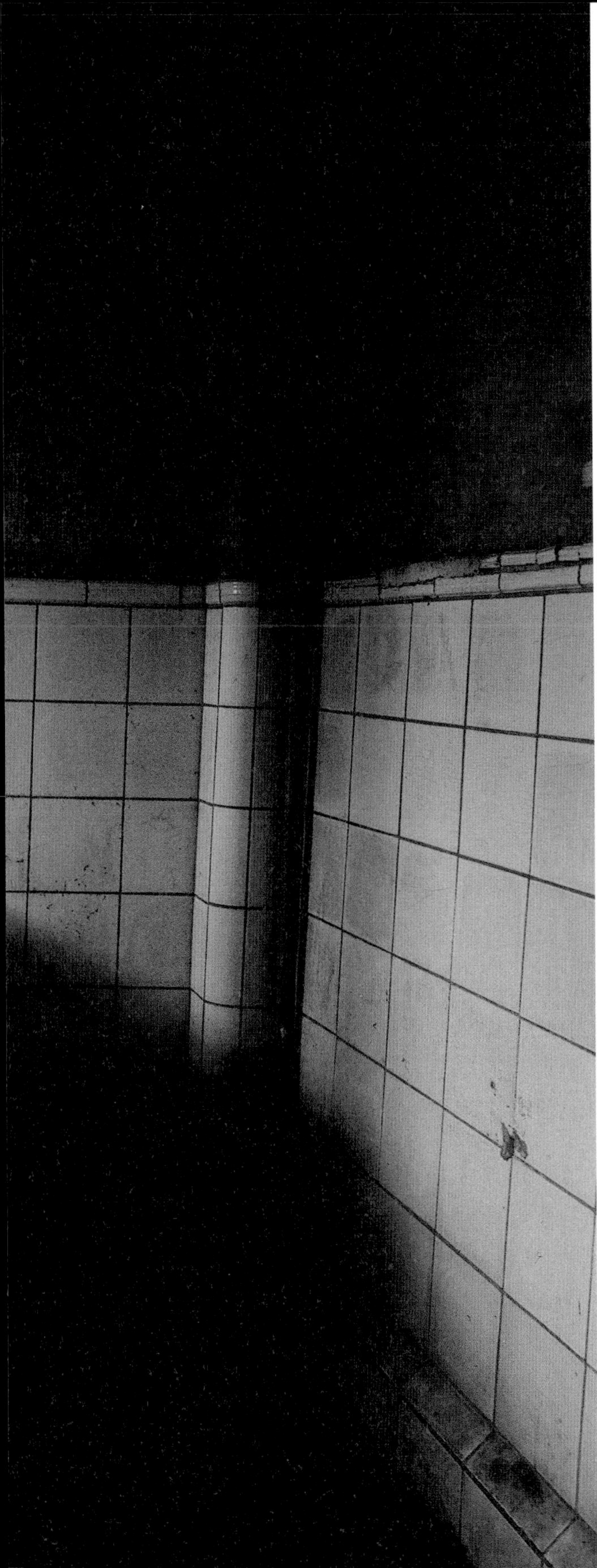

731 → Information Center

hello
layers
lives are
here.

of an idea, but when the villagers who were meant to live there refused to settle in it, the attempt to create a new community with no real economic or social justification was revealed as a costly mistake. From his own writings about the project it also became clear that Fathy's true concern was with his reputation among his First World architectural peers,[23] not his poor "subjects" or his Third World colleagues. Nevertheless, thanks to the publicity about his effort to adapt indigenous architectural forms, Fathy became considered something of a guru among Third World architects. Today examples of Fathy-like architecture are widespread in the Egyptian landscape, often feeding the myth of Egyptian vernacular architecture that it supposedly emulates. It is clear from this typology that the manufacture of heritage as commercial enterprise and the consumption of tradition as cultural demand are two activities that cannot be separated from each other. This explains why many countries are now actively inventing or re-creating their own heritage, and using tourist revenues toward this objective. Their design agenda thus have two components: a self-servicing political aspect and economic sustainability.

Here lies the dilemma of globalization: Because of the importance of the heritage tourism industry in the economy of nations, regions and cities, preserving heritage has become important not only for their economic sustenance but also in terms of global competitiveness. The paradox is that investment in heritage may encourage further nationalist sentiments, often reinforcing a sense of superiority and therefore isolationist tendencies. The destruction of the Babri Mosque in Ayodhya, India by Hindu fundamentalists and the ensuing riots is a good example of how conflicts over heritage sites are redefining the political agendas of many countries in this global era. As Kevin Robins has remarked, "Globalization pulls cultures in different, contradictory, and often conflictual ways. It is about the 'de-territorialization' of culture but also involves cultural 're-territorialization.' It is about the increasing mobility of culture but also new cultural 'fixities.'"[24] While cultural encounters across frontiers can create new and productive kinds of cultural fusion, hybridity and global citizenry, restoring or rebuilding could also enflame further social unrest and division. Indeed, the great danger lurking in this new global citizenship, of course, is the erosion of its own public sphere.

Disneyland and its Main Street have captured the imagination of visitors as the most quintessentially "American" of all places. Newspaper reports have indicated that its story may have come full circle. Marceline, Missouri, and Fort Collins, Colorado, were the towns that originally inspired the design of Disneyland's Main Street. Marceline was the hometown of Walt Disney, where as a boy he first sketched barnyard animals and fell in love with trains. Fort Collins was the birthplace of Harper Goff, Disneyland's first director in the 1950's. However, as *The New York Times* reported in "A Tale of Two Main Streets," a reverse flow of cultural capital is now taking place from the copy to the models from which it was derived.[25] According to the article, when Marceline and Fort Collins began to experience economic difficulties, both seized upon the expression of their ties to Disneyland's Main Street as a strategy for survival. In particular, the citizens of Marceline renamed its downtown street Kansas Avenue "Main Street U S A" to cement the connection to Disneyland. The town tour now attracts several thousand visitors each year, and the train depot has been transformed into a Walt Disney-Santa Fe Railroad Museum. Meanwhile, in Fort Collins, the article reported that the preservation of its downtown had begun to look "suspiciously like Disneyfication."[26] These examples clearly show how in today's globalized era, where communication, tourism and heritage industries reign supreme, the notion of authenticity has sometimes been cut completely loose from its moorings. The image of the original has now actually replaced the original itself.

In addition we are not all equal in this authenticity equation, and indeed at times its confused nature may border on the absurd. At Disney World's EPCOT Center in Florida, the Moroccan pavilion was actually subsidized by the government of Morocco, and Moroccan craftsmen were sent by the King to secure the country's place in the new global order.[27] One must ask what kind of authenticity or legitimacy the Moroccan government thought it was buying by investing in such an enterprise, especially when none of the wealthier nations represented at the exhibit, such as France or Italy, provided any such funding for their pavilions. Morocco did not want to be left out of the copy, lest it also be left out of the real.

In this regard one might also remark on the Cairo street created for the Paris Exposition of 1889, for the construction of which the curators felt compelled to import actual dirt, donkeys and caretakers. The concern for authenticity was so great that several details of an actual historic structure – a Quranic school for children and a water fountain – were disassembled, shipped to Paris, and installed in the copy.[28] Perhaps the supreme irony is that, one hundred years later, when a foreign preservation team working for the Egyptian government wanted to restore this structure, the only surviving clear and detailed representations of it were the exhibition publications.[29] Here the copy of the original became the means by which it could continue to exist, and the relationship between the two became mutually sustaining if not constitutive. This also explains why the Venetian casino in Las Vegas established a special fund for the preservation of the Venetian buildings it replicated.

However, the events of 9/11 necessitate a different reading of scholarship on endings and on the fate of tradition in the global era. They also beg the question of the "end of tradition" in the built environment. The articulation of this dilemma is complex and depends largely on what one really means by tradition. I argued some fifteen years ago in the first conference of IASTE (International Association for the Study of Traditional Environments) that tradition must not be interpreted simply as the static legacy of the past but rather as a model for the dynamic interpretation of the present. I still believe that this view is sound, and it complemented Yi-Fu Tuan's position that tradition was always about constraint or absence of choice.[30] Hence, our work in IASTE was challenging the very concept of tradition itself and the parallel belief that the landscape has some authentic connection to a discrete population. Other colleagues in this debate have suggested that we turn our attention away from a search for the "authentic, the characteristic, the enduring and the pure, and immerse ourselves in the active and the impure, seeking settings that are ambiguous, multiple, often contested," and examining points of contact and transformation.[31]

I also suggested in the mid 1990's that in the current climate of globalization, while settlements are likely to become homogenized, their inhabitants are showing greater awareness of their ethnic, religious, and racial differences.[32] I concluded that "identity" and tradition, in the era of globalization, are likely to become less tied to locality and more informationally based. So, then, is this the end of tradition, particularly in built material form? The scholarly emphasis on the re-evaluation of tradition, its role in the production of environments, its relative efficacy of transmission, its demise in the face of globalization, etc. suggest its possible "end." Indeed, if tradition is merely the dialectical fabrication of modernity, then does not the end of tradition as a meaningful object of inquiry suggest the end of tradition as an objective reality? Jane M. Jacobs has argued that tradition has indeed been brought into being by modernity's own imaginary, and, under globalization, has been reshaped and enlivened in a range of unexpected ways in the same place. Rather than doing away with tradition, she asks us to think about tradition and modernity as being in an ever-changing vibrant couplet within which the terms are *both* co-dependent *and* mutually exclusive, or, in her formula, "tradition is (not) modern."[33]

The emergence of the idea of a global culture supermarket adds another challenge to the legitimacy of tradition as a stable frame of reference. Gordon Mathews argues that the earlier idea of culture as "the way of life of a people" should be combined with the more contemporary concept of culture as "the information and identities available from the global cultural supermarket." This is to say that in a global era it is necessary to adopt a view of culture that is shaped equally by both the political state and the economic market.[34] Tradition, like culture, has now become – at least for some – a matter of choice, because both information and alternative identities are now available in this global supermarket. Tradition should also be viewed today as the arena of mediation between the hegemony of national or local culture in a given society and the exercise of choice by some members of that society. According to a Hong Kong newspaper article, for instance, when a reporter asked members of a motorcycle gang in China why they were obsessed by Harley Davidsons and the American dream of freedom, he was told, "Cultures… are like the dishes on a table. You just pick up what you like."[35] People everywhere increasingly identify with more than one tradition and one culture: They develop multiple, flexible and simultaneous identities, no longer mediated mainly or only by the state. In our current media-crazed world, tradition is further manipulated by the cultural and material global supermarket. However, the situation is not one that exists universally, either. For the traditions that shape the cultural landscapes of ethnic and minority groups will continue to be molded by their practical resistance to the dominant culture and their stronger allegiance to a community identity.

So it would seem that what has ended is not tradition itself but the idea of tradition as a harbinger of authenticity and as a container of specific cultural meaning. What has ended is tradition as a place-based, temporally-limited concept, as a static authoritative legacy, and as a heritage exclusively owned by specific groups of people. We must recognize that lasting tradition today is "the transient, the fleeting and the contingent."[36] Tradition, like "fashion is not innocent of history… in fact it continually scavenges the past for props, masks and costumes."[37] Ultimately, not only does the distinction between the fake and the real become meaningless, but the fake and the simulated become the real in and of themselves. In other words, the "real" and the "reel" have become mutually constitutive codependent entities where one cannot exist without the other.

Tradition is not dead and in this case has not ended. What should end is tradition revered as the authentic and the exclusionary. Tradition is no longer found only in "real" places. It lives even in the most fake of all places, where it is being reborn everyday in the social practices of those who inhabit what used to be the space of fakery. A good story for conclusion has to do with New York, the quintessential American city, and its Times Square. In the 1990's, Rudolf Giuliani took over the mayorship of New York City vowing to clean up Times Square of all its prostitution, drugs, and informal street hawkers. The campaign to achieve this end included appropriating several establishments, selling property, rezoning, and a package of benefits to encourage major corporations to take over this public space.[38] By the end of the 1990's, Times Square was totally remade, with Disney and other large global corporations occupying a major part of it. The Square has now been made safe for tourists and citizens alike, but at the expense of making it more like a Disneyland or a Las Vegas. No longer are the homeless there; no longer can we see prostitutes and pimps. The hawkers, prostitutes and pimps still exist in New York, although not in its most important public space anymore.

In Las Vegas, a place no one even called a city a few years ago, a new hotel casino named New York / New York was built in the mid-1990's. The casino, with a skyline that emulates New York with a scale model Brooklyn Bridge in front of it, has become a popular place among tourists who have never been to the "real" New York but feel that New York / New York is as much as they can or want to experience. But while

New York / New York remains a private casino inside, its public space on the strip is being taken over. After September 11, informal street vendors selling all forms of New York souvenirs from firefighter T-shirts to police officers' memorabilia took over the sidewalk in front of the Casino. Also in front of the casino, men and women may be seen distributing cards with pictures of prostitutes who can arrive at your door in 30 minutes. The cards promise prompt service, credit card confidentiality, and that the person who comes will at least match the advertised image. The cards go on to identify rates ranging from $50 for half an hour for a "brunette" to $80 for the same period for an "Asian beauty." In front of the casino's hotel, mounted riot police may be seen on weekends controlling young teenage crowds – children of the casino employees – mainly minorities and predominately Hispanic. None of these forms of behaviors exist in the real Times Square as they are no longer tolerated today. Yet, in Las Vegas the ultimate fake city, these traditions are alive and well. Has Las Vegas become the real city that New York City used to be?

The paradox is that Las Vegas, designed as a utopia streamlined for unfettered consumption now exhibits the "messiness" of a real city. This should remind us that the end of tradition does not come when a highly circumscribed utopia ceases to exist. Rather, it arrives when we realize that tradition is what we make and sustain everyday and everywhere through the occasionally contemptuous act of living.

I would like to conclude with a personal anecdote. On a field trip during a conference I attended in Cairo in 1998, I met an American academic on the Giza plateau at the foot of the Pyramids. Looking down toward the Sphinx, he said, "Oh, but it is so small," really disappointed. His comment puzzled me, and it took me some time to figure out what he meant. He turned out to be a professor at the University of Nevada, Las Vegas. His city housed the famous Luxor Hotel and its casino, built as a glass pyramid with a Sphinx enlarged three times at its entrance. The professor was used to parking his car in the hotel's lot that faced the giant Las Vegas Sphinx. When he was in Giza, he became disappointed, not because the reality did not live up to its image, but because along the way, the reality ceased to be relevant when the image became the principal frame of reference.

This is reminiscent of a tale of mimesis once told by Jean Baudrillard: The cartographer of an empire draws a map that is perfect in every detail and eventually becomes a substitute for "the real" it represents. The map is slowly rotting in just the parts where the territory in real life becomes deserted or occupied by other nations. "Simulation is no longer... a referential being or a substance. It is the generation by models of a real without origin or reality..."[39]

Much of the material included in this article is based on various arguments presented in my two recent books, *Consuming Tradition, Manufacturing Heritage: Global Norms and Urban Forms in the Age of Tourism* and *The End of Tradition?*

New Scenarios

After the dissolution of alternatives to the Western model, the present debate about cities seems to oscillate between two irreconcilable poles: the one being a nostalgia for the traditional city, made of stone and defined enclosures; the other, an ever-increasing attraction to the enticements of suburban comfort. Both models present obvious risks; both traditionalism and relativism, even if they appear to be polar opposites, are, for all intents and purposes, equally counterproductive to the healthy principle that sees the project of cities as a model for the future. Even when taking this dichotomy into account, or more generally even considering all the risks and uncertainties that arise when one argues about the use of models, it is our conviction that we need to start once again from the principle that architecture is an activity that must be capable of transcending the single building. The single building, in fact, must emerge in its intimate meaning as a reflection on cities and territories as such they currently exist.

The activity of planning thus appears similar to that of Sisyphus, who uselessly hauled a great rock up a mountain, knowing only too well that the gods would inevitably hurtle it back down into the valley. Sisyphus, however, as Albert Camus imagined him (and like many of the best planners and architects), is neither entirely unhappy nor desperate. He knows full well that without the apparent futility of his action, he will lose the heroic aura that so clearly distinguishes him, that way of elevating himself above the fetters of everyday life.

Whether or not everyone accepts this view, it is certainly demonstrable in the modern tradition, and in the tradition that sees the project of cities and territories as a highly intellectual work, aimed at defining the forms suited to the needs of the future. In postmodernism currently the issues are considerably more complicated. Cities and territories increasingly show a congenital rebelliousness towards the project, and planning proves itself increasingly indifferent to urban or territorial design. This is a sign of changing times that seem to have rejected the argument for models, which are now seen as buried under the ruins of ideologies, all of which is given and evident, an inescapable expression of how a post-industrial democracy establishes itself in a territory. Under such a condition, which it is logical to define as anti-Platonic and inherently contrary to a priori ideas, it seems difficult or nearly impossible to think of the project as a relevant expression of a much larger matter.

The question that we pose is similar to the question posed by scientists throughout the last century, the same question that gave rise to the discipline of the philosophy of science: is it possible to have models and prescriptions all the while knowing that these will inevitably be disregarded in a situation that is increasingly more complex and contradictory than we are capable of imagining? A way out of this impasse is based on a twofold observation: any given theory is false, in that it selects and arranges certain data and not others; while, at the same time, one cannot live without theories, in as much as dogma, or at least a certain amount of dogmatism, is necessary for the dissemination of knowledge. Thus, if the prescriptive idea of the city is dogma, and that of the building is an empirical elaboration of it, then we must allow the two aspects to live together despite the fact that they are both refutable elements, in some ways false or fallible, because they are the precondition for the accumulation of successive errors and disregarded rules that constitute the essence of the most beautiful cities in the world, from Rome to New York. It is necessary to begin with the facts, to select their decisive articulation, so that they can then be arranged into new categories, all the while knowing that all of this is a process of fabrication, destined to be undermined by other theories equally fictitious, yet hopefully more interesting.

Let us begin with the category of *territory-city*, always keeping in mind the idea of describing an apparatus suited for generating, in the actual building, the conceptual surplus value which is capable of transcending the simple event of building. Territory-city encompasses those places of low-density living, imported from the United States, which are increasingly structuring the geography of Europe. The main characteristic of the territory-city is its configuration as a hybrid landscape, where nature, infrastructure and architecture tend to blend together as a whole: a landscape where the hierarchies are muddled and where everyday short-term needs surpass mid to long-term ones.

The concept of territory-city is substantially different from the seemingly analogous one of *city-territory*. City-territories were, indeed, entirely different in that they originated from a planned reality; more specifically, they emerged from the ideas of architects in the late 1960's, who believed, along the line of Hegel's idea, that history proceeded according to laws. The idea of that era was to define the gigantic building organisms that absorbed into their interiors the functions of city life; that would make it possible, according to Marxist theory, to overcome, once and for all, the division between urban and rural. Such building organisms, of which forms have been recorded on paper despite their indescribable dimensions, could still refer to the classical idea of the city, in as much as they are closely packed hierarchies, unitarily designed. The current territory-city model is exactly the opposite. It is anti-hierarchical, disseminated and antithetical to urban design in the way that it tends to blend topography and building development into a configuration that opposes the concept of an exact, planned unity.

The result is, nonetheless, already well known as the diffused city model, the inherent informality of which is nothing else than the exact transcription in the territory of the needs and the economic and social dynamics of our model of development, essentially based on consumerism and mobility of the overall population. Like it or not, this is the current European scenario: an endemic and highly important scenario in which all pretence of a return to a united and formally defined origin of the city or territory is shattered. It is, however, misleading to think that the territory-city corresponds to a territory lacking in quality, ultimately detrimental to the urban logos. This is an inadequate simplification which, above all, does not take into account the puzzling capacity that this model has for adaptation, the indubitable vitality that allows it to renew itself through its own errors and inherent contradictions. Although the territory-city is indeed a parthenogenetic reproduction, its own elementary structure elevates this model to the status of an ideal container for current mass yet fragmented society.

We bring these preliminary remarks to a close with a question that is really very simple, but exactly for this reason no less urgent. One must ask if, in fact, it is possible to think of a type of architecture that would be a figurative or metaphorical reflection of new scenarios, or if we must, instead, definitively renounce all that transcends mere appearance and finally adapt ourselves to an architecture of sheer event – an expression of Western society which, even though powerful, is, in the last analysis, in crisis, given that it lacks values and, hence, shared planning skills.

Obsolete Parameters

In the not so distant past, the theoretical laboratory for architectural planning and building, particularly in Italy, pursued the so-called consolidated city in which the historic center incorporated the surrounding suburbs. The operative hypothesis was based on the principle that the arguments for a building should be in tune with the context, which history had honed and polished into one final and organic whole. "Architecture of the City" was thus defined for all practical purposes as an ideology, surely a fascinating system of references, especially for us in Italy, yet that also suffered from all the imperfections of the prescriptive systems of thought as it is also conceived and enforced top down. It also fell into the simplifications of dogmatic thinking, in which the city was reduced to a few single elements: boulevards, squares, perhaps a radial configuration and peripheral industrial areas or the like. In other words, the model was the 19th century city.

Walking around Venice, the mistake appears obvious; the urban sequence is much more articulate and variegated than any dogmatic model. For the actual city includes other elements – in Venice these include calli, campi, fondamenta, porteghi, sottoporteghi, rii, rii terà, etc. – which are equally important and can be neither made to fit into a plan nor reduced to a few elements, except at the risk of an inevitable semantic impoverishment.

The mistake appears even more clearly when one passes from the consolidated city to the territory-city; here the categories literally implode upon themselves. It is all the more vain to speak of texture and morphological laws inherent to the urbanized territory. Postmodernism has in fact imposed a prescription even more invasive and devastating than modernism did; consumerism and mobility, the two main principles of present-day development, have proven even more radical than industrial expansion has been, resulting in such a complete disappearance of any traces, plans or signs that searching for them could be likened to an act of necrophilia.

We are speaking then of new scenarios and obsolete parameters even if the main question still stands. If in fact one begins with the presupposition that in order for architecture to be legitimate enough to go beyond its own appearances, that is, if it must once again become "architecture of the city," or better yet, architecture of the territory-city, what are the new parameters on which we are to rely? In other words, is it still possible to think of a city that is definitely no longer abstract and prescriptive, but rather unconstrained in its thinking and yet resilient enough to shape the architecture it encompasses?

Necessary Considerations for the Consolidated City and Territory-City

In the recent past, what held the consolidated city together, at least from one theoretical viewpoint, was the idea of permanence. By identifying the types of permanent structures it was possible to establish the grounds for a subsequent and adequate building development. In the territory-city the permanent structures are reduced to one type alone: the infrastructural networks, both the visible ones, such as the plotted courses of streets and railway lines, as well as the hidden ones like power lines and their relative connections and routes. What undergoes change is the building, an ever more transient and ephemeral event, and with it the building fabric, ever more frayed and no longer homogeneous. The long-term design is, however, an infrastructural one, and as such it is the only structural element on which to anchor a reflection that seeks to oppose the relativism that has by now dismantled the idea that architecture can be considered to be a part of a whole. By beginning with the assumption that infrastructures and their layout are the permanent elements, one is able to lay the foundations for a workable alternative.

What else needs to be said about the consolidated city, or about the historical city centers and their relative surroundings or suburbs is that the common practice, though a mistaken one, is to regard such as city as a completed organism, frozen in certain respects. Among the closely woven stitches there exist lacerations or rifts in the city fabric, discontinuous moments, real and proper omissions that gradually increase as one draws away from the center. Generally these omissions are classified in the inclusive category of empty urban spaces, which, among others, increase in direct proportion to the city's capacity to transform itself and to its economic instability.

Usually there is an effort to introduce in zoning laws the features of the consolidated surroundings, even when these zones are of large dimensions. The case of the reconstruction of the city of Berlin is instructive in this regard and shows all the effects and limitations of this backward-looking intent. The proposed alternative is completely different: the urban or sub-urban empty spaces, even if enclosed, display traces of a history that have little to do with the consolidated surroundings: They are closed enclaves and probably should be considered as such. The arguments and formal proposals for such cases should probably be applied to the territory-city and introduce these embedded historical or environmental features and variables to the surroundings while at the same time allowing for their own development.

It is also easy to see how the historical city centers are really very different from what they appear to be. In Italy, for example, we have truly witnessed a quite obvious "museumization" of the historic city centers. It is indeed an ideology of reclamation, based upon the orthodoxy of restoration, for centuries alive and resistant to change, finally crystallized. Also here, what was born as a social concern, has become over time such an insidious ideology that once natural sites of urban complexity have been turned into mono-functional enclosures where the mono-culture of tourism rules. From one theoretical point of view, this change has once again overturned earlier certainties. These places and their history, which once embodied the idea of the city itself, were increasingly reduced to a a schema not so different from that of sub-urban. Thus, the scenario has not only changed in the territory-city; it has changed everywhere, and the new parameters can no longer be bound only to the vague shapelessness of the territory-city.

Architecture as Urban Thought

In the celebrated painting of Pala d'Urbino, a promised city is shown depicted in the splendor of its architectural supremacy. In the picture nothing alters the magnificent balance of the conscious game between architectural volumes and structures illuminated by an infinite peak of light, which privileges a single spectator's viewpoint. In the painting we encounter intellectual production that establishes itself amidst the disorder and imperfection of everyday life, deliberately eliminating the unforeseeable. The argument is a Platonic one drawing on innate ideas, uncontaminated and accessible only to a chosen few who have had the privilege of entering the cavern. No natural elements or people are shown in this representation; rather the scene has been constructed so as to present the observer with the most perfect possible relationship between architecture and city.

This relationship, which in truth preceded Renaissance thought, was for centuries the fundamental element of European urban identity despite its adaptation, from time to time, to different styles. And it remained more or less unaltered until the modernist architecture of the 20th century, when the symbolic aspect of architecture was relegated to second place and the social aspect took precedence. Despite the transformation of the city into a palimpsest in the making and despite the crisis of hierarchies and set rules that subsequently occurred, the Western notion of architecture as art for prefiguring the city has not only survived but is at the height of its intensity. The Futurists, Tony Garnier, and Le Corbusier, as well as Archigram or Superstudio, despite considerable differences, based their work once again on the research of a dialogical relationship between the city and the architectural object, this time turning their attention to a utopian future ever more extreme and radical.

The dialogical relationship between architecture and the city, however, quickly crumbled in postmodernism. The short yet significant phase of refusing modernism which took place in the 1970's and 1980's did indeed produce such a split. The regression into outdated cities and its architecture through intellectual nostalgia was the prelude to our current situation, in which architecture, despite its return to modernism, seems to have once again refused to surpass its own appearance, considering itself incapable of any symbolic representation. Indeed it seems that Fukuyama's premonition of the end of history has come true concerning architecture, that it is impossible to describe events other than in a causal and finalistic way.

In truth there have been a few exceptions where one has not surrendered to the concept of architecture as art which prefigures the city or territory. One of the most striking of these is offered by the Dutch school. It understood how to combine in an organic, if not picturesque, idea of housing, both domestic culture and the sublime, so to speak, culture of large-scale urban phenomena, such as Rem Koolhaas's well-known theory of urban congestion. The success of contemporary Dutch architectural thought is not fortuitous, but rather the realization that the idea of urban and territorial architecture can no longer be considered absolute; it cannot, as it were, produce a perfect unity. Thus, its approach is to accept the apparent contradictions, allowing apparently very different concepts and situations to respond and react to one another, and working among the debris that the disjunction of disparate approaches inevitably warrants.

New Themes for New Landscapes

It is not a given that what appears to be an endemic condition of postmodernity – or the definitive split between the idea of architecture and that of cities or territories – must remain as such. In other words, it is not clear that the present-day practice, in which buildings are created as expressions of autonomous power or as purely distinct events, is destined to persist forever. At the same time, it is quite clear that the strength of this relation is unable to manifest itself in the scenario of consolidated cities; rather, in our opinion, it can be seen in those territories described earlier that, even though poised between the urban and territorial, between abandonment and misuse, increasingly show a remarkable potential that is representative of our time.

In these territories of dormant identity and representation, too often confined to narrow urban perspectives, we are likely to find the track of the hedonistic tendencies of postmodernist architecture interrupted. It is clear that the relationship in question can be neither prescriptive nor designed with preconceived generalities. Rather it must be adjusted to the visible negotiation between the temptations of the large scale and the consoling resignations of the small scale, while on the other hand interrogating the territory bound by and relative to the questionable rules and their negation.

All of this can seem flimsy if the characteristics of the new projective themes proposed in these territories are not considered. The landscape of infrastructures and networks is certainly one of these territories, and it is perhaps the most interesting to consider if for no other reason than that its developmental model depends largely on the organization and management of interchange systems. In the case of networks, the difference in scales that we mentioned earlier can appear more clearly. The objects which do indeed determine the landscape of infrastructures can be briefly defined by a simple classification: first by the technical, repetitive positions of the same networks, and, second, by the series of all the elements which we will define as support features or objects.

The difference in scale is enormous, and yet in both macro and micro-scale planning, its quality still lies dormant. In the current situation the definition of the networks and relative support objects is almost entirely the prerogative of those in charge of the technical design and planning, who are in general indifferent to the aesthetic substance of objects that have always been considered mono-functional. The result is that the actual distant traces and routes from which we perceive the territory fall into the debate on the mechanized repetitiveness that degrades the natural geography and urban conditions. At the same time, aesthetic discourse or architectural design has difficulty in finding a plausible, operational space that is not simply drawn from ornamental catalogue solutions that are by now obsolete.

Thus, if one starts with the principle that the reclamation of the landscape must begin with the infrastructure networks, no design or planning operation can be confined to the solution, however brilliant, of the single case. In other words, our concern must be with the actual aesthetics of network designs, and that, by nature, involves an approach as a model that can be applied to similar cases. Hence, although from a purely spatio-temporal point of view we can hypothesize the painting, Pala d'Urbino, in terms of infrastructure and landscapes, we must always consider these infrastructures within the context of a unitary whole as environmental representations or forms located between the realistic and the utopian, and developed through the empirical treatment of the theme with a view to creating a model. We must first know how to begin from the empirical in order to rise to the level of the model form, and then be able to return to the materiality and pragmatism of each specific case. The operation is certainly not easy and the need for a unitary prefiguration of the landscape of infrastructures is unavoidable; adding extra aesthetic value to infrastructures is an extremely costly operation and feasible only if approached from a wide perspective, proposing clear models with all their opportunities and risks defined in advance.

The aesthetics of infrastructure design is even more complex and tricky than this. Under current legislation, network infrastructure is protected by a bare strip along its paths that skirt the peripheries. This restricted area can be seen as a true no-man's land, destined to deterioration and abandonment. It is where intervention needs to take place, and it is also where an infinite number of the experimental design themes can take shape: from the embankments of rivers and lagoons to areas bordering streets and motorways, from the border zones between different urban plans to the formal upgrading of active industrial areas, from street furniture systems inside new urban zones to the access points of specialized areas (e.g. archaeological sites, natural reserves, sport parks, areas catering to tourists, etc...) as well as restricted areas under landscape protection laws. Once the themes are identified, the overall plan concerning these areas acquires greater credibility as opposed to a simple formalistic solution of peripheral infrastructure. Kevin Lynch's research, which focused on the perception of the large scale through diverse and changing connotations, from sign systems to monument markers and regulatory indicators, is an example.

One sees that the themes listed above are characterized by their "non-volumetric" features, in as much as they are devoid of any internal space. Our research is focused precisely in this direction; we believe in investing effort in non-volumetric architecture (intended as a comprehensive activity involving architecture, engineering, art and design) so as to confront once again the truly unresolved theme of modernism and post-modernism: public space.

> When modes of music change,
> the fundamental laws
> of the state always change with them.[1]

This essay is a reflection on a specific characteristic of the relationship between the modes of architectural composition and production in the context of the current environment, where digital apparatus dominates among production technologies. Considering all that digital technology contributes today to the design of architecture – and yet given that architecture still remains essentially a hand-made product, unlike, for example, automobiles – it is critical to reflect now on the relationship, or the interface, between actual and virtual modes of architectural design production. This reflection has to do in large part with the great disjunction between the idealism of the virtual and the realities of the actual. How are the contemporary technology and its idealism actually implemented in the *composition* of culturally iconic and formally avant-garde actual architecture today? With this in mind I engage specific examples from the recent history of music and discuss some direct and some implied parallels that can be drawn between these musical events and architecture. My main point in making this analogy is to highlight the fact that in both disciplines, there exist comparable efforts relying on the techniques and procedures of notation and representation in the conception of the end product. Therefore, I have attempted to concentrate on the procedures of *writing*[2] as a primary means of creation in both domains and their effect in the enterprise of both disciplines vis-à-vis what lies outside their disciplinary conventions.

The central issue here is that techniques of re-production are the primary modes of architectural production today, analogous to those of music ever since the invention of the phonograph. This mechanized aspect of reproduction is paired with examples of music production and, specifically, the attempts by Nam Jun Paik and John Cage to reorganize the performance-product relationship. In this discussion I take up notions of the conflict between institutionalized science and the imaginary, noting the experiments of Cage and Paik, namely the idea of *subversion*. My key point is that a series of subversive experiments issues an essential challenge to and modifies the canon of a given aesthetic genre, while on the other hand, within the apparatus structure, a resistance or a safety is devised in order to reduce such subversive elements' frequencies and intensities. The main issue in this discussion, in my view, is the incorporation of an apparatus into one's personal and professional life to such an extent that it becomes the very means of measuring the vital signs of one's worth. Central to this is obviously how the apparatus does what it does in order to fully understand and to be able to verify such process. Ultimately, my objective in this essay is to discuss the scope and *potentiality* of digital architecture, rather than its instant gratifications and fascinating wonders.

A quick survey of any architectural design studio, either academic or professional, will demonstrate how capable we are today of disassembling, rearranging and recreating our temples, in countless variations, in three days or less. Even while this ability appears to follow the recognizable pattern of an uncontrolled proliferation of cheap images and artifacts, it also presents an opportunity for a critical assessment of architectural production as a mixing of parts and fragments that can be reorganized and reconfigured toward a richer and more diversified perspective. Without debating whether this is good, bad, or ugly, I would like to entertain the question of how and if the digital process in architecture, its narratives and symbolic qualities – most of all its representation in the age of digital omnipotence and the seemingly uncontrollable stockpiling of fast, cheap and out-of-control image making – could become conventionalized beyond automation and maximization of human capacity. The term *convention* here refers to a process within which the tactical decisions of everyday practice rely on a pattern of play between the simultaneous satisfaction of both personal and public agendas and is therefore a bridge between the desires (fantasy) and the necessities (knowledge) that any architectural project is expected to embody. In between these polarities one could find an area where convention becomes the process of assessing how the volatility can be accommodated and managed in a specific context. The term *context* is highly problematic as its definition inherently contains a set of assumptions that can never be made unbiased, and therefore the subjectivity of organizing and classifying information again becomes the issue of authenticity and authorship vs. the objective common denomination.

This conventionalization of the digital production process in architecture can be approached by analogy to music in its re-production of performance – rather than the actual performance itself. In the music of the 20th century, the invention of mechanized instruments created the techniques of recording, editing and mixing capable of creating the everyday reality of aural experience previously limited to actual theatres. At the core of this enterprise of reproducing music for daily consumption and entertainment was a new genre of codification that demanded certain expertise quite unlike that which was required for the actual performance. It also created the ideological and economic criteria of specialization in distinguishing and isolating noise, the identification and classification of the undesirable, which may be impossible to remove completely but which must be made manageable. The history of the reproduction of music can even be understood as centered on and reduced to the single issue of noise control. Furthermore, the idea of an apparatus – today's ever-present software-hardware combinations – that can actually distinguish, classify and prioritize sound and its sources has enormous implications for creative (or intuitive) processes, be it in music or in architecture. Such an apparatus-controlled dimension already assumes a certain level of automaticity that lies beyond the variables of the actual. The systematic organization of this apparently unconstrained operation, whether intentional or not, has been made inevitable in the production process. This process is driven and made possible only by the "automatic" apparatus, of which the sole purpose is the replication of human labor (and perhaps ultimately replication of any natural animate beings) beyond the limitations of its natural capacity.

In 1913 Luigi Russolo, one of the founding figures of Futurism, declared in his "The Art of Noise" that the noise made possible by the machine age "*reigns supreme over human sensibility*." In this manifesto, he further declared,

> First of all, musical art looked for the soft and limpid purity of sound. Then it amalgamated different sounds, intent upon caressing the ear with suave harmonies. Nowadays musical art aims at the shrillest, strangest and most dissonant amalgams of sound. Thus we are approaching noise-sound. This revolution of music is paralleled by the increasing proliferation of machinery sharing in human labor.[3]

His ideas opened the door to the reorganization and expansion of the conventions of music by annexing many types of noise-sound into the realm of music. This is, in essence, attributable to the production of music beginning with the notational process in which music is *written* preceding its aural realization, the performance of the text. We also witness the notation (writing) as a process that is beyond expressing human comforts and pleasures as the primary objective of expression, as exemplified by such writers as Velimir Khlebnikov (1885–1922), with his onomatopoeic, "beyonsense" and "zaum" writings[4] and later, Antonin Artaud (1896–1948), who proposed the evolution of Western theatre beyond its language-based tradition (*The Theatre and Its Double*, 1938).

As is the case with music, architecture is heavily dependent on the practice of writing, not only the writing of treatises but also in its need of drawings and specifications for its materialization. In architecture we can also consider the dimension of "noise-space" relative to our capability to mix and remix elements. As countless studies of the symbolic and iconographic evolution of architecture and its profound reliance on the codices of the past could attest, we are indeed engaged in the process of sampling, mixing and remixing architecture every day. More specifically, the issue at hand is, as in music, the classification and treatment of what we consider to be noise-space in architecture and its cultural context. In this framework, how can the convention of the architectural notational system contain noise as a legitimate element of composition? By definition, noise-space in architecture should not occur. It is supposed to occur only by accident, when architecture fails in its duty to appeal to the positive senses, because architecture is supposed to provide *solely* safety, comfort and pleasure, even more so than music or painting, since architecture is supposed to provide the experience of sensorial *totality*.

to be continued on page 233

Tucson – Nogales

Josef S. Green

LEONARDO

El Karajo
8
TECATE
Light
PIOS
TAXI
TAXI

14 RUTA
PERIFERICO
REFORMA
TIANGUIS

PINTURAS
145

DR. SERGIO
DE LA ROSA
Medico Cirujano
TEL: 2 24 37
SE RENTA
31 2 38 20
31 4 62 44
EXTENCIONES
MAQUILLAJE
FORD

ALTIMA
VYD-26-35

As we often see today, the global popularity of certain types of music suggests a pattern by which certain types of architecture could similarly proliferate, not only under the banner of an individual "superstar" artist but in broader terms of stylistic and technical compositions. Today, the most striking feature of music, predominantly thriving in the phase of reproduction, is its capability to mix and remix itself according to the inclinations of the producers and the musicians, the managers and the functionaries of the production process. The resultant product more often than not determines the goal of what the performance itself is: the production value establishes the position and prominence of a particular performer and performance, and therefore their economic viability. In the end, the control over the reproduction process with respect to determining the degree of sound manipulation and what is to be removed as extraneous noise is at the heart of the recording industry, and this has a direct and profound impact on the economy of music.

The idea and technique of sampling as a serious experiment in music and sound making date back to the research work of Dick Raaijmakers, under the pseudonym of "Kid Baltan," a resident composer at the electro-acoustics division of the Philips Research Laboratories, known as NatLab, and of Tom Dissevelt, who, between the 1950's and the 1960's, developed compositions by electronically generated sound fragments and splicing magnetic tapes.[5] In the history of music production technology these compositions represented a significant step in the evolution of the conventions of how music should be composed, produced, stored and distributed. The research initiated by Philips for this project was motivated, ironically, by the prospect of creating "popular" electronics for making and storing music, primarily targeted for the consumer market. Again, the project started, similarly to many other breakthroughs, in a vision that someday a person in a living room will be able to replace an existing institution, for example, the orchestra, by means of technology – in this case, an electronic keyboard, first produced in 1963 under the brand name, Philicorda – that can emulate the full sonic spectrum of an orchestra. As has been also the case with architecture, this process demonstrates a pattern of exploiting existing materials, the extraction of certain parts and fragments and their reassembly. This process also includes the vision of "fully synthetic" machination of an existing organic production.

Thanks to current digital technology, today's architects can go beyond the efforts of the pioneers, cutting and splicing numerous types of images generated by and collected from even more diverse sources that range across many segments of cultural activities and periods. As with Philicorda, the electronic home orchestra Philips envisioned, this case explicitly represents the tendency in which the process of mechanization that intensifies fragmentation and re-constitution forms the very concept of production essentially as management. In other words, the most important issue now is not the actual making of tangible objects; rather, at the center of the production process is increasingly the management and manipulation of the apparatus. In this process, even though one could also argue that the process allows the product to approach the state of certain state of perfection, nonetheless the point is that such presumed perfection is in the end a sum of managerial decisions in the operation of the apparatus.

Along with this development at Philips, another major event in the composition and production process of music took place at the opposite end of the technological scale, with two of the most prominent artists of the same period, Nam Jun Paik and John Cage. Paik is regarded as the inventor of video art, and Cage has been highly influential with his compositional method based on a random, indeterminate process using the *I Ching*. The two artists' work presents a compelling example for architecture in that both had a very strong notion of an exterior condition, that is, the *other* that lay outside the specific boundaries of a discipline conceived in terms of its canonic definition; and both resorted to techniques that intentionally contaminated those boundaries. Both have also often approached their work by intentionally *misusing* their instruments

Random Access, Exposition of Music-Electronic Television, Galerie Parnass, Wuppertal, 11~20 March 1963

of choice, for example by placing a magnet in front of a TV set in order to produce patterns of distortion, or by inserting random objects – stones, spoons, nuts and bolts, etc. – in between piano strings.

In his installation project in Wuppertal in 1963, entitled "Exposition of Music – Electronic Television" at Galerie Parnass, Paik presented two variations of an interactive installation called "Random Access." The first version consisted of strips of magnetic recording tapes mounted on a wall in a random crisscrossing pattern, on which a performer (or a visitor) would rub the head of a tape player, thereby generating random sound patterns dependent on the particular movement of the performer.[6] The second, subtitled "Schallplatten Schachlik," consisted of stacks of records, a turntable and a radio, and viewers were invited to play with the sequence of the records by moving the pick-up head of the turntable across and up and down different LP's and also adjusting the volume. This performance by Paik also laid down a challenge by proposing that the essence of music lies in the act of physical performance, however random and arbitrary that performance and its sound may be. The music becomes the expression produced by that specific physical act with all its inconsistencies and imperfection.

Obviously, the outcome of this performance as music making did not conform to the normal conventions of "M"usic. The importance of this particular performance is that it was an attempt to gauge the increment of electronic precision in relation to the conventional humanistic principles of music making, thereby implementing the contamination of the singular. This is important in terms of not only the technological apparatus but also its resultant product, which is transformed into the other – that which is contaminated and made "noisy." This experiment was counter to the ideals of traditional music making in general and to the burgeoning industry of the electronic reproduction of music at the time, which can be

Random Access (Schallplatten Schachlik), Exposition of Music-Electronic Television, Galerie Parnass, Wuppertal, 11–20 March 1963

conceived of as a process of removing spurious elements from recordings: the mechanized manipulation intervenes as an interface between the apparatus and its abstraction (reproduced music) of a physical phenomenon (music played by a musician in actual time).

In parallel to Paik's performance, Cage's "Prepared Piano" presents another compelling point about an instrument and its singularity. By randomly inserting objects between the strings, he altered the relationship between the *domestic* nature of the instrument and how it was meant to be performed. This experiment transformed the functionality that was its purpose. In other words, it became *useless* in the traditional sense. The piano no longer served the purpose of its notation; instead, the assembly of parts itself, its physical composition, made manifest the product of its utility (at this point, highly questionable) as an instrument of music production. Again in this particular case the totality of a piano as an instrument with its own inherent mechanized logic has been questioned and the integrity of that has been violated (or abused) by making it perform *other* functions. On the other hand, in order to accomplish the indeterminacy of his compositions, Cage's process was a highly *conventionalized* one that contained and accommodated its variables as inherent components of the process by employing the *I Ching,* also called the *Book of Changes*, in which various narrative fragments (or oracles as Cage puts them) are organized in hexagram sequences and probabilities. Cage describes his compositional process of indeterminacy in *Imaginary Landscape No. IV* (for 12 radios) and *Music of Changes* (for piano):

> Three coins tossed once yield four lines: three heads, broken with a circle; two tails and a head, straight; two heads and a tail, broken; three tails, straight with a circle. Three coins tossed thrice yield eight triagrams... Three coins tossed six times yield sixty-four hexagrams... read in reference to a chart of numbers from 1 to 64... Charts are made of an equal number of elements (sixty-four) which

James Tenney preparing a piano

> refer to Superpositions (one chart) (how many events are happening at once during a given structural space); Tempi (one chart); Durations (n, the number of possible Superpositions, in these works, eight charts); Sounds (eight charts); Dynamics (eight charts).[7]

The relevance and importance of this to the architectural process resides in the fact that today the production of architecture has turned to the precision and the simultaneous mutability of architectural imagery, which are made possible by means of digitally controlled research, composition, design and engineering processes. The seemingly antithetical technical processes of music making by Paik's magnetic tape *sound graffiti* or Cage's *prepared piano* present possible potentials for architectural production; these processes can be seen as ways of creating a *device* to define and characterize certain spatial variations. This also points toward the basic instrumentality of the idea of re-production as a creative genre liberated from the patronage patterns of a particular historical tradition. This example sets forth the problem: what is the way to produce architecture as in music with contingency and dissonance (noise or the subversion or disturbance) and incorporate them; and, in addition, how does one make a place for the absence of marked difference (silence or the voided)? Obviously the ultimate discussion in this regard is between the potentiality of notions such interference, extraneous formality, spontaneous variables, the multiplicity of temporality, etc. and the object-centered clarity and efficiency the vision mandates.

The modernist architecture was ultimately annexed to the competitive market economy, and corporate glass box headquarters are now the best known popular representation of both. This follows an established pattern in cultural practice wherein the specific boundaries of a discipline are refined according to their acceptability to the prevailing economic and political regime. Eventually this also led to the self-adjustment period in architecture and its countless examples of iconic revisionism as a means of repenting for what were considered the modernists' sins. Perhaps this was indeed inevitable and necessary. Perhaps we are now entering a similar phase, in which the pursuit of high-fidelity in production and reproduction is relative to the development of technological apparatus as the means of determining what is acceptable and what is not, i.e. what the managerial standards are to be, and also as a precise measurement for systematic identification and elimination of "noise-space" or the dissent in general. According to Allen Weiss:

> Recording is always more than representation, bearing the stamp of both the technical aspects of the apparatus and the stylistic demands of the technician. We know that Thomas Edison… could not stand complex musical textures or pungent harmonies; he found tremolo to be a distinct defect of the human voice, and believed that a voice without vibrato was preferable, … and even wanted to know whether a tune could be written solely with thirds and sixths; and, in his scientific perfectionism, he detested "extraneous" noises, such as the squeaking of flute keys, the thumping of piano felts, the turning of pages, gutteral vocal sounds – and even breathing![8]

This presents another issue, because it magnifies the problem of precision in reproduced music as a hygienic purging process that reduces the deviation to the minimum determined by the technical standards of the apparatus. A rapid development toward sonic purity has spawned a technocratic ideology that is in effect the codification of systems that can single-handedly determine a clear differentiation in an exclusionary process; and this process creates an exclusive management and self-corrective regime to determine what is desirable and what is not. This occurs by means of its digital codex and its inherent opacity to inspection and verification; its product is very often irreproachable, subject merely to comments as to whether or not something appears *interesting* as a product. Such a codex of digital technology is by nature insular and detached from the variables of *composition*.

We now have the technological means which enable the process of architectural composition and production to accommodate and express *difference* and move beyond the historical notions of architecture, a still-life, immovable and fixed in a frame in time: the subordination to what is presumed to be "real" is no longer acceptable. The case in music demonstrates a unique opportunity for architecture, in that the composition (the codification and its notational system) is directly tied to the practice. Yet the symbiosis of the codification and its execution produces, in both disciplines, specific differences that are dependent on individual interpretation on many levels. The uncertainties that reside in every aggregate of the performance produce the difference that is about the same object but different. With the rapid spread of disposable image-driven styles, including those of architecture, the results could easily attract the kind of criticism once directed toward modernist architecture, with its ideology of utopian oppositional politics and its call for the "better and improved," but this time around, the pursuit of ever changing ideals based on technocratic specifications rather than a set of static ideological ones. In architecture today there also exists the absurd proposition of androgynous optimized buildings (or blobs) springing up, covering the globe – although still in their developmental stage but nonetheless analogous to the glass boxes envisioned in the early 20th century and to their countless grotesque reincarnations regardless of the local specificity. Presumably they will eventually establish the ideal of the anonymous value-pacified globe constructed according to this optimized prototype. Perhaps this is not really a danger, but rather the realization of the prophecy that eventually the globe will become the ultimate art object of human kind.

The danger is necessarily an ideological one: the excessive enthusiasm for and reliance upon an instrument, of which automaticity (more often than not opaque and invisible) outweighs considerations for any factors outside the specifications of its black box. The necessity of formal generation is largely dependent upon the exclusive codification by software-hardware applications and systems; for this codification is designed to perform and produce a specific set of effects intended by yet other authorial standards (the programmers'). It still remains to be seen whether or not this new codification system will yet again promise health, liberation, and freedom and eventually lead to the prescription for yet another cure-all. However, this automaticity of technology could, at the same time, provide a possibility for architecture that is unprecedented in terms of its diversity and scope. Inserting the idea of various domesticities (contingent frequencies) into this process can take it beyond the lavish naming and narrow perspectives of naive panaceas, which often result only in thoroughly forgettable formal gymnastics that become flaccid even before they are exercised. They are dead as soon as they are built as architecture. We see only what they once were – swirling tornados or swarming birds and bees – and are content with the specimen captured in a jar of formaldehyde. Indeed we could all become immaculate connoisseurs, whose paramount importance is taxonomy (or taxidermy?) and its thoroughness.

What this new capability could also bring is a numbing mix of architectonics as dull as the beats of techno dance clubs, after all modes of production have passed through the bottleneck of the apparatus that prescribes a particular set of operations. On the one hand, we may now be close to being able to control and design every square inch of the globe, and, on the other, the lens of this codification also generates a view in which the human population progresses into sexless androids residing in sanitized perfection. Perhaps this is the vision of the *Gesamtkunstwerk* circa 21st century, with everyone living happily ever after, as was the case with recording technology, given the cleansing power and rapid deployment of the disparate narratives made possible by today's nimble digital technology. Today, the digital technology's ability to sample and repackage disparate aspects in an attractive container makes the messiness of mundane human constructs seem clean and safe, just as Descartes' ordering system made the bloody realities in his time appear clean and safe; the center of this system was of course the Sun King (and the benevolent God), the coordinate (0,0).

Today, we see that a vast array of techniques in music reproduction have necessitated a fundamental re-examination of music as a disseminator of certain values that were formerly attached to the institutionalized cultural framework (the *royal* regime) of a specific locality and its culture. As a result of this technological development – cassette tapes, CD's and MP3's – we see the contemporary genres of music that are entirely focused on the remixing of sound fragments, that is to say, the composer has become an *editor and manager*, whose decisions are primarily based on the location and flow of fragments and how they function within the whole collective.

We move into the realm of architecture as interface device. It is not so much the box (whether decorated or not, or the duck) but the *device* that is used to fulfill the function of codifying the historical, the canonic or otherwise purely imaginary narratives of a place and its cultural domesticity. Narratives in history used to represent particular versions of events, whether royal or subversive or otherwise prevailing in fragments and unwritten, in order to steer and reinforce a group's tendency in a direction within the context of certain belief system. Satisfying the programmatic functionality of a building also reflects the overall narratives of a given site as a cultural, political and economic entity. Therefore, architecture no longer serves, as the early modernists hoped it would, a certain *truth* in the widely perceived conflict between the revolution of the subversive and the status quo of the canonical as represented by the archaic continuity.

The optimization and value-engineering of architectural process by mean of the digital management has also accelerated the production of buildings at a rate that is tantamount to the uncontrollable growth of fatty tissues that result in obese, unhealthy and eventually indifferent and depraved space. For many architects, architecture is a matter of managing parts of which the production and consumption process tends towards the maximization of its material value per weight per hour per dollar spent (value-engineering and trans fatty acid). The data that affects this value structure is the essence of managers' architecture. And yes, the data can be sublime. Then again, this defining data represents a particular narrative of the value system and its manager, if not the entire regime of its appropriation.

By moving the notion of architecture as a narrative and communicative medium into a legitimate political debate, this position occupies the peculiar and rather uncomfortable spot where an architect could be an antagonist and, at the same time, a subversive "free mason" who no longer follows and satisfies the wishes of his master as a faithful minister, but rather becomes someone who makes *noise* and dissents. Yet this politicized position of the architect (the independent manager and functionary of the product of his own labor at the same time) also raises another important question. Can we continue to see architecture as the primary provision of comfort and safety (at least that is the presumed intention), if the means of extracting and re-presenting the narrative power of architecture and its role have so fundamentally changed? Again, we are at a point where the consideration of "noise space" is crucial. What do we consider music and what do we classify as noise in architecture today? Is there still such a distinction? If so, do we engage in the suppression of the noise without even thinking about it for a moment, seduced by the shining surfaces on our computer screen? If we include the noise-space, what do we make of our architectural canon? In doing so, will we come closer to a *pure* architecture, akin to what Artaud proposed as "pure" theatre?[9] Perhaps architecture, as a particular mode of thinking, will reveal more of its potentialities when we begin to examine its noise-space, where the architect aims at "the shrillest, strangest and most dissonant amalgams" of forms.

Returning to the notion of liberation by means of technological advances, architecture also shares a parallel with music. One feature to note is the different layers of cultural consumption in general and specifically in music and other forms of popular entertainment. Around the world, at least in those areas where the necessary technological infrastructure exists (and where it doesn't, we speak of the disadvantaged technological underclass), we can also distinguish people by the kind of the music they listen to, and this predilection is today shared in that particular membership regardless of the physical location. For example, radically different groups of people, whether in Kansas City or Bombay, subscribe to the same cultural products, which are currently dominated by the US, Europe and Japan.

It is a part of human desire to want to experience something that is supposed to be popular, in demand. This desire for what supposedly everyone wants and must have is carefully managed and relentlessly propagated with a promise to claim membership to the culture of image and material possession. Liberation is achieved by material possession: you are what you possess, the main motto of branding and image-making. In this managed environment of desire for possession there lies the danger of the local imagination being purged and lost forever, just as music has been managed in such a way as to exclude what has been determined to be irrelevant and undesirable, or simply, noise. On the other hand, the same technological regime also presents also an ever more compelling opportunity to remix and reinvent a certain locality by the inclusion of the noise-space and impurities caused by various sources of volatility.

In architecture, too, the aspiration toward exclusive membership creates the cult of the superstars, parallel those found in music, as we see buildings designed by the superstar architects dotted along the lines of money, power and politics, displayed by the dominant nation-states, corporations and individuals. The most distinctive manifestation of this is the so-called "The Bilbao Effect," named after Frank O. Gehry's Guggenheim Museum in Bilbao. After the success and superstardom of this project and its contribution to the city's prestige and economy, we have seen a wave of superstar projects rolled out from London to Dubai, and from Beijing to LA and New York. The problem is not so much that such star-studded gala projects are created, or whether or not reliance on such projects as a means of certain economic opportunities is warranted; it is the fact that they become the references, of which success is to be emulated, and therefore the fallacies of status objects with all the glitz, vulgarity and violence found in much of contemporary popular mass media.[10] According to Jacque Attali:

> No organized society can exist without structuring differences at its core. No market economy can develop without erasing those differences in mass production... It itself becomes undifferentiated, goes anonymous in the commodity, and hides behind the mask of stardom. It makes audible what is essential in the contradictions of the developed societies: an anxiety-ridden quest for lost difference, following a logic from which difference is banished.[11]

In this regard, for architecture today, the opportunities lie where the sources of differences are located. One such source is the narrative that is specific, though not necessarily unique, to a particular place and its culture. When we consider the nature of specific narratives, whether canonical and royal or subversive and *vulgato*, what we find is the memory of times and places that have fragmented and receded into the past. The potentialities in architecture today reside in the permutations of such mnemonic fragments that can actually pronounce and amplify the difference and therefore provide a means to embody the volatility in undifferentiated noise-space.

Image Credits:
Manfred Montowé p. 234
Rolf Jährling p. 235

Notes on Architecture for Globalized Bodies

Diego Barajas

This is an approach to city users in the context of globalization. It is employed in an attempt to identify new operative parameters by exploring the relation of architecture to an emerging *imaginary* in that context. Globalization is explored here, above all, in its spatial aspect, as observed in users' experience of territorial production and consumption.[1]

This text is a part of an ongoing study focused on the lifestyle of transnational migrant communities, how they are manifested in space in different ways, and how they construct the city on the "glocal" level, often

This is Natalia on her father's television, in one of many videos he keeps of his daughter. She lives in Tuluá, a small city two hours away from Cali, the main city in the Valle del Cauca region of Colombia. She knows more about Madrid, where her father, Harold has lived and worked for years...

operating at the margins of established models, but still able to survive at the edges and flourish, making use of the most modern capabilities as these emerge among new communication technologies. Migration here implies not just a *move*, or a *change of position*, but a continuous relationship of tension between *arrivals* and *departures*, whether those are physical or non-physical places or concepts. The two concepts of arrival and departure should not be taken as fixed, for they tend to multiply, overlap and continually interchange.

In the process of migration, the results of tensions between forces of de-territorialization and re-territorialization have very clear spatial manifestations. It is possible to grasp social potentials within the spatial structure and operational logic of dispersion and of new forms of collective life. It is also possible to analyze the relationship between users and the new hardware that makes these processes work, and to investigate its possible implementation in urban planning.

In the current context of accelerated mobility, migration among transnational communities presents simultaneously advanced and marginalizing experiences of globalization, along with global forms of production and consumption emerging at the bottom of the socio-economic scale. These seem to be presenting us with alternatives and paradigmatic social models for a broader distribution of a latent, new Globalized Body.

Globalized bodies possess multiple prostheses,using technology to occupy a large territory, a fragmented habitat, or a swarm structure. Although these exist at different scales,[3] their spaces are all shaped by multiple mental paths, and expanded spatial experience of them is determined by the constant stimulation of the senses. Globalized bodies are constantly migrating bodies, the consumers of territory.

They are also heterogeneous bodies acting against monolithic entities, and their identity is neither linked exclusively to a geographic place nor defined by the traditional territorial structures of the nation-state. The globalized bodies can be viewed as a particular concept attached to individual imaginations though subjected to and conditioned by the disjunctures[4] created where contradictory pressures intersect: between self-determination and commoditization, homogenization and differentiation, transnational powers and local absorption. They exist as very

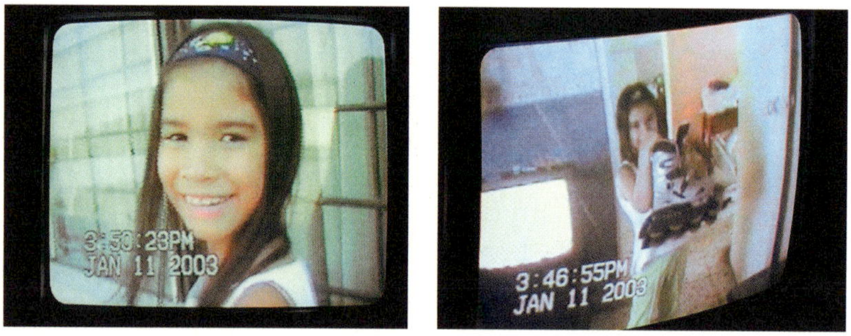

Because Harold is an "illegal" according to Spanish migration policy, there is no legal way that Harold can bring Natalia to live with him in Spain. So they occasionally exchange home videos made with borrowed video cameras, or communicate in faltering telephone conversations and in front of a web cam in local locutorios,* in Madrid and Tuluá, paying 2 euros or 2000 pesos for half an hour, in a low-resolution simulation of a familiar conversation. Harold regularly transfers money and sends packages to Colombia, usually carried by transatlantic commuters from either country, who often offer their services in locutorios and other migrant oriented shops.

artificial, dispersed re-connected landscapes, lying between forces of de- and re-territorialization.

Parallel to the expansion of the mass media, smaller networks organize themselves at the glocal scale, sometimes in almost invisible ways, and multiple spaces emerge around them as heterogeneous processes in the city and alternatives to flat homogenization.

The Cape Verdean glocal networks in Rotterdam, Netherlands, present a paradigmatic example of these self-regulating organizations, which are the alternative to such flat homogenization: historically a dispersed and decentralized society of archipelagos that grows and reinforces its national archipelago model within globalization processes, it is the result of different tensions and forces occurring at many scales. It challenges traditional social and territorial models such as the nation-state by bringing a national aspect to Rotterdam's urban interior spaces, expanding it, as well, to large, transcontinental scales, between Boston, Lisbon, Rotterdam and other port cities in Brazil and Angola.[5]

Dispersion

Dispersion is an urban pattern, a spatial way of inhabiting, fragmented and reconnected by artificial means. As it grows inside globalization and individualization,[6] dispersion marks the natural habitat for a transnational body as a fully spatial experience: a body that experiences space in multiple elastic scales.

In modern urban history the impact of new inventions like electricity, the train and later the car in the shaping of the cities of sprawl is remarkable, as are Fordist and later Taylorist models of decentralization.[7] Yet the enormous impulse this process has had in the last decades constitutes a big difference today; and its effect is growing, increasingly fuelled by shifts in production and consumption habits, constantly stimulated by the progress of communication technologies. The multiple dislocations between production and consumption have not only changed industry but also the intimate ways that we relate to places and to others. Fragile territories are spread around the world, positioned in ways that do not respond to a society characterized by masses of people and serial production, but rather to different lifestyles, and to a networked production system.

24 / ESPAÑA EL PAÍS, lunes 26 de abril de

LOS PROBLEMAS DE LOS INMIGRANTES

Euskadi abre sus puertas a los 'sin papeles'

El Gobierno vasco les ofrece alojamiento, sueldo y formación, y tramita su regularización ante el Ejecutivo centr

TOMÁS BÁRBULO, **Vitoria**
Inmigrantes de varias razas, ataviados con trajes típicos vascos, miran sonrientes a la cámara. Bajo su imagen, esta leyenda: "Puertas abiertas para todos". ¿Se trata de otra broma del cineasta Bajo Ulloa, que en su película *Airbag* se mofaba de las tentaciones racistas de Sabino Arana mostrando a un *lehendakari* negro? Nada más lejos de la realidad. Estamos ante una campaña diseñada por varios municipios y financiada por el Gobierno de Vitoria. Su objetivo: integrar a los inmigrantes.

Ese cartel no es una anécdota. Detrás de él existe un plan de inmigración trienal avalado por 43,5 millones de euros para los 28.000 inmigrantes regularizados y 11.000 más *sin papeles* que viven en Euskadi. La cantidad es apreciable, sobre todo si se tiene en cuenta que el presupuesto del último plan trienal de la Comunidad de Madrid, donde los regularizados ascienden a 355.000 y el número de *sin papeles* se acerca a esa cifra, fue de 12 millones de euros. En resumen: el País Vasco invierte 60 veces más dinero que Madrid en la integración de cada inmigrante.

La oferta gratuita de Euskadi para los extranjeros, con o sin *papeles*, incluye alojamiento, tarjeta

Los nuevos vascos

Basque government campaign to assimilate migrants. March 2004

As the physical distance between us and our objects of desire becomes geographically bigger, a counter-response develops that tends to bring them closer, making use of artificial means and operating in a cyclical, never-ending consumption machine, partially controlled by large-scale corporations, partially self-organized by one's individual agenda. Dispersion is not only a spatial phenomenon but also a social and cultural phenomenon. It is often seen exclusively as a by-product of the West, with its forces of globalization and the expansion of capitalism. However, here within the "network society," this seems not to be the case. Instead, dispersion is pushed by very diverse forces. We could say that dispersion appears as a multiple phenomenon.

Mechanisms of Fiction

Dispersion is a physical and spatial condition, but it also constitutes a primarily mental condition, an imaginary one. This imaginary is activated by diverse fictional mechanisms that are based on tangible mental constructions. Simulation strategies are the main architectural means of bringing forth artificial de- and re-territorialization. The mechanism to initiate activation, such as the communication systems, employs different sorts of combined artificial means. These range from internet web cams,

Advertising campaign in Madrid metro offering phone calls to countries in Latin-America. September 2004: You are here (Spain) but also here (countries in Latin America)

video cameras, mobile phones, thermal jackets with communication and GPS functions and multinational magazines, to interior atmospheres, which are environments with particular client services, specific aesthetics and programs, such as shops, religious buildings and all manner of social and economic facilities.

Belhuis in Rotterdam: Condensers of Globalized Bodies

The *belhuis*, literally meaning "call house" in Dutch, is a communication facility found in Rotterdam and other Dutch cities that is a part of a broadly international type of telephone call center similar to *locutorios* in Spain or *télécentres* in Senegal. They constitute a new kind of public space across multiple scales in the city of dispersion.

Cabo Line: Bottom-up Customization

On Nieuwe Binnenweg 177 is Cabo Line, a belhuis often visited by Cape Verdean residents of the neighborhood. But the owner of Cabo Line is actually Pakistani, as is the case in the other Cape Verdean places in Rotterdam. The Cape Verde flag appears next to others on the entrance, above the picture of the Cape Verde islands' blue sky and the catchy name, "Cabo Line."

Here the territory of the Cape Verdean nation has been established in the urban dimension in a totally different configuration and socio-economic structure. Like the owner of Cabo Line, Ijaz, many other Pakistanis have set up belhuis in different areas of the city. By simulating a piece of Cape Verde for its people, Ijaz has successfully targeted his business to a specific community's need for communications service. He knows well that many Cape Verdean people maintain strong family ties, so calls to the homeland are quite frequent. In fact, according to the surveys by KPN, the Dutch telephone company, because most of the foreign-born population keeps strong family ties, they are frequent callers even inside the Netherlands.

Infrastructures of Re-territorialization

These call centers serve as interfaces, allowing members of migrant communities to call their home countries. The call center is more than just a community phone booth. It facilitates the operability of the dispersed territories, acting as an interface between "here" and "there." The call center has the obvious function of providing the means of communication over long distances and many time zones. In this way, it concentrates diverse sub-cultures and even sub-societies, making it a very particular transnational space in the city of Dispersion.

In the Netherlands the call centers became known to the general public through the mass media only when several were, in some way or another, operating outside of local regulation – some evading taxes and others

Cabo Line

accused of money laundering. They later became more infamous after investigations into the train bombing in Madrid on 11 March 2004 revealed that Locutorio Nuevo Siglo in Lavapiés in the center of Madrid had been a key location in its planning and execution.

Frequently on the edges and marginalized, living in a type of *soft anarchy* beside the ghosts of paranoia and real danger, dispersion opens new landscapes of communication.

Belhuis Evolution

Call centers in Europe are often opened clandestinely. Their origin is said to date to the early 1990's, and they started to become visible and common in the Netherlands since its decentralization of the telecommunications market in 1997. Today, in most cases, some degree of their initial clandestine nature still exists and the level of legitimacy ranges wildly. Despite the local rules against hybrid programs at these call centers – for example, combining with calling service the sale of imported products or longer operating hours – they continue to thrive.

The globally scaled operations which characterize the functioning of the belhuis are beyond the limited scope of local regulations, which often cannot be applied outside their rigid jurisdiction. Therefore the call

Waiting space functions under maximum concentration where the interior atmosphere creates a new locale, an artificial condition of feeling at home

centers in the Netherlands are in a legal limbo. This condition reaches a state of *soft anarchy* fluctuating between the space of new publicness and a pretext for occasional violence. Indifference has also allowed the call centers to blossom as an extraordinary new social prototype and at the same time an effective hub for underground activities.

Belhuis Stimulator: Territories for the Imagination

A Pakistani caller enters a belhuis and he is suddenly surrounded by a space decorated in a Moroccan fashion that brings him to the Sahara. While waiting, in this short time, he also meets a Surinamese woman buying a cover for her husband's mobile phone with a picture of Paramaribo on it. In the Netherlands it is noon, but in Surinam it is early morning. The belhuis begins to shift slowly through the world time zones, drifting from Sahara to Aruba, and as more Surinamese enter, the more Caribbean it becomes.

The Moroccan owner lets the Pakistani caller know that he can now use a booth to make his phone call. Then he is suddenly in another place, back with his family in Pakistan, seamlessly connected. As he leaves he will pick up a flier on the counter about bargain flight offers from an Indian travel agency. As he leaves the belhuis, he is mentally not in the Netherlands but with his memories in Pakistan. Next month he might as well fly to Pakistan, thanks to the special offer by the Indian travel agency he found today. The caller's immersed experience has stimulated another territory within the city; the streets of Rotterdam overlap with those of Casablanca or Paramaribo – images that remain in the memory of callers well after they hang up. The urban landscape is destabilized through private mental constructions through electronic communication.

Space of memories and imagination...

Action space operates through maximum global diffusion: Porosity is replaced by smoothness

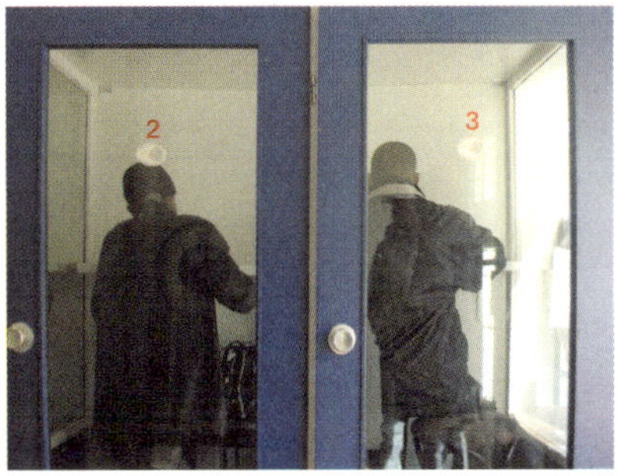

Mobile Ladder Labyrinth, New Babylon, 1967, Constant Nieuwenhuys

Hyper-programming

Hyper-programming is about a high density of programs as much as the speed of those programs' actual change. Because of the unstable character of the belhuis, additional services have begun to appear in the waiting area in partnerships between the belhuis owner and, for instance, an Arab hairdresser offering special hair treatment and skin cream, or a belhuis-internet café, or a Bollywood video shop for the Hindu-Surinamcustomers. Leasing space for other services has become more than a smart business alliance; it also creates a hybridization of programs and social activities that enliven the interior of the belhuis at different hours.

Different devices make up the system of operations in the belhuis. These devices have different origins and some – such as Nestlé ice cream freezers – belong to other business entities. Devices range from local

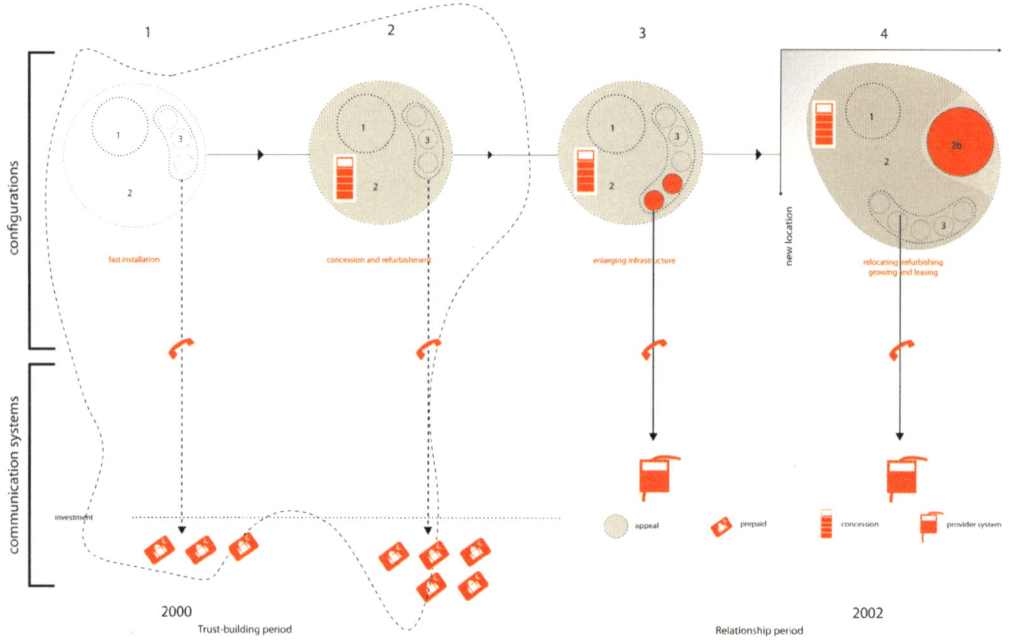

Belhuis transformations from "trust-building period" to "relationship period" 1. Spatial configurations program: Over time, zones undergo changes in configuration and character as for example when additional services are introduced by other owners or when the space is refurbished. An open relation between specialized entities and the hybridization of programs becomes the best way to optimize the performance – not only commercial but social – of 40 square meters of space. 2. Communication systems: During a trial period, the owner is able to build up a reputation that will ultimately enable him to install a long-term service in the form of an ISDN (Integrated Services Digital Network) box. For a new belhuis the most frequently used system is one of prepaid telephone cards, which is more flexible; later, usually when the business stabilizes, a solid relationship with providers is acquired. This diagram explains a Moroccan belhuis in the western part of Rotterdam, a case study showing transformations of zones in four different stages over a period of two years. These steps do not always occur in the same order; rather they tend to follow non-linear trajectories. Some steps can be skipped while others are carried out all at once

---

The *belhuis* constitutes a *migration stimulator machine* as an essential piece of hardware within the city of Dispersion

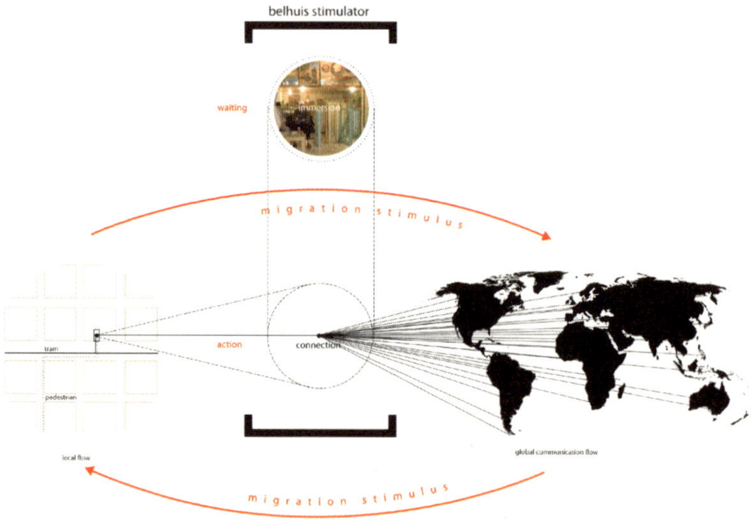

objects, such as handcrafted wooden cornices by Moroccan carpenters to sophisticated German alarm clocks made in Hong Kong. We see high-tech surveillance cameras and screens as well as the traditional security guard.

It is this relation between autonomy and interdependency among elements that not only makes the belhuis a functional structure but also determines its aesthetics. The aesthetics of its atmosphere more closely resembles a sponge than a blob, cloud or a wave. What the constituents of a belhuis present is a construction that resembles the logic of the Bo Bardi exhibition at Museu de Arte de São Paulo in 1969[8] rather than a simple time line. Among those elements, hierarchies do exist, but they are powered by their own fragility and instability. Production of space here is no longer a single-enterprise monopoly as in the old Fordist ideal, but a network of large, medium, and small entities.

Systems: Interior Design is Urbanism

As a station within a large urban configuration, the belhuis operates through different internal systems: *administration*, *security*, *waiting*, *commerce*, *ethnic media*, *communication*, etc., each using its own specific devices. Here the performance of the interior is based on not only specific products but also on specific processes in which the emotional involvement of the users is essential.

In the belhuis, the scales of urbanism and interior design are merged. Interior design functions at its traditional scale: it immerses one in an entirely artificial interior landscape and, at the same time, functions in an urbanistic way, connecting and organizing entire large territories, even entire nations. It is urbanism because it is a system that configures and articulates the relations between different entities over extremely heterogeneous territories. Far from Disney-like, flat and monolithic simulation, the belhuis presents a model for alternative ways of fiction in the city, an open and hybrid system, a fictional, multi-layered device.

Very different from the common use of written rules and contracts, here the system at the local scale depends, as in older times, on human relations and emotions, not only between customers and owners but also between owners and providers. Bankruptcies and other sorts of failures are common in belhuis transformations, as they are part of a fragile process very much dependent not only on legal conditions, but also on economic circumstances linked by human communication, likes and dislikes.

Searching for ways to maximize their profit, the belhuis businesses internationalized their communication system even before the national telecommunications companies did, and the system was to able connect any call in the world through the US system, proving once more the slowness and obsolescence of public utilities that still remains nation bound, when others are operating worldwide.

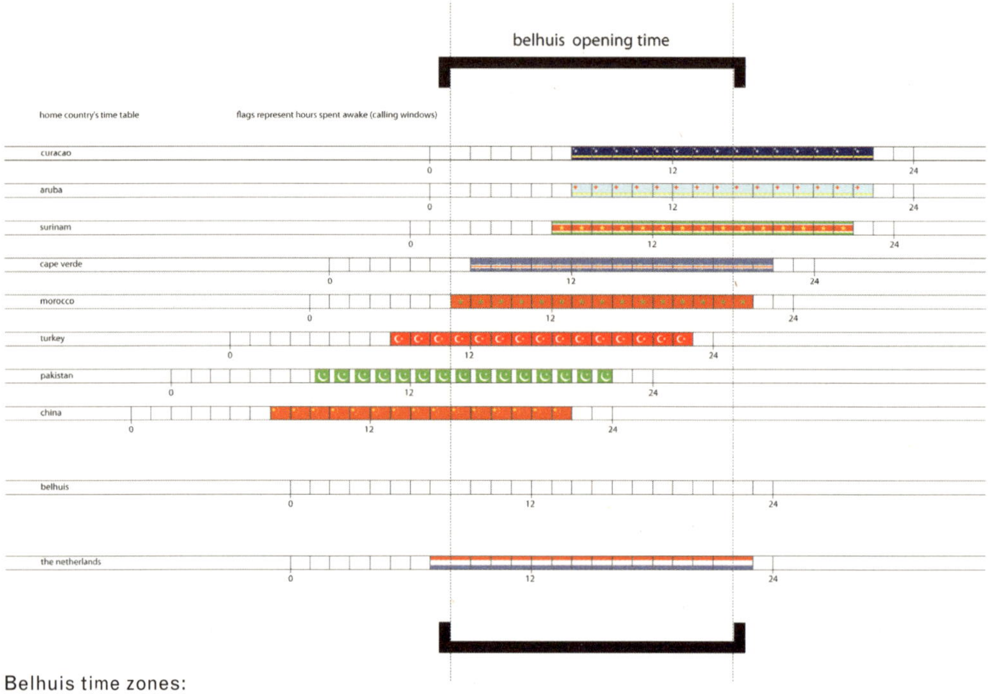

Belhuis time zones:
Condensers of globalized bodies

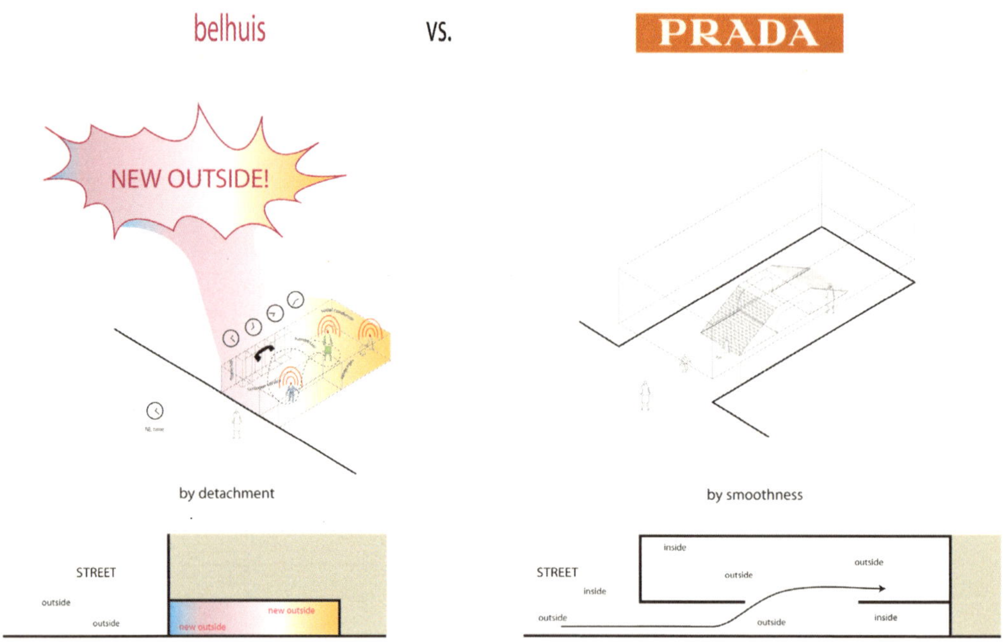

Belhuis public space strategy:
by detachment vs. Prada Public
space strategy: by smoothness

A New Hardware for Publicness within the City of Dispersion

More often than the city street or avenue, spatially measured in traditional architectural scales, what city planners are facing today is totally new hardware or infrastructure, like telecommunication and atmospheric interior design strategies, which are fundamental to the spatial organization of the city of dispersion. The new structures, often unseen by planners, constitute a complete artificial experience, establishing new ways of making the city, and forms of re-constituting the public sphere. Architecture is no longer only the support but very much the infill too. Habraken's[9] infill is not software but a new architectural hardware, and this publicness is no longer determined by the void but by the fullness of different fictional means ranging from *hyper-programming* to *make-up* techniques that bring specific qualities into the territory.

Strategies of Detachment

As if it were a contained fog, a domestic atmosphere surrounds customers as soon as they enter. If migration implies de-territorialization, thanks to architecture's design and creation of atmosphere people can hope to find artificial re-territorialization. The whole immersion ambiance created in the belhuis acts as a stimulator of distant objects of desire, a strategy of detachment from the immediate surroundings.

Different notions of daytime set by telephone communication with the interior micro-environments activate a new glocal collective, a new sense of community. It is not the bourgeoisie's public space, not an idealized and all-inclusive public domain of a nation-state. It is based on disputes rather than unity.[10] Its publicness works on scales very different than those of the traditional pedestrian space so often idealized by architects. It works on scales simultaneously narrower and broader.

By using different techniques of simulation in interior design and communication systems, the belhuis constitutes an entirely artificial urban condition. Inside, the essential cohabitation of the infrastructural systems of the telephone technology and the immersive systems of fiction stimulate a mental transformation in the subject, a particular mental state that enables the spatial processes of migration, de- and re-territorization, and the reconstitution of collective spheres at different scales and locales. The belhuis is an exemplary device for mental dispersion. In relation to other services of migrant communities, the belhuis – and also locutorios in Spanish cities and other sorts of call houses elsewhere – is a socially congested structure; a new public space within the city of dispersion, but not within the traditional concepts of "public space." Paradoxically – and in opposition to the traditional architectural discourse of fluidity and erasing boundaries – in the belhuis there exists a radical detachment from the surroundings, like a bubble in terms of interior atmosphere, client service and also the time zones experienced by the telephone connection, which is what makes this shop a collective place on a local scale as much as on a global one.

Belhuis vs. Prada

In July 2004 the new Prada shop designed by OMA opened on Rodeo Drive in LA. Unlike Gucci and Brioni just next door, whose doors are always closed just as are those of most luxury stores, this Prada store is completely open to the street on the ground floor. Rodeo Drive Prada is just one example, probably the most recent and spectacular, of an old modernist tradition of *opening the Cube*, of opening architecture to the city. This is what modern buildings aimed for, and it was largely implemented with, for example, the pilotis: bringing the outside to the inside and vice versa, a valuable idea although often linked with the more questionable modern hygienic concept of transparency.[11]

But when this concept is brought literally to the contemporary context of Rodeo Drive, within LA's extreme fragmentation and urban sprawl, the *public* effects of this openness seem much more questionable. How public can the door-less shop be experienced in a city that is not linked by walkable open streets but rather by thematized streets and highways experienced only while driving and through virtual communications of telephones, faxes, internet and airwaves? And when a society is no longer a homogeneous mass sharing the un-programmed space of the streets but a swarm of interactive networks that select precise routing according to lifestyles and convenience?

The belhuis again questions this traditional notion of "outside." This new outside is constructed not as a measurable territory but as a multi-scaled and multi-dimensional one and as a psychological territory as well. The belhuis does not follow the streets any more and in many ways even denies the space of the street. Its publicness is not established by the dissolution of the physical limits, but through the detachment from and confrontation with them.

Belhuis vs. Cellular Phones

The use of cellular phones is increasing, even among the economically depressed immigrant communities. In a context of more accessible and lower-cost advanced technology, mass customization, and large-scale production, manufacturers such as Nokia have been able to reach diverse and extreme market segments. However, the cellular phones and the belhuis are not mutually exclusive. In fact, belhuis customers often bring their phones inside.

Examining the contemporary manufacturing processes allows us to compare the belhuis to cell phones and not only with respect to the close relationship between the architecture of dispersion and mass-produced communication products but also with respect to the deep difference between the belhuis as a communication center based on place and body, i.e. a self-customized product, and a mass-commodified one. This helps to explain why cell phones do not replace the belhuis. More crucially, it shows that we should investigate the inherent spatial qualities of the belhuis' interface architecture relative to current shifts in the relation between production and consumption, and also initiate the study of new forms of collective life in the context of new production processes.

Nokia and Belhuis: Emotional Production Modes

As most companies had access to the same level of technology, Nokia sought a competitive edge. Aesthetic appeal, marketing and branding became the focus of the company's production process and the key to its tremendous success in sales. "In the new era of cellular competition… style becomes substance." stated Jorma Ollila, the president of Nokia at the time.[12]

The aesthetic appeal follows the design rules connected to lifestyle, which are increasingly different from what the functionality of the communication device dictates. Although primarily concerned with the final product, this appeal is also linked to the structure of production and organization, the increasing differentiation between the internal functions and the external appearance specific to customer preferences in both global and local markets. This division is most extreme in the case of Vertu,

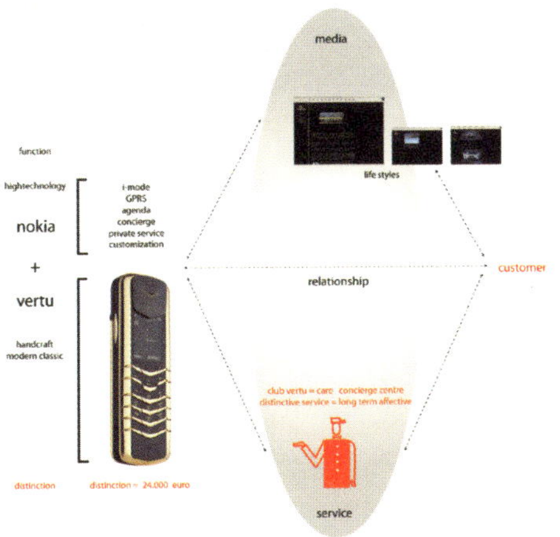

Vertu: distinction by coalition

Nokia's extravagant cellular phone subsidiary launched in January 2002. Vertu's handcrafted phones, which feature an 18 carat gold or platinum case and a sapphire crystal screen, are reserved only for the super-rich, costing as much as $30,000. With this product line, appearance and service have become completely detached from communication. Nokia provides the technology for the communication service and Vertu provides the styling and distinction available only at exclusive jewelers and boutiques around the world.

In the case of the belhuis, something similar happens. The local managers take care of the shop, its decoration, the specialized local client services and its overall atmosphere, while the infrastructure is efficiently controlled by providers both small and as large as KPN. Form follows no longer a function but a style: in the case of the mobile phone, a particular aesthetic and economic class, and in the case of the belhuis, the immersive experience. In both products there is also a tendency towards an important shift in production terms, because of a longer-term relationship between production and consumption linked with the concept of service.

Continuing with Vertu, we can think of its customer service as a "special concierge center" that provides high-profile attention, accessible worldwide. By simply pressing a button you can have a hotel booked or a new phone battery delivered within minutes. On the one hand, this establishes long-term customer loyalty and turns the product into a service in itself. On the other hand, this enables a close contact with the client, which ensures a constant update of the service-product, according to customers' demands. It implies, therefore, a constant transformation of the industry and its products. This is even more evident in other industrial segments, such as automobiles, for example, in the manufacturing concepts as "Just-in-Time" and "Built-to-Order" developed by Toyota, concepts that are leading the shift from the Fordist to the Toyotist model of production, in which a tighter and more precise relation between production and consumption is established.

In the entertainment industry today, production and consumption grow ever closer. In this industry the manipulation of emotion becomes crucial as the product here is not necessarily about the tangible but about certain feelings, stimuli or excitement in the subjects, which becomes the product itself.[13] These emotions in the subjects lead to Negri's concept of *bio-production*, a step further in the shift from an experience into a transformation of the economy.[14]

Architecture as Migration Experience: De-territorializers and Bio-production

The effects on the subjects generated by the artificial interior environment of the belhuis also produce a transformation: stimulus migration. The bio-production qualities of the belhuis lie in the properties of physical immersion that are inherent in architecture-plus-connection. Immersion is in fact a common strategy used broadly and in a variety of circumstances for creating experiences on behalf of industries such as entertainment and advertising. Consider the campaigns around Star Wars re-editions that aim to continually introduce the story to the "expectator," to insert the story into the consumer's mind not only while the movie is playing, but in an extended consumption period created by sets of interactive games, toys, accessories, cloths, soundtracks and books.

Fundamental differences appear, then, between cellular phones and the belhuis regarding the experiential relationship of the product to the customer. With cellular phones, the design refers to a personal style; the appeal of the device lies in its capacity to relate to an individual's identity. The cellular phones are marketed as a type of prosthesis – a cyborg-like extension of the body's own faculties. In the case of the belhuis, design is applied to the creation of atmospheres of domestic appearance in which the globalized bodies are immersed and increasingly familiarized with each visit. The physical and social contact that occurs in this immersive stimulation experience cannot be replaced.

A stimulation experience of de- or re-territorialization feelings toward a distant place, whether physical or imagined, is what makes people continue to patronize the belhuis even if they often pay more than they would to call from a normal KPN phone booth. In fact, belhuis are rarely less expensive today, but still they continue to appear. As its cost-efficiency wanes, its cultural and emotional value increases.[15]

On one hand, the belhuis reveals the close, often intimate links that frequently exist between informal and spontaneous consumption phenomena and the all-absorbing corporate commoditization machinery. Looking further in this direction we can see that, by taking the idea of a transformation economy in a perhaps unexpected direction, the three-dimensional character of the belhuis, with its multiple production modes,

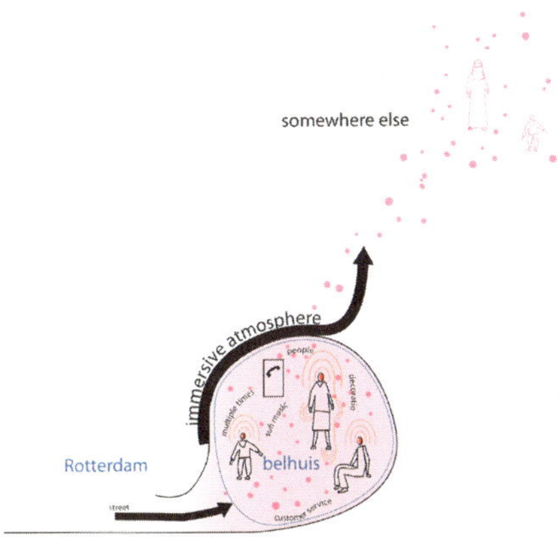

Belhuis atmosphere: condenser of globalized bodies

is not only similar to the industrial design industry, but far ahead of it.

On the other hand, the belhuis' collective life, and the psychological effects it produces, tell us about significant ruptures that appear in the models of discipline and control established by mainstream production and consumption models, thereby showing us a possible path somewhere else, contesting the flow not from the outside but from within. The belhuis presents alternative options for other kinds of publicness, other aesthetics, and also for a discourse on how human relations can be re-addressed.

Image Credits: Stills from research and video documentary on Natalia by Lucas Nieto, p. 243, p. 244. From *El Pàis*, 26. April 2002, p. 245. Constant Nieuwenhuys, p. 249. All photos and illustrations by the author.

CONVERSATI

NS

Architecture of Iconography, Representation and Convention

Robert Venturi and **Denise Scott Brown** Philadelphia

In conversation with Sang Lee

Interior Street, Nikko Spa & Hotel, Kirifuri, Japan

Representation and Scenography in Las Vegas

Robert Venturi A comparison of the old and the new in urban Las Vegas is revealing. The old involves, basically, two-dimensional signage and the decorated shed, and the new involves three-dimensional, scenographic reproduction. The old derives from the auto-dominated landscape of The Strip, and the new is the landscape of Disney. Scenographic architecture is an architecture of reproduction. To us, it seems irrelevant because it doesn't relate to the technology of our time and it doesn't accommodate the culture and scale of the automobile. Whereas an architecture of representation – where information in depicted in two-dimensions on flat surfaces – seems appropriate for today, especially when the representation engages the electronic media of the Information Age. We're particularly interested in techniques that exploit the electronic iconography of now.

Another aspect of representation involves content – what is represented. In our Nikko spa and hotel in Kirifuri, the hotel lobby is a representation of a Japanese village street. Although the design is scenographic, it employs two-dimensional representation rather than reproduction. Flat elements – signs that represent the scene and the theme – face you as you walk up and down the street. Our symbolic street learns from the Las Vegas of the 1960's, not the Las Vegas of the 2000's.

When we first suggested that we design a representation of a village street, our client said, "We want to make sure what you are doing does not become a Madame Butterfly!" This reply was amusing but it also showed great understanding, and of course we agreed with him. Our aim was nearer to that of the American Pop Artists, who represented ordinary / everyday elements in a new medium, new scale and new context, so you perceived them in a new (extraordinary) way.

Cross-cultural Representation and Symbolism

Sang Lee I would like to continue with this idea of representation and symbolism in different parts of the world where you have done projects. Now we have reached a point where information can be extracted

Fabric Designs for Nikko Spa & Hotel

and transferred into different contexts and used to formulate new narratives. It seems to me that the origin of such a source has become by-and-large irrelevant. The cut-and-paste process in architecture and planning tends to hinge upon the impression of authenticity, not necessarily on the materiality of the object, nor on its historic reality. You mentioned that your observation and experience of a culture, your discoveries within the native context, come into your architecture not necessarily simply emblematically or through appearance. How do you begin considering representation and symbolism in your design process?

Denise Scott Brown The origin and appropriateness of a source are highly relevant for us, even though we use collage, allusion, and cut-and-paste to adapt the source and don't aim for historic accuracy. Wherever we work, we do a *learning-from* study. We try to catch and set down our first impressions, as artists, and to let these help formulate our designs. Our clients are often amused by our different view of aspects of the environment familiar to them. Our mentor in Japan, Akio Izutsu, loved the fact that we had not deeply studied the country before going there, because he could watch us responding intuitively to our first impressions. Through our eyes he saw the familiar in a new light.

One example concerned a book we discovered in Tokyo on Japanese indigo cotton fabrics.[1] Made by peasant women and used for working clothes, they were part of Japanese social history. Their amazing variety of patterns, all in shades of blue, sparked something in us. We reinterpreted the patterns for fabrics and wall coverings in the rooms of our Nikko-Kirifuri hotel.

These wonderful rural designs, used in a new way, formed part of the project's intercultural debate about the project. As with the village street, our client encouraged us to react to this Japanese cultural resource, personally and professionally. But they also provided an advisory committee, to ensure that our borrowings and allusions did not outrage Japanese sensibilities.

New and Old

SL Given the worldwide proliferation of Western architecture, the destruction of the local is often inevitable. What possibilities do you see for bringing in new development that relates positively with the old?

DSB Throughout history the new has replaced the old. A Christian cathedral was built on the site of a pagan temple. The question is when to preserve the old and when to obliterate it for the sake of the new. The issue is one of balance. We need to take a Situationist view of the problem – to deal with the *realities* of each situation we work in.

RV The Modern movement promoted a revolutionary ideology of urban design. Le Corbusier's Ville Radieuse and Frank Lloyd Wright's Broadacre City had this in common, despite the fact that these architects agreed on almost nothing else. But within urban development there are times and places for evolution and reevaluation rather than revolution. During the slow evolution of European cities, the varied forms and symbols of Romanesque, Gothic, Renaissance and Baroque architecture were juxtaposed. And today, evolution is still, we feel, generally more appropriate than revolution for cities; and it should be accomplished pragmatically rather than imposed ideologically. Nevertheless, in the evolutionary process, some demolition will inevitably take place.

Whether the new dominates the old may be less worrisome than the fact that the new is frequently of poor quality, and is too

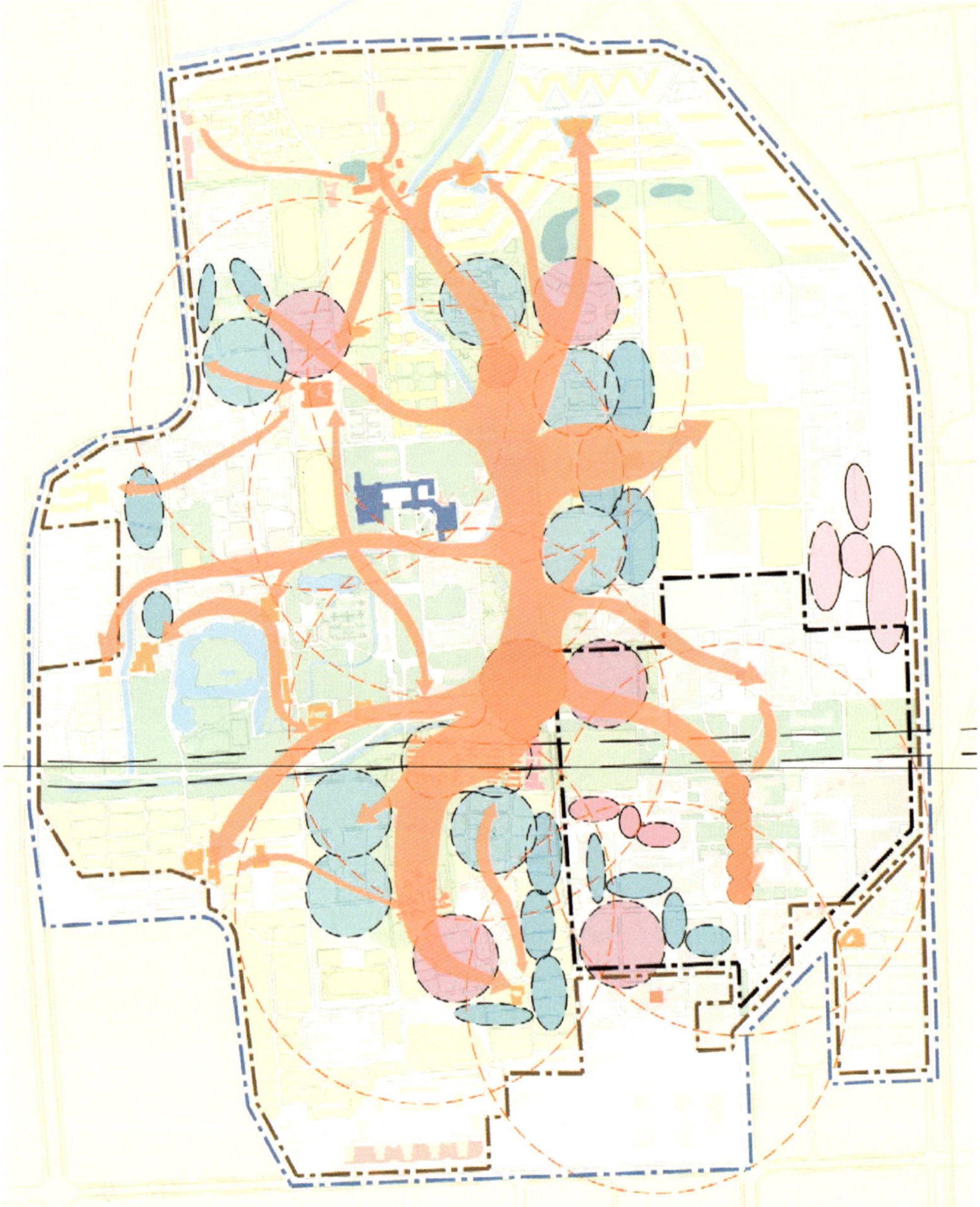

Tsinghua University Campus Life Map

often a *dramatique* and / or expressionistic monstrosity. Good architecture doesn't have to be egotistical, original, or "show-off." It can sometimes be *recessive*. I like to point out that Michelangelo was not original. He didn't invent a new vocabulary. He was simply *good*.

The issue is the *quality* of the architecture. We *should* of course worry about whether or not the new is demolishing the old, but old and new can exist together in a wonderful way, and the drama in their juxtaposition should come from analogy *and* contrast. However contrast should not derive from the expressionistic *dramatique* of current Neomodernist architecture.

In building for our complex and contradictory world, *universality* – mostly involving the technical, structural and electronic systems of architecture – confronts *multiculturalism* – engaging the social aesthetic, expressive, and symbolic elements of architecture. Today's urban context should be pragmatic / varied / rich – not pure; and aesthetic harmony should be achieved via contrast more than via analogy.

Cross-cultural Influences and Cultural Hegemony

SL The debate on globalism and cultural hegemony includes a discussion of the destruction of historic cities. For example, current massive developments in China cause us to consider the loss of what has been around for centuries.

DSB Global hegemony has a long history. It's not recent American invention. Globalism that is hegemony projects its influence from an economically dominant to an economically dependent culture, and in that direction only. But in our experience, influence may occur in both directions, and without an issue of dominance or dependence. For example, there is so much to be learned in Shanghai for architects with sensitive eyes and a knowledge of urbanism. We were fascinated by the city's historical multiculturalism and by Chinese adaptations of Western building types.

I would love to run a research studio in China, to discover building typologies unknown in the West but relevant for us today. One example is the *shikumen linong* housing complexes. They have Western-derived entry archways that open on to long lanes, densely lined with small houses. Another is the "scholar's garden," a small, intense urban landscape, designed to seem larger and more extensive that it is. Professor Xiaowei Luo showed us the clever techniques landscape designers evolved to suggest depth in these cramped urban sites. I would love to interpret the principles of the scholar's garden in a downtown site in an American city.

SL You mention the discovery of what already exists somewhere today, the importance of a convention, and technology's capacity to modify this convention. Do you think these interactions lead to constructive contrasts between the domestic and the foreign that could be more mutually beneficial now than before, say in the 1960's or 1970's?

DSB "Constructive contrast" figures in our current work in Beijing advising Tsinghua University on their campus plan. Its administrators say, "We have seen in some American universities qualities that we admire and feel Tsinghua needs." In American campuses they sense a *culture* and an *artistry*, as they put it, and a set of values about learning and education that have to do with interdisciplinary communication and with learning as a social endeavor – factors that the administrators feel will be important to the future of their university. Although they don't intend to imitate American universities, our client asked us to explain and interpret American

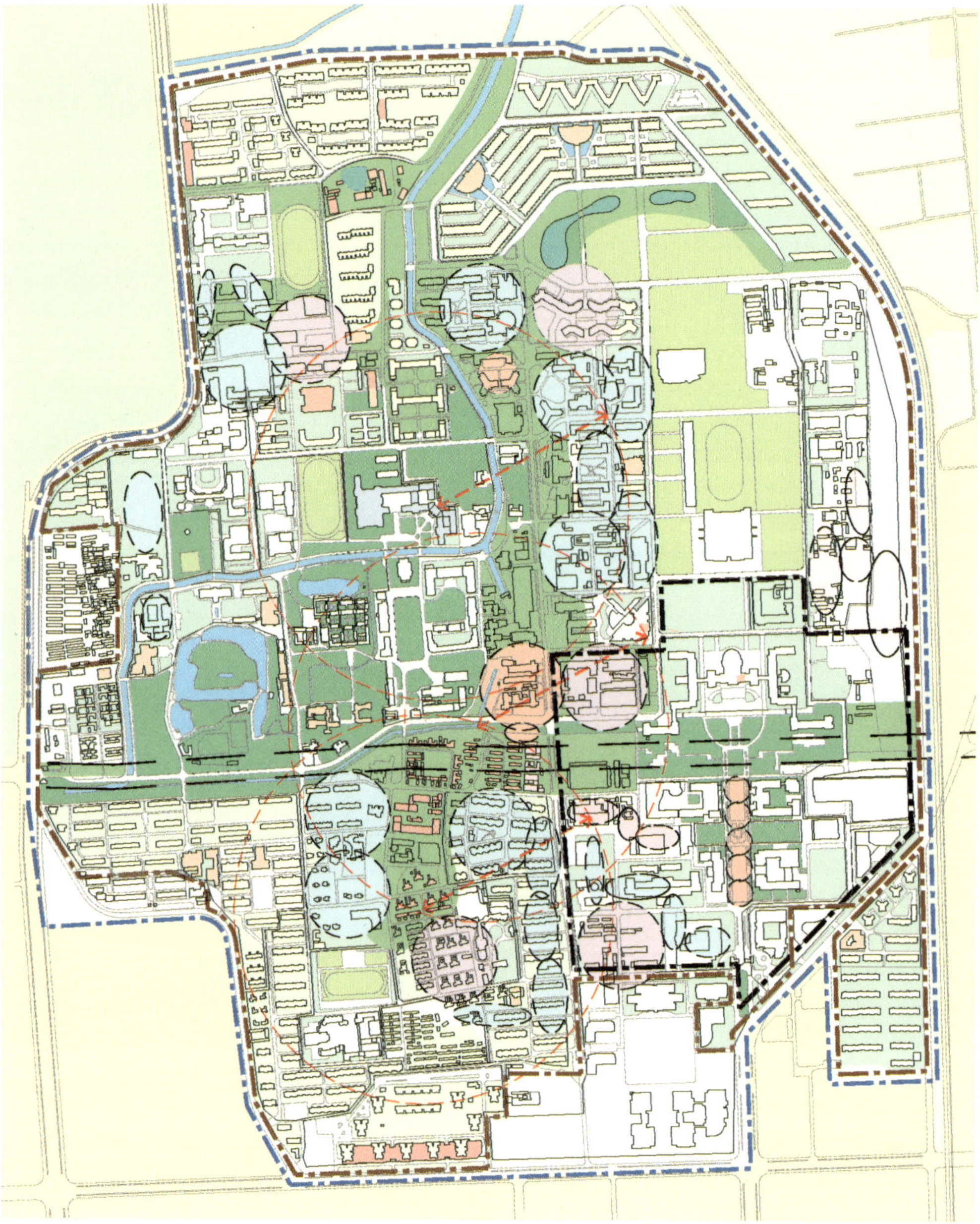

KEY

Existing

- Symbolic Greenspace
- Common Greenspace
- Athletics
- Residential Lawn
- Public Park
- Greenway Buffer
- Water

- Master Plan Boundary
- Tsinghua U. Boundary
- Study Area Boundary

5-Minute Walking Radius (400M)

Suggested

- Symbolic Greenspace
- Water

N

January 15, 2005

0 100 200 400 M

0 300 600 1200 FT

SUGGESTIONS FOR CAMPUS LANDSCAPES: MAIN CAMPUS

Tsinghua University Campus Planning
Base Map Information Source:
Urban Planning & Design Institute of Tsinghua University

Venturi, Scott Brown & Associates, Inc.

Tsinghua University
Landscape Map

campus planning in ways that would be relevant to Tsinghua.

We started by analyzing the activities on their campus. Using computer mapping, we described current patterns, then disaggregated certain variables – activities (academic, residential, social, recreational), structures, landscapes, circulation, and so forth – then overlaid them to see what new patterns or new interpretations might emerge.

Because educators today feel learning should take place not only in the classroom but through all activities and places on campus, we suggested new patterns of activities and structures that could help integrate life and learning across the campus. We paid particular attention to facilities having to do with student residential and recreational life.

During our cordial and open-minded collaboration with members of the university, we compared cultures and philosophies of learning and offered comments and suggestions based on our own experience. Learning and teaching flowed both ways.

SL In this specific case, nonetheless, doesn't that allude to what they would consider a *desirable model*, in this case American universities? I am sure they are familiar with your campus projects at Princeton University or the University of Pennsylvania.

DSB I don't believe Tsinghua looked to us to produce American brick-and-limestone architecture on their campus. They wanted us to help them understand the *patterns* of their activities and landscapes and to discuss how a physical campus might reflect educational policies. Our maps showed that places of busy activity today are not near the university's beautiful and historic landscapes, and therefore the university community does not sufficiently benefit from them.

We were asked to suggest ways of extending the atmosphere of Tsinghua's historic green campus to the hard-edged places where the students actually live and study today; to advise on ways to change the patterns to bring them in line with the lives of students; and to suggest how activities can come together to make a true cultural environment.

Design and Administrative Process

SL Related to this, many decisions about architecture today – in terms of the appearance of the buildings, design styles, or even the choice of architects – are made by an administrative process, whether by a governmental bureaucracy or a private corporation. Do you see different approaches by the administrators?

DSB We did not discuss architectural styles at Tsinghua, but in the US, recently, there have been trustees' revolts against *Neomodernist* design. Over the last decade or so, numerous Neomodernist architects have been brought, mainly from Europe, to American campuses.

RV In America now you will not be hired for a prestigious cultural project unless you are a *foreign* architect. America is experiencing a cultural inferiority complex. In Philadelphia, most important projects are done by foreign architects or ones from New York.

DSB A colonialism of the mind exists today in America, regarding architecture. Cultural institutions want to import the good stuff, the high-class stuff, from another place. They seem to feel inadequate to do it themselves. This is the view colonials have. It's the result of the earlier cultural hegemony of Europe over America.

The latest importations were initiated by American museums and their directors. They were intended to show, through architectural pizzazz, that their institutions were forward-looking and deserved funding from donors. But when the "advanced" buildings turned out to have extravagant budgets and late schedules, trustees on various campuses said, "From now on *we* will control the style of architecture on campus, and it's going to be Georgian."

These trustees were worried about their budgets and schedules, but they also *liked* the traditional architecture of their campuses and were against the trend toward Neomodernism.

SL But doesn't that particular point also indicate that the role of "star" architects in many parts of the world is essentially to provide their international and global clients such *pizzazz*?

DSB To some extent, but giving architects their heads may also have to do with the urgency of the project, or with lack of administrative processes. For example, immediately after the Russian Revolution, architects were given considerable freedom, as there was an urgent need to build and no time to set up a building bureaucracy. Constructivist architecture resulted. But when people saw it, there was a backlash.

Technology and Materiality

SL What makes a particular architectural environment more or less visible also has to do with its type of materiality and that of its context. And it is related, as well, to what the buildings represent, and how such representation is formulated. The idea of the "decorated shed," in a way, foresaw what I would call the disappearance of tactile experience.

DSB That is an interesting point. Tactility disappeared from architecture in the 1920's and 1930's and again in the 1950's, after World War II, when Modern architecture was expected to take over the world, and industrialization and lightness were architects' mantras for a great new society. Buckminster Fuller once asked, sarcastically, "Madam, how much does your house weigh?" He meant that *real* modern buildings are light-weight, *immaterial*. But today, when we plan campuses, we find that the buildings of the 1950's and 1960's have not stood the test of time. Those of the 1930's have done better, and those of the 1890's, a lot better.

RV There is much irony here. The aesthetic of the 1950's buildings was supposed to express the fact that their technology was supreme and up-to-date. The results were, in the long run, unsuccessful, partly because the new and revolutionary didn't benefit from the advantage of past experience. But another reason for the calls for demolition of these buildings today is taste: we don't like the architecture of our recent past.

DSB The space standards of many 1950's buildings are too low for today; their construction is not sturdy enough; and they were too specifically planned to be able to adjust to new programs. I feel the stress again today on *immateriality* might cause the same problems to arise.

In the early 1950's Le Corbusier was expected to lead the way toward soaring glass architecture, but he produced Ronchamp, the exact opposite. Now, soar and swoop are with us again. But Bob and I are more concerned with architecture as communication, as signs, and as systems and patterns.

SL Many architects today have moved on to where they consider buildings to be the material *traces* of techniques. They are therefore distanced from information-giving or the narrative intent… the codex, the iconography.

DSB You're probably right that some architects would consider this moving "on." We think it's a return to 1960's architec-

Lehigh Valley Hospital, Allentown, Pennsylvania, USA

tural navel-contemplation – the outlook that caused architects to be considered "part of the problem" during the civil rights movement.[2]

The Narrative of Technique-driven Buildings

DSB But buildings that are evolved fairly directly from techniques need not lack an architectural narrative. Albert Kahn, the architect whose industrial buildings influenced Mies, designed some wonderful academic buildings at the University of Michigan. They have the qualities we admire in traditional lofts: sturdy construction, big structural bays, and large, evenly-spaced windows. That was the prototype we learned from for the design of our life sciences complex at Michigan. But, given our programs, we could not match Albert Kahn's scale. So we tried to find an overall pattern for the façade that would simulate his scale, be appropriate to the historical campus, and yet seem new, as well, and suitable for the future.

Our buildings are simple, yet they come together and tie the campus together in complex ways, and there is complexity in the patterns of movement and activity they engender and support. The whole is planned for meeting, and the interdisciplinary life of scholars and researchers.

RV Urban and architectural planning should create a sense of community, so that people can live together and communicate with each other. We try to work toward that purpose.

DSB Our maps show all the connections that can happen between the activity patterns via the circulation systems. We would have liked to provide more communication on the façades of the buildings, but we could not; however, the surfaces of some inner spaces communicate on the outside. These buildings are "decorated sheds," par excellence – or, to use your terms, buildings which bear the material traces of techniques, yet carry a narrative as well.

Signs

RV Another issue is signs and American's hatred of them. Sign phobia is in part an aesthetic snobbery derived from the mid-20th century, when abstract art was the right kind of art. It comes also from

Americans' fear of being considered materialistic/commercial. But we believe the billboards of today will hang in museums in the next century, right next to quilts, as great examples of craft art.

In our project for a hospital in Lehigh Valley, we designed a sculptural H, standing along the highway.

It was 80 feet (24 m) high and light blue in color. Our client loved it but it was turned down by the local review board. They said architects do not create art, they create buildings; therefore our H was not sculpture but signage, and couldn't be allowed.

SL If you go to Tokyo, you would say the opposite, since, in many places, you can hardly see buildings because signs have become a dominant form of urban expression. Times Square today, more than ever, is similar to what you would see in Tokyo.

RV Signage is not new. The architecture of ancient Egypt is covered with hieroglyphs. And the Gothic stained glass windows we consider art are only *incidentally* art – their main purpose was to provide *messages*. The great murals of the Renaissance essentially gave instructions. They were signs that were done very well, and therefore incidentally became art. The same goes for Byzantine mosaic murals and the Baroque murals that try to convince you not to become a Protestant: they inform and persuade – advertise? So architecture as a carrier of signs and messages is not new.[3] But in the 20th century the idea was lost.

I should also mention that Times Square is our favorite urban place of right now. It is one of the most significant urban places of today, our equivalent to the Piazza San Marco. It is essentially a place where there is *architecture as signs*, many of them now electronic. It does not engage the old-fashioned idea of *space*. Space is so irrelevant, a Modernist cliché that doesn't mean much today. We should instead consider shelter and communication. Shelter and signs are more important than space and form.

The Evanescent and the Concrete

DSB After the 9/11 attack, American flags appeared on Times Square buildings, almost instantaneously, via. The buildings could and did change their communication very quickly.

The historical equivalent could be an ancient Hindu temple with blossoms on its altar – the temple one thousand years old, and the blossoms changed every day. In urbanism, banners, flags and flowers are evanescent; but infrastructure – roads, walls, bridges – can last a thousand years.

Architecture as "decorated shed" can approach urbanism's dual time dimensions. The shed's generic form can accommodate multiple lives and varying functions over decades, while its communication system, if electronic, can change on demand. But this technology will allow (or will cause) the decoration on buildings in Times Square to be produced by graphic designers, not architects. Both the *message* and its *content* will be taken over by others. Will architects of the Information Age accept this condition? Where it pertains (not in *all* buildings) will they produce *sub*-decorations, *sub*-textures and *sub*-tactility in other parts of the building? How will they manage the adjudication between evanescent and concrete in given design situations?

The Loft

RV Let's consider the decorated shed that is a loft. We love to acknowledge the distinction between the building as glove, where "form follows function," and the building as mitten, where there is room to wiggle. The loft allows flexibility inside.

It is a mitten. Its long tradition includes the Italian palazzo, which started as a dynastic family residence but could later evolve into a library, an embassy, a museum or an apartment building. The great industrial mill buildings of America are lofts, and so are many of our early academic buildings – Nassau Hall (at Princeton University), Harvard Hall, or the William and Mary Hall by Sir Christopher Wren. These too have accommodated ranges of programmatic, spatial, and technological change over time.

The *loft* building is not articulated in form. (Louis Kahn's Richards Medical Research Laboratories at Penn, which *is,* doesn't work as a laboratory.) The loft does not derive its architectural aesthetics from being *dramatique* or *original* in *form.* Its form follows a *convention*, just as most historical building types did – people knew what a house or a church looked like. Modernism threw out these conventions: conventional came to mean boring, unoriginal. But convention is a beautiful idea, and the loft is a conventional building that can last many years, while its surfaces change to become new. It provides a wonderful combination of the valid temporary and the valid eternal.

The Universal and the Local

RV There is also the issue of universal vs. local. Today both are acknowledged and we think it significant and appropriate that they work together. An example of the universal from the recent past is the high-rise complex with Corbusian slab buildings, set in a Ville Radieuse-like park. Arrive at almost any airport in the world and, from the plane, you will see this type of urban complex below.

The Renaissance was an earlier universal style that originated in Florence but traveled to France, England and beyond. On its journeys, it was inevitably modified, that is, localized: English Renaissance architecture is different from French or Italian. And for a vital and valid world architecture of now, we too can combine and juxtapose the universal and the local, to create a duality involving *both-and.*

I think Modernist ideology favored the *universal mode,* but expressed this preference in terms of style – Le Corbusier was universal via his stylistic vocabulary. I think we, too, can choose the universal, but now no longer as a style. The universal can be manifested today via the loft that is *recessive*, but can nevertheless have dramatic, ornamental *and* information-giving surfaces. So architecture can be recessive in its form and aggressive in its surface ornament, and local culture can be acknowledged via iconography!

I love Le Corbusier's Cité-Refuge de l'Armée du Salut, in Paris of the 1920's. In the background it is a loft structure – a *slab* building. In front – but still part of the same building – is a complex of low, articulated wings. This combination of a loft for general, evolving uses and specific pavilions at the front may be appropriate for now. But Le Corbusier's was a diktat *sans* iconography!

DSB In his urban plans, Le Corbusier moved from lofts to high-rise slabs and towers. This had vast urban as well as architectural implications. The form of the pre-industrial city was dictated by the technology of wood. Apart from fortifications and some civic and religious buildings, the urban tissue of an African village, a European medieval town, a Japanese city (or even Levittown) is clearly structured by the spanning dimensions of wood. But in the late 19th century there appeared high-rise commercial buildings. And in the 20th century, the economics and technology of slab and tower design created another building norm, and a resultant urban form with much broader physical dimensions than those derived from the properties of wood. And the new diktat is global: for a while last year, one half of the tallest construction cranes in the world were building office towers in Shanghai.

Surfaces

SL Returning to the idea of a loft and its surfaces, I was once struck by Frank Gehry's remark (in 1990) that his current work would not have been possible without Complexity and Contraction in Architecture. Related to the decorated shed, he also mentioned that he first constructs what he calls a "practical model," essentially programmatic elements as boxes of various sizes with circulation in between. And then he dresses up this model with skins.

This is similar to what you have mentioned about the loft-façade relationship and the decorated shed. In your projects how does this idea work?

RV I feel more comfortable – indeed, very comfortable – when Frank's curved elements are essentially two-dimensional *potato chips* applied to a *shelter*. This is significantly different from when they are explicitly three-dimensional, and themselves make the building. There is a difference between two-dimensional decorations applied to a shed and three-dimensional curvy elements composed explicitly to form the shelter as a whole!

Then there is the architectural element of *layering*. The Villa Savoye is my favorite building of the 20th century. I learned very much from the way it accommodated valid contradictions between inside and outside elements and programs. Another example is la Casa del Girasole, in Rome by Luigi Moretti, where there is the idea of *duality*. The diagonals at the top of the façade, via their inflection and symbolism, engage both the element of duality and the element of shelter.

The building accommodates *contradiction,* via layers, one surface dealing with one thing and others behind with others. My mother's house connects with all these ideas.

Process and Pattern

SL What you have just mentioned sums up by and large why I find your ideas on architecture can be so difficult on many different levels. Your idea always tends to be a complex mixture of many different components, in other words, a deliberate construct aiming at a more complex view rather than a singular still-life. How do you organize all the components for an idea? How do you start working with all the different layers you want to take into account?

DSB One way is through thinking about architecture *urbanistically*.

SL Given the particular attention you pay to the context, how do you relate your urbanistic analyses to historical and contextual components or *codes*?

DSB On one level, we look upon the context as *patterns* – social patterns, patterns of circulation and activities – and we *grow* them, we extend them, into our building. We think urbanistically *inside* the building. We pull a pathway from the outside into and through the building, seeing the building's circulation system as streets that link the activities within and support their patterns. Then the life of the inner street dictates the location of the various activities – the elements of the program or brief. Major meeting places occur at intersections of the main vertical and horizontal circulation ways; activities requiring quiet or privacy are off less frequented paths.

So we do urban land use and transportation planning *inside* buildings. We like, as well, to design a public and a private sector

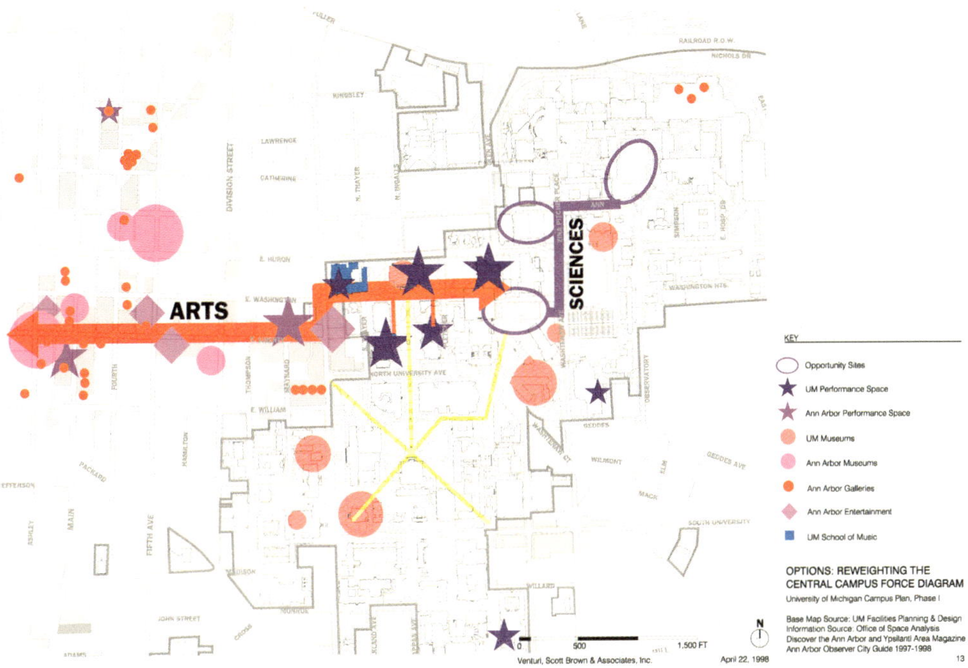

University of Michigan Arts-Science Axis map

within a building, and to consider it as composed of typologies of spaces and structure – for example, a grid of modular lab spaces and informal lounges. Then we consider how the generic and the *unique* spaces relate.

In our high-tech lab buildings, the relation between lab life and recreation life, between work space and meeting space, is carefully arranged. The lab parts are repetitive, with regular bay sizes, set for flexibility, but there are coffee lounges or a larger cafe-meeting place, perhaps irregular in plan, set *off* the grid and designed to purvey a different *identity,* a sense of community, relaxation and comfort. The lounge has a different view. It says "meeting, informality, conviviality, serendipity." The modular labs and the comfortable lounges offer two interrelated ways of working in research.

We design the outside of the building to communicate with you. As you approach, it is seen in a certain way and as you get nearer, in another. The cone of vision of the human eye demands that this communication on the exterior be strongly hierarchical.

RV It is so important that we allow for future flexibility. The program will change – often before the construction of the building has been completed.

DSB The changing program requires us to take a different, more generic, view of functionalism, but for us, rationalism and functionalism haven't disappeared. We think functionalism was the *glory* of early Modern architecture, and we consider ourselves involved with it. We are interested in functionalism not only for practical and moral reasons, but also for aesthetic ones.

The Computer

SL What does computer technology contribute to your practice?

RV We often try to use computer-operated electronics to communicate from the surfaces of our buildings, but we don't get many opportunities because it is still expensive and it's considered vulgar. Also you cannot do much with electronics in the rural campuses, where we have many of our projects. These are only rarely an appropriate context for this technology.

DSB A computer is a *tool* with its own limitations. You can't match by computer the sensitive variations of a great hand drawing, but those who draw well with their own hands are best at computers. What you do with the computer is open to your imagination. For example, the beautiful reflection on water in our Whitehall Ferry Terminal night view was created by computer.

We use computer mapping in campus and urban planning and design, basing our techniques on those we've learned from various urban planning disciplines, particularly from *regional science*. This is a branch of economics that adapts the notions of gravity and potential from physics to the study of settlements and cities. It tries to understand laws and principles of urban growth by mapping and diagramming urban variables such as land use, density, travel time and cost, speed and so forth, and uses computers to both map and analyze the data.[4] In so doing, it produces beautiful patterns that are evocative for designers. Although we're guided by the precepts of regional science, it's not just a question of following the laws. Sometimes we break them. But then we have to support the breaking really well, which requires understanding.

SL Does the computer have a role in the disappearance of the *hand?* In other words, with the computer, have the methods and techniques of architecture exceeded and become something other than human capacity? Does the *automaticity* of the technology induce a paralysis, not only through the invisibility of its operations, but also because very often, the criteria for judging the outcome of digital technology is problematic? In some cases, it seems criteria are abandoned altogether, and computer outcomes are called "output" and taken for granted…

DSB I am chagrined when I see my carefully designed computer maps attributed to "computer printout." It's as if a hand drawing were attributed to "pencil." We like to push computer technology. I think architects need good IT training. They must also understand the concept of GIGO – "garbage in, garbage out." Human judgment is still (even more) necessary and, for this, architects need full minds and hearts, good education, strong knowledge, and wide cultural preparation – and an ability to integrate these within their professional lives. This will allow them to make creative use of the computer – this, and the continuing presence of their hands in their work.

SL Another interesting aspect of architecture today would be the increasing separation of the architectural triptych, plan, section and elevation. I am mentioning this because what has made architecture so interesting has been the complexity of seams, so many different lines, corners and edges, and how they project the conditions of one surface meeting the other.

RV In an exhibition I saw on digital architecture, the designs seemed so linear. There seems to be something wrong when a methodology of working and presenting has this effect on the design.

DSB Do you mean plan, section and elevation are breaking down in digital architecture – and that orthogonal architecture is disappearing? This does seem the case in Neomodernism today. But it doesn't go too well with the fact that people stand upright. I think people are *tuned* to orthogonal planes because of where their eyes and feet are and how gravity works. Are we surrounded by orthogonal architecture for those reasons? There are places, but few, where horizontal and vertical planes are not required.

RV Mies van der Rohe *is* orthogonal.

DSB Buckminster Fuller isn't.

RV He isn't around anymore.

The World Trade Center

SL What do you think of the new World Trade Center project?

RV I am sure I would disagree with the approach and what they build in the end. It would be wonderful if we could get involved, but it would also be absolutely hopeless.

SL A dynamic particular to New York City is that there seems to be such an overriding domination of the local machinery when it comes to architecture.

DSB They say New York is *ungovernable* – that you can't govern *with* the forces at play and you can't govern *without* them. This affects architecture and everything else in the city. I can't even begin to guess what the hidden agendas are at the World Trade Center. But I feel power play in New York and the irrationalities surrounding the project will grind down any rational or artistic design solution. Development will be done, as it often is in New York, in the way the most powerful stakeholders want it to be done.

RV Denise wrote a very good Op-Ed article in *The New York Times* about rebuilding after 9/11.[5]

DSB I suggested Manhattan take its time, because no one knew what the trends would be. Given that there was movement away from the area even before the attack, how, I asked could they decide, so early, on the amount of floor space needed?

I haven't seen a ground floor plan of the scheme that shows how they propose to tie it into the activity and movement patterns around it, or to bring the city into the complex. City physics would locate foci of intense development where people emerge from transit systems and become pedestrians – where they change, *en masse* or in small groups, depending on the mode of transportation. How and where the transit system gives people access to the complex should help determine where entrances to buildings are placed and how stores are oriented to sell goods; also where elevators are needed and service access is located.

Then, within that system, how do you deal with the enormous irrationality of a huge and deadly hole? How will and should city physics reassert itself – as it always does – against a very big impediment that distorts everything – and should be allowed to do so? How can you help to create patterns both with and against the hole? That's a great fascination of the project.

Image Credits:
Nikko Hotel & Resort: Photo by Kawasumi Architectural Photograph Office, p. 261
Fabrics: Photos by Venturi Scott Brown & Associates, p. 262
Drawings by Venturi Scott Brown & Associates, p. 264, p. 266, p. 273
Lehigh Valley Hospital: Photo by Matt Wargo for Venturi Scott Brown and Associates, p. 269

Comments on the Production of International Architecture

Arata Isozaki Tokyo

In conversation with Jörg H. Gleiter

Semiotics and Criticism

Jörg H.Gleiter Years ago in Kenchiku Bunka you published a series of essays entitled *Counter Architecture*, in which you took a position against the incessant commodification of architecture in the global capitalist market economy. As a reaction to this, your generation instead turned to the practice of semiotization of architecture: you were trying to find a new scientific basis beyond the instrumental reasoning of technology and the global capitalist market economy.

However, today, from a distance of more than 30 years, we can see that the so-called linguistic turn opened up the first round of global discourse in architecture: if anyone, it was your generation that laid the ground for the global cultural logic of architecture today. I believe that any discussion with you about the domestic and the foreign in architecture should begin here…

Arata Isozaki According to my understanding, it was already the mid-1980's when we began to revise critically this process of semiotization. However, in the 1950's, when I was a student, the International Style architecture of the 1930's was all we were taught. Program, function and the use of industrialized building materials were the only tools given to us. The cultural heritage and the public's demands for architecture were hardly ever thematized.

By turning to semiotics we were trying to emphasize architecture as a cultural practice beyond its mere functional determination. We were convinced that everything was meaningful and that each element and form, and the building as a whole, had a special meaning for society. Considering this we automatically had to go back to the history of architecture, our culture and different levels of our social life altogether. Therefore, semiotics became a very important tool. Ultimately it was a method to engage in architecture production creatively. The point was to shift from the generalized modernist concept to cultural specificity, away from the homogenized global regime of function, budget and construction.

At the same time, with semiotics the different meaning structure of architecture could be discussed within a broad and general discourse. For example, over a period of 30 years central to the discussion in Japan has been how to introduce the ideas of modern architecture and integrate them into the Japanese building tradition. This all started in the 1930's when Bruno Taut first came to Japan and lasted until Kenzo Tange's design for the Olympic Games in 1964. There was very much discussion about how to merge the Japanese tradition with Western technology without getting too close to either Western or vernacular architecture.

Although the historical elements of architecture are territorialized – obviously Schinkel stands for the German tradition, the Ise Shrine for the Japanese tradition and the Forbidden City for China – I myself profited greatly from Le Corbusier's La Tourette as well as from the Parthenon and the Katsura palace in Kyoto. Even though La Tourrette and the Parthenon do not belong to the Japanese tradition, on a semantic level they all maintain the same proximity to me and our time. Their respective meanings differ greatly but on a broader architectural level we do not necessarily have to differentiate their different origins: They all belong to the world heritage and the textuality of architecture. Just as each language, its structure and narratives form part of the great history of literature, the history of architecture does not belong to a single region. History must be understood as the common archives available to anyone anytime. In this context it is important to understand that only later were these ideas used to revise our view of modern architecture. For example, critical regionalism aimed at reterritorializing and instrumentalizing these elements in a regional context.

We should not evaluate the architectural heritage according to categories such as a style, a vernacular tradition, high art and the like. In terms of semantics they exist first of all on the same level, free of value. I called this method the method of quotation. That means to take certain images or forms, extract them from their regional and historical context and insert them into a new context. You may take the colonnades of the Acropolis, transfer them to somewhere else and eventually combine them with sliding doors from the Katsura palace or a high-tech lighting system. However, most importantly, before being combined with other elements the quotation must be liberated from its origin. It cannot and will not stay the same.

JG You just argued for three distinct techniques of semiotization in architecture: The first one, breaking with high modernist ideology, and the second one, concerning the local or regional issues, especially the specific Japanese problem with the introduction of modern architecture and how it may be reorganized within traditional Japanese culture.

On the third level, and maybe most importantly in your practice, semiotization is a critical technique. According to my understanding, the method of quotation or collage not only affirms architecture in its function as a symbolic device – to reassure it of its role within a given regional culture – but also as a critical tool with respect to the concept of cultural identity.

AI The method of quotation means nothing without the recognition of its inherent critical potential. Simply to choose, transfer and combine certain elements means nothing in itself. Of course many architects used the method of quotation without any understanding of its critical potential. This we call postmodernism in architecture today. It is very low on a conceptual level.

For example, our friend Charles Jencks, very much into semiotics in his writings lacked any criticism. He was simply gathering and combining different elements, which is very commercial. One must take it further to the level of criticism in architecture or its history. The question is how to find a method to consider and evaluate individual architectural elements, and by doing so, evaluate the process. Just arbitrary quotation is really terrible and simply about fashion. In fact fashion took over postmodernism and postmodernism became fashion.

JG Does this mean that the transformation of the universal architecture heritage into something specific or domestic can only be accomplished by a technique of criticism, ultimately a trope that involves incongruity?

AI I think so. Especially in the mid 1980's, the technique of quotation and irony played a very important role. Irony itself is always a technique of manipulation, transforming the given and at the same time keeping it a distance. It has very much to do with these universal archives of architecture; for architecture in general without any direct mediated connection to the object is almost meaningless. But in the processes of transformation we can find some sense of humor or paradox which, together, turn into irony.

JG After the critique of enlightenment reason, is it your position that any cultural identity, be it global or local, domestic or foreign, may only be achieved by a negative definition, criticism and irony? Is it the case that today we can no longer define our cultural identity by positively referring to the past but only by a negative dialectics and critical use of our cultural legacy?

Then what about today's digital design practices? They are very far from the semiotic subtleties, if they have any at all. Their relation towards the formal issues in architecture is a very affirmative one, based on the universally applied design application and providing little alternative to the only numerical logic of the digital medium.

Digital Technology and Architects' Work

AI Yes. After the introduction of the digital technologies, architecture in some way was trapped. However, for the integration of the new technologies into the design practice there are new ideas coming up. Just take a look at the competition entries for the Florence train station. Our idea is based on Gaudí's concept of structure – it looks a little bit like Gaudí's – but those forms cannot be found in his work unless you look at the upside down experimental model he used for the Chapel of Colonia Güell. It is important to note that our scheme is somehow close to that, while at the same time it is very far from the simple or parabolic geometries Gaudí used. Since we were looking for the most rational and optimized form for a given size, height, span and material, they of course must be different from Gaudí, just as he was trying to find the best solution for his own specific needs. While Gaudí tried to determine it by his string model, we instead used the computer.

Obviously in Florence we had no intention whatsoever to copy Gaudí. But we adapted his ideas and tried translating them with the computer to a totally different formulation. It is today's computer technology that provides the optimization of

Gaudí's process. It was the structural engineer Prof. Mutsuro Sasaki who, through the diploma thesis of a student, was the first to become aware of the digital formulation for structural optimization. He immediately understood its immense potential. Sasaki later on gave it the name ESO or *Evolutionary Structural Optimization*. Of course this is completely based on the computer technology. The idea behind it is similar to Gaudí's, except that Gaudí had to invent his own technique, his three dimensional string models.

JG Even though computer technology offers new possibilities for the realization of ideas related to the realm of building technology, I still see in your latest design method a strong consistency with your idea of the architectural archives and their availability for contemporary architectural practice. You seem to be still engaged in adapting and transforming ideas from the archives, but now adapted to the new technology.

AI Let us turn to the form itself. In structural terms the Florence scheme is determined by a computer-generated process. Therefore it is absolutely optimized. It means that every part is determined in the most rational way. This is the way I think contemporary computer technology should be used. My office is now working to develop this idea further. Soon we will be able to realize the first building. As a matter of fact, two years ago people were afraid when we first proposed this structure for the Florence train station. They considered it to be unbuildable and so we lost the competition. But we used the same method again in a competition project in China, and once again people were afraid of it. Finally in the city of Doha in Qatar it will be realized.

JG You just made a plea for what one might call, referring to Ernst Cassirer, the speculative logic of architecture versus the numerical logic of the digital medium. For the latter we have seen many examples at this year's Venice Biennale.

AI The problem at the Biennale was that most of these complicated forms appear to be simply generated by the computer with no theory behind them. They produce only strange forms, total arbitrariness. However, in our project in Florence we had a clear objective. Just as Gaudi did with his string model the computer, we programmed the computer to find the optimal form to cover the span of 250 m. This marks the difference from the general usage of the computer in today's design practice.

For example, Frank Gehry's design is always the result of a momentary impulse. With the help of an aerospace application, he could analyze and calculate handmade shapes. Gehry is a great master in this. If he wants to change something, he can do so easily. But with the ESO, we cannot change the form, since it is not arbitrary but clearly determined by the digital process of optimization.

At one point of course I had to stop the computer and freeze the process. This is the architect's work, not necessarily to draw but to control the process, and for this we need theory. In the 1920's, the main interest in philosophy was focused on the process of decision making, with Rudolf Carnap and Otto Neurath being the main protagonists.

JG Is this exactly the point where the speculative logic enters the architectural domain?

AI That's right and Jacques Derrida's major concern had always been the concept of undecidability. There are always many different solutions to one problem, never only one. That means that someone has to decide which solution. But today almost nobody is able or willing to make a definitive decision, since no solid cultural

CrossSection, New Entrance to Uffizi Gallery, Florence, Italy

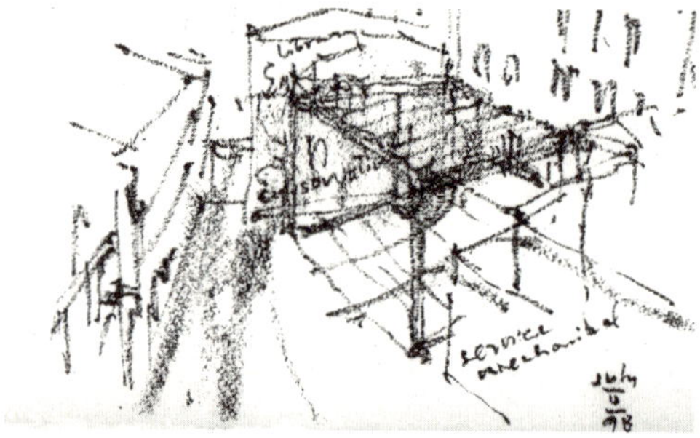
Sketch for New Entrance to Uffizi Gallery, Florence, Italy

Rednering, New Entrance to Uffizi Gallery, Florence, Italy

foundations exist any more on which people could easily base their decisions. However, in our digitalized culture today decision making occupies 99 percent of the design work.

JG Do you mean, after the end of the author – as propagated in the 1980's by the deconstructionists – an architect now turns himself into a decision maker?

AI That is right. But the author returns as someone who is able to make a definitive decision within a given range of possibilities. If his decisions are wrong then the result will be terrible. The more technological complexities there are, the more the possibilities for errors increase.

JG Let's turn once again to our topic: the reciprocity of the domestic and the foreign. Your architecture always stood out for its strong autobiographical expression, a kind of idiosyncratic body of work. This means that in your work the architect as an author is always present. How much of it is determined by the cosmopolitan architect, and how much of it by a Japanese?

AI One part of your question that I actually object to is the association of myself with a certain nation-state. Of course I have a Japanese passport, so I am a Japanese national. But psychologically I do not want to belong to Japan, especially Japan as a modern nation-state. As you are familiar with the Japanese mentality, its history and architecture, in your case it might be different. But almost everywhere in today's so-called globalized world people want to pin me down to a representative of Japanese architects. It is always the same stereotypical questions I am asked: why as a Japanese I want to come to a foreign country and do a project there. This kind of question I am asked almost everywhere. Maybe less in the US or Europe, but in many other countries, especially in China.

For example, at conferences or selection processes for competitions, Rem Koolhaas is always stamped as Dutch, Steven Holl as a typical American and I am the Japanese. This is how it works at Chinese conferences: you are always classified. They want me to play the Japanese as they want Steven Holl to play the American. The situation in Italy is similar to China. As you may know some years ago my scheme was selected for the new entrance to the Uffizi Museum.

I already secured the contract and we were ready to start construction, but at the last minute they decided that this was too important a museum to be built by a "Japanese" architect. One of the arguments was that as Japanese I would just be the kind to destroy or violate the Italian treasures. I heard nothing like that in Germany or even Spain. In China recently I won three first prizes for projects but eventually lost them because of this kind of attitude. That is why I refuse to play the role of the Japanese architect. As already mentioned today identity can only be achieved through a critical attitude and process.

JG Only a week ago this became big news. This highlights the problems that an international architect is faced with… However, if today an architect is a decision maker, then we cannot deny that the architect somehow also functions as a kind of mediator, between different cultural practices.

AI In general, yes, this must be the architect's job. But the point is that I don't want to be politicized in the frame of a certain nation-state. Just consider Immanuel Kant, who has to be regarded a citizen of the world. He lived in Königsberg, not at all the center of Prussia, and he never left it. His thoughts were never centered on matters specific to Germany but on the universal idea of mankind. The world has to have some structure, but not the nationalistic one. So if you called me a citizen of the world or cosmopolitan architect, I feel quite comfortable…

Paradigms and Iconography

JG In 1990 Peter Eisenman and you founded the ANY conferences. They were set up as a global enterprise with a similar universal claim.

AI Indeed, Peter and I were the two founders of the ANY conferences, which were held eleven times in different countries in different continents. Each time many of the participants were selected among the local architects and scholars. Even though the problems in architecture were similar all over the world, the subjects of discussion were not at all related only to the specific place or region where a conference was held. On the other hand they were not only global in terms of the architectural subjects discussed but also respecting philosophy, art, poetry, technology and psychology. At the core they were also interdisciplinary in their basic concept. So any subject matter, whether of local or global interests, was discussed within a wide range of different positions. Although the conferences were documented in ten ANY books, I actually don't know how to evaluate them as a single enterprise. Recently I tried to look back on what happened then, but I could not find any definite subject that had emerged.
The experience was completely mixed…

JG …and decentered. One question,

which seems central to today's discourse on architecture in its global perspective, is one Fredric Jameson used to discuss, namely the general shift of the cultural dominant in the 1980's from the modernist paradigm to the post-industrial information society. K. Michael Hays pinpointed it as a shift from object production to image consumption resulting in the dissolution of the boundaries between the world of objects and the post-industrial world of images. In other words, we are confronted with a new heterogeneity of the semiotic surfaces and a displacement of architecture's collective communicative-symbolic function. It seems to me this eventually will also blur the notions of the foreign and the domestic, which until now has been strictly separate.

AI I also think we are witnessing a real paradigm shift. I would point out that iconography is a key concept for us to consider today. Of course already for a long time architects have been working with iconographic representation, but now with the digital technology it is becoming even more important. Through the digital technology, icons can be extracted and transferred easily. Everything is digitalized today and reduced to codes. But in the instant we receive information, it is transformed into iconic images or forms. Even though words or letters are also a kind of image, after the introduction of the digital technologies images are more important than ever before.

JG Dissolution of the boundaries between object and image means that the traditional idea of space is subject to a drastic change. As a technique of spatialization architecture has been always engaged in shaping local character, the genius loci. In the digital age the concept of chora, which you repeatedly refer to, seems to dissolve.

AI In regard to space I think you pointed to an important fact. As you know, the concept of space became a key issue in architecture in the late 19th century. Before that nobody talked about space, everything was about iconography. But now for already more than a century the idea of space and partially also that of time completely occupy our discourses. Or, more accurately, they became basic features of architecture. But if it comes to information technology there is no space, nothing – it can neither be expressed nor experienced. Just like space, time, too, is reduced to just a distance between one object and another, between one point and another point.

But once we get away from the media and the computer and turn to the built environment, space and time become important again. Here it is the human body and movement with which we experience buildings, linking space and time. Space and time are features of our bodily experience: we cannot conceive of them outside of the body. In such an approach to built architecture, space-time is important.

Body and Technology

JG If the body becomes a central reference point for the experience of space and time and therefore of architecture, then according to Hegel's Phenomenology of Mind, we are back to the beginning, the pre-intellectual state of human consciousness, the mere Sinnliche Gewißheiten, i.e. Sense Certainty of human existence.

AI Yes exactly, sensuality!

JG As you know, *Sense Certainty* marks the lowest possible point in Hegel's philosophical system, which culminates in *Absolute Knowledge*. In this regard we may say that with its semiotization the spirit of architecture was never again as clearly articulated as in the 1970's and 1980's. However, contrary to the ever faster pace of the development of global technol-

New Station, Florence, Italy

ogy today, we find ourselves in a state of cultural regression – regression to a mere bodily condition, a kind of extremely local condition. Universal technology and the individual bodily experience seem to mark the two dialectical opposites in today's digital age.

AI Before we talked about actualities and virtualities: there are two opposing aspects of the experience of an object, its recognition and the feeling we have towards it. But without the body this dichotomy cannot come together. So virtuality and actuality are mediated through the body. As a psychological condition objects are virtual, but by seeing and feeling them they become real. Without our body we cannot touch and feel. In this regard I am very much interested in the phenomenon of *otaku*, a group of people and their mentality as this is called in Japanese society. They cannot differentiate between the reality of their bodies and the virtuality of the digital medium. They cannot distinguish between the actual world and the virtual one. Sometimes, just as easily as in the movies they murder, a dangerous development because they don't understand that right in between the real and the virtual is a human being. Just like our eyesight, hearing or tactility all of the senses are mediated through our body. As a matter of fact the *otakus* are a very strange species totally absorbed by a worldwide bodiless communication through the internet.

JG So the body has to be referred to as the local or domestic condition, while literally the internet represents the global and universal condition…

In regard to global strategies in architecture culture, let's turn to another aspect. In the 1990's computers became a serious design tool in architecture. While many architects first ignored the technology, virtual space immediately became a sort of playground for the deconstructionists, who were operating beyond any spatial and temporal limitations.

AI Yes, with the computer the deconstructionists could even more easily manipulate architectural forms. Finally everything could be deconstructed, there were no limits anymore.

JG While already at the beginning of the 1990's architectural deconstruction had exhausted itself, the digital space immediately became a dream turned reality for the deconstructionists, but at the expense of the bodily experience in architecture.

AI On one side the real building has to relate to the body; and on the other, the virtual world to the mental and psychological condition of mankind. Together they constitute our reality today. The body is always in between. Today I am mostly occupied with this mediating position of the body, especially in regard to its relation to and functioning with respect to technology in general, and specifically the digital.

The fact is that the body is very primitive. Unlike the computer it is unstable and never definite. This instability and uncertainty is probably what Jameson and Hays are referring to when they talk about the imminent shift in the cultural logic. But what makes that shift? I think it is technology although not limited to information technology – technology in a broader, more general sense. We have to take technology seriously, especially in times of no solid foundation. When Nietzsche said that God is dead, instantly the old style humanism was discredited, and with it, the clearly determined cultural foundations. Today's world is based on a certain nihilistic idea. This idea makes many people extremely nervous, but we have to observe that the world is still around. This is why we can approach history only through criticism.

Technology and Invention

AI If there are no longer foundations to relate to, if our base is nihilism, then all theories, too, become unstable. I also find in history situations of disorientation similar to today's. For example what makes Brunelleschi such an outstanding architect in history? In his time the Gothic style was the cultural paradigm. But he rejected it, sensing that something else had to come. As a matter of fact he found no reliable foundations any longer for Gothic design but at the same time he did not know yet with what to replace it. Led only by his intuition he found Roman architecture quite interesting. Yet in a time without any valid theoretical foundation he became aware that he could rely only on technology. This is how he created this incredible cupola of the Duomo in Florence, by setting aside all his intellectual scruples and by relying solely on pure technology.

The point is that great things happen at times when solid foundations are lost. However, these are very short periods. This is what we can learn from the Florence of the 14th century. Immediately after Brunelleschi's death, Alberti, on the basis of humanism, worked out a new architecture and art theory. With the anthropomorphic humanist concept he gave architecture culture new intellectual foundations. Alberti is a revisionist who, by theorizing, transformed Brunelleschi's technologically based concept into a humanist concept. Even as recently as Wittkower, Colin Rowe and others like them, contemporary historians all worked (or are still working) within in the frame of Alberti'sconcept of humanism. Though they were relying heavily on the new technologies, even the

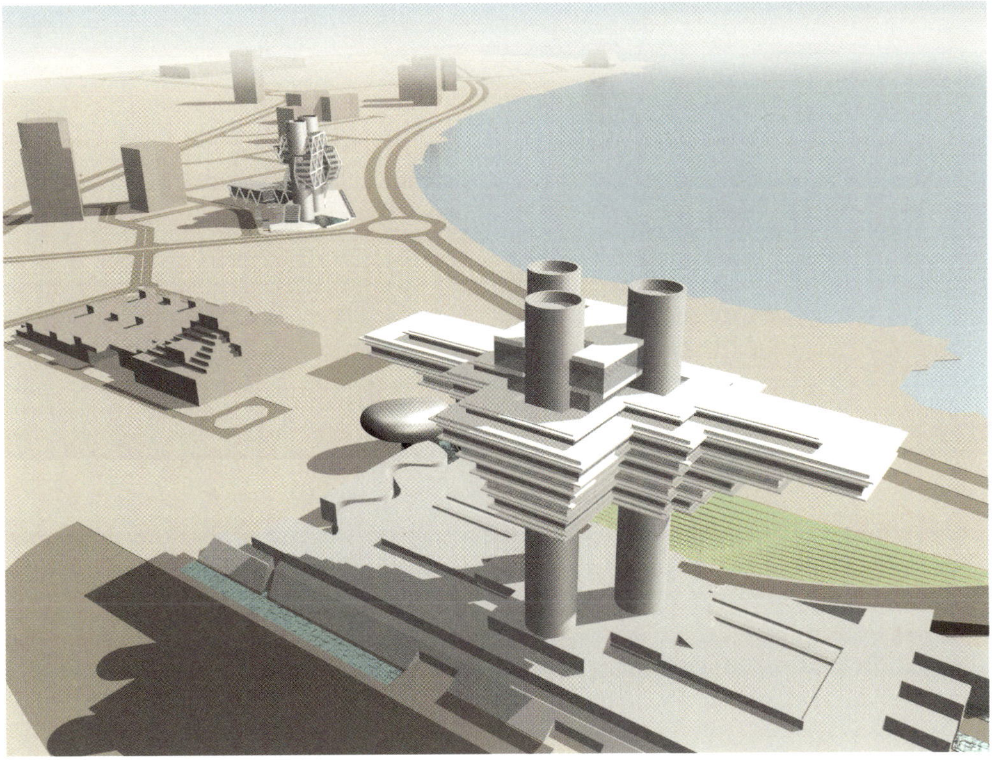

Qatar National Library, Doha, Qatar

modernists like Le Corbusier were still typical anthropomorphists, i.e. Albertian humanists.

JG Are you proposing that with the critique of humanist thought and with the advent of the new computer technology we are again at a historical turning point similar to that of the early Renaissance?

AI Yes. The reason is that we have lost the solid foundations of the last 500 years.

JG Therefore, in order to build a new cultural logic we cannot but rely on technology – it's the only thing we can count on?

AI Since our topic is globalization in architecture, in this regard just let me add that I found a similar case to that of Brunelleschi in Japanese history. I refer to the Japanese Buddhist monk *Chogen* who built the first Todaiji temple in Nara, which burned to the ground in the 12th century. In my view this architect produced an incredible work and his thinking was the same as that of Brunelleschi. He also relied only on the most highly developed technologies of the time while neglecting all the traditional decorations and ornaments. Soon a book is coming out with an essay of mine about the work of Chogen, along with other articles concerning the Katsura Palace and the Ise-Shrine.

Globalization and Diversity

JG It seems to me that the issue of technology is somehow at the center of your concern about the globalization processes in architecture.

AI Of course, but globalization today is still based on the idea of 19th century high capitalism. Until today it has been the major force for promoting the globalization process, mainly in the underdeveloped countries. For example, in Africa the idea of global capitalism is directly linked to that of modernization of local feudal systems, seemingly a necessary step in the development of each individual country.

Historically and culturally the world is very different: everywhere there are different topographies, political situations, and the histories themselves are never the same. Though an inevitable part of the globalization processes, the capitalist market economy will also contribute culturally to what I call an accumulated situation. However, underneath the surface things will react with each other, creating a whole array of very diverse things. Finally we will accumulate patterns of countless small, very specific cultural islands.

In today's Tokyo, the *otakus* have already changed the Akihabara district. The *ganguro* girls – the young girls who like to dress themselves in crazy costumes and present themselves in the streets of the Shibuya district – produce yet another, very particular look. And young Japanese architects create the translucent architecture along the Omotesando Avenue in Harajuku district. Here are three very distinct examples of cultural expressions, just to name a few, in Tokyo. We can take Tokyo as a reduced model of the globalized world.

Tokyo is obviously transforming itself into an increasingly heterogeneous urbanscape, just the opposite of Hilberseimer's model for a modern city of the future. Within the context of Tokyo's global market economy, absolutely unpredictable things emerge. We cannot judge them as good or bad, well or badly done. Some say that they like the *ganguro* girls but find Omotesando just horrible or vice versa. Typically there is no single majority anymore. Very soon in the sea of globalization we will see many more such cultural islands appear.

JG Then we can no longer talk about the *domestic* and the *foreign*. It is applicable only to the 20th century, and now that opposition is becmoing obsolete.

AI The domestic situation will change. Already today we may call all of the three examples in Tokyo equally typical for the domestic situation in Japan. But this doesn't change the fact that Akihabara, Shibuya and Harajuku are rather local islands of only limited size. In the near future the global condition will be comparable to the concept of an archipelago. No doubt the world will become an archipelago, that is, a collection of countless islands floating in a world of dissolved homogeneous matter.

Image Credits:
All images by Arata Isozaki & Associates

An Italian Perspective on International Architecture

Paolo Desideri Rome

In conversation with Ruth Baumeister

Ruth Baumeister With your partners – Arlotti, Beccu and Raimondo – you run the architecture firm of ABDR in Rome. As a typical Roman architect whose work is highly esteemed outside Italy, as well as at home, do you think it is an advantage or a disadvantage to work in the context of the many layers of Rome's architecture and urban history?

Paolo Desideri I consider the presence of history in Italy very important, because it provides the source of enrichment for architecture and requires the practicing architect to pay attention to the context. Therefore, the real issue is not about the presence of history and tradition but about the context formed by such history and tradition.

RB Would you characterize your design as a reaction or response to historical contexts and does history therefore provide your references?

PD Yes, but not in a stylistic sense. My reference to history is always linked to the experience of space. We try to work with the volumetric relationship between the individuals, the building and the space, because the great architecture of any period in Italy always had the capacity to connect with the *genius loci* and the context; therefore contemporary architecture should also strive towards this example.

RB Last year, ABDR designed a housing and commercial development project in the United Arab Emirates and an urban rehabilitation project in China. In both cases, you were invited to the competitions because the clients wanted *Italian style*. How did you respond to their request, especially when it was based a stereotypical image of a nationalist style?

PD Let us consider the Chinese project, because it is a very interesting case in this respect. The central government of China launched an international competition to develop a master plan for the Italian quarter in Tianjin.

We applied just as we do in many other international competitions and we were selected. Our task was not to design a new quarter in any specific style but to rehabilitate the old Italian part of the city. Tianjin is a city on the east coast of China, 200 km from Beijing, basically the capital's harbor. Besides the Italian, there are three other historical, autonomous "European" quarters: the German, the British and the French, all designed and built around 1910. The Chinese government chose one firm for each sector: ABDR from Italy, Von Gerkan from Germany, AREP from France and Hsueh-Li from Taiwan. It was a unique and interesting project for us, because we had to develop a master plan for a typical Italian city of the 19th century, which during the 20th century underwent a lot of changes. Many layers were superimposed on top of the original pattern, and we tried to redefine the Italian structure of the urban space, which was something different from what the government expected from us. We avoided any stylistic implications in our design and proposed simple volumes, very minimal in a stylistic sense, but the volumetric composition and the production of space were really *Italian*.

RB What exactly do you mean by a "really Italian" production of space?

PD In my opinion, the experience of space in Italy is the real resource that we have in our culture, and therefore we tried to design an Italian urban space, by creating piazze, corsi, sottoportichi, etc. We wanted to achieve a typical Italian pattern of streets and squares, of pedestrian and motorized circulation, of high and low volumes in the city, but this had no relationship with any particular style, even though it is commonly understood as such. In other words, by "Italian space" I mean that the project consisted of the kind of urban spaces that are typical of Italy and its urban typology

RB Do you know why the Chinese government wanted to rehabilitate this area? Do you think the European neighborhoods – French, German, Italian or British – appeal to them as something exotic or unique and that the area could possibly further promote commercial activities?

PD They wanted a huge shopping mall in the Italian style where well known Italian brands, such as Ferrari, Brunello di Montalcino, etc., would be sold. Together with AREP, we won the competition and developed our scheme. Last year, they cleared out the area completely in order to start the development. Unfortunately, soon afterwards they put a hold on the project due to some programmatic problems. Obviously, there was no demand for something like this anymore.

RB Did you initially go to China and look at the site?

PD We went for the presentation of the project and stayed a week longer to look around. That was interesting, because at the moment it is an *El Dorado* for architects. I do not know what will come out of it, but for us, at the moment, there is no future in this kind of work.

RB Let us now consider Italy itself. During the economic boom from the 1950's through 1980's, cities expanded mainly by speculative projects in the peripheries. Simultaneously, in the urban centers, housing had to make its way for administrative use. Both developments meant a lot of work for architects and engineers at that time.

During the 1990's the building sector slowed down, and in Rome it basically came to a total halt. Therefore, many architects worked on theories, started teaching at universities or went to practice abroad. One could claim that Italian architecture during that time could be saved only by leaving its domestic territory and those who stayed had to trade the building site for academia. What is the situation today? Did the opening of national markets in the time of globalization change the production of architecture and urbanism in Italy?

PD Italy is a problem! I generally agree with your reading of the present history of Italian architecture, but it lacks one important detail. In the 1950's Italy was at the highest level of international production in architecture. If you consider international firms, such as Saarinen or SOM in the United States, Arup in England, or Atelier Le Corbusier in France, the equivalents in terms of quantity and quality also existed in Italy, such as Pierluigi Nervi, Riccardo Morandi, Sergio Musmeci, Ignazio Gardella, or Gio Ponti; they could certainly compete at an international level for high-end projects in both quantity and quality. Toward the end of the 1960's, though, the demand for architecture in Italy changed completely.

RB Why do you think that drastic change occurred?

PD The masters we had in the 1970's, 1980's and 1990's were very different. Aldo Rossi, for example, in a certain sense was the opposite of the examples that I cited before. He produced sketches after sketches that were so deep and rich in a semantic sense that somebody else had to develop architecture from it. This was also different from the situation in the rest of Europe.
I cannot think of any example where the master would produce *only* sketches, *only* preliminary designs. This occurred only in Italy; in all the other capitalist countries in Europe and the US the tendency was more towards the integration of both architecture and engineering, in other words, of the sense of form and the complexity of the building process.

RB Are you implying that Rossi's architecture did not meet the quality of his poetic sketches, because of the separation of drawing and building. Do you think that Rossi's "semantic depth," as you call it, could be achieved only through sketches and that he could not translate them into architecture? What do you see as the reason for the separation of the production of the "semantic" and the actual building?

PD I'm in particular talking about the architecture developed for the engineering society society between 1980's and 1990's, which started from Rossi's sketches. The *Centro Direzionale di Perugia* no longer conveys the same power as the *Teatro del Mondo* floating on the Venetian canal did in the 1980's.

At the same time, the Teatro del Mondo is a good example of the fact that the "semantic depth" of the initial sketches can be implemented by great expertise in structure. In my opinion, even the most delicate and poetic of any ideas can be transformed into architecture, and I would say this is the task of any "high" architecture. One of the main problems for architects is to maintain the coherence of the work. On the one hand, they must retain the semantic depth of the sketches and, on the other, build at the same level of poetic expression, because there is no shortcut between the two, and the architect has to follow all the stages and maintain responsibility for his project from the emergence of the idea to the end of the building process.

RB I understand that in Italy, in general, you argue that no consistent development exists anymore between the initial drawing and final building. What is the practical implication of this state of affairs?

PD During the 1970's and the 1980's the

Street Elevation, Italian Scenic Area, Tianjin, China

relationship between the design process and the building and construction industry was crazy. We had a complete separation between the production of the drawings and that of architecture. Today, we have to reorganize and reintegrate the process of design and production so that we can compete on the European and global markets. Here lies the main problem of contemporary Italian architecture: we completely lost the capacity to integrate formal and spatial designs, technology, industry and economics. In a certain sense, it led to the *banalization* of the building process. I would argue that in Italy today no school is able to manage the complexity of today's architecture projects.

RB You are pointing out the separation between the conceptual drawings and the actual buildings. This is a common criticism in architecture today after the introduction of digital technology and media in the profession.

PD Yes, exactly. But, it seems to me that back then – in the 1970's and the 1980's – the Italian design approach was still within the *Beaux-Arts* tradition, but certainly not in a beautiful and fantastic manner. Until the 1990's, in Italy form played a completely autonomous role within architecture. Today, we need to find a way to define form so that it can create an equilibrium between the many contradictory aspects within the design and building processes, instead of producing form just for its own sake, thus avoiding the kind of contradiction that would eventually cause the system to collapse, because architecture is neither just form nor just function, but rather the equilibrium between the two. This is what is uniquely central to architecture in contemporary practice thanks to our substantially increased capability to design and build.

RB You describe this as a typical Italian problem and thus distinguish it from those in other countries. Does the fact that Europe is in the process of economic and cultural unification have any influence on the Italian dilemma? In other words, did the recent developments within Europe have any impact on Italian architecture or the Italian construction industry, leading them to become more compatible in the global market?

PD No, absolutely not. Italian architec-

ture in general has no role in this scenario, which certainly does not mean that no good Italian architects exist. It is not only a crisis within the architect's competence but also a huge problem in the culture of construction and management. It is absolutely necessary to reorganize the entire system of architectural production.

RB How about your students, the future generation of architects? In Weimar, I recently noticed that we started receiving many Italian exchange students, very open minded and much more cosmopolitan than earlier generations I am familiar with. They are also highly motivated to compete in an international environment.

PD The students are the patrimony of our next future. Compared to the students of my generation, they are definitely much more professional and have a strong desire to venture out into the rest of the world. At the same time, they seem less sure of their ideas, and, unfortunately less curious.

RB Some global players in architecture have recently received prestigious commissions in Italy. In Rome, for example, Zaha Hadid won the competition for the museum of contemporary arts in 1999. Richard Meier has recently completed the millennium church and at the moment his congress center at the historical site of the Ara Pacis is under construction. The latter, especially, has raised a lot of polemics, centered on a core question, "How much architecture, neither conceived nor designed by Italian architects, can the Eternal City bear?" What is your opinion of such modification of the historical context in the case of Rome?

PD The issue is not the relationship between contemporary architecture and the historical context. There is a widespread resistance towards any form of transformation of territory in our society, which derives from a suspicion that each of us harbors and which is worse than anywhere else in the world. Let me give you a practical example. Since the 1930's, we have had a beautiful open-air theater for Lyric Opera in the ruins of the ancient Baths of Caracalla, which was unfortunately closed by the archeological commission in 1990. They claimed that it would harm the archeological remains. Subsequently, the city launched a competition to transfer the theater to another, quite beautiful site nearby. The project was then abandoned and came to be used for drug dealing and prostitution. We proposed a reorganization of the theater and provided a park with a central open arena, and we won the competition. When we presented our scheme to the authorities, however, they were very opposed to our suggestion. I finally asked whether they preferred a spot for drug dealing and prostitution to a park with culture and music and, surprisingly, they were all for drugs and prostitution. This shows the current paradoxical situation, which generates fear of any kind of transformation in Italy. There is absolutely no trust in the work of the architects, builders and the administration: in general, there is no culture of transformation.

RB Is this the reason why Italians are often considered to dwell in history instead of looking toward the future?

PD No, I do not think so. There has been a paralysis, especially in the transformation of territories during the past 30 years. During the 1950's the situation was different, because people were not so afraid of it.

Let me point out another typical Italian example. Between the 1970's and the 1990's our cities increased by up to 100% in size and thus underwent a drastic transformation…

RB …except that it took place almost without the involvement of architects and urban planners…

PD Yes, it is incredible to realize that, but this transformation was completely subversive. It happened beyond any professional planning, meaning that our cities increased by illegal construction and building. In the 1970's the peripheries in Italy were like the ones in Lebanon or Cairo, where today you see the illegitimate activities of the speculators with the collusion of the authorities. Anyone in the middle of the country could build his or her banal villa or a *toppolino*, a kind of Mickey Mouse house. In general, the construction industry in Italy was shabby. This very low quality of construction trade and building management produced a form of predatory economics with no comparison anywhere else in Europe.

RB How do you see the situation today? Is there any trust or respect in the profession of architecture in Italy?

PD The contemporary condition is schizophrenic. On the one hand, there is a celebration of a very few architects in the media and, on the other hand, there is no common concept of what an architect is or does on a daily basis. Recently, the *Order of Italian Architects* conducted an opinion poll on the public's view of the profession. The result was that the French, when asked about an architect's work, said it is the design of public and private buildings and/or urban environment, while the majority of Italians answered that an architect is the person who chooses the color of apartment interiors or restores monuments.

RB You are drawing a rather bleak picture. What do you think are the prospects for the future?

PD This clearly shows that in the past 30 years architects in Italy did not have a significant role, and because of this, the general public doesn't recognize the profession. But, at the same time, Italy at this moment is a very important market for architecture, because public projects were put on hold for so long that in the future it will certainly provide many projects. It has been about ten years since a new general master plan of Rome replaced the previous one from 1962. With the exception of Berlin, there is probably no other European city with so many impor-

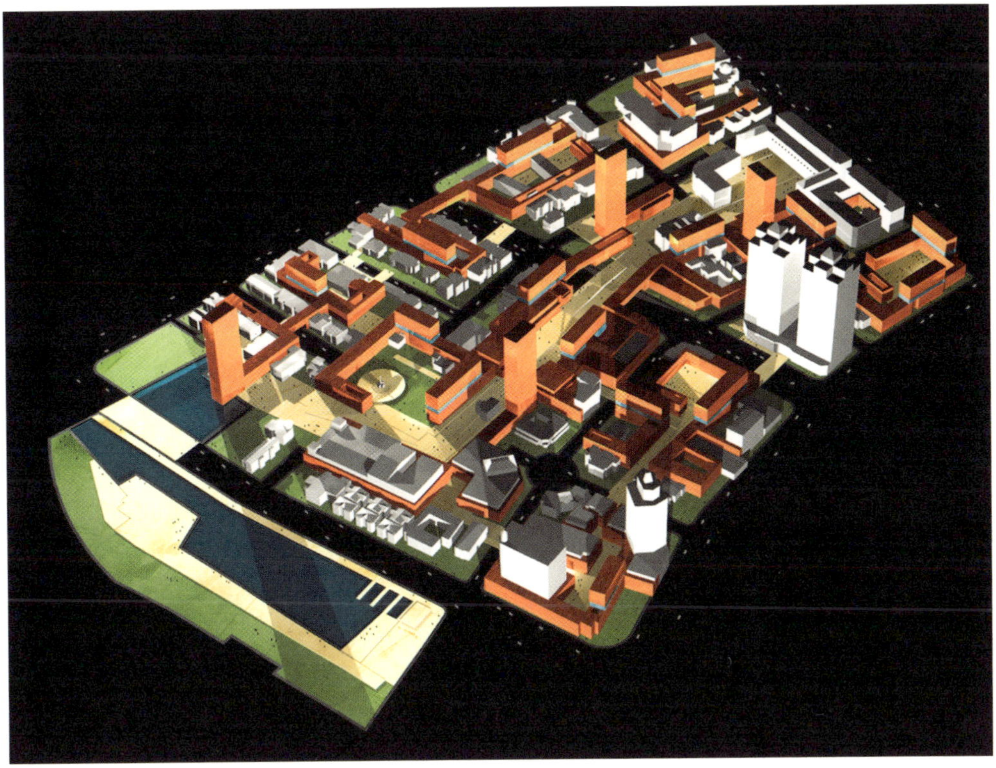

Master Plan, Italian Scenic Area, Tianjin, China

tant recent buildings. Numerous public projects are being developed at the moment, such as the Tiburtina station, Pallazzo di Esposizioni, Metro B Uno – all designed by my office – the Cloud of Massimiliano Fuksas in EUR, the MAXI of Zaha Hadid, the extension to Galleria Commuale d'Arte Moderna by Odil Deq, Galleria Nazionale d'Arte Moderna by Diener & Diener, Ara Pacis by Richard Meier, and so on. It is incredible that in this situation only two offices in Rome can compete. This reveals a dramatic problem. International competitions for the high-speed train stations in Naples, Rome, Turin and Florence, for example, were won mainly by foreign architects. In Turin, Wiel Arets won the competition, and in Florence Norman Foster got the commission. In Naples, the winner was Zaha Hadid, and with the Tiburtina project in Rome, I was the only Italian architect who managed to win one of these four major Italian commissions.

There exists the risk that, although Italy will be a very important market for European architects, Italian architects themselves will have big problems competing in their home market. It is not a question of whether or not we are capable of designing, but of whether or not we can build good architecture at the scale these projects demand. In Rome there are probably only two or three offices with the capacity to work at that level.

RB Your office takes part in many international design competitions, some of which you were invited to participate in and have won. What is the biggest challenge for you, when you work in contexts outside your domestic, Italian one?

PD There are sectors like fashion and

New Tiburtina Station, Rome, Italy

industrial design, where the Italian design approach is recognizable, for example, and I would like to see something similar happen in architecture. Unfortunately, though, that is impossible at moment, because the Italian architects are too few and too indifferent. For example, Renzo Piano's is probably the most international architectural practice we can find around the world at this moment, but he is not at all recognizable as Italian. In a certain sense, the same is true for Massimiliano Fuksas, who produces beautiful work, but he comes more from the French than from the Italian context.

RB Do you think an architect's nationality or national affiliation today is still important to the production of architecture?

PD No, not necessarily. In order to find and develop a *typical* Italian architecture today, I think it is important that the practice grows within this culture, taking into account its specific qualities, that it not be external – therefore, indifferent – to it. In this respect I am proud of our practice and of my role in creating it, because it is one of the few that is *native* to Italy. Of course we were always looking toward the international market, but our perspective remains internal, maturing and accumulating the unique experience offered by the contradictions, economics and culture of Rome and Italy. I hope that in near future other offices, such as Gino Zucchi's in Milan and Marco Casamonti's in Florence, with a background similar to ours, will develop and mature. This might eventually lead again to a recognizable *Italian* design approach in architecture.

RB Do you think that these offices, because of their background, are able to produce a less generic architecture? In other words, do you think that the precondition for *Italian* architecture is that its architects must remain at home and work immersed in the country and its culture?

PD Yes. My hope is that the Italian way in architecture will be recognizable again when a couple of large practices grow inside the country yet are still capable of working in the international market. But to achieve equilibrium between the global and local, which is to realize what is often called "glocal," I do think that it is necessary to be present in the local. You have to stay local and look at the global.

RB Since you work in many different places and cultures, you have to deal, on the one hand, with the context you find yourself in, and, on the other, with your personal *signature* as an architect? How do you negotiate between the global and the local in your daily practice?

PD In our work, there is a kind of schizophrenia between the local and the global, which became especially obvious in our project for the new Tiburtina station. This project is suspended between the contradiction of the global and the local, and, at the same time, this was already inscribed as a condition in the competition outline. A high-speed train station in some way has the same programmatic requirements as an airport, but an airport is in the periphery and a railroad station is in the center of the city. We were challenged to design something suspended between the atopia and context, a local atopia so to speak. The programmatic requirements were similar to what you would need for an airport in terms of safety, security, customs and circulation. At the same time, the local administration asked us to realize a program that ran completely counter to those requirements. They envisioned a bridge, similar to the Ponte Vecchio in Florence, with stores that are open 24 hours a day, a piazza, completely accessible to the public at large – anything but what one would expect to see in this new type of train station.

RB How did you resolve this conflict?

PD Let me give you an example: in order to obtain approval for the Tiburtina station – by the way, this project is a train station financed as a public building, not a commercial development – we spent a whole year trying to achieve a consensus among 35 different public authorities, such as the archeological commission, the department of public works, the department of the environment, etc. They all searched for a miraculous common consensus, but each single agency was in conflict with the other. This is very typical for the complex process of a public project in contemporary architecture in Italy. What an incredible challenge for the architect! The architect will probably be the only one left to survive this system with its struggles for political power and over representation. In order to achieve this, I had to be willing to channel all my creativity towards this goal. Within this process, form is the only means to create equilibrium among all the conflicting parties. If you imposed an auto-referential form – one that is related only to you and God – you might stress the system even more and possibly risk its collapse. In any large scale project your design has to resolve the multi-facetted nature of the conflict. At the scale of urban design, it is located between various systems of authorities, all of whom have their own interest in the territorial conflict. At the scale of construction, it is between the structure, design, technology, builders, economics and engineering in general. In my opinion, you can only negotiate this conflict through your handling of form, and this is my personal approach to architecture in a situation such as this.

Extension to Il Palazzo del'Esposizione, Rome, Italy

RB As a professor of architectonics and urban composition at the University of Gabriele d'Anunizio in Pescara, what is your approach to teaching the future generation of Italian architects?

PD In Italy the situation in academia is no better than it is in the construction sector. At this moment, our universities are full of professors incapable of designing anymore. But please note, I do not mean to say *build* but design! The reason for this is that the majority of our design professors have actually never designed anything. They never participated in or won a competition and, therefore, they have never built anything. Their design approach is completely *literary*.

RB How did they become professors then? Are you suggesting that nepotism and corruption are still big problems that happen also in Italian universities?

PD I'm afraid you are over-reading my comment. I would like to say that even here, when it comes to the ability of innovation and transformation, Italy is not flexible. In some ways, the situation today is still similar to that of the 17th century when the *bottega* was handed on from father to son; just as for the notary, this could also happen in the case of a professorship. This is not the place where I want to imply a moral judgement, but I'm strongly interested in stressing that all of this is an indicator of deep-seated discomfort: a vital country is a place with powerful wishes of transformation, without this we'll slip back into the glorious Baroque twilight.

RB Is there anything you, personally would do about this problem?

PD When I was a student during the early 1970's though, most of my professors split their activities between teaching and the practice of the profession. In the end, the professors and the profession came to have the same *code*. For me, it is easy to be a professor, because I do have something to offer, and this is my approach in design, too. I have something to offer in practice. But at the moment, very few of us have the possibility of teaching what they learned over the years through practice. Thus, most professors today lack sufficient practical experience. This is a very big problem and has contributed to the paralysis in Italian architecture for the past 30 years. The situation has to be rectified. But I strongly believe that the origin of any good professional faculty is good professors – whose strength lies in having had the *possibility* of accumulating a large body of practical experience. I recommend to my students to be curious, to travel, to observe, to read architecture and its history, and, finally, to spend time under the sun, preferably at a beach on the Mediterranean. I trust the Mediterranean approach to architecture…

Image Credits:
All images by ABDR Architetti Associati

Being a Local Architect in New York

Frederic Schwartz New York

In conversation with Sang Lee

Projects in China

Frederic Schwartz Right now we are competing for one of the world's largest projects, in Shanghai, for the World's Fair Master Plan in 2010. The post-World's Fair then transforms to a model for the city of the future. It includes a proposal for the world's tallest building at 718 meters (2183 feet).

Sang Lee Can you talk about the program for it?

FS The program is similar to any typical world's fair, with international pavilions and gardens, great exhibition halls and grand plazas… But what makes it very interesting is that this area of Shanghai is planned to become a model sector for future cities. Designing for 2010, for a city growing exponentially is quite a challenge. In China, 50% of the population is moving from the countryside to cities, which *The New York Times* calls the largest mass migration in the history of the world.

On July 4th, 2004 the *New York Times Magazine*, instead of writing as they usually do about the current state of America, dedicated the whole issue to China. I have been there five times in the past year. This is the first time I have been on a trip to another city and returned to find New York looking small. As far as the eye can see, the density and growth in and around Shanghai is staggering.

The site is right in the heart of Shanghai, in the underdeveloped Pudong sector, and our Master Plan is equal to the area from the southern tip of Manhattan to 34th Street. We partnered with Robert A. M. Stern's office and the Southeast University of China in Nanjing (SEU).

SL When you did this proposal, did you get a sense from the project organizers what they are looking for as a cultural project? If the large rural population is rapidly migrating to an urban environment,

Master Plan, 2010 World Expo, Shanghai, China

there must be some sort of cultural changes and adjustments to consider in addition, especially if many foreign architects will be involved in the project.

FS China's idea about foreign architects is changing. They recognize that they have their own talent and don't necessarily need to rely on foreign architects. For the 2008 Olympic Games they invited many international "star" architects, and the local firms would compete for the construction documents phase of the work because of both the inexpensive labor market and the legal requirements.

What makes our situation unique is that we work as equal partners with the Chinese. We didn't just do the conceptual design and farm out the rest. We went over to China for a week at a time and worked together. It was really a team effort and an amazing experience in terms of the substance of the collaboration.

The program was absolutely culturally oriented. We put forth a cultural program because we believed in it and stressed important environmental issues to offer Shanghai new models of sustainability. The site is on both sides of the Huangpu River – also called the mother river – equivalent to the East River here in New York. Our master plan took off from one of the ideas we explored as the THINK team for the World Trade Center, which was the Sky Park.

In Shanghai, one of the densest cities in the world, we proposed giant-scale man-made mountains and vast open green areas. The idea is about multiplying the land use by building habitable structures underneath vast, useable green roofs that double as public parks. This idea is obviously very closely related to sustainability issues. While the Chinese cities are growing, they are also becoming extremely polluted. There is a constant haze of smog in Shanghai that makes Los Angeles look clean.

SL As an architect from New York City, what was particular about the domestic culture of architecture in Shanghai, compared to New York or other cities you have been to? Did you have anyone engaged in the critique of your work?

FS We are partnering with our Chinese colleagues. We were listening and learning, breathing and absorbing the culture. We would meet with a Feng Shui master who would review our design in the middle of the night and discuss the project. Here in America, Feng Shui is taken lightly. But in China it is like a zoning code. You cannot do a project in China without it.

Another partner, Eric Sun, was born in Shanghai and educated at Yale. We were immersed in Chinese culture. Also we have in our office a very skilled young architect from China, Tza-Ping Leng; we hired him independently of this project before we were invited to participate.

SL How does this compare to your experience in New York on large projects?

FS This makes Ground Zero, then considered one of the largest, seem small by comparison. Ground Zero is 16 acres (6.5 hectares) and this site in Shanghai is 1 600 hectares (3 954 acres). I have been very lucky to work on large projects, and I enjoy working on large projects not because of the size but because they bring so many complex and interesting issues to consider. Take the Westway project in Manhattan, where I was Project Director for five years while at VSBA (Venturi, Scott Brown and Associates): it stretched for five miles along the Hudson River from Battery Park City to 42nd street. It was the largest urban project in the country at that time, valued at $2.6 billion. World Expo 2010 and Westway are comparable in terms of complexity, but the fact that I was working in such a different culture makes it far more interesting.

Let me expand on this a bit more. What's happening in Shanghai is that when you go there you sense instantly that it's more commercial and capitalist than even New York City. Actually, every city I visited in China was teeming with this spirit. With all the advertising, buzz and vibrancy it felt like the Wild West in Asia. I was prepared since I grew up in New York City and I am

FUDU Mansion Tower, Shanghai, China

"from the streets," so to speak. If I had been from a small town in the American Midwest for example, I might have been completely overwhelmed and had a different opinion.

Architecture in New York City and the World Trade Center

SL I am asking this question because New York City is one of truly global urban centers in the world. But yet it is not that easy to find strong outside influences on architecture. Do you agree with that? Why do you think it is the case?

FS I do agree with that. Architecture in New York City is controlled mostly by large corporate firms servicing real estate interests that are geared to squeezing out the maximum profit per dollar. That's why you see so many terrible buildings in this city, one after another. Outside my office window, I am looking right now across the Hudson River at New Jersey. Paul Goldberger recently wrote that the Shanghai of New York is New Jersey's Hudson River shore – and that is not a good thing. In Shanghai, so many buildings are also terrible. You don't know who designed the buildings, most are anonymous. None aspire to anything that is particular about architecture. They are just real estate. Herbert Muschamp of the *New York Times* wrote best about this, that architecture in New York is largely real estate, not architecture, controlled by big corporate firms. There are major firms with a lot of mouths to feed that pretend to do relevant architecture once in a while, but mostly that's in between corporate buildings – real estate.

Now, obviously much has changed because of Ground Zero, and architecture in the post-9/11 era as design is becoming re-recognized as an important part of our daily lives. So in New York City, now we are starting to see buildings that are Architecture with a capital A. Only last year Richard Meier designed his first signature building – now he has three – in Manhattan. His practice has been based in New York City for decades. I worked for twelve years on Whitehall Ferry Terminal, which opened in 2005, and now people have started to recognize it as significant public architecture. I think with the work on Ground Zero by our design team, THINK, and by some others like United Architects and the team of Eisenmann, Meier, Holl and Gwathmey, people started to get excited about the possibilities of collaborative urban architecture, no matter what the size was.

But unfortunately architecture is still governed by real estate first in New York City. You can see the great potential and possibilities to do significant architecture at a place like Times Square. There are very few places in New York where the priorities are about architecture rather than real estate.

SL Do you think this is also the reason why there are so few architectural competitions in New York City? For Ground Zero, the Port Authority initially just hired the architects they already had a relationship with.

Some would say that to be able to work on civic projects in New York City, you have to collaborate with big corporate firms or very well known foreign "star" architects. Do you feel that way, given that your firm is still very small in size and native to New York?

FS In the first six plans for Ground Zero, people were outraged by what they saw. I have been very fortunate in my career to work with the right people at the right time. We are a small, growing firm but we are able to work on the biggest projects in the world because we collaborate. We are now beginning to get much larger projects on our own, but I still prefer collaboration. It is much more interesting. We just won two important international competitions, the New Jersey September 11th Memorial and the Westchester September 11th Memorial, collaborating with Ove Arup for the engineering component. But for large projects in New York you just can't compete in the selection process with the firms such as SOM (Skidmore Owings and Merrill) and HOK (Hellmuth Obata Kassabaum) on a level playing field, given their size and resources, unless you collaborate or are invited to compete. Even the large firms team up for the big projects – for example Meier and SOM on an East Side public project.

For 25 years I have been in practice, and I have participated in lots of competitions – perhaps over 100 – I should count. Within the past five years, I have completed over

White Hall Ferry Terminal, New York City

The Wave, San Diego

40 competitions in various situations. As a sole practitioner, I believe I might have probably completed the most competitions in the America. Most of my colleagues have never done even one competition in their entire careers – not even a single one!

In New York City, the Whitehall Ferry Terminal competition in 1992 was the first competition sponsored by the city in over 100 years. New York City stopped architec-

Coney Island Theme Park, Brooklyn

tural competitions at the turn of the last century because McKim, Mead and White won all the time. They were the SOM of their time.

Rafael Viñoly and I have just teamed up again – we have collaborated on the Ground Zero master plan – to design the largest project on the West Coast, located in San Diego, three million square feet in one mega-structure. It was a competition by developers, an international open competition for qualifications, and then they selected 6 teams. We designed "The Wave," an idea we hadn't tried before. All the other schemes were as usual. They did exactly what developers always want. You couldn't distinguish one from the other, because they were all more or less the same. One might be better or worse than the others by a small degree but basically they were all the same. They were all scaling down, instead of scaling up in terms of the quality of the design work. Of course the situation is more complex than that, but the developers were essentially looking for conventional buildings with no risk instead of a THINKing master plan given the project's size and density.

SL For Ground Zero you have worked with an international cast of architects. What was your experience in that collaboration?

FS None of the work at Ground Zero by THINK would have been possible without that specific collaboration. It was one of the most enlightening moments in my career in terms of education for myself. I learned so much from others in the team: what they think, how they work and how they interact. I don't believe that type of project should be done by one architect – especially when a personal ego is involved.

I believe that we won that project, but something else happened politically. But that's another story. We shared a great work ethic. We never stopped working and still continue to collaborate.

SL When architects come from the outside, even those considered prominent, historically they seemed to have a hard time with projects in the city. For example, Le Corbusier with the UN complex – it is well known that he had a bad experience. Mies also had a hard time with his Seagram building, because his open public plaza in front broke the uniform street façade line of Park Avenue.

Why do you think it is so difficult for foreign architects to execute projects in the city? Do you feel that New York City is resistant to architects from the outside?

FS At this point, it is changing. In the past, yes, it was very difficult, not just for foreign architects but for all architects except for a few well-established ones in the city. Right now, though, Enrique Norton's office (TEN Arquitectos) and my office are both working on very progressive, large new projects in Harlem with government support and public participation that are only possible because of the change in the climate and the support of the present administration. The city's very complex zoning laws can put you in a shoebox. But one of the reasons that there is a change is that we now have a mayor, Michael Bloomberg, who cares about the arts and architecture, and a Commissioner of Planning, Amanda Burden, who I think is the best to date. So there is more flexibility, more possibilities and positive thinking from the administration, based on a new sensibility about architecture and planning and its possibilities, post-9/11.

Whether foreign or domestic, whether it is the fashion of "star" architects, now people see more value in architecture. I am not a star architect but in terms of the work we did after 9/11 and after my proposal for the design study that the *New York Times* sponsored, I see more doors open for me. That is one of the reasons why someone like me can do a very large public project such as the one in Coney Island, a vertical theme park and entertainment complex with three million square feet of floor space.

SL After the LMDC (Lower Manhattan Development Corporation) competition for the new World Trade Center complex, you and your design team became in the end the runner-up. After that, were you invited to contribute any further to the project by the LMDC?

FS No!

SL After the competition concluded, even though you were officially the second place winner, and given the enormity of the project, was there no possibility for you to be involved in the project at all?

FS I wasn't asked for any further involvement.

When we submitted our scheme for the Ground Zero competition, the committee voted unanimously for our design! It was not even a tie, which the governor would have had to break in such a case. Our scheme was the choice of the committee, but something else happened and we were removed. I cannot tell you exactly what happened, but that was the end of it.

SL Now the first building, World Trade Center No. 7, the building SOM started designing even before the competition, is almost finished. How much of the former WTC complex was put up for the competition?

FS Even though it is a building in the World Trade Center complex, the building was initiated independently from the LMDC, so that 7 WTC was not in the scope of the LMDC's World Trade Center competition. It should have been. The

Vertical City, Sketch for the new WTC master plan

16-acre area of the original Twin Towers was the specific scope of the competition. There are many buildings around that area, of which 7 WTC is a part. Now the former Deutsch Bank building has became a part of the project as I always said it should. So the extent of the project boundary has been modified.

When I proposed my idea for West Street in March 2002, I took on all of Lower Manhattan. I stated that if we look at *only* the Ground Zero area, we will fail! I thought that by examining all of the Lower Manhattan area including West Street we would open interesting possibilities. Many felt the same way, but when the LMDC briefed the architects about the competition, they specifically made it clear to me, and everyone else from around the world, that we were not to touch West Street. I thought it was a big mistake.

SL Also, now Santiago Calatrava has designed the transportation hub at the WTC site. There was a substantial competition for the master plan with a great potential, but if I look at the process and where it is heading, it seems in the end there will be many buildings plugged in and around the site, designed by many different architects selected by many different interests. How do you think this will work?

FS A good master plan would allow architects to express their designs – I don't mean this as a comment or critique of the situation on the site at the moment, whether it is good or bad – but a good master plan would accommodate flexibility and may change all the time and not be so prescriptive in the expression of an individual piece of architecture. I think it is healthy that now we can have someone like Calatrava and many others of his caliber. The buildings at Ground Zero shouldn't look all the same. That is why I am critical of both Battery Park City Master Plan and the current World Trade Center Master Plan.

SL Do you think there will be other competitions for any buildings at Ground Zero?

FS No, there will be no more competitions at Ground Zero. They will do it by a closed-door selection process as usual. They will select architects based on the qualifications that the legal guidelines specify for public projects. That way it is easier for the Governor to control the design. I am all for competitions because that is the only way I and other small offices like mine will have the opportunity to participate and design these kinds of buildings. As for the legal guidelines, the authorities will make their decision based on how many large buildings I have done, and in that case I cannot compete. They rely on the safety of such a process for the governing agency, because it's easier to pick someone and then have them directly under their control.

SL So you mean that such a process in this particular case is a political decision, before anything else.

FS If you look at the Ground Zero competition, in the end the decision was political.

Context and Architecture

SL When you have projects overseas, in different cultural and political contexts, how do you start?

FS I start by immersing myself in the environment: history, politics, art, food, music and reading as much as I can about the culture and its architecture. I try to absorb as much as I can to make the project *relevant*. By this, I don't mean in terms of historicism but a bigger picture. I can see that with the kind of technology we have today the world has really became global and that time is moving exponentially.

When I am in San Diego, Toulouse or Shanghai, it seems many places are becoming similar. Perhaps that means that it is becoming easier to *read* those places. All these places used to be very different from each other: Even though Los Angeles, San Diego and San Francisco are along the same coast line of California, they are three entirely different cities. When you are in those cities to design architectural projects, you are aware of those differences, not to mention the differences you would certainly notice in a place like Shanghai. But as different as they are, now they share many of the same characteristics. They are as much the same as they are different.

I was amazed to see Shanghai even more commercial and capitalistic than New York. Even just ten years ago, you wouldn't have felt that way. Exponential changes!

So, on the one hand, I try to absorb what the local culture is at a given place and at the same time I find a lot of its features becoming shared in many different places. This could also mean that globalization somehow makes it easier to be in those places, yet at the same time you try to find what is particular about them to make the local special today. I have learned a great deal from Donny Deutsch, who is the most important person in advertising and branding in the US. We designed his offices in New York, Chicago, Boston and LA. All Deutsch offices in the USA share the same branding idea but Donny also stressed the importance of finding the particular in each place. In every Deutsch office you go to, you know clearly that it is a Deutsch office, but at the same time each of them has a particular local persona.

SL How subtle or apparent are the local differences in this example?

FS Their headquarters are in New York. But when I designed the Los Angeles office he specifically asked me that it should be distinctively Los Angeles. Not Deutsch New York transplanted to Los Angeles. When people walk into the Los Angeles office they should be able to see clearly that they are not only in a Deutsch office but also in Los Angeles. And they do because we tried to reflect the local difference of LA compared to New York. It's both national and regional branding.

SL In architecture, how do you think the type of branding could work on a global scale and at the same time the representation of the local?

FS I try to make both aspects work. If I design a project in Coney Island, for example, I would like to see both these aspects (local and global) and a sense of where it is coming from among others. Certain architects, to their credit, are brands. They could be brands whether you like or dislike them. You know that they are brands when you refer to them by their first names or last names, not both – Gwathmey, Meier, Rem, Piano, Venturi, Zaha, Gehry. I think it is good that someone can be so good with what they do that their projects are referred to by their personal names.

Star Architects

SL Do you think there is architecture beyond the individual architect's branding aspects?

FS You could find many types of architecture designed specifically for certain social, political, cultural and economic groups. You could draw a map of architecture and find all these different types. I aspire to finding my own voice and my own way in architecture. I don't want to do the same predictable architecture all the time. Just yesterday, someone called me from Chicago and wanted to discuss a project at the river. They said that they looked everywhere and found my work overwhelming in terms of its variety. I feel that's where I want to be. I don't want somebody to be able to predict what I am going to do next as I don't know what I am going to do next. I follow a certain intuitive direction but at the same time always try to look at every project from a fresh, new and different angle. Denise Scott Brown calls it "non-judgmental" architecture.

SL If you look at the work of the "star" architects, they are wanted because of their particular signature expression that may be reiterated in many different places.

FS They are. For example, Frank Gehry is great at what he does. He put architecture back on the map with a capitol "G." I think it is great he does what he does best and only he can do it. He invented his own style and language. There are those who think that his way of doing architecture is problematic, but I disagree with that opinion, and he definitely helped open up many new possibilities in architecture. This debate has been going on probably as long as architecture itself. I am sure the Pope's court probably had the same debate about Michelangelo.

SL What kind of problems have you had because of your point of view or architectural language?

FS I had problems with certain commissions because some of my projects in the past made the clients think I will do the same thing. But sometimes I also get work for that very reason. You know it is a struggle to have a growing firm. But it is also a unique position that is possible because of the number of architectural competitions. You always have to compete for projects. Commissions almost never get dropped in your lap. Competitions allow me to beat SOM. I cannot beat them in interview selections because I am not asked for the interview in the first place.

SL Did you have experience with a community opposing or protesting against your design?

FS For the Westway project, yes, but almost always quite the opposite. We had enormous local community, national and international support for the THINK team's World Cultural Center at Ground Zero. Right now I am working on one of the largest new projects in Harlem, where I recently presented the design to the community board, and they approved it unanimously at the first meeting. Unlike other mostly commercial projects in Harlem, the design is specifically about the relevant culture. I worked with Jack Travis, a very talented African-American architect, who helped steer us through what the spirit of a building in Harlem should be. The community understood that. It is very difficult to do this in Harlem, not to mention other communities.

SL For a long time I have wanted to discuss something uniquely New York: Philip Johnson and his power. It is extremely rare to find someone who has had so much prominent influence and power for so long over the profession.

FS He was so powerful because he could deliver a commission to any architect of his choice with one phone call. He could make MoMA include you in an exhibition by simply saying so. He was the Pope of architecture and also the Godfather. It was as simple as that. In the end that's what architecture is sometimes all about: Power and influence! H. H. Richardson said that the most important part of architecture is getting the project.

SL Do you think Johnson's power and influence on the profession had a positive side?

FS The positive side is that he helped a few talented architects get very important commissions and then they did great work. But at the same time he prevented those who were not in his favor from getting projects. For the few on his *list* he was great and for the others, well, just too bad. There are always power brokers in every city. But he really consolidated his power nationwide in terms of who would get major commissions. I met with Philip one day and the very next day received a phone call for a project. Nothing came of it, but he did it just to show off his power. This type of power in architecture is very much magnified in New York, just like everything else in this city. During the World Trade Center Competition, Eisenman met with Philip to get his blessing on their project and influence the process somehow. I got wind of that, so I had my audience with Philip, too. He said it was amazing with a typical devilish, gleeful laugh of his – and then he said it was the best thing he had ever seen!

Understanding Cultural Sensibility

David Chipperfield London

In conversation with Ruth Baumeister

On International Practice

Ruth Baumeister For over 20 years you have been building projects in Japan, China, the United States and several European countries. Your work is highly esteemed throughout the world, and this makes you a global player among architects. How do you find your commissions?

David Chipperfield Nearly exclusively through competitions. Either a design competition or sometimes we participate and get short-listed in an interview process.

RB How do you organize the projects that are built far away from your home office? Do you establish branches?

DC We have two offices, one in London and one in Berlin, where we do both design and production. All of the work in America, Spain or Italy is done from the London office. For the rest, we team up with contact offices all over the world. With the exception of one local office in Shanghai, we do not set up our own local offices; everything is done in collaboration.

RB Do these local offices also have an influence on the design process?

DC We try to integrate them in the design stages so that we benefit from their input. We also try to make contact early, and sometimes these partnerships turn into long-term partnerships. Of course, there is no ambiguity in terms of the leadership; we lead the projects through the design stage, but we conduct workshops with the local offices. They have, first of all, very good technical skills, and we rely on their knowledge of the local conditions. But even more than that, they often contribute greatly to the design. While you can't necessarily expect it, we find that we do get a more personal commitment and collaboration, which in 90% of our projects is very successful.

RB How do you find these "partners"?

DC It varies. Sometimes you already know them; sometimes they are recommended; sometimes you have to go and look. Generally they've become quite close friends, like our contacts in Naples, Milan Barcelona, and America. You cannot have only a technical relationship, since you rely on them to fight for you.

RB You have people from various countries working in your offices. Does this affect the way you conceive architecture?

DC Yes. Someone recently told me that in our London office we have 22 nationalities represented. We have a majority of foreign people there: only four out of 50 people are English. I am sure it does affect our way of conceiving architecture. We try to be very open, and working in many different places all the time keeps us from being an exclusively English practice. We are not influenced solely by the working environment that we would have to deal with if we were anywhere here in England. And to some degree that has meant that it is more difficult for us to get work in England.

RB Are you considered to be an international firm, rather than one which is completely familiar with the British scene?

DC I think it is partly that our foreign experience does not give us credibility in England. So when someone there is looking for an architect with a certain amount of experience, they would still say that we do not have enough, even though we are doing the Museum Island in Berlin, and, in Barcelona, the largest public project in Europe. So that is one thing about the English condition that at a certain point I guess we get a little bit impatient with.

Domestic Conditions and References

RB What exactly do you consider to be the English condition?

DC Generally it is very commercial; there is not much public work. Essentially,

Figge Art Museum, Davenport, Iowa, USA

a very heavy emphasis is placed on project management, which is a very American condition. On the one hand, America has a very commercial orientation, which is quite difficult for architects to deal with; on the other hand, there is a lot of private money available that goes into projects like museums or university buildings and that provides a very good creative opportunity for architects. In England, we do not have that same situation. It is not very easy for us to get work there.

RB Despite this, you still keep your practice there?

DC Yes, I live there, and Heathrow is one of the best airports. There is no necessity for me to live where my business is located.

RB If you start a project, do you work with a certain design method, and are there specific conditions you consider particularly important?

DC We approach our projects in an analytical way, in terms of both program and context, as most architects would. Probably because we work in so many different cultures and in so many extremely different places, we are more likely to make comparisons between projects. If you build in Madrid, what are the opportunities that you can enjoy there, that you can't enjoy in Berlin? What are the opportunities you can enjoy in Alaska that you can't enjoy in London? What are the programs that you need to confront in Alaska that you don't confront somewhere else. I suppose that, like a tourist, you are sometimes more enthusiastic about trying to understand a city than are people who always live there.

RB Do you try to define basic principles or standards?

DC You have to make generalizations, enormous generalizations, which are

obviously dangerous in one way, but maybe positive in another. So that is one thing; and the other thing is that I try to identify every project with a purpose. I am not particularly concerned about functionality as a determining strategy. It is something that you have to do; if you write, you have to be able to spell. If you design a building you have to make it work. Therefore it is not enough to say that the buildings are functional, because that is just the technical aspect of the process. But what I do think is important is to identify a kind of purposefulness. In every project, we are trying to understand what this should be about. What are the issues in terms of the building's location, and also, culturally, in terms of how people might use it? We are very concerned that people have definite opinions about certain things. So, when you design a museum, it should be your idea of what a museum should be like. When you design a house, you should be trying to push your idea of what living should be about. For me, that is more important than pushing an idea of what architecture should be like. In the beginning, instead of starting with a fixed idea such as a particular material, we consider the client and what he or she loves and make sure that the house satisfies the needs of the client, as opposed to beginning a design process in such and such materials, or in this or that shape. We work on the formal language later in the process.

RB You mentioned context as one of the major determining categories in your design. Fortunately, your architecture proves to be a creative interpretation of the context, resulting in something new, rather than only a consequence of it. Do you consider the design process to be a dialogue with the existing context, and, at the same time, do you try to establish your own position in this process?

DC Yes, I would hope so. Moreover, it is a matter of forming an opinion about something and identifying what you value. I think you have to give values to things. I've never really recovered from Louis Kahn's statement about trying to discover what a project wants to be, and I still think that this is a very interesting place to begin. Of course, as we gain more experience we bring more prejudice to a project, but that also means that we can arrive faster at an idea. I think it is clear that the more you build the more prejudice and preconception you have.

RB You mentioned Louis Kahn as one of your points of reference. Have you been influenced by other architects or schools, and are there certain icons in architecture history that had some influence on the way you understand, see and conceive architecture?

DC I am not someone obsessively looking at other people's work because there is never enough time. But I would like to look at others' projects to see how they work. At school I was influenced by great modern architects such as Le Corbusier, Aalto, Asplund, and, to some degree, Louis Kahn. In my early practice, especially in England in the 1980's there was basically either Postmodernism or High-tech. I was very much looking towards Moneo and Siza and Snozzi, who were very important to me in my formative professional years. Therefore, their visions represented a really refreshing and optimistic alternative in that period in England. Many contemporary figures closer to my generation, such as Koolhaas, Herzog, Diener, and de Mora, continue to impress me by the very high quality of the work they produce. The world is full of very good architects.

House in Corrubedo, Spain

Generally, I would say that I am quite relaxed about other architects' work, and I don't have a great ideological resistance to someone who works in a very different way than I do.

RB As sources of reference for your daily practice you mentioned several contemporary architects and some classic modernists during your studies. Do you also connect with other times, other centuries?

DC We, like all modern architects, are impressed by buildings of any period. I do not think that we are immune to the power and beauty of architecture. So there are certain buildings and certain places that I find enormously inspiring. In England, I certainly think we were very fortunate to have people like Wren and probably even more, in my opinion, Hawksmoor.

Technology and Architecture

RB Since you received your architectural education, a major revolution in production techniques has occurred in architecture. How did the introduction of the computer and tools like CAD and Photoshop influence your own work and the way that you conceive architecture?

DC For us, the process is obviously very important. I am always very nervous about the influence of computer simulation and, to some degree, the tendency to replace idea with image. It is a very dangerous tendency, but quite difficult to resist. Clients want to see what the buildings might look like very early now. And they want to get that sense probably before you have even decided. There is also a great danger for the team in the office that, once having produced an image, they will assume there is no need to have a concept. As long as you have an image, you do not have a concept. That is a dangerous idea, because we now produce images that look very convincing and somehow give viability to a project. In the days before you had that, viability was guaranteed only by continuously testing it intellectually and through discussion and description, and that could, in a way, create a more rigorous atmosphere, whereas the montage can create a less rigorous atmosphere, because everybody can relax and say, well, this looks really nice. Later, you realize that the project has been developed and that there was never an idea.

RB Can you fight this tendency?

DC That is what we try to do. We have a way of resisting more and more the requirement to produce that type of image and have always used physical models a lot, because I do not have any trust or interest in virtual simulations.

RB This raises a very important issue. Architects are accustomed to and capable of reading plans and models, which is not necessarily the case for clients. So, by using computer technology in architecture, you are able to present a project like a TV commercial, and this might be easier for the client to understand.

DC If it is a way of communicating with a client and it is used as a tool. Then I don't think it is so dangerous, as long as you know why you are using it. It is more dangerous when the client is a group of people, and the process of choosing a project becomes a beauty contest. At that point the most powerful image wins, not necessarily the best concept.

RB Computer technology and modern means of communication allow us to be anywhere at anytime. Particularly in architecture, this fact leads to endless discussions about the global and the local. I would like to focus this question explicitly on the production process in architecture. As someone who is building all over the world, is your choice of construction and materials in any way dependent on the local market or the local traditions of the various countries you work in?

DC I think that there are cultural prejudices, opportunities, and climatic considerations that occur everywhere. There is a tendency to globalize technologies. For example, if we are doing an office building, we know that there are going to be certain companies that are doing facades and are working all over the world. The tendency is to make everything the same and that is inevitable. There are cultural considerations which sometimes resist that tendency. This may have to do with regulations; for instance, German regulations are enormously different from the American ones. There are things that you can technically do in England that you certainly cannot do in Germany. Of course, there are some materials that you

Palace of Justice, Salerno, Italy

feel comfortable with; we know that if you build in concrete in Switzerland you will probably get a good result, and we know that if you build with concrete in Spain that result will not be quite so good.

RB Does this also determine your choice of materials or the techniques that you use?

DC It may. Getting good quality concrete in America is even more difficult. So there are always things that push you one way or another in terms of your decisions. But you know we have overcome the need to limit ourselves to only certain technologies and materials when building in a certain location. It is possible to do a concrete building in America and it is possible to do a wooden building in Spain. The location does not dictate your starting point.

RB What are the meanings of borders or thresholds between cultures for you?

DC As an office working between London and Berlin, we are all interested in this opportunity to explore several cultures. We take different qualities from different cultures. This is an increasing advantage and privilege that our culture offers us.

Difference is not only inescapable; it is also enjoyable.

RB Do you also feel sometimes you have to overcome that?

DC Yes, completely. Every condition has its different issues, and each culture has its different situations, whether that is a different point of view culturally or different professional or procedural issues. Every place has different conditions, both good and bad. And I don't have much time for the idea that one place is better than another – I am often sitting in Berlin with teams when they say that in Germany it is terrible because of this or because of that. Try working in Italy, try working in America, you will sit there and worry about different things. So just take all the good things and enjoy them rather than complaining about the bad things. God made sure that we had all a fair distribution of qualities.

Understanding the Foreign

RB You did your first major building not in England, but in Japan. How did you get your commission there?

DC I did a shop for Issey Myake, the fashion designer here in London, which he liked. So he invited me to go to Japan and I spent one year doing different shops for him, which professionally was not very interesting; to be honest it was quite difficult. But culturally it was very fascinating. It coincided with the bubble economy, and because of that climate, and because I was spending so much time there, I was able to get other projects.

RB Why was commercial work like this professionally not interesting for you?

DC Because they were little shops, and it was difficult to understand how to operate professionally in that situation. Doing a shop interior, in any case, has limitations. And doing many of them in department stores was really not very interesting architecturally. It has more to do with branding and interior design, which was not something I was specifically interested in. I wanted to do shops when it gave me the opportunity to do something quite architectural.

RB Kenneth Frampton once went as far as calling you a Japanese architect because of your great sensitivity to and understanding of the Japanese culture. Do you think that nationality has any importance for your own personal understanding and the way that you do architecture?

DC The strange thing is, I did my first building in Japan. So professionally, I had not established a position and was much more open. Had I built a few buildings in England and then been invited to go to Japan, maybe what I would have done would have been similar to what I had been doing in England. Instead, I had to design my first building in Japan, not sure whether I was an English architect doing an English building in Japan, or whether I was an English architect doing a Japanese building in Japan, or maybe something in between. So that is one consideration The other, if I make a generalization about the British, is that we are quite good at going to other parts of the world and enjoying them, in finding something there, and in absorbing other cultures. I think the reason why the British became big colonists was not only because of their power, but also partly because of their island mentality and their openness to other cultures. The history of Europe has been such that the French, the Spanish the Germans had to define their own nationalities, and I think in England we have been a bit more relaxed about that. The island condition sometimes allows you not to have to keep defining your own character. Again, all generalizations are dangerous and they are obviously not completely true. But I do think that the English have been quite good at going somewhere and being quite open, and that is also to a certain degree my own history.

Dolce & Gabana Stores

RB Did this work in Japan also change the way you conceived architecture once you came back and built in Europe?

NinetreeVillage, Hangzhou, China

DC Yes, I think so, it must have. Especially their idea about space, and their notion of making space connect to the outside. That is a very Japanese approach. I benefited greatly from that experience.

RB While you were practicing in Japan, did you experience the cultural context as really foreign compared to what you were used to in Great Britain? And did you try to translate this into your architecture?

DC It is completely alien. I've been there more than forty times, but I still find it very difficult. I adore it and I really enjoy being there, but I still find it very difficult to understand anything, not just linguistically. Everything is different in many ways. What I was interested in was what things people could be held in common. That was a very important lesson to me. If you do certain things, in a way it does not matter whether you are German or English, Japanese, Chinese, or an Eskimo. There is still a certain comprehension, and the more you deal with physical things and experiential things the less you are subject to cultural confusion. The sea, for example, is enjoyable in any country. Light coming through a window is not something only the English enjoy. A reflection on the water is not something which is culturally enjoyed in one place and not another. I look for things, which are, if you like, common. And one of the things which I enjoyed very much in traditional Japanese architecture was the connection of the inside and outside, and that was something I played with. This is also where the reference to Ando comes in, because he was doing this and he was the person I looked to. He was the person I had to look to, to identify those traditional qualities, and who had found a way of expressing them in modern architecture.

RB Did you feel the presence of a native tradition in architecture in Japan?

DC Yes and you do continuously experience the presence of a different sensibility. Say someone puts a cup of tea down in front of you, and they turn it just a little bit, you recognize that if they put it down, they do it with care; you realize that this is a very different way than a Western person would do it. There is hardly a single thing which happens there that is not really loaded with cultural difference. What I enjoyed and have taken from Japan is the idea of giving importance to normal things and elevating them: placing of a cup of tea is invested with importance, not just in a tea ceremony but also in a coffee shop. They look for ways to make the normal things very special. And for me that is a very important lesson.

RB This shows your careful observation of daily life and the rituals within it. Can you use this as a source for your own architectural work?

DC I think that should be true for everything. I think that all architecture is a frame within which daily rituals are lived out, and the responsibility of the architect is to create the right frame for us to do those things. It is possible that architecture can make those activities and rituals of daily life more enjoyable.

Image Credits:
Christian Richters, p. 310–311
Hélène Binet, p. 312
Dennis Gilbert, p. 315
All other images by
David Chipperfield Architects

Structure as Architecture

Cecil Balmond London

In conversation with Ruth Baumeister and Sang Lee

Ruth Baumeister How would you describe the relationship between architecture and structure in your work? It certainly would be different from what we know as a traditional relationship between architects and engineers.

Cecil Balmond For me, there is no such relationship between architects and engineers. In my opinion, it never enters the equation, because in my view structure *is* architecture. That does not mean that it is all of architecture, but it is a part of architecture. Engineering is the calculation of structure. All my work with people like Rem Koolhaas, Daniel Libeskind, Toyo Ito or Enric Miralles has been, essentially, what Rem calls the input of a conceptual rigor.

Essentially, when working with an architect, I try to understand at an early stage the premise of the architectural hypothesis for that specific situation; then I subvert it, transforming or taking it somewhere else completely. The architects that I work with expect this. We are collaborators. Later on, it is just a matter of words whether we are labeled engineers or architects. I contend that structure *is* architecture, because I see structure as a punctuation of space – episodic and rhythmic. These are wholly architectural concerns.

I feel that I am interrogating space when I carry out a design. I look for patterns of movement for the eye. I look for metaphors. I negotiate these through very strong and clear conceptual diagrams of a process.

RB I think that is very important, because, over the years, when I looked at your diagrams, I found they were very clear and needed almost no words… It is obvious that they are the driving agent of your work.

CB Exactly. In fact, when I put together my recent book, *Informal*, I first fell into

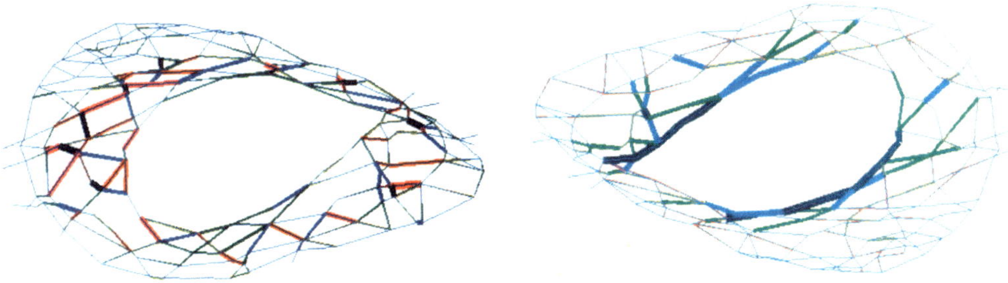

Roof Structure Analyses, Chemnitz Stadion, Chemnitz, Germany

the trap of thinking about pictures, text, layout and all that. The designers I was working with realized that the diagrams were really the story, rather than the photos. So we devised the book in such a way that the diagrams provide the key part of the story. The text simply supports the diagrams. When we had photos, they were just fillers – unlike most architectural books, which fundamentally rely on pictures.

SL So the diagrams become a more effective interface between yourself and an architect. A kind of meeting ground… How do you see the role of narratives in architecture? Narratives, or simply put, telling a story or using something analogous to what can be readily recognized. For example, at some point you mentioned a cloud or a forest for a certain structure.

CB They become headlines, often. When I worked with Peter Kulka and Ulrich Konigs on the Chemnitz Sportstadion in 2002, and we were initially discussing how we would work it out, Kulka talked of "cloud," "earth" and "forest." I do not imitate nature or have any such narratives, so I stripped away the metaphors and used simple abstract diagrams. Since the word "cloud" meant "turning." I did, for instance, also put down "turning" at the relevant place. What is the essence of "cloud"? It leads to rotations, arc upon arc. The word "forest" denotes serial planting, and we created this by duplicating a grid and rotating it, using the scatter of the nodal points for inclined column positions.

RB Going back to the first issue you mentioned – the relationship between architects and engineers – I would like to ask something more. Does there exist a distinction between content and form, since both architecture and structure must strike a balance between these two primary concerns? Could you call it a representational relationship?

CB A form does not stand alone. The form is *almost* a product of the content. I think that a form creates its own archetypes in our memory and emotion. We have three kinds of internal space for memory: emotional space, intellectual space and physical space. They are all interrelated, and good work brings all three together. When we bring them together, we get a different kind of space than what we are actually looking at. If you look at a building's form, and if that form is *right* for the space and for the building's purpose, then you get quite a different feeling about the building. Good architectural work always has this *other* dimension: the other layers come through – as if there were another building, a phantom building within it.

SL You just implied the issue of the *sublime*, that is, the nature of the sublime and what is beautiful. It seems that architecture, through its unique devices, influences human perception: it is something that is grand, beautiful and at the same time, perhaps, even terrifying But if you look at architecture, at least of the 20th century, in many different ways it has been about the *description* of space, not necessarily its performance.

Now it seems we are heading in a direction where the description *itself* becomes the form that actually suggests the specific instrumentation and performance at the same time. Returning to your earlier comment, you do not see the separation of structure and architecture; rather, they form one singular body that performs in a certain way.

CB I would like to comment more on the performance issue. The Kunsthal in Rotterdam is a good example of structure giving rhythm to architecture – in this case, by simply carving up the volume into four sections, letting the circulation flow through. The building is just that. Inside are many different inventions. There is a release of many structural forces and, in a sense, the Kunsthal became a kind of small catalogue of structures. What is important is the *configuration.* The configuration leads straight into metaphors, narratives and all sorts of things. I spend a lot of time thinking about configuration: it underlies our basic reading of a form.

RB Instead of applying *standards…*

CB I have never done that. When I was working with Jim Sterling, I pushed for imposing columns in the temporary exhibition gallery [in Stuttgart], which we did not have when we won the competition. I began to think that we should puncture the space, and they became the famous "ice cream cone" columns. It was not just about inserting columns because of structural necessities. It had more to do with interrupting space and not having uniform structure.

SL Of your projects, the Villa by Rem

Structure & Circulation Diagrams, Kunsthal (OMA), Rotterdam, The Netherlands

Koolhaas in Florillac describes perfectly what you were saying about performance and configuration being interrelated. The architectural form and the structural performance are so intertwined that the very existence of the building depends on all of these elements.

CB That is a great example. You cannot separate the two. How does a building levitate? We posed that question. In the whole footprint, there were only two supports to the ground: the staircase and one column. I drew all kinds of test diagrams to make it stand and levitate, but it needed a new configuration to make it work. We did not know how it would pan out: there was no previous frame of reference. It was like a ball at the top of a hill, and we rolled it off to see what would happen. If I were on the customary path of traditional design and then tried to experi-

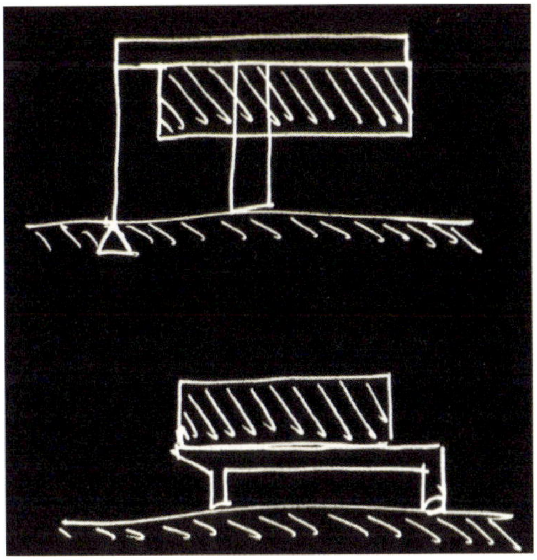

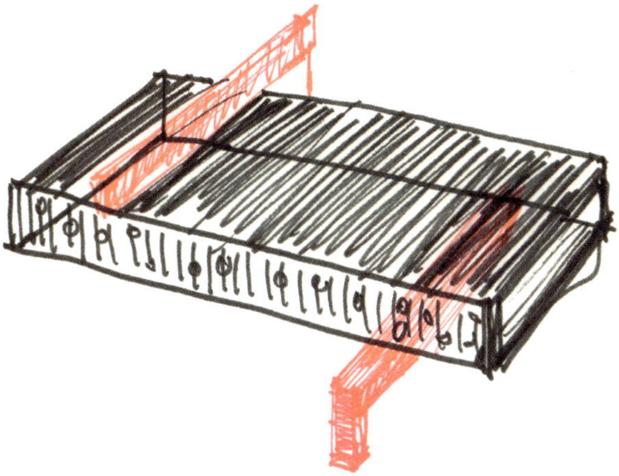

Structural Concept Sketches, Bordeaux Villa (OMA), Florillac, France

ment, I would have become a deconstructivist by definition; to get up that hill, I had to take what was known and push it apart.

SL What I thought of the house at first was how to keep the concrete counterweight in the ground and, then, how to keep the materials balanced so that they do not crack. Because as simple as the concept might have been, it actually demands very great control and working within the smallest tolerance, and that seemed a great accomplishment in it own right…

CB In the end, in pure structural terms, there was a moment when I realized the whole building hung together by only two bits. Suffice it to say that the collaboration between an architect and an engineer starts in the zone where there is no distinction between them. It is the concepts and configurations that first appear, and downstream my team became engineers and Rem's team became architects. Discussions went backwards and forwards from team to team, and then Rem and I would come together again and we would return to the configuration and re-examine it all over again.

RB Your work is deeply rooted in research. What motivates you to begin research on a new topic?

CB I believe strongly in research on two fronts: development of theory and new forms, and geometry aligned to the non-linear. The non-linear for me also embraces the linear. I am not excluding the Cartesian world. This is very important. The Cartesian world is a limiting space, even though it is a *good* space: we use it and inhabit it. However, we know that there are other geometries. I want to resurrect geometry, in the best sense of the word, in the Greek sense, as a living organizational idea, with a philosophic root. For the Greeks, it was philosophy. In addition, there is the idea of "*techne*," the art of building: architecture and engineering were all wrapped up together, coexisting without a distinction. Also, the idea of symmetry was very dynamic, not static.

I wanted to bring "*techne*" back. I take the view that geometry die, and that this led to proportion. Yet that also died – although it enjoyed some new life in the Renaissance with Palladio and Alberti. Gradually geometry became a *residue* of shapes, not an active agent. With the digital age, and

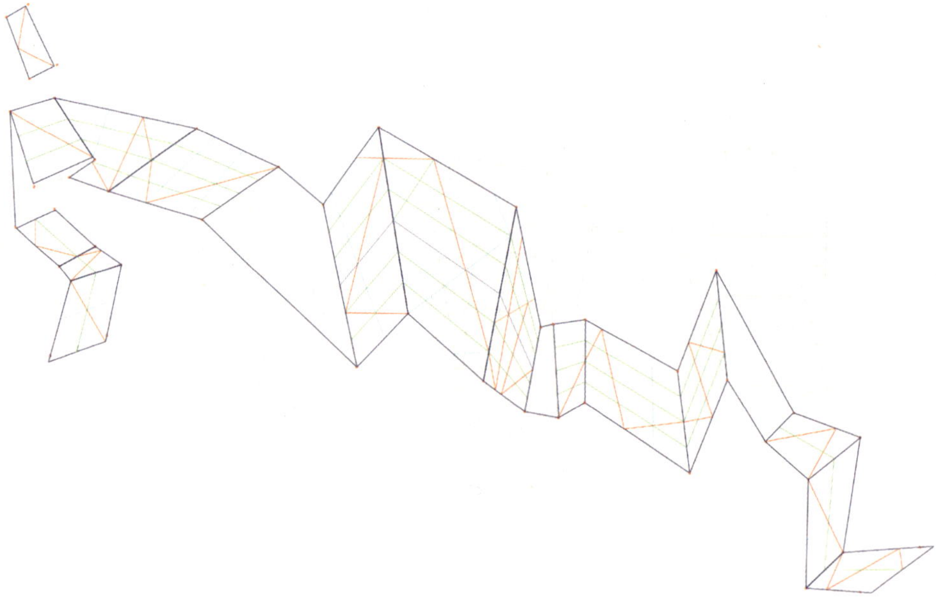

Folding Diagram, Serpentine Gallery Pavilion 2001 (Daniel Libeskind), London, UK

its yet unreleased new power, there is an obligation to articulate geometry again – geometry of a new kind that can be dynamic and vibrant for architecture. That is ultimately what I want to do: build buildings, not just theorize. I tried to educate myself in order to build and create my own manifesto and theory. Over the years, by interrogation – and that is where the teaching has come in – I have tested some very new ideas, prior to their construction, and seen ways in which I might develop a new methodology.

My main interest is to either invent new configurations or revisit the fundamental ones, as I have done with the Bordeaux villa or Chemnitz stadium.

My work at the Serpentine Gallery in London is another perfect example of my interest in *configuration*, which comes from my *root* interest in patterns, again a very old-fashioned idea that needs to brought back. For me, patterns – Libeskind completely understood this – have layers: a priority layer that is the structural pattern, a secondary layer of architectural motifs, and other successive layers which bring back the idea of ornamentation. I suppose this is a reaction to the stripped-down modernism that I really reject: more and more glass boxes, fewer and fewer columns. In the end, the minimalist pure box has nowhere else to go; it must vanish. To get *impure* again, to be rich and textural again – that is where I want my research to take me.

SL Despite all the discussions of globalism – the news media mention it day in and day out in many different contexts – there is still really no definite understanding of what it is. It seems to me that the only possibility to discuss it in architecture is through the discussion of purity or hybridity. What do you think is there materially?

RB Or how do you express intangible conditions materially and give them a body – which is in essence what architecture does?

SL Modernism came to a point where its description did not seem very relevant anymore, because of the new architectural

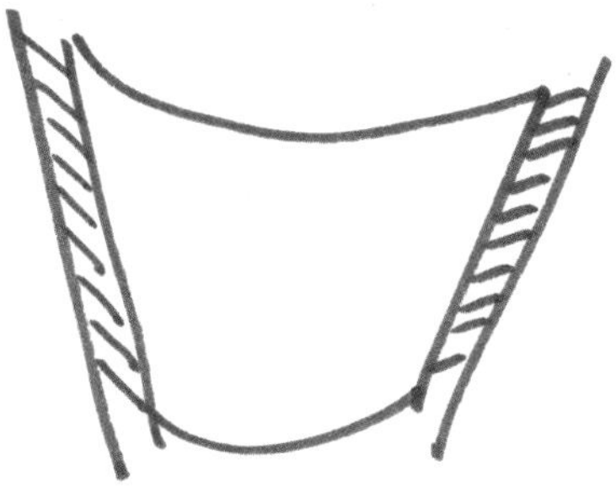

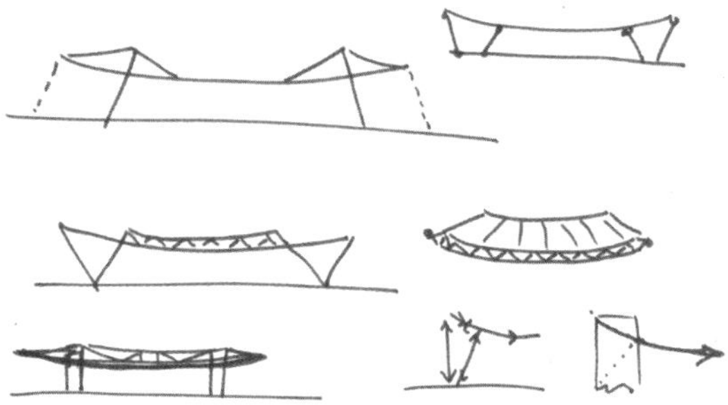

Structural Concept Sketches, 1998 World Expo Portugese Pavilion (Alvaro Siza), Lisbon, Portugal

conditions that you just mentioned, and because of the direction we wanted to move in. In the case of the Bordeaux villa, it was a process of taking something and turning it in such a way that it worked programmatically, which had a lot to do with the cultural aspects of living, and structurally, this had very serious implications for the materiality.

How do these discussions develop in your practice working with architects? What would be the force behind doing something more diverse or impure? Do you ever discuss a project in such a manner with an architect?

CB That is inherent – a given – with personalities like Koolhaas or Libeskind, and I never had to add those points. With Alvaro Siza, I found it interesting that as a purist in form-making, he understood the material significance of what I was trying to do. When I was hired by the Portuguese authorities, they wanted a high-tech, cable-and-wire structure for the Expo Pavilion. When I thought more about the sensibility of Siza's own work, I decided to do it in concrete. I made a choice that was crazy in so many ways. The span was 80 meters: you do not traditionally use concrete for such a structure, but rather light metal. It was a very big risk. I decided then that the materiality of concrete had to be denied, which ultimately gave it a feeling of levitating weightlessness. It was an instinctive move to deny the rigidity of the plate, because I knew at the same time it was in an earthquake zone. I wanted it to jiggle, if it were shaken, like a woman's necklace…

SL We are at a time when many aspects of life are driven by a certain ideology and its economy. High-rise building could be an example of the architecture of purity in that it represents a singular economic system. If you look at high-rise buildings by high-rise architects going up in the US, they have all the formulas pinned down: from curtain walls to elevator cores, they must have specific dimensions… I do not know how difficult it has been for you to pursue your own detours, so to speak, to get to an idea, and not to be forced to move on a single track…

CB My colleagues in the US cannot get architects to create anything interesting… They have all the solutions cataloged. It is what I call *extrusion* architecture. I think there is an economic imperative towards accepting a pure condition of structure and form. *Streamlining*, *extrusion*… these are manufacturing metaphors, extruding window gaskets or high-rise buildings. I reject such a pure condition, feeling that it is a by-product of an impure condition – the non-linear world contains the linear, so the impure contains the pure. I explore what appears to be confusion, diversity, variety and chaos, in order to probe what the rules of engagement are. That is what my research is directed towards.

It was very difficult to initiate this, because I also had to reject my own company and training. I was rejecting the high-tech school for which the firm had been famous. This company created it. I was rejecting the *given* condition that cannot reinvent itself anymore, that is, the crane. If you could do a crane, that was it. You cannot have a twisted or buckled crane. The main battle is always with the economy as a measurement that sets a price on fear. The unknown or the impure is always priced as a penalty condition.

RB It is always considered a danger, a danger that is primarily conceived in terms of a financial calculation, and therefore in direct conflict with capitalist ideology…

CB It is a concept that can be quite hard work to explain – for instance, in relation to a project like the Victoria and Albert Museum. You have to go further to explain it fully.

Going back to the global condition, a paradigm shift is occurring – which is global in my sense of the word, but not in the economically measured general sense – a shift in organization. From the strictly authoritarian or hierarchical models of the past, we are submitting to increasingly *informal* ones.

I was surprised to find out in 1993–95 that printing machines could run on fuzzy logic, a non-linear organization. I did not expect this of machines! Economists have known about this: namely, how non-linear organization works in stock markets. I started looking into cell growth and was interested in how the human brain works – which I always believed was a completely non-linear organization, not configured at all the way the conventional view would suggest. It is a simultaneous activity of many parts, connected to create coherence. Again, the simultaneity of seemingly chaotic local events leads to coherence, stability and equilibrium. It is essentially a turbulent medium, or a medium built with instability, such as our ecosystem. Stability is only an exception… There is a move toward a different organization everywhere. Architecture is the only discipline not to understand that.

SL When you discuss these points of view, philosophical frameworks or narratives, it seems that the discussion of globalization, especially concerning narratives, is very difficult to carry on outside the ideological and political framework of hegemonic nature as to the proximity of those to the project and how they will do it. Is there such an architecture that is in tune with the local and its dynamics, or is it necessary to cause a disruption?

I am curious as to how someone who is engaged in the delicate balance of formal and functional issues at the same time – in the middle of this ideological and cultural debate about architecture and its specific localities – would deal with it. What do you find of value in the debates on global issues in architecture, on those occasions when you work in a very different place, such as China?

CB This is a difficult question with many levels to it. As a pragmatist who, in the end, does want to build, I never dilute the ideas: they come before I engage with the local culture. However, of course there is a reference to the client's aims or ambitions: big, small, iconic, functional, etc. There is a sort of imperative to deal with, but then I find that each culture has its own negotiation process for realizing a project. In this realization process, I directly respond to the local dynamics. They are very different from each other in different phases. Some are more onerous in the conceptual phase, and some others are that way in other phases.

RB How do you find out these differences? Also trying to respond to the local could also compromise your conception and development of a project…

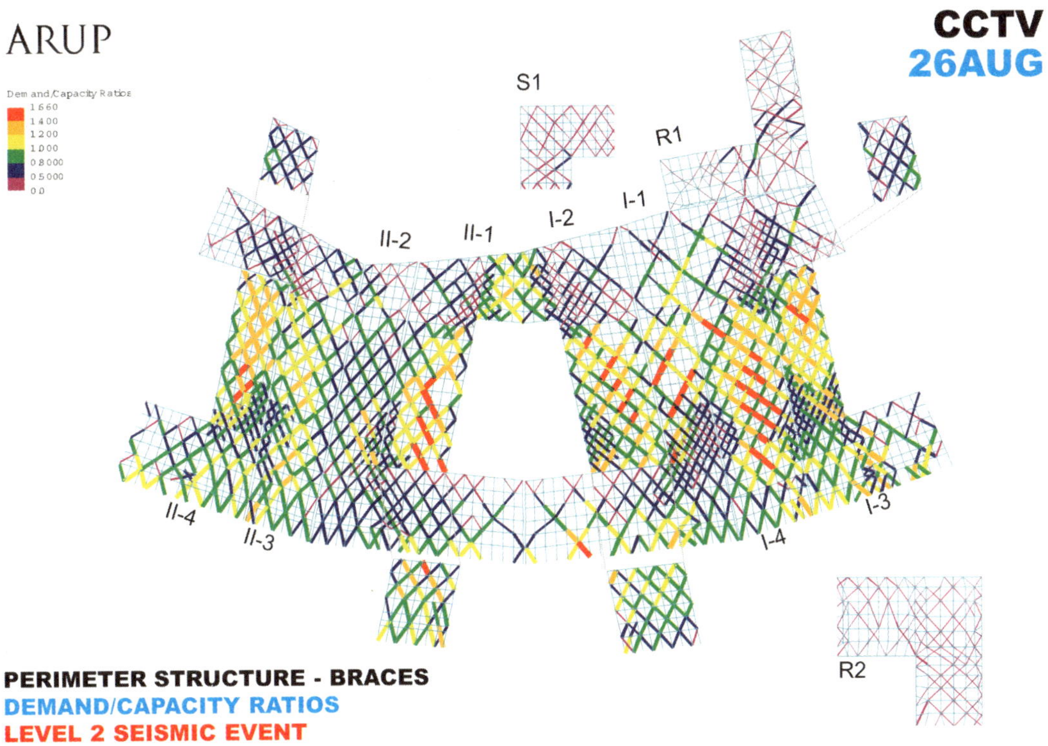

Seismic Analysis, CCTV (OMA), Beijing, China

CB There are no books to teach you how to do this. Of course there is a collective wisdom, and some would warn me against this or that: but the collective wisdom is not necessarily always true.

My Chinese clients have completely astounded me. They are very demanding, but what is amazing is that they appear – at least for now – brave and forward-looking, and they embrace work that displays a certain iconic power. They seem to be willing to take risks and undertake work that many European clients would not touch. Conversely, you have to negotiate a completely tangled web in order to procure money through the machinery of China's shifting economic structure. Grasping the infrastructure of decision-making – understanding how the decision happens – is the key to all my jobs.

I would not work in certain places in Europe where I know the infrastructure of the decision-making process is either hidden or frozen, and therefore there is no way the project that I have in mind will ever be achievable. So I have to either abandon the concept or walk away. However, if you are a professional and are smart enough, you don't put yourself in that position! It has never happened to me yet.

SL But even if that happened, it would be a speculation in itself, which may not be anymore valid than your original concept.

RB You would feel that you had not tested the idea fully and fairly, if you did not fight it through…

CB That is true. You would not know until you had gone through with it.

SL Basically, what you mentioned is that it is not the material expression in itself that counts, but how that depends on the performance of the configuration with

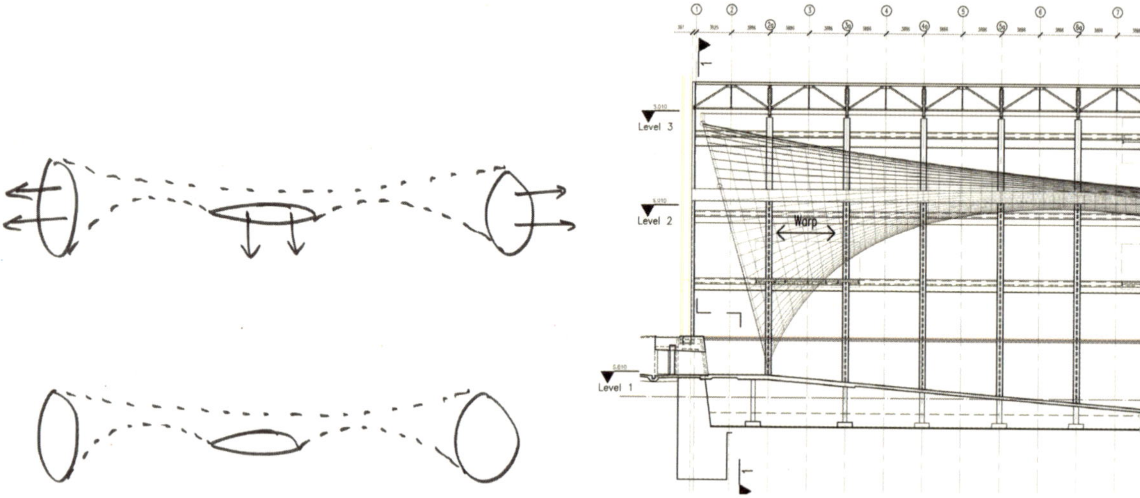

Concept Sketch and Structural Drawing for Anish Kappor's Marsyas, Tate Modern, London, UK

which you are working. Again, that ties in to the whole issue of architecture as a material practice that has no certain inherent form to it to justify it as what it is.

RB Or predictable standards. Consider how often we find ourselves saying something cannot be done because it doesn't meet the *norms*…

SL This is quite interesting to think about. If we look at the so-called post-modernist period, there was a strong consensus that architecture was what it was because of where it had come from. Therefore, many architects devoted their main effort to replicating historical *codes*. So, in terms of historical codes, what is the typical discussion when you present your scheme to a client's decision makers – such as with the V&A or CCTV? What makes the communication possible in different political and cultural contexts?

CB Almost always, I demythologize architecture. In their minds, many clients brace themselves to encounter something nonnegotiable, untouchable. I go completely the other way. My fundamental approach is to engage the minds of the people I relate to, but also to show that what has been done – whatever it may be – is as a literal constructive process of putting things together.

I would put together, for example, an animated presentation that shows the concept as something that compiles space. We, as children, all played with building blocks. We put things together. It is a fundamental human need to build and make your mark. By the end of the presentation, they engage their minds in some way with building the project. Then it becomes easier to discuss specific structural elements, not just as a given didactic. If you did present it that way, there is not much to say, other than "there it is" and "it is going to cost this much money," at which point they begin to feel uncomfortable because they cannot do much with it. You have to start to engage, and then they know that they can work with you. Otherwise you get flushed out.

If you look at my presentations, you can see how the projects are put together; and they are beautiful to look at. They have to have some poetic essence. That is a universal condition. Again, they may be culturally different but there are certain

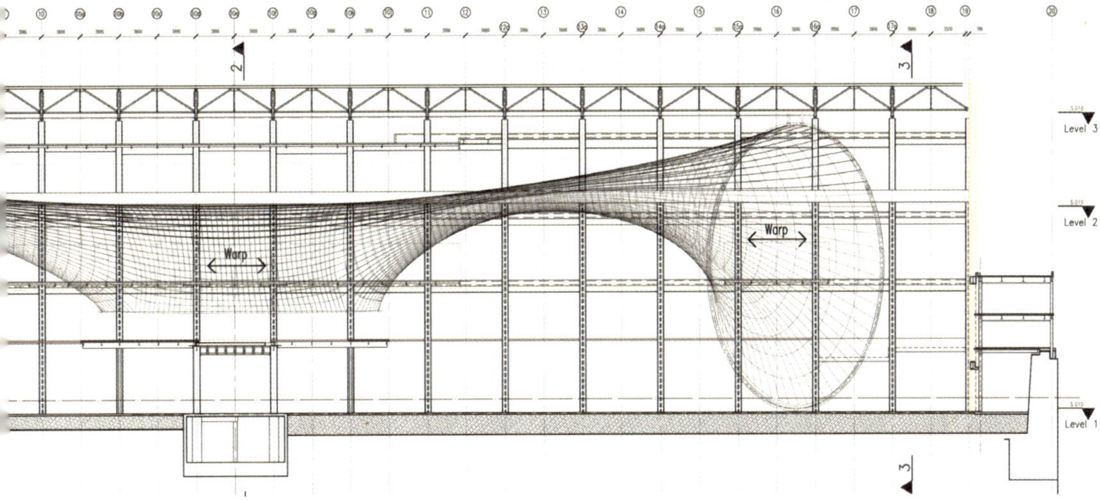

lyrical qualities that are universal. People react to these qualities, which transcend cultures.

RB In terms of the practical realization of projects, your website states that Arup has offices all over the world. Would you say that the brain is here at the London HQ? Or would you compare the idea of the non-linear world to the actual operation of Arup as a business entity?

CB We are established all around the world, and stand for a certain quality – wherever you may encounter us. In design terms, however, the Advanced Geometry Unit that I created with Charles Walker is based in London. It undertakes the research programs, and only works on very special projects that will test and develop my hypotheses.

In relation to cultural issues, technical design in particular definitely has a cultural reference. The realization of a building is wholly local. Each country is completely different. In architectural terms, the US has a very constrictive process of value-engineering that breeds conservatism. China, however, is an open territory for exploration, because they have not yet fully set up an infrastructure to support the process. Europe at present is comprised of an in-between balance of invention and functionality – a nice blend in a way – though there are also still closed pockets.

I think traditional architects – as a non-violated species with an overriding grip on the design process – are disappearing. Clients are going to others to define projects, and architects often come in merely to put their signatures on the project, rather than to control the whole process. Over the last 20 years, there has been a slow but steady decline in the power of architects to control the process.

The Advanced Geometry Unit at Arup consists of both architects and engineers, along with mathematicians and physicists: when we explore a research agenda, we need all these different specialists because of the type of research I am doing. It is led by Charles Walker, an architect and engineer.

RB How do you form a collaborative with architects?

CB In the past, usually the architect would ask if I might be interested in a project. However, nowadays it does not generally happen in this way. I am diversifying a lot more. I am working, for instance, with Anish Kapoor on a sculpture at Tate Modern, and also collaborating with the sociologist Richard Sennett, who is interested in using my ideas and theories for societal models and crowd definitions.

I am exploring radical systems of form appropriation, which can emit light and sound. What looks like architecture – when physical – is really light in another dimension. I am currently working on an installation of light in an old church in Philadelphia, and as the system can extend to music, we may also invite someone to provide this. The university I am working with has been good enough to say that they will sponsor the project, and we hope to have it built by the end of next year. This will be an exploration of organizational systems.

RB Earlier you mentioned that architecture is the last discipline to understand the shift in complexity. Also architecture takes a long time to produce and lasts very long, compared to an installation, which is a more immediate process...

CB Master planning is quite interesting: it allows you to see the ideas of an animated – as opposed to a static – sense of motion at the site. It is the processes that are interrelated, and this has to do with the individual's sense of space evolving around them as they move through it.

SL Another point of discussion is about standards. This could be related to the ideas of branding in commerce, such as Nike, which the other competing brands might have to try to match. For example, if Arup set the standard in so-called high-tech architecture, how do you see this standard functioning in difference places? Does it have any relevance in the production process of architecture or to our understanding of how things should be made? Is there some other way of establishing a minimum that needs to be achieved? Or is there, for example in China, a notion of standards to operate by?

CB Each building is a prototype. Many people would say thatwe should have standards for constructing buildings. Every few years someone produces some standards, but they change every time, because someone else always finds special conditions to counteract them. We end up with every building being a prototype between a particular architect, the site and a particular client... The ingredients keep changing... The only elements that do become standard are the compatibility of materials and the quality of workmanship – we insist on certain minimum standards there, no question.

RB Even then, in terms of your work with Koolhaas, if I look at how the buildings are detailed and the way materials are used together, it seems to me they very often depart from commonly used standards... Such conflicts, I think, are what make those buildings interesting.

CB There are standards of control, such as environmental systems, but they are technical and not architectural... You are right. There are still standard typologies, such as boxes everywhere. You cannot deny that, but that was based on the philosophy of modularity in modernism. I think that is now dead, or at least has been superseded.

We all used to iron out conflicts and unique conditions in the name of some ethic of efficiency. "All fits one and one fits all." There were endless discussions about modularity, endless discussions about cladding modules and window modules and so on. No one was talking about the architecture, but just about the modularity. Now that that is gone, no one talks about it anymore – even about the facades. We talk about the glass type, the light quality,

Algorithm Sketch, Serpentine Gallery Pavilion 2002 (Toyo Ito), London, UK

intelligent systems, transparency, reflectivity, etc. Modularity has taken a back seat because of the digital techniques that can produce any desired shape or size.

I also often hear people saying that something cannot be done. They are correct in that it cannot be done if you rely on the conventional language of the material, but the moment you reject that – and if you employ a different mix of materials – suddenly it is possible. This is the whole idea of hybridization: suddenly you find the potential within the materials to realize certain ideas. This area has hardly been touched on, and there are presently very few examples of hybrid materiality.

SL One of the most interesting parts of this whole discussion is this very issue – that the particular, the specific, determines the whole; and the general is actually a collection of the particulars.

CB Absolutely. That is innate to my understanding. Differential equations describe the world. They have two parts: the general solution and the particular solution. The particular solution fits around the exact boundaries of the problem: it is site-specific. The general solution is like an eternal engine that is just there. It is a beautiful concept: the general made real by the local condition, the particular integral.

Globalization has always been a series of collected moments. What is important is the organizational structure and the configuration that allows it to work. To deny the Chinese the right to be Chinese and work in the Chinese way is crazy. Additionally, to say that they are not global because of that is also crazy, because they are a particular part of the system. We were also trapped by the thought that globalization was about a monolithic idea that would spread world-wide. That was an erroneous idea. You have to have local outlets that are very lively, and completely in tune with at the local level, and then the internet, company structures and so on ensure the global aspect.

I would like to write more about the local culture, the local hybrid and the local juxtaposition of events as an organizational system with great flexible power. This stands in opposition to a static monolith, a centric, ordered system, or even a pyramid, where you cut the head off, and it is gone! In the case of the local culture, a more amoeba-like system grows, fits together and ultimately acts in unison. So I am very much interested in the ideas of the local, and essentially these ideas are algorithmic, repeating themselves: as the order grows, so does the interrelationship.

Image Credits:
All images by Cecil Balmond and Ove Arup & Partners

Traveling in Becoming and Being an Architect

Ettore Sottsass Milan

In conversation with Ruth Baumeister

Traveling as Learning

Ruth Baumeister Traveling as a means of inspiration, investigation and learning has always been a major component for becoming and being an architect. In the 19th century, young artists and architects traveled on the *Grand Tour* of Greece and Italy in search for what were then considered to be the classical tradition in architecture and in order to expand their vocabulary for their own domestic environment. This has certainly changed over time, but even today there is still the desire to venture into "other worlds." What is it that we can only see, observe and learn by physically traveling? One of your more important trips was to India in the 1960's. Why did you choose to go to India in particular?

Ettore Sottass India has a certain way of doing philosophy, thinking, or tricks for survival, and I was curious about that. In the beginning, I read a big book by an Indian historian, which was very exotic and appealing to me: speaking of abandoned temples in dark, mysterious forests; speaking of a different kind of religion, and peoples of various ethnic backgrounds. I was also reading poetry and writings by Westerners about the Indian religion. It was very interesting and, in comparison, I felt my life was very boring. So I went to India in search of some confirmation of cultural necessities that I thought they had and I needed at that time.

RB What exactly do you mean by confirmation?

ES By *confirmation* I mean that I wanted to see whether it was possible to live in another way than the one we were living in and whether I could have another relationship with life in general and religion. With colors, for instance; the so-called rationalistic era did not want anything to do with them. They taught us not to paint over materials because that was very corrupt. I

A blue house in India, 1988

thought the contrary. For me color is an element of life and through color you can tell stories. The Parthenon was all colors. The history of colors in Indian decoration is very important and I did not notice very much interest about the problem of colors by architecture critics and historians. I had the feeling that I had to go to a place where life and design were different from the way of the *Bauhaus*, for example, or other kinds of rationalistic approaches. It was a working trip without really having any work to do.

RB Did you travel with a specific plan in mind; were there certain monuments you wanted to see?

ES I had no goal. When you are in love, you are in love. Eventually, you have goals. You might want to go to bed, but in the beginning, you are just in love. You do not know why or what it is, you just feel it. Later on, my travel became more and more sophisticated, because I not only went to India, but to Katmandu, to Japan, to China two or three times, without having anything to do there, just for the sake of it. Travel responds to curiosity. It is an intellectual curiosity, which has to do with the idea of food, climate, and social relationships. It is another world and you travel to see what is happening there. Immediately, once there, you can see if the people are surviving or not, if they are happy or not. The happiest people I found were in the forests in Thailand. They had a small canal as a bath, they could run around... They were happy, happy people... The problem is that you do not find happiness somewhere; you have to build your happiness *while living in the life conditions in which, as it happens, you find yourself.* But you want to be happy.

RB Could you describe in more detail what you were searching for and what you experienced in India?

ES I was in search of another kind of possibility. For instance here, in our civilization, you never see a funeral as a part of daily life. There, when I looked out of my window in the morning, I could see lots of people with flowers carrying a dead body in white linen, covered with flowers. In a boat on the river, I saw them burning a body and I was very shocked. But then, I thought, how beautiful to disappear like that. They believe that smoke is the soul. Burning is a nice idea.

RB What other differences did you experience and how did this impact your work?

ES People in India develop the highest possible sense of color. If you go into shops where they sell silk, you will realize that here all the colors are plastic, but there every color is a mystery. I do not know how they make them but they have a very special sense of color. They also have a

A Wall, Hampi, India, 1991

very different sense of food. Once we went to a very small village in the desert. The most desert-like place I ever saw in my life. Sometimes there was a small valley where the very rare rain water was collecting and in those valleys some bush was growing and the bushes had berries. That was all. The people of the village invited us for lunch, and made small dishes of what they find in the desert. The food was fantastic, *molto semplice,* and very poetic in some ways. I am very much interested in food. Food is another way to tell stories.

RB With your trip to India, you entered into a world which was sensually much richer and a lot more appealing to the carnal body than to abstract rationality. Would you say this also changed your own existence?

ES Yes, exactly. For instance in the rationalist culture, if they have a table, they consider it a geometrical event. It is a surface and material is mainly thought of as an intellectual vision of the surface. I try to deal instead with the relationship that this material has with our senses. So this table, which we designed here in the office, is a volume. See how thick it is? It is not just a surface. Its volume and also its weight is something you feel with the senses. All these small elements were of no interest to the rationalists. Even though I have to say that I like the rationalists very much. I came from that culture when I was

Interior Court, Cheng Qi Complex, China, 1994

young and therefore don't deny rationalism, but I do think you have to give another form to rationalist inventions.

RB I understand your travel was prompted by curiosity to experience something that was unknown to you, or even lost. Were you also in search of another life that you could actually live, maybe different from the one you could have in your own home country?

ES Yes, exactly. I was in my 30's then, not young anymore, because the war took eight years of my life. At that time, traveling was to me a necessity. But not only to me, it was a necessity to the whole generation of 1968. In fact, it had started around the 1950's already, after World War II, after all the massacres and horrible things that had happened. We felt that there should be another kind of life. The life that brings wars was not what we wanted to go through

Cheng Qi Complex, Yongding, China, 1994

again. We wanted a more direct contact with life and existence. Therefore we were searching for places that were untouched. That was one reason. The other reason was that we were feeling too much imprisoned in outdated conditions: we needed maybe new religions. In America, it was the period of hippies and the beat generation: new religions, new ways of living, new everything.

India today is a different place and that is why I do not travel anymore. Nowadays, I find cars, radio stations and TVs, I find shops all over: it is the American way of life.

RB Does this mean that you stopped traveling entirely?

ES No, these days, I have to travel for work. At the moment we have a project in China, but I did not go there yet because I am too old and get very tired when traveling so long. I might go to see the place in spring. The project is a recreation center near Nanjing. It is very big and other architects are working there. Arata Izosaki is building a hotel nearby and Jean Nouvel some residential buildings, etc.

Practice and Traditions

RB Your work is highly esteemed worldwide. When you have so many international projects, how do you organize your office? Do you have branches or is everything done from the Milan office?

ES Basically everything comes out of here. Years ago, when the office was really big, we always had at least five different nationalities represented on our staff, because I like very much to mix cultures and architecture. Now the office is a little bit smaller, because one of my younger partners left: as always happens, young people at a certain moment need their own professional independence. They are right. I had to reduce my work in the office so that I could work more for myself.

RB In describing your office, you just said that you like the mix of cultures and the same would probably be true in talking about your work. At the moment you have a project in China. How do you go about working in a different cultural context?

ES First, I want to see the land, the climate and the immediate environment. I went to China several times before, because I love the history of Chinese architecture. The first time I flew there, I saw the round houses built in the mountains in one of those airplane magazines. But I could not read where they were and no one knew the place. Finally a young girl said that this was where her family was living and she told me where it was. When I had to return, I knew that I wanted to see it.

RB Why did you find this house so attractive?

ES From what I could see in the magazine, it was a very big complex with about fifty apartments. Later, I learned that the people living there, a very famous tribe, built it themselves. When Genghis Khan invaded from the north, people fled south and built this complex in order to isolate and protect themselves from the inhabitants. A Chinese friend of mine arranged for me to go there with a Spanish girl who was studying Chinese in Beijing. We went to one of the houses and talked to the people and a man even offered us his bed. Can you imagine that someone in a Western country would offer his bed to an unknown traveler?

It was a very big round house where all the families lived, a kind of commune. The children played in the center court; they had a small chapel in the middle and a spot where they could wash. It all came together. Not so much on the outside: that was just a wall with small windows. But in the inside it was a piece of furniture, all built of wood, with balconies also in wood, and they were sending down things in small baskets. It was very interesting, not in a superficial way, but because this was a way of living, an idea of life. More difficult maybe, but more tender. People who have difficulties develop passion.

RB How did the observation and experience of this special house and life influence your own work?

ES I might make a proposal that a town could be made of big courtyards, instead of roads. So the cars are around the courtyards, where you do not see them. Inside it is calm and there is room for trees and benches for old people. In small villages in France, I also saw piazzas like this and they were very nice. A nice system – not for a metropolis, but for a small village. This was a trip that taught me a lot of things. Maybe I cannot apply this, but I can apply this to life if not to architecture.

RB This sounds like a nice idea, but mainly, as you said, for projects on a small scale. What about the metropolis? If we stay with the Chinese example and look at the developments of cities such as Beijing or Shanghai within the last ten years, not much of this traditional architecture is left. Do you think that there is a way of saving this tradition in architecture?

ES I don't think it is about *saving* the tradition. But why design and build a town considering just the business necessities? When discussing a way of living, you cannot say you will build the underground from here to there, so the ride will take only one hour. Should every man or woman have a one-hour train ride to go back and forth every day? What do they do during this hour? I do not recommend repeating this system. I just say that probably some of the solutions in different ways, with a

CIPEA Recreation Center, Nanjing, China

very close attention to the way people are living, could make a more happy future for people than just generic skyscrapers.

RB Would you say there are certain permanent conditions that make or shape life? How do you work with these conditions as a designer or architect?

ES Yes, there are, but history is changing all the time. For instance, marriage is a permanent condition, but there are very different kinds. Eating is also very different everywhere, depending on what is available. I would say there is almost no solid starting or repeating point. In my opinion, the only thing that stays is a convention, for example that people agree that black is used when you die and white is used when you marry. These systems of conventions in different groups define them and at the same time make the group think that it is the reality.

RB Is this a permanent condition?

ES Yes, but sometimes this changes very slowly. From the laws of Hammurabi three thousand years before Christ to the ones of today, they are still "the laws," but they are different. Consider the law about sex. Ten years ago, you couldn't have seen a naked woman on TV. But today, from noon on, you can see this on TV. So you see that the laws are changing. Some still remain, for instance, you must not kill your neighbor. But then again you can identify yourself in a way that redefines the situation and say that you are in a war or that it was self-defense.

RB You just talked about your understanding of tradition, convention and permanent conditions in society. Can you also describe whether these categories have any impact on the design process,

A Wall, Los Angeles, 1987

for example the project that you are doing at the moment in China?

ES In the beginning, I saw the site because they sent me some photographs and they told me what the program was. Then we went through books of Chinese architecture, just to see how they used to do it. They used to build into the landscape, small elements connected to small roads, so that you feel you have traveled in the landscape and not just in front of a monument. Then they have different materials and different traditions in the sense that they are much related to the earth, very much as in ancient times. Because this was a possibility, I did not need to build a skyscraper. I asked to let us try to break it down, to build a small village. So the Chinese were very happy, because in some way they had also had this in mind.

RB It seems that they could identify themselves with the project, on the one hand and, on the other, they were also fascinated by the *foreign*, the unknown aspect that you could bring into the project because you come from another cultural tradition. In other words, why do you think people in China would hire Ettore Sottsass to design their project?

ES Yes, you are right in some ways. Again, it was not only the tradition; it was a way of approaching the space more generally, the relationship with nature, and so on. As I said, I do not copy tradition, but to me tradition is nourishing. Nourishment in Italy comes from having pasta; but you have to cook it and you do that in many different ways. You know that you are repeating the effect, since you have pasta on the table and you do something with it.

A tradition is often modified and I think that it is a patrimony of knowledge. There are different possibilities and you have to discover this. You should have the vocabulary. In the 18th century for instance, when Italian architects went to the court of the Czar in Russia, they brought their own ideas about richness, power and so on. It was an export of a way of life that the Czar liked.

Personal Experience

RB I would also like to address your trips to the US after the war. In general, I feel that you are very critical of American culture. There, even more than in Europe at that time, one could observe a loss of the values you were searching for in your travels to India. What was the reason for you to travel to the US?

ES First of all I am very "critical" of everything including myself. Anyway, you could say that these two worlds, India and the US, have nothing to do with each other. But I went to India later, in 1956; whereas I went to the States in 1951. I think that the trips to the States also gave me the reason for later going to India. I wanted to see another possibility, another way of life. From my American friends such as Ginsburg and others I learned that you could do things that are not necessarily always in opposition.

I first went to America in 1951. At that time, I was quite poor. I had an opportunity to fly to the US, because of my first wife, Fernanda. She was a writer, working, in particular, on the current American situation. She won a stipend and so I went to America with her, even though I did not have the money.

Before this, I had met George Nelson here in Milan and he said to me he could pay me if I came to the States and worked for him. I agreed, and he offered me $125 a week, which to me at that time was an immense amount of money. So I went and worked for him. Two days after the secretary wrote me the first check, the tax people took out 30% of it. And the room, in the most horrible hotel on Broadway, cost me another $50. I had almost no money to eat and I went around eating pizzas, the most horrible pizzas you can imagine. But I was so happy to be in New York that I did not feel the poverty that much. It was part of the game to be cool.

But the main result of this trip was that finally I felt the presence of "industrial culture," in the sense of anthropology, in the sense of industrial production. When I returned to Milan, I completely changed my culture, from the idea of producing an artistic design – at that time I was painting, action painting and so on – to the idea of producing symbols of living.

RB Did you only work either in New York or on the West Coast?

ES With Barbara – the girl I met after Fernanda and with whom I've been living for the last 25 years – I went to California also because we had and still have a very good and nice friend there. He thought very highly of me and my work and so we stayed in his house in Malibu near Los Angeles. He gave us a big Buick to go around in. A very beautiful life! But there was also another reason. I was still working for Olivetti then, and they had established a relationship with La Boule, an electronics company in France, and GE in the States. Therefore, I was traveling to meetings in Phoenix, Arizona, in Los Angeles and in Paris. For every trip I did for work, I tried to spend another week traveling to see what was there. I was supposed to find a way for big companies to produce computers and other electronics. It was very difficult partly because the technical tradition was stronger than other traditions. The French had a certain idea about how the business should be run; the

Americans were changing their president every six months; and the Italians were another case.

Unfortunately, I could never bring them together; I could not even get them to agree on common colors. The Americans wanted to use some kind of white. I found it the most horrible, yellowish kind of white. It didn't seem human. In meetings with American and French designers to talk about the colors for new machines, there was simply no way of agreement. Another problem arose when I was designing a typewriter for Olivetti and wanted to slightly change the keys. I did not realize that in America there were maybe thirty thousand typewriting schools and countless secretaries using the IBM system. So, if you wanted to sell typewriters in the American market, you had to go with the IBM system. We had to keep the tradition of keyboards and there were other problems – we could probably talk another two hours about changing technological conventions. They are stronger than any kind of revolution.

RB And why, in the first place, did these companies want to cooperate?

ES Perhaps they thought that it would be nice for business to have some basic shared elements and later on to produce different machines. For instance, electronics in the beginning were built on a rack. The rack is a support for the telephone and all the elements are 59 cm. This dimension was at that time the only basic measurement used by Italians, Americans, and everywhere everyone else. But today electronics are – how should I say this – like mashed potatoes, you can use it with anything… We have electronics in our pocket. The electronic idea is used not so much to produce machines, prostheses in our life, but to produce products.

RB That is true, but still, what you described beforehand shows clearly that if you design in various cultural contexts you have to address many different issues. Developing something on a global scale means that you have to deal with so many layers of different conventions that it sometimes becomes almost impossible.

ES Yes. For most of my lifetime electronics was only used in business centers, universities and sometimes banks, where they made big calculations. The computer was as big as a room. Today that is just history, because all the industries were quick to produce something different from the others just for marketing reasons. Competition happens, not with simple instruments only, but with instruments of life and death at the same time. So, if you look throughout the world today, different places like Japan, China and others, everyone could build an atomic bomb.

RB But, as you explained before, in everyday life there are still a lot of obstacles to overcome. For example, once I had to go to London. While preparing for the meeting in the hotel, I realized that I unfortunately forgot to recharge the recorder, and in the center of London there was no chance of finding an adapter for it. This was a serious problem.

ES Yes, they will never overcome that, just as they will never overcome driving on the left-hand side. When we talk about globalization, I will say that the first thing to do is to change all the tubes that are still in inches. At the moment "globalization" doesn't mean that different traditions are meeting together to find out how everybody may survive with their own original DNA in the new environment, sometimes as barbaric as ever. "Globalization" as it works today means that different traditions meet together just to listen to "orders" or "diktats" by the most powerful army, by the most powerful of banks, of insurance companies, of religious institutions.

Image Credits:
Ettore Sottsass / Photology Milano,
p. 331, p. 332, p. 333, p. 336
Max Rommel, p. 335

Navigating the Local

Rem Koolhaas Rotterdam

In conversation with Sang Lee

Local Forces and International Practice

Rem Koolhaas There are some preliminary issues I would like to mention. One of them is that I have a very weak sense of the domestic inasmuch as I spent a large part of my youth not in the Netherlands but in Indonesia after it became independent, and thus not in a colonial but in a post-colonial situation. I studied in England and then spent 8 years in America. I would say that my entire relationship with architecture is foreign. For instance, the language in which I discuss architecture is English. When I speak about architecture in Dutch, it is incomprehensible and clumsy. I also write about it in English. As I come from Holland, my domestic environment is very limited. It is a tiny country, almost a pinprick. Those two things gave me, first, the motivation to go beyond Holland and, second, early familiarity with shifting and operating between different cultures. If you come from a limited domestic context such as Holland, you must try to overcome and expand it, and, at the same time, cultivate flexibility in dealing with the foreign.

SL In terms of the position of architecture in culture, if you think about your own practice, with projects in different parts of the world, what do you see as the relationship between those architectural projects, on the one hand, and on the other, the environment, the locality and the people involved? If you consider, for example, the CCTV HQ, how do you view it in terms of its specific locality and therefore its own cultural presuppositions?

RK I should say that in each culture we try to work within the "given" of that culture and make it influence our work to the extent that we can control it. For instance, we just finished the library in Seattle and are now finishing the concert hall in Porto. These two are extremely different buildings, and that difference is

Massing Model, Seattle Public Library, Seattle, USA

really generated by the different cultures in which they emerged. I think that is an interesting fact that people really don't recognize at this moment, namely the fact that the domestic is still very vigorous and still defines not only the political but also the material terms of a project.

The Seattle library is a project for a board of trustees, and therefore a kind of project that is based on negotiations in a country that works in steel and through value engineering. That makes it a very rigorous and harsh project. The Porto project was for the Portuguese government, and we worked with five different governments and five different administrations. In terms of the material, it is a concrete building and really is in every aspect thought out in concrete. However, looking at the political bodies and the material processes involved, you can immediately recognize that understanding the local forces can help you define the scope of and the strategies for the project.

Therefore, from those two experiences in the West, you can reconstruct both certain openness to the influence of the domestic and also a critical reading of the domestic. Of course, it is the case that in Seattle we worked mostly with Americans and in Porto mostly with Portuguese. There is always something exaggerated in the assumption that if I look at a condition, it appears foreign to me given the fact that I have an organization that also contains or is based on a number of American thinkers. And the same is true in Europe.

I am basically taking these two examples in order to talk about China. Although, in my opinion, there is no bigger leap between, for instance, Holland and America, or Holland and Portugal, than there is

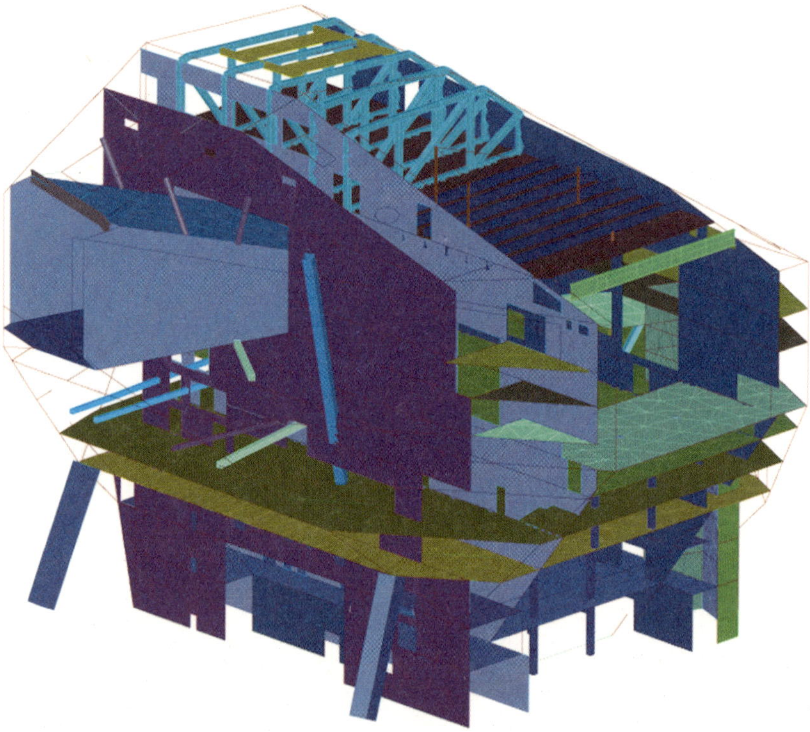

Structural Configuration, Casa da Musica, Porto, Portugal

between Holland and China, but of course somehow – I don't know whether that is a form of sentimentality or connected to any other issues – we still think that Asia is more foreign than America. For me it is not really the case. It is a bigger leap for me only in terms of assumptions, and therefore it's a more delicate operation.

Many things are the same in the sense that when we worked on CCTV we had 80% Chinese in the office. Many things are also the same in the sense that the building is very carefully designed in terms of what China can do and what is possible in China at this moment. What is also true, of course, is that the project has to engage politics in China, which is completely different from everywhere else. In that sense, I don't know whether you can call China domestic, but I deliberately inscribed the building inside the political possibilities of China, which I think don't exist anywhere else. I think that only in China could you do a building that is so intensely programmatic in terms of integrating all the process of TV production inside a single building.

I think that everywhere else the forces of the market economy would have been stronger, and the tendency would have been to take it apart. So, in that sense, it is very carefully inscribed in China's domestic political and material situation. Now I am also very deeply aware that in China there was a big controversy about the building; it generated both enthusiasm and opposition. And I've not only addressed the issue in writing; I also organized a number of events in China – they were not public events but – where I answered the opposition. We had a meeting in Chingwha University and another one in Tongji

University, where basically I invited people who were against it as well as for it to comment. In a certain way, by making myself a part of the context, it has also become less of a foreign entity.

Politics and Architecture

SL How big a factor is the political system in China when architecture is involved? It has certain similarities to the Constructivist period in Russia; the government promotes a certain expression in architecture because it needs it. Then comes a point when those needs are met, or when they think those needs are met, and the scene of architectural production completely changes. By this I mean the substance of the architectural process: how it is promoted and done and who the participants of a project would be…

RK I think it is very true. Of course I came to architecture with the example of Constructivism, which really triggered my interest in architecture, and I pursued that interest as a scholar. That also made me aware of the extent to which the political system can abuse an aesthetic movement, the possible alignments and uses that can be made of it. But what is really interesting is that this process it is more transparent in China today. One would think otherwise, given that it is a highly centralized government with a high concentration of power and control at the center. That level of transparency is there; for we are very aware of the thinking of Mao and Deng, and so are able to construct a certain history and direction in terms of the way China is moving.

For that reason, we are confident that, compared to such a situation, what happened in Russia will, in the end, be very dissimilar. There may be a similarity in terms of supporting a political system, in terms of where and how it wants to evolve

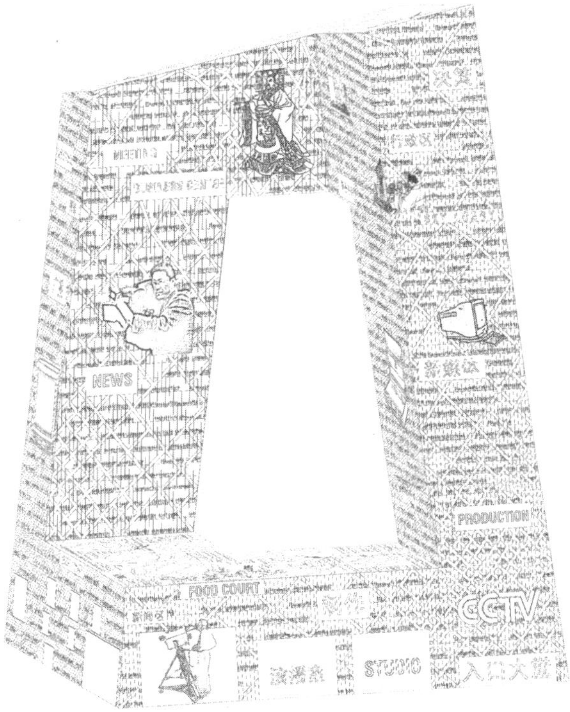

Elevation Model, CCTV, Beijing, China

and in order to support the notion that it is indeed evolving, or to create the avenues for it to evolve. But, at the same time, I think, first of all, the situation is sufficiently transparent to make reasonably sure that that an evolution is actually taking place and, second, that China is now so much a part of the international community that the kind of implosion that happened in Russia is extremely hard to imagine, because unlike Russia at the time of Constructivists, China is firmly connected with the rest of the world.

I think it is very clear that how China develops is an issue not only for China itself but also for the rest of the world, and that we all have an interest in shaping the outcome. For that reason we convinced ourselves – I am not sure everyone would follow us there – that it is more important to work on things that make a *difference* than what is harmless. Basically we have been accused in the press, or found controversial at least, not only in China but also in the West, because of what we try to do and for proposing an agenda for it. Well-known articles telling us that however understandable and excellent it may be to do such work in China, we should work on housing or hospitals. I think that there is a strong reason to work on what is crucial in terms of how China thinks it needs to develop.

Architecture as Apparatus

SL Keeping those issues in mind, what kind of differences do you see in the approach to material possessions characteristic of different cultures and political systems? What I mean by this is that each culture defines itself, or more specifically its own environment, in terms of objects – and thoughts attached to them – accumulated through its historical legacy.
Now, because of technology and its global proliferation, it seems to me that this situation is changing everywhere. Formerly there was an emphasis on objects designed for our gaze; now there is a shift towards the making of the apparatus relationship: we are surrounded by objects that contribute to a more dynamic and complex system. It seems to me that architecture is becoming increasingly about the instrumentation that provides the formulas. It is not really about space itself but about the constituents that can produce a certain notion of space. In this sense, the notion of architecture as space-making seems to have become irrelevant – although I am not sure about this point…

RK In that sense, I am really handicapped. I have always thought the notion of "space" is irrelevant because it is not possible to conceive of a notion of space without first understanding the components, or devices, that make such a conception possible. That's not really news. In addition, I always thought architecture was a device, rather than an object. It is a device, as you mentioned, an apparatus that describes and defines the human environment. Therefore in this way by nature architecture is a device or an apparatus. Maybe I am living through the advantages of my handicap, i.e. I could never bring myself to do what you call *gaze* architecture…

SL When you talk about doing an architectural project, you will necessarily involve a series of objects. Over the years, architecture as a body has been becoming less and less substantial, both conceptually and materially, that is, less of a corporeal entity. Now it has been replaced with apparatus that projects it own autonomy in a more complex manner. What has been your experience of the relationship between a particular culture and its architecture, considered in terms of the culture's relationship to material objects?

RK I think that we at OMA have been able to benefit less from the changes in culture than most architects, and that we, more than most architects, have our own agenda and interests. In that sense, it has been harder for us to benefit from, or surrender to, general tendencies in architecture. I think really interesting moments occur only when our interests intersect with others', which may be outside the profession. So it's not so much a question of whether we can capture the movements, but that we are intersecting with other movements… Maybe this is not a very good answer…

SL It is an interesting idea, the intersections between ideas, movements, materials… etc. More likely, the references we need to work with are always about the ideas of intersections. So unless you have an intersection, how would you have any reference with which you can operate… ?

Let's pursue this question, the idea of apparatus objects and digital technology: how do they affect architecture? We have the internet [now turned into a cultural apparatus], and specifically with regard to architecture, we now have all these new instruments made possible by digital technology. How do you see all that developing in architecture? What makes architecture interesting appears after all to be the seams or the intersections and joints that explicitly demonstrate and project the conditions of an idea.

RK The transitions, the frontiers… Are you implying that seamless architecture therefore cannot be interesting? I can answer with regard to place of the digital. As an office [and also speaking for myself personally], we are entirely digital and see architecture basically as information; and the information about architecture is as important as architecture itself. I think that is partly an effect of digitalization, that is, how we consider and manipulate images, information, forms, etc.

The way architecture is now expecting some kind of profound effect of the computer in terms of form making is incredibly naïve and embarrassing, and hopefully it will be over very soon… I don't know if you were in Venice and saw the Biennale in 2004. The fact that so many intelligent architects who participated in it were humiliated by all the similarities. It makes it very clear to me that this is not the way one should employ the digital. One should, instead, be concerned about one's position and the ease of establishing reciprocal movements between reality and fiction – perhaps one should even completely question that contrast.

SL I found it quite interesting that there are all kinds of architects engaged in this digital architecture; but the critique of it is misguided, because I think it is not about the generation of forms or what kind of forms but rather about why we are generating these forms… if we can talk about it in those terms…

RK I think you raise an important point. In the past ten years, criticism has totally disappeared. There is no voice left with any authority. You have to wonder why that is. There are still a few voices with authority, such as Robert Venturi and Denise Scott Brown. They still have integrity, and therefore authority. But consider Peter Eisenmann – who I think is a really fantastic guy – his voice has no authority anymore.

Why do these authorities disappear? I think that is partly related, again, to the issue of the domestic and the foreign. It is hard to define a position of authority based on the foreign because then everyone becomes so skeptical about that issue and about the possibility of having a singular vision that is able to critique different domains. I think there is a strange situation that a few have authority only in America, some other few only in Europe or only in Asia. I do not know exactly how it works but really feel that this problem is connected to this question of the domestic and the foreign.

For instance the last time criticism was connected to the domestic was perhaps with Frampton and his critical regionalism. In retrospect, it was an attractive theory, and I think that perhaps it was a better theory than he realized. I think the weakness of that theory was that it was not about critical internationalism. The world is globalizing, but in a distant valley in the Himalayas, there is a still a local culture. It is more interesting to say that in true globalization, new local conditions emerge and they are as different as they used to be just between valleys.

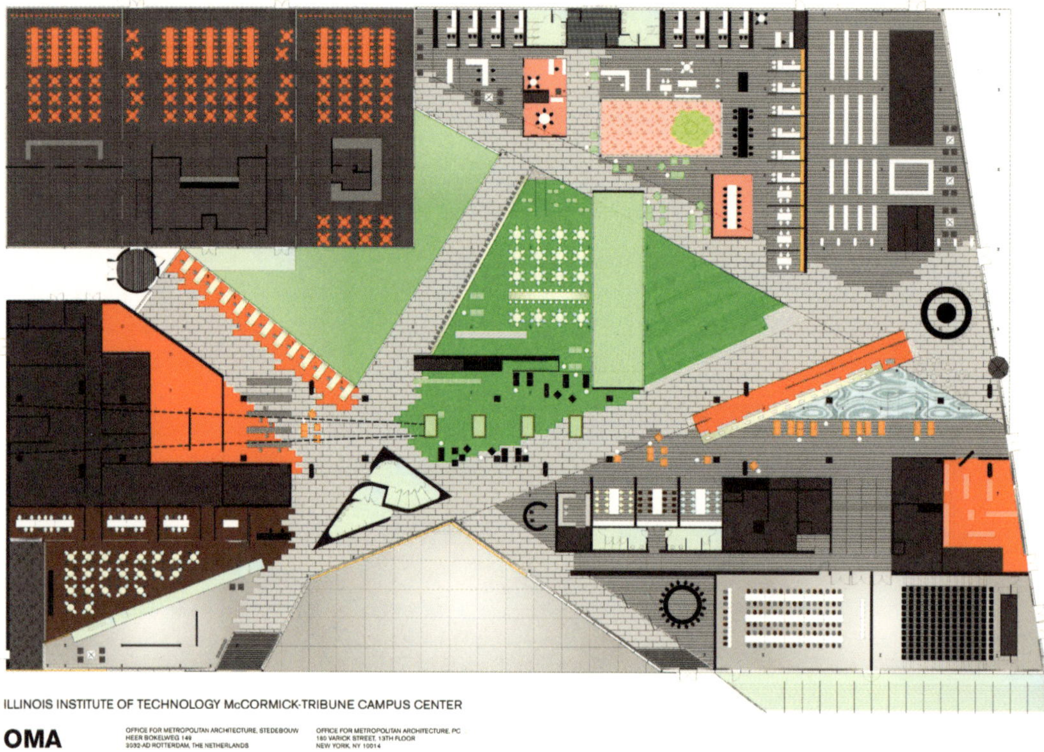

Floor Plan, IIT McCormick Tribune Campus Center, Chicago, USA

Ideas and Representation

SL Going back to the digital production of architectural forms, I think one of the more important points to address is the idea of the separation of body and skin, so to speak. Somehow, it seems much of architecture today is about the skin, about the wrapper, or how to present it. How would you approach this idea, architecture as information, or architecture as a collection of membranes that work as a filter in different contexts? You can have a set of programmatic issues that needs to be wrapped, filtered and transformed. Do you approach the idea of the skin and envelope relationship in any particular way relative to a given context?

RK I think it is very important simply in terms of the fact that we are very aware of the context and realize we have to operate in the field, which is defined by the interpretation of digital architecture as a fluid architecture, and partly by the definition of architecture as wrapped condition. But it doesn't mean that we always conform to it. In certain cases, we try, with more or less success, and sometimes we fail. In certain cases, we propose alternatives. I think the three conditions you just mentioned [i.e. wrapped, filtered and transformed] happen at the same time. Therefore, it is not a very pure condition.

Even though I don't want to talk about the Prada store as if it were a potential answer to anything, when we did their store in LA, I think we were more successful in the design process in terms of doing one thing as an apparatus and basically having almost an independent media aura device that was a part of it but not defining it in its entirety. Sometimes we do two extremes without making any attempt to join them.

The concert hall in Porto is a harsh concrete building, but inside there are things definitely defined as skin, for example the interior of the concert hall.

SL How about the student center at IIT? Again, this project seems heavily dependent on the definition of skin, bringing us back to my comment on apparatus architecture…

RK That is where we really tried – actually I think it is one of the more interesting projects recently, in a certain way more radical than the Seattle library – to experiment with information architecture and skin architecture. On the other hand, we have always done that. It's always a matter of emphasis and improvisation.

SL To move onto something a bit more practical, how do you work with different professionals within a project? For example, when you start a project, do you already have some ideas and try to test and develop them?

RK No. We never have ideas at the beginning. Ideas only emerge in our discussions and are dependent on the individual case. In initial discussions we always have engineers, almost always graphic designers and almost always either an anthropologist or a curator. We almost never have a purely architectural thinking process. Impurity is for me a very important part of what we do, because we do not consider architecture as one of those hermetic disciplines. Architecture is in essence about formulating and assembling a version of information and its flows. Therefore we cannot work on a project unless we have a team that can deal with many different aspects, and I think the majority of those aspects today are not architectural in the traditional terms of the profession.

SL How do you assess the condition of impurity? One way or the other, being impure always assumes a type of measurement. If you were doing a project in, for example, Mongolia, what you do there, one way or the other, will end up being *impure* relative to the domestic condition as the natives see it. But how do you actually *measure* such a degree? Or is there any difference in the degree of impurity?

RK What we try to do in every case is to have not only the project but also a narrative of it – I think the narrative is almost equally important. I think the narrative is really the record of both the generation of the project and also our own best attempt at describing how we measured it, our own exploration of all the issues we thought relevant. This is not an attempt to create criticism, but it allows us to be more explicit about what we think we did, and to provide our own assessment.

SL The process of writing or describing a project is a way of qualifying for a specific architectural project…

RK First, a presentation and then writing… In our case the two are always very close.

New York City

SL What do you think about the practice of architecture in New York City, when you consider it now, compared to when you published *Delirious New York*? You also have an office in the city. How about the new WTC project, for example?

RK I have written about it in WIRED, and also in *Content*. I thought the original WTC buildings by Yamasaki were unbelievably inspiring indications of the future, even though at some point they looked really old-fashioned. I was deeply attached to them as symbols but also as realities.

I think the architecture proposed at the WTC site right now is not able to generate new impulses the way it could and should. It is no one's fault, neither Libeskind's nor the city government's. But I think if you look at Venice and the WTC site and try to find a way to relate the two, you can see that our vocabulary in architecture has become very rich but our arsenal has become very limited…

SL New York works in such a way that financial priorities supersede almost everything, probably more so than in most other metropolitan centers. Architecture in New York is a part of that condition. Therefore, somehow you have to deal with that situation one way or the other. How do you operate in such an environment with your New York office?

RK If you look at the Harvard Book on Shopping, you'll see it was all about the theoretical assessments of how the conditions of architecture and the conditions in which architecture is produced are changing today. Especially in a city like New York, they are all about the shift from the public to the market economy and therefore the predominant influence of money.

But if you look at what we did recently as architects – a house for a disabled person in Bordeaux, a public library or a public concert hall – you see that basically our work is, in a way, old-fashioned; and with the theories we have been articulating, such as the "Generic City" and "Junkspace," we are really trying to describe what's happening in the world.

The critics have been unbelievably stupid in the way they have reacted to all this… They still talk about us as people without a moral compass, people who would do anything. Critics have interpreted all this work and its intent – including the one about Lagos looking at the *human* conditions of that region – as ultimately corrupt and a form of selling out because they misunderstood it as a proposition to promote further and legitimize the kind of commercial architecture they thought we do. Though, now, people seem to be less negative about it. Maybe their architecture is different or has nothing to do with it anymore…

The irony is that we theorized about this but never actually built very much for developers… Maybe we will do it. Still, we have to address whether we could do what is good or significant enough under the circumstances. I don't think it is hopeless per se, but I think many architects are not doing it in an intelligent or honest way.

Architecture and Business

SL But don't you think that has a lot to do with the fact that the relationship between architect and client really hasn't changed all that much at least since the time of the Medicis?

RK Yes. I totally agree.

SL It happened – that separation, or the disappearance of political and social subjugation, between those who commission and those who produce, for example Mozart – in music, literature and fine arts. It seems architecture may be one profession which has experienced very few changes in this regard…

RK Architecture is still Mediaeval economically. This is what I have been trying to say. Every profession has been inspired by the market economy but we are still stuck in some kind of esoteric guild.

SL Do you see the possibility of an architect being a financier or a developer?

RK There have been examples, of course. But I am not sure if that is really an essential question. I think I would feel very uncomfortable if I could do whatever I wanted. I would not be very challenged or inspired. Thinking about money and development in a different way is, I believe, both possible and necessary. We have a new managing director, who used to be a banker and worked for Schiphol airport. We want to address that issue now…

SL Let's talk about working with limitations or obstructions – not only as potentially negative influences but also as new opportunities for inventive solutions. How have they affected your projects?

RK I would say, if you look at the world and draw a map of risk taking, in America it would be 0, in China, 90%, in Europe, may be 55%, and in Africa between 0 and 100%. I think risk taking is a very important factor…

Inevitable Aspects of Architecture

SL Going back to China, given the nature of the government there, what kind of limitations did you have to work with…

RK When we were working on CCTV we were very surprised by a number of things. First of all, the transparency of the process: it was a competition and very clear, with no political influences at work. Then, once our scheme was chosen, we had to go through an approval process. But the process was much less political than we would have assumed. For a long time, there was a conflict between the city of Beijing and the client. It is on a 4-block site, and the client wanted some kind of a clear definition of the perimeter, while the city wanted the traffic to continue to go through it.

Getting approval for the structure also involved a long and very arduous process, but it was very systematic and transparent. In that sense, the linearity and the transparency of the process have been very revealing of conditions in China: no political power pushed us around or interfered…

SL Thus you didn't have to deal very much with political agendas?

RK It was a new situation, and handled very carefully. Things were taken seriously, and there was also an awareness that the world was watching and that certain processes had to take place before the next step could be approved.

Let us consider another issue concerning architecture in developing countries. Here, too, the question of digitalization arises. It seems many architects dispose of a certain repertoire and that they exploit it by re-configuring or re-collaging bits and pieces. Because of digital technology, it is easier than ever to produce a narrative that is specific to local conditions… Do you find that is becoming a problem, or does it sometimes lead to positive results?

RK In fact it is often re-shuffling… What we are increasingly trying to do is to escape, to a certain extent, from all the inevitable aspects of architecture. So we started AMO. With that, we are trying to really engage conditions that in themselves imply and demand completely different conditions. For instance, we are working on the Hermitage Museum in St. Petersburg, and we are determined not to introduce anything new but, instead, to work completely with the existing conditions. We are also trying to create in Beijing an area characterized not by renovation but by preservation. Thus, in a number of fairly unique conditions in the world, we are trying to find a relationship beyond architecture. The stupidity of architects is that they are always compelled to change the existing conditions, even those existing conditions may be superior to what they could offer as an alternative. Here most architects try in a very simplistic way either to preserve them or to transform them into some cultural operations – or just simply look at it as Lego blocks they can play with. As architects it's important for us to find the domestic conditions that enable us to sever ourselves from that kind of predictable pattern.

SL In that case, isn't it a problem – this might not be relevant – that the evidence of your work may not be visible?

RK No. On the contrary, it's a positive issue. You can do what may be invisible on the surface but eventually improve the local condition.

SL It seems to me that it is not necessarily about the physical heft of architecture but about how it is skinned. Probably one project from OMA I am referring to and appreciate most in this regard is the student center at IIT. I thought that was a wonderful play between the Miesian cut, an attempt to slice an empty space by very simple moves, and the idea of skin as interface...

RK I agree. But that kind of project became *unreadable*. People still write about heroic things...

SL Given that, do you think about the monumentality and symbolism of architecture, and whether or not there is a place for monuments anymore? When the CCTV project is completed it will be a monument, even though from what I have seen I don't think it has been designed as a monument. It is very anti-monumental in many ways, a kind of a *disembodied* monument...

RK Of course, you are always aware of those contradictions. It is always interesting to proceed and see what happens. We don't claim to know exactly the effects or the results of what we do.

SL With "Junkspace," you described architecture in which all kinds of debris and found objects coagulate into an obese body, the pathological architecture we see often defined by all kinds of uncontrollable found objects of value engineering...

RK Yes. Found objects, but at the same time the combination of architects ignorant of that fact and yet insisting on architecture's autonomy. It's really the grotesque interaction between the form and the formlessness and how our architects' naivety always forces us to make such new *contributions* that are simply junk...

Image Credits:

All images by Office for Metropolitan Architecture

Introduction
pp. 13–33

1 Homely vs unhomely, unknown, uncanny; whereas „heimelig" means "homely," in a more literal sense; „heimlich" also contains the notion of being secretive or clandestine.
2 Ernst Jentsch: „Das Unheimliche" (1919), Georg Simmel: „Die Grossstädte und das Geistesleben" (1909).
3 „Das Unheimliche" (1919).
4 Originally published in "Global Village: Perspektiven der Architektur" 8. Internationales Bauhaus Kolloquium, Weimar, 14.–16. Okt. 1999; Rf. Thesis: Wissenschaftliche Zeitschrift der Bauhaus-Universität (Weimar, nos. 4–5. vol. 46, 2000), pp. 16–25.
5 Mafredo Tafuti and Francesco Dal Co: *L'Architettura Contemporanea*. (Milan: Electa. 1976); the 1st English edition: *Modern Architecture* (New York: Harry N. Abrams, Inc., 1979).
6 A Dutch word for "call center."
7 Both books were published by Actar, Barcelona, in 2000 and 2002, respectively.
8 This description of Aoyama Dojunkai has been provided by Arie Graafland, Antoni van Leeuwenhoek Professor of Architecture Theory at the Delft University of Technology.
9 "Border Patrol Finds Body of Mexican Man" in *Arizona Daily Star*, "Tucson Region" section. 23. Aug. 2006.

A. Dirlik: Architecture of Global Modernity, Colonialism and Places
pp. 37–46

1 Even the politically sensitive (and radical) Kenneth Frampton has nothing to say on colonialism and architecture in his important survey, *Modern Architecture: A Critical History* (London: Thames and Hudson, 3rd edition, 1992). It may be that colonial architecture does not attract much attention in architectural history because it was derivative, and produced nothing of great originality, as Robert Fermor-Hesketh writes in his Conclusion to Fermor-Hesketh (ed.): *Architecture of the British Empire* (New York: The Vendome Press, 1986), pp. 186–215, pp. 186–187. But this world also indicates an obliviousness to the spaces of everyday life as opposed to celebrity-oriented architecture, something that many writers complain about. Paul Rabinow and Gwendolyn Wright have also pointed out the important part the colonies played as "laboratories" for experimenting with different kinds of urbanism which could then be transported back to the "mother" country. Rabinow: *French Modern: Norms and Forms of the Social Environment* (Chicago and London: University of Chicago Press, 1985), and, Gwendolyn Wright: *The Politics of Design in French Colonial Urbanism* (Chicago and London: The University of Chicago Press, 1991), esp., chapter 2. Especially important, in light of recent developments in architecture associated with postmodernism and "critical regionalism," is the effort in colonial projects to "localize" architecture. I will say more on this below.
2 Roxann Prazniak: *Of Camel Kings and Other Things: Rural Rebels Against Modernity* (M. D. Lanham: Rowman and Littlefield)
3 Shanghai has become the talk of the town, so to speak. For recent reports that are typical of the excitement – and anxiety – created by the Shanghai boom, see, Ron Gluckman, "Bright Lights, Beautiful Bund," http:// www.gluckman.com/ ShanghaiBund.html, 3 pp.; Pepe Escobar, "Shanghai Rocks," Asia Times Online http://www. atimes.com/atimes/China/ EJ29Ad02.html, 5 pp. For the architectural frenzy, see, Ron Gluckman, "Flash City," http://www/ gluckman.com/ ShanghaiArchGeo.html, 8 pp.
4 The role of global architectural firms in the making of the new Shanghai is documented in Kris Olds: *Globalization and Urban Change: Capital, Culture, and Pacific Rim Mega-Projects* (Oxford and New York: Oxford University Press, 2001). Note especially the photograph (p. 214) of foreign architects atop a Shanghai skyscraper, presumably discussing the city's architectural future.

5 Jan Morris writes of the development of British imperial architecture that, "by the middle of the 19th century the imperial architects had been feeling their way towards some such synthesis... of east and west, rulers and ruled. The old hubris of Empire was somewhat tempered by then, and the imperialists yearned for forms which would imply a blend of command and cooperation." Jan Morris: "In Quest of the Imperial Style," in Fermor-Hesketh, op. cit., pp. 10–31, p. 25. The "hybrid" style that emerged went by the name of, variously, Indo-Saracenic, Hindu Gothic, or Renaissance Mogul. But the British retained control over the style, as well as over native architecture. See, Thomas Metcalf: *An Imperial Vision*, op. cit. Similar considerations guided the institutions and architects who produced a "Sinicized" modern architecture in China – especially in the case of universities and even churches. See Jeffrey W. Cody: "Striking a Harmonious Chord: Foreign Missionaries and Chinese-Style Buildings," Architronic v5n3, http://architronic.saed.kent.edu/v5n3/v5n3a.html, 22 pp.

6 "China's Vice-Commissioner," *World's Fair Bulletin*, 4.10 (Aug. 1903): 2–5, p. 3. Atkins & Dallas. A list of their projects, along with sparse biographical information, is available in Zheng Shiling: *Shanghai jindai jianzhu fengge* (Architecture in Modern Shanghai) (Shanghai: Jiaoyu chubanshe, 2003), pp. 323–325. I am grateful to Laikwan Pang for locating this source for me.

7 "Dedication of China's Building Site," *World's Fair Bulletin*, 4.12 (Oct. 2003): 2–4, p. 4.

8 The principal of the firm was assistant engineer to the Shanghai Municipal Council. See, "China," in Sir Banister Fletcher's *A History of Architecture*, 19th edition, edited by John Musgrove (London: Butterworth's, 1985), Chapter 35, pp. 1233–1243, p. 1233–34.

9 Peter R. Rowe and Seng Kuan, Ti/Yong: *Architectural Encounters with Essence and Form in Modern China* (Cambridge: MIT Press, 2002), pp. 24–55.

10 The first major study of the history of Chinese architecture was Liang Sicheng and Lin Whei-yin, *History of Chinese Architecture,* published in 1943.

11 Not only did foreign architects play an important part in the production of this style, but Chinese architects themselves were trained abroad, mostly in the US, and took modern architecture as their point of departure in the creation of a new synthetic architecture. Many of the Chinese architects also worked for foreign firms, which already were "transnational" in their practices. See, Rowe and Kuan, pp. 55–107. See, also, Jeffrey W. Cody: *Exporting American Architecture, 1870–2000* (London: Routledge, 2003).

12 Wang Zhenxia: *Zhongguo jianzhude wenhua licheng* (Cultural Formations of Chinese Architecture)(Shanghai: Renmin chubanshe, 2000), p. 298.

13 Barry Hirst and Graeme Thompson: *Globalization in Question: The International Economy and the Possibilities of Governance* (Cambridge: Cambridge University Press, 1996).

14 For some groups in the population, this may appear as an ideological reversal of an earlier colonialism, when many leading figures found in colonialism an escape from the social transformations wrought by industrial capitalism that undermined hierarchy at home. These colonialists found kindred souls in native elites, whose collaboration in turn made possible the "indirect rule" characteristic of British colonialism. See, David Cannadine: *Ornamentalism: How the British Saw Their Empire* (Oxford and New York: Oxford University Press, 2001).

15 For the TCC, see, Leslie Sklair: *The Transnational Capitalist Class* (Oxford: Blackwell Publishers, 2001). The emergence of such a class does not imply equal distribution of power globally, needless to say, which still is centered in the triad areas of North America (New York), Western Europe (London) and East Asia (Tokyo). Architectural practice is very much part of this structure, not just because firms follow capital around the world, but they are themselves part of a structure of global capital. The centers of global architectural practice are New York, Los Angeles, Chicago and San Francisco, in North America, plus London and Tokyo. Architectural education itself is transnationalized, with students from around the world flowing to institutions in these areas, while these institutions become centers for studying global cultures in order to achieve greater transnationalization in design and, we might add with a bit of cynicism, access to local markets. P. L. Knox and P. J. Taylor, "Globalization of Architectural Practice," Research Bulletin 128 of the Globalization and World Cities Study Group and Network, http://www.lboro.ac.uk/departments/gy/gawc/rb/rb128.html, 14 pp. In some senses, architectural education and practice have been transnational all along, as witnessed by the training of Chinese architects earlier in the 20th century (See above, note 12). For the implications of globalization for architectural practice, see, Nina Veregge, "American Designs on the Pacific Rim: International Architectural Practice and 'Globalizing Cities,'" http://www.geog.ubc.ca/iiccg/papers/Veregge_N.html, 6 pp. For the premises guiding international studios, see, Julio Bermudez and Robert Hermanson, "Pedagogical Migrations: Constructing New Worlds," Proceedings of the 1998 ACSA International Conference (Rio de Janeiro, Brazil: ACSA Press, 1998), pp. 66–71. In one such studio, between American and Argentinian institutions, students ("immigrants") "engaged in the art of exploration, colonization and occupation of new praxial territories." (p. 66).

16 Robert Rydell: *World of Fairs: The Century of Progress Exhibitions* (Chicago: University of Chicago Press, 1993), p. 62. For further discussion of the colonial in the global, see, Arif Dirlik: "The End of Colonialism? The Colonial Modern in the Making of Global Modernity," in boundary 2 (forthcoming).

17 For this collaboration in the case of Shanghai, see, Fulong Wu, "A Real Estate Development and the Transformation of Urban Space in China's Transitional Economy, with Special Reference to Shanghai," in John R. Logan (ed.): *The New Chinese City: Globalization and Market Reform* (Oxford: Blackwell Publishers, 2002): pp. 153–166. Other essays in this volume offer important discussions of the urban poor, and the new geography of poverty. See, part IV, pp. 183–226. There is, of course, also a new geography of wealth that brings together the Chinese and the foreign elites.

18 Rem Koolhaas, "Architecture and Globalization," in William S. Saunders (ed.): *Reflections on Architectural Practices in the Nineties* (Princeton: Princeton Architectural Press, 1996), pp. 232–239, p. 237. Examples of such projects are to be found in an interesting volume, *Shanghai Reflections. Architecture, Urbanism, and the Search for an Alternative Modernity*, edited by Mario Gandelsonas (Princeton: Princeton Architectural Press, 2002). A collaborative project between Princeton, Hong Kong University and Tongji University in Shanghai, the volume discusses designs for the renovation of a catholic church (Dongjiadu) and its environs in Shanghai. Despite the "alternative modernity" in the title, and cliches about "an 'alternative modernism' that China has recently forged as it opens itself to a dialogue with the West," what is remarkable about the various commentaries and the projects discussed is how little they have to do with their immediate human context, including the residents of the area discussed. The "dialogue," of course, is initiated and carried out by Princeton, in this case, and is exemplary of the studios that US architecture schools have been conducting around the world – much as US business schools are opening up branches abroad.

19 A celebratory note on the tabulae rasae is audible in another work co-edited by Rem

Koolhaas with colleagues in the Harvard Design School (this one on the Pearl River Delta in Southern China), when the editors write that, "only the tabula rasa can enable possibilities otherwise hindered by the traditional obligation of cities and architecture to be stable." Chuihua Judy Chung, Jeffrey Inaba, Rem Koolhaas, Sze Tsung Leong (ed.): *Great Leap Forward* (Boston: Harvard Design School, 2001), p. 111. Nancy Lin, the contributor of the section on "Architecture" (mainly in the first Special Economic Zone of contemporary China, Shenzhen), writes that, "Architecture has become a channel for investment. Building construction has become such a profit-making tool that a building's primary function is no longer to serve human needs. The traditional concepts associated with architecture such as aesthetics, comfortable environment, advanced building technology, and human occupancy have been suppressed to emphasize quantitative measures like construction volume, capital investment, construction time, cost and profit return." (p. 165). Also see below, note 34.

20 John Morris Dixon, "The Crisis of Confidence in Architects and the Public Design Review Process," in Saunders, op. cit., pp. 20–25, p. 21. For the Shanghai slogan, see, Susan Balderstone, Qian Fengqi, and Zhang Bing, "Shanghai Reincarnated," in William S. Logan (ed): *The Disappearing "Asian" City: Protecting Asia's Urban Heritage in a Globalizing World* (New York: Oxford University Press, 2002), pp. 21–34, p. 28.

21 Paulina Bozek, "Architecture and Globalization: the relation of Space to Place," http://www.vitamin-free.blogspot.com/globalization.html, 4 pp., p. 3.

22 I am grateful to my colleague James Mohr for coming up with this term.

23 Hans Ibelings: *Supermodernism: Architecture in the Age of Globalization* (Rotterdam: NAI Publishers, 2002), p. 66. Marisa Carmona refers to the present growth of urban areas, associated by many with globalization, as a "second modernity." See, Carmona, "Introduction: The Return of Large Plans: From the First to the Second Modernity," in M. Carmona (ed.): *Globalization, Urban Form and Governance: Fifth International Conference, Alfa-Ibis Proceedings* (Philadelphia: Coronet Books, 2001), pp. 15–31.

24 Koolhaas, "Architecture and Globalization," pp. 237–238, 239.

25 Richard Marshall: *Emerging Urbanity: Global Urban Projects in the Asia Pacific Rim* (London: Spon Press, 2003), pp. 193–194.

26 Ibelings, op. cit., p. 151. Prominent among Ibeling's "non-places" are airports. He should derive great comfort from the recent movie, "The Terminal," where Tom Hanks not only manages to make (build) the "twilight zone" of the terminal into a place, but becomes a working-class heron in the process.

27 Kenneth Frampton: *Modern Architecture: A Critical History*, (London: Thames and Hudson, 3rd edition, 1992), p. 314.

28 I have already discussed this problem from the perspective of modern China. For illuminating studies covering other areas, see, Lawrence J. Vale: *Architecture, Power and National Identity* (New Haven and London: Yale University Press, 1992), and, Sibel Bozdogan: *Modernism and Nation Building: Turkish Architectural Culture in the Early Republic* (Seattle and London: University of Washington Press, 2001). For a discussion of the postcolonial production of national identity in architecture, see, Vikramaditya Prakash, "Identity Production in Postcolonial Indian Architecture: Re-covering What We Never Had," in Gulsum Baydar Nalbantoglu and Wong Chong Thai (ed.): *Postcolonial Space(s)* (New York: Princeton Architectural Press, 1997), pp. 39–52.

29 For a splendid global overview, see, Liane Lefaivre and Alexander Tzonis: *Critical Regionalism: Architecture and Identity in a Globalized World* (Munich: Prestel Verlag, 2003). This overview is critically sensitive. The two articles by the editors, which trace critical regionalism historically, are focused mostly on critical regionalism as a response to universalism, but have less to say about the relationship of the regional to the national, which has been problematic all along. Bozdogan offers an interesting account for the case of Turkey, where the national both presupposed the international as its point of departure, and sought also to appropriate the internal regional. See, Bozdogan, op. cit., chapter 5, esp. pp. 255–271. Bozdogan also shows that a limited kind of critical regionalism (and associated themes of architectural postmodernity) were implicit in the nationalization of Euro / American forms.

30 Manfredo Tafuri: *Architecture and Utopia: Design and Capitalist Development*, translated by Barbara Luigia La Penta (Cambridge: The MIT Press, 1976), p. 181.

G. Mathews: Cultural Identity in the Age of Globalization: Implications on Architecture
pp. 47–54

1 This is attested, for example, by the recent series of volumes published by Cambridge University Press on "Modern Architecture and Cultural Identity," among other writings.

2 See E. Hobsbawm and T. Ranger (eds.): *The Invention of Tradition* (Cambridge: Cambridge University Press, 1983), and Benedict Anderson: *Imagined Communities* (London: Verso, 1991).

3 See, for example, Arjun Appadurai, "Disjuncture and Difference in the Global Cultural Economy," in M. Featherstone (ed.): *Global Culture* (London: Sage, 1990), pp. 295–310, and Ulf Hannerz, "The Global Ecumene as a Landscape of Modernity," in: *Transnational Connections* (London: Routledge, 1996), pp. 44–55.

4 Gordon Mathews: *Global Culture / Individual Identity: Searching for Home in the Cultural Supermarket* (London: Routledge, 2000).

5 For example, Joel Kahn: *Culture, Postculture, Multiculture* (London: Sage, 1995).

6 For example, the influential journal *Cultural Survival Quarterly*.

7 See Benjamin R. Barber: *Jihad vs. McWorld: How Globalism and Tribalism are Reshaping the World* (New York: Ballantine Books, 1996).

8 As was proclaimed by former British Foreign Secretary Robin Cook in a speech on British national identity given on April 19th, 2001.

9 Peter Hall: Cities *of Tomorrow: An Intellectual History of Urban Planning and Design in the Twentieth Century* (Oxford: Blackwell, 1988), p. 214.

10 Peter Hall, op. cit., p. 238.

11 Chris Abel: *Architecture and Identity: Responses to Cultural and Technological Change* (Oxford: Architectural Press, 2nd edition 2000), p. 170.

12 Chris Abel, op. cit., pp. 156–159

13 Kenneth Frampton, op. cit., pp. 306–307.

14 Kenneth Frampton, op. cit., p. 327.

15 Udo Kultermann: *Architecture in the 20th Century* (New York: Van Nostrand Reinhold, 1993), p. 248.

16 Quoted in "Arata Isozaki, Tsukuba Center Building" in Sabine Thiel-Siling (ed.): *Icons of Architecture: The 20th Century* (Munich: Prestel, 1998), p. 150.

17 See, for example, G. Mathews, "Fence, Flavor, and Phantasm: Japanese Musicians and the Meanings of 'Japaneseness,'" *Japanese Studies*, 24 (3), Dec. 2004, for an argument on the varieties of cultural identity claimed by musicians.

18 In his *Architecture Without Architects: A Short Introduction* *to Non-Pedigreed Architecture*, (Garden City: Doubleday, 1964), Bernard Rudofsky offers a radical brief for a democratic, unprofessionalized architecture; in his *Architecture for the Poor: An Experiment in Rural Egypt* (Chicago: University of Chicago Press, 1973), Hassan Fathy shows how such a program can be implemented.

19 Chris Abel, op. cit, p. 160.

H. Yatsuka: Fragmented Subjects in Former Colonial Cities
pp. 55–64

1 Chu-joe Hsia. (2000b). *Building Colonial Modernity: Rewriting Histories of Architecture and Urbanism in the Colonial Taiwan*, paper for an international workshop on Urban and Architectural Histories under Colonial Rule in Asia, The Institute of Taiwan, History Preparatory Office (ITHPO) and the Program for Southeast Asian Studies (PROSEA), Academia Sinica, Sept. 6–7.

2 Edward Said: *Orientalism* (New York: Patheon Books, 1978).

3 Michael Hardt and Antonio Negri: *Empire* (Cambridge: Harvard University Press, 2000).

4 Rf. *Cinema and Desire: Feminist Marxism and Cultural Politics in the Work of Dai Jinhua,* Jing Wang and Tani E. Barlow (eds.) (London: Verso, 2002).

5 "At the End of the Century: One Hundred Years of Architecture," The Geffen Contemporary at MOCA, The Museum of Contemporary Arts Los Angeles.

6 "Japanese Art after 1945: Scream against the Sky," Guggenheim Museum SoHo, September 14, 1994 – January 8, 1995.

D. Hauptmann: A Cosmopolitan View on Thinking and Being-in-Common
pp. 81–93

1 Ulrich Beck: *The Cosmopolitan Vision* (Cambridge: Polity Press, 2006), p. 26. Originally published as *Der Kosmopolitische Blick oder: Krieg ist Frieden* (Frankfurt: Suhrkamp Verlag, 2004).
On the use of the term cosmopolitan it is perhaps important to note the following passage: "This choice of words is an experiment – and an open question. Anyone who finds this meaningless, nominalistic, a form of language fetishism devoid of any sense of scientific conceptual rigour, has not grasped that actions grow out of language, one way or another, and that the total negativity of the Holocaust may well have a formative effect on history," p. 111.

2 From Aristotelian, Stoicism, Hebraic tradition (Book of Numbers), and Pauline Christianity, to Marx, Simmel, Goethe, Nietzsche, or Adam Smith and John Dewey, to name only a few.

3 See: Immanuel Kant, "Idea for a Universal History with a Cosmopolitan Intent" (1784) and "Definitive Article in View of Perpetual Peace" (1795).

4 Jacques Derrida "On cosmopolitanism," in Stephen Cairns (ed.): *Drifting: Architecture and Migrancy* (London:

Routledge, 2004), p. 58: "Kant seems at first to extend the cosmopolitan law to encompass universal hospitality without limit. Such is the condition of perpetual peace between all men. He expressly determines it as natural law (droit). All human creatures, all finite beings endowed with reason, have received, in equal proportion, "common possession of the surface of the earth." If Kant takes great care to specify that this good or common place covers "the surface of the earth," it is doubtless so as not to exclude any point of the world or of the spherical and finite globe (globalization), from which an infinite dispersion remains impossible; but it is above all to expel from it what is erected, constructed, or what sets itself up above the soil: habitat, culture, institution, State, etc."

5 Derrida, op. cit., p. 49. Derrida's challenge is not merely to rethink the notion of cosmopolitanism; it is to consider whether or not the city might be able to reorient the politics of the state. My own paper will not address the geo-political forms of policy which Derrida approaches in his work as here cited (Derrida's paper was presented in Strasbourg, 1996, to an International Parliament of Writers on the topic of "Cities of Asylum"). However, the disposition of his work, which inclines towards the individual as a member of a community of "others," remains of central importance to the argument I am presenting here.

6 A similar deliberate treatment of the terminology that surrounds the term *urban* can be seen in the work of Henri Lefebvre. For instance, his 1970 *Le Révolution urbaine,* whereby he substitutes the term "post-industrial society" with "urban society" in order to make an operative distinction, in much the same way as Beck immediately notes the distinction between the "global" and the "cosmopolitan."
It is also worth mentioning that Lefebvre also believed (see note 1 above) in the linguistic play of words, designations, terminologies, etc. in order to "open understanding" of the city to such things as "tendencies, orientations, and virtualities."
I have dealt with this in some detail in "Problematizing the Virtual: Lefebvre and the Urban Problematic," in S. Read & C. Pinilla (eds.): *Visualizing the Invisible: towards an urban space* (Amsterdam: Technepress, 2006).

7 Beck, op. cit., p. 9. It is important to note here that the term "cosmopolitanization" can take two forms: the first being something that occurs "unconsciously," its effects being generated "passively" as "side effects of global trade or global threats" (p. 19). Yet, when he applies his own prefixes, i.e. "scientific," to cosmo-politanization, he is intending to suggest a methodological (as opposed to a merely theoretical) approach to this phenomenon.

8 Beck, op. cit., p. 50: "We are witnessing an invasion of politics by culture. Dividing lines between civilizations are mutating into threats to international stability and global order. The democratic values of the West and the premodern values of the Islamic world are confronting and colliding with one another in ever more menacing and hostile ways, both within nation-states and between different global regions."

9 One might add here that Beck will consistently offer a reading of these modalities which suggests that by their own internal dichotomies they have been prevented from addressing the reality of social and cultural difference in a positive manner.

10 For Beck's account we should add to this, that it is in the form of the law and social sciences that such an "everyday" social ontology will be encountered. For those unfamiliar with *The Cosmo-politan Vision* it is necessary to note that throughout this work Beck is taking issue with methods practiced within various disciplines, specifically that of sociology, in terms of how they approach their "object" of analysis; in fact, in order to open up a new way of thinking about cosmopolitanism, Beck offers many correctives to research methods. However, commentary on this aspect of Beck's work does not fit in the limited scope of the present work.

11 Beck, op. cit., p. 48. He will here also draw a distinction between a "realistic" or "social scientific" view of the current potential of cosmopolitanism from what he sees as the idealisms ("philosophical") of past perspectives.

12 Beck, op. cit., p. 49.

13 Beck, op. cit., p. 55.

14 As a 10 year resident of the Netherlands I can offer anecdotal observation that this "principle of tolerance" has been one which is indoctrinated into the minds (if not the heart) of almost every Dutch citizen. Now the "truth" of this system, the actual evidence of its founding principle (Erasmus) has, to my mind, been greatly obscured. In fact, one might suggest that given the current pressures of socio-cultural integration this term "tolerance" has been reduced to little more than ideological rhetoric.

15 Beck, op. cit., p. 66, 67.

16 Étienne Balibar: *We the people of Europe? Reflections on Transnational Citizenship*, translated by J. Swenson (Princeton: Princeton University Press, 2004), p. 29. Originally published as *Nous, citoyens d'Europe: Les Frontières, l'État, le people* (Editions la Découverte, 2001).

17 Beck, op. cit., pp. 28–29. One way or the other, both the generic and the over-particularized alternative when taken as doctrine, Beck argues, can amount to "cultural suicide."

18 D. Hauptmann, "Turning Turning in the Widening Gyre," in OASE, issue 58: "Scratching the Surface" (Amsterdam: Sun publishers, 2002).

19 This paper does not afford me the opportunity to do so, but to address this point further it would be necessary to take issue with Beck's argument regarding either the idea of "interventionism" or "inevitability."

20 With this I would also include Bruno Latour's notion of "thinking between." See: Bruno Latour, "Why Has Critique Run out of Steam? From Matters of Fact to Matters of Concern," in *Critical Inquiry,* vol. 30, no 2, winter 2004, pp. 225–248.

21 Douglas Rushkoff, for instance, in his book *Children of Chaos* (1997), writes on a current manner of processing stimuli into information, and of information into knowledge under the terms of "recapitulation." He distinguishes the presentation of information directed at knowledge from that of data directed at the accumulation of information into categories of storytelling: "instructional" (real-life exchange of experience as a survival method in pre-history -literal), "metaphorical" (narrative exchange or experience which functions with the "like me" recognition of similarity through empathetic recognition – symbolic) of and "recapitulation" (the intentional distancing from emotional reality through "self-conscious awareness" – non representational). Of course, it is the last which interests us here for it addresses the "change in experience" which today constitutes our memory, the virtual and the real, the actualized and the lived. In other words, the "self-conscious" recognition of the "self-similar," not the "like me reflection" of parable, but the "actuated me" of recapitulation.
I have discussed this in "The Past which Is, The Present that Was," in D. Hauptmann (ed.): *Cities in Transition* (Rotterdam: 010 Publishers, 2001).

22 Beck, op. cit., p. 30. He here wishes to make clear that while the national outlook, in practice and in principle, excludes the cosmopolitan outlook, the latter, nonetheless, includes the former.

23 Beck, op. cit., p. 32. Although this will not be addressed in this paper, it is worth noting that while this sentence captures the geo-politics (see note 5), it leaves out the city (*cite*), on which, in both Derrida and Nancy, this argument heavily relies.

24 Beck, op. cit., p. 33

25 The former is typically related to history (and, rightly or wrongly, memory); while the latter assumes a primary role in discussions within most fields dealing with (global) economy, sociology and urban geography, amongst others.

26 Beck, op. cit., p. 76. In a forthcoming paper I will offer an extensive commentary on Henri Bergson's last major work, *The Two Sources of Morality and Religion* (1932) in which Bergson outlines what he understands as both the natural and cultural basis on which both "open" and "closed" societies have developed. Bergson assigns "tribalism" to a closed system; and this is an argument which Claude Lévi-Strauss used in his book *Totemism*, in order to correct Émile Durkheim's reading of the structural function of the totem as it applies to a tribe or a clan.

27 Beck, op. cit., p. 76.

28 Beck, op. cit., p. 77.

29 Balibar, op. cit., p. 29. Here Balibar goes on to argue the following hypothesis: "the two extreme situations turn out to be unlivable, if not absolutely impossible, in practice, which means they mark permeable, fluctuating borders between the normal and the pathological. One of these extremes is represented by the absolute univocality of identities, their forcible reduction to a unique social role from which we cannot deviate whether it be a private role, such as 'good' or 'bad' child, father or mother, servant or boss... or public role, or at least a role exhibited in public, such as activist, soldier, or civil servant. On the other extreme we find infinite multiplicity, the continual passage from one identity to another, which has become a certain postmodern ideology of liberation from authoritarian figures of the constructions of personality, at the risk of lending itself to another form of subjection: that imposed by the model of the universality of 'exchanges,' that is, the market and its own 'libidinal flows.'"

30 Beck, op. cit., p. 77. It is worth noting that here we might suggest that Beck is caught in the classic clash between thinkers in sociology, geography, etc... between those who claim that our current thinking, since modernity, remains temporal (i.e. Ed. Soja) and those who argue that postmodernity has, in fact, undergone the shift to spatiality (i.e. David Harvey).

31 Beck, op. cit., p. 77.

32 Jean-Luc Nancy: *Being Singular Plural*, translated by R. D. Richardson and A. E. O'Byrne (Stanford: Stanford University Press, 2000), p. 35. (Originally published as *Être singulier pluriel,* Éditions Galilée, 1996).

33 Although this current paper does not seek to provide a more comprehensive account of the notions inherent in a discussion of simultaneity and succession, I would direct the reader to the work of Henri Bergson. Bergson offers a philosophically sustained treatment of these issues, from his earliest work on Aristotle, *Quid Aristotoles de loco senserit* and *Essai sur les données immédiates de la conscience,* both of 1889, through to his well known work *Matière et Mémoire* of 1896, and perhaps most significantly, in the work in which developed a critique of Einstein's theory of space-time, *Durée et Simultanéité* of 1922.

34 Nancy, op. cit., p. 61.

35 Nancy, op. cit., pp. 24–24. "It is here that the critique of abstract rights comes to the fore. However, the 'concrete' that must oppose such abstraction is not made up primarily of empirical determinations, which in the capitalist regime exhaust even the most egalitarian will; rather, concrete here primarily signifies the real object of a thinking of being-in-common, and this real object is, in turn, the singular plural of the origin, the singular plural of the origin of 'community' itself... All of this is undoubtedly what is indicated by the word that follows 'equality' in the French republican slogan: 'fraternity' is supposed to be the solution to equality (or to 'equiliberty' ['égaliberté']) by evoking or invoking a 'generic identity.'" What is lacking there is exactly the common origin of the common. pp. 24–25. On the idea of "fraternity," Nancy is here referring to Derrida's Politics of Friendship (London: Verso, 1997).

36 In fact, we see in this work a constant opposition to the kind of analysis that takes globalization as "the" reality through which social research should advance.

37 Beck, op. cit., p. 79.

38 Balibar, op. cit., pp. 54–55. Furthering this distinction Balibar takes recourse to Jurgen Habermas' thinking on the nature of democracy as it extends beyond the traditional boundaries of the nation seen as a self-sustaining and independent body. Here Balibar, citing Habermas: "'the normative model for a community that exists without any possible exclusions,' that is, humanity. All this confirms that the logical space situated between communitarianism and cosmopolitanism, within which the 'civic nation' would be situated, is highly paradoxical; or yet that the mode in which the nation institutes belonging and engenders a form of identification through the universal, by understanding itself as the historical incarnation of the universal, hides profound antinomies." (p. 56)

39 See: Étienne Balibar, Immanuel Wallerstein: *Race, Nation, Class: Ambiguous Identities*, translated by Chris Turner (London: Verso, 1991), p. 93. (Originally published as *Race, nation, classes: les identities ambiguës*, Paris, 1988). Conversely, with regards to the "nationalization of identity," Balibar and Wallerstein write that "(a) social formation only reproduces itself as a nation to the extent that, through a network of apparatuses and daily practices, the individual is instituted as homo nationalis from the cradle to grave, at the same time as he or she is instituted as home œconomicus, politicus, religious..."

40 Nancy, op. cit., p. 41.

41 Nancy, op. cit., p. 22.

42 It is also worth noting at this point that we will be dealing with the "individual" from a philosophical perspective and not only from a political one.

43 Beck, op. cit., p. 79. He addresses this by "promoting the conceptual disclosure and empirical elucidation of the growing interconnectedness and interdependence of national spaces."

44 Beck, op. cit., p. 27: Here Beck makes reference to Zygmunt Bauman's use of the concept of "liquid modernity" (see: Z. Bauman: Liquid Life, 2005) to discuss the difficulty in sustaining a model dependent on axiomatic conceptions of a "nationally closed society" in light of notions developed under the terms of flows and networks (whether economic, cultural and / or social) or imaginary communities etc.

45 Beck, op. cit., p. 81.

46 Beck, op. cit., p. 91.

47 Balibar, op. cit., p. 26.

48 Balibar, op. cit., p. 221. Earlier in this book Balibar also outlines a notion of community, or more precisely, the possibility of a "citizenship without community" that addresses the problem of agency within more tradition models of cosmopolitanism. The problem being that a community is defined, "in fact," by an oppositional position with regards those who belong (insiders) and those who do not (outsiders). Arguing that this opposition even remains contained in the inverse proposition of an all inclusive community of all humanity; as "found in the modern cosmopolitan tradition, from Kant to Habermas," p. 65.

49 Balibar, op. cit., p. 67.

50 Beck, op. cit., p. 89.

51 Examples of this can be found in my recently edited volume entitled: *The Body in Architecture* (Rotterdam: 010 publishers, 2006).

52 Unfortunately, architecture (except in terms of policy) is too often seen to lie outside the political (this has been often argued by Foucault in his interviews, for instance, with Paul Rabinow). However, at the level of environment, which impacts experience at the site of the individual (the body-politic), architecture as urban practice remains well situated to "act."

F. R. Jameson: Globalization and Architecture
pp. 94–122

1 Rem Koolhaas, *Pearl River Delta Project*, p. 367f.
2 Rem Koolhaas, ibid, pp. 367–368.
3 Rem Koolhaas, ibid, p. 205.
4 Rem Koolhaas: *Manifesto for an Abstract "Generic City,"* p. 1035.
5 Rem Koolhaas, ibid, p. 1035.
6 *Oeuvres Completes*, Vol. 1 1910–1929 (Zürich: Boesiger 1929), p. 60.

G. Ritzer: Can Globalized Commercial Architecture be Anything but Highly McDonaldized
pp. 123–145

1 Non-commercial architecture presents a much more complex picture and would require a separate, and somewhat different, analysis. Nevertheless, it, too, is characterized by McDonaldization and nothing.
2 George Ritzer: *The McDonaldization of Society* (Thousand Oaks: Pine Forge Press, Revised New Century Edition, 2004). There have been some efforts to apply the idea of McDonaldization to architecture and cognate ideas (e.g. McGuggenheimization) have also found their way into the literature. See, for example, Roger K. Lewis, www.globalpolicy.org/globaliz/cultural/2002/1102arch.htm; http://www.islandsonline.org/pdf/shsd/Deda.pdf.
3 George Ritzer: *The Globalization of Nothing* (Thousand Oaks: Pine Forge Press, 2004).
4 A caveat: I am not an architect and have no great expertise in it. I will focus on my ideas and their potential relevance to architecture. I will, of necessity, say a few things about architecture, but they should be taken with a grain of salt and evaluated in light of this caveat. However, my conclusions are not out of line with recent books in the field of architecture. See, for example, Hans Ibelings: *Supermodernism: Architecture in the Age of Globalization* (Rotterdam: NAI publishers, 2002), an analysis that was influenced, in part, by my work on the cathedrals of consumption (see Footnote 6).
5 http://www.wordspy.com/words/generica.asp
6 George Ritzer: *Enchanting a Disenchanted World: Revolutionizing the Means of Consumption* (Thousand Oaks: Pine Forge Press, 2nd edition, 2005).
7 I would like to thank Professor Deborah Oakley for discussing these matters with me and for alerting me to them.
8 Richard Scofidio and Elizabeth Diller: *Blur: The Making of Nothing* (New York: Harry N. Abrams, 2002).
9 Marc Auge: *Non-Places: An Introduction to an Anthropology of Supermodernity* (London: Verso, 1995).
10 www.junkfoodnews.com/largerstmcdonalds.htm
11 Although they may have complexity of another type derived from a multitude of inputs from many locales. For example, scholarly work often derives much of its complexity from the multitude of intellectual inputs and the idiosyncratic way in which a particular scholar puts them together. The currently popular fusion cuisine is another, more mundane, example of complexity stemming from a variety of ingredients and recipes from many different parts of the world. Much the same can be said of great architecture that integrates styles and

materials from many different areas.

12 Hyphenating time-less here gives it a different meaning than timeless. The former means a lack any ties to a given time period, while the latter means that something has attractions that transcends any given time period.

S. Bulle:
Architecture as an Object of National-Transnational Imaginary
pp. 146–155

1 Cf. Edward Said: *Orientalism*, (New York: Pantheon Books; London: Routledge & Kegan Paul, 1978).

2 Expression by the French Historian, Fernand Braudel, in: *Grammaire des Civilisations* (Paris: Flammarion, 1987). According to Fernand Braudel, evolution and its means are linked to the general history of the World.

3 Arab Palestine extends to the east from Israel. The Palestinian Territories count around 6 millions inhabitants including West Bank and Gaza Strip.

4 One knows that the peace agreement was de facto broken by the resumption of the Palestinian Intifada in 2002. The failure of the universal peace agreements must be seen as one of the limits of the cosmopolitan state. In 2002, during the agreement of Camp David, Israelis and Palestinians mutually refused to normalize their relations. The disagreement was on the questions of Jerusalem, the absorption of Palestinian refugees, and the borders of the State. Israel evoked safety reasons and the risk of destabilization of its State. On the other hand, the Palestinian delegation judged unacceptably the proposal for a delimitation of the new Palestinian state, fragmented and reduced to three zones, the West Bank and Gaza.

5 Palestinian territories and their resources in fact still remain controlled by Israel and became more fragmented in the West Bank and Gaza. It became impossible during these five years of the peace process to move from Ramallah to East Jerusalem, which still depends on Israeli's municipality and administration.

6 Benedict Anderson has emphasized the role of imaginary and of the collective signs in the constitution of nationalism, in: *Imagined Communities* (London: Ed Verso, 1983).

7 The contribution of the Diaspora in investments and philanthropic activities was evaluated to approximately 400 million dollars in 1996 and 1997. In addition, the international community financed the whole of Palestinian modernization (the phase of pre-national construction) since 1993. With the signature of the peace agreements in 1993, nearly 3 billion dollars were allocated by the international community, directly or indirectly, to the Palestinian Authority for the construction of its institutional framework for urban management as well as for the whole of its infrastructures.

8 This notion of cosmo-politanism refers to Kant's concept on the universal idea of peace. See also the analysis of Habermas in: *La paix perpétuelle* (Paris: Ed du Cerf).

9 David Harvey's expression developed in: *The Urbanization of Capital: Studies in the History and Theory of Capitalist Urbanization* (Johns Hopkins University Press, 1985).

10 Between 1990 and 1994 during the Oslo Accord the land and real estate prices have shown a considerable increase, due to the speculation system and the monopoly of private investors, from approximately $90 000, the average sale prices of a 70m² apartment of in Al-Bireh (Ramallah). The contribution of the Diaspora to the real sector would have been 197 billions in 1997, according to Sari Hanafi, "Contribution of the Palestinian Diaspora to the Economy of the Territories" in *Maghreb-Machrek,* no 161, Novembre 1998, Paris, la Documentation Française.

11 The agglomeration of Ramallah counts around 200 000 inhabitants.

12 Since 1994, one needs a permit or must be registered as a citizen of Jerusalem by the State of Israel to be able to go to Jerusalem.

13 Deleuze has summarized the Foucaltian approach: Subjectivation is the production of modes of existence or life styles in: *Pourpalers* (Paris: Editions de Minuit), p. 156.

14 According to the terms of Appadurai: "where thre is consumption there is pleasure, and where there is pleasure, there is an agency" in: *Modernity at Large: Cultural Dimensions of Globalization* (Minneapolis: University of Minnesota Press, 1996), p. 7.

15 The veneration of the white stone of Jerusalem exists as well in the Jewish, Christian and Moslem culture. *It* will be noted that they are the English administration with the help of Patrick Geddes, know Scottish urban planner planner who contributed to his valorisation of starting from a plan of conservation in 1918.

16 Disaster of the war of 1948 for Palestinian.

17 The first constructions are within a few kilometres distance.

18 Title of a part of the brochure on history of the operation edited by *Bethleem 2000* in 2002.

19 During the period of occupation (1967–1994) and re-occupation (since 2003), a large part of the ancient heritage of Nablus, Gaza, Ramallah and Hebron, has been devastated by the Israeli Defence Forces, in military operations. The urban and labyrinthine fabric serve urban guerrilla between by Palestinian resistantce and Israeli army.

20 See the editorial of *Public Culture* no 1 (A. Appadurai ed.), University of Pennsylvania, 1988.

21 Refugees living in East-Jerusalem or in the Palestinian Territories do not have any citizenship and civil rights as they still depend of UNWRA (humanitarian offices of UN).

22 Among the critics concerning the studies on globalization and hybridization or the subalternist anthropologists, we note those of Jonathan Friedman addressed to Lisa Malkki and her studies on African refugee's identity: «Des racines et (dé)routes, tropes pour Trekkers», in *l'Homme* no 156, 2000, pp. 187–206.

23 Hannah Arendt: *The Origins of Totalitarianism* (New York: Harcourt, Brace and World, 1st edition, 1951).

R. Baumeister: The Worldwide Proliferation of Bauhaus and Its Cultural Legacy
pp. 156–178

1 Mies van der Rohe in his Inaugural Address as Director of Architecture at Armour Institute of Technology, 20. 11. 1938. Published in: Fritz Neumayer: *Mies van der Rohe on the Building Art* (Cambridge: MIT Press,1991), p. 316.
2 Orig. „Harmonisierungslehre."
3 Klaus-Jürgen Winkler: *Der Architekt hannes meyer* (Berlin: Verlag für Bauwesen, 1989), S. 89.
4 See the student rosters for Weimar, Dessau and Berlin in: Hans M. Wingler: *The Bauhaus Weimar, Dessau, Berlin, Chicago* (Cambridge: MIT Press, 1968), p. 615ff.
5 Folke Dietzsch: *Die Studierenden an Bauhaus*, Dissertation Hochschule für Architektur und Bauwesen Weimar, 1990, Bd. 2, S. 336.
6 Adolf Behne: „Das Bauhaus in Dessau" (Reclams Universum, 43, 1926/27), Bd. 1, S. 318–19; translated by the author, original German text reads as: „Die Lösungen, zu denen das Bauhaus bis heute gekommen ist, sind das Resultat gemeinsamer Arbeit der besten künstlerischen Kräfte Europas. Denn mit vollem Recht hat das Bauhaus stets alles aufgenommen, geprüft, verarbeitet, was irgendwo im neuen Geiste geleistet wurde, und in der vortrefflichen Reihe seiner Bauhausbücher... hilft es ja selbst, die kameradschaftliche Gemeinsamkeit dieser europäischen Arbeit zu verbreiten."
7 Comp. Magdalena Droste: „Unterrichtsstruktur und Werkstattarbeit am Bauhaus unter Hannes Meyer" in: Bauhaus-Archiv Berlin / Deutsches Architekturmuseum, FFM (Hrsg.): *Hannes Meyer, 1889–1954* (Berlin: Ernst & Sohn, 1989), S. 136 f.
8 http://artlog.co.il/telaviv/list.html provides a wonderful example for this phenomenon.
9 "The Architects Collaborative, Inc."
10 Walter Gropius: "Systematic Preparation for Rationalized Housing Construction (Systematische Vorarbeit für rationellen Wohnungsbau)" in journal *bauhaus*, (Dessau), Vol. 1, Nr. 2, 1927.
11 E.g. his building at Weissenhofsiedlung in Stuttgart or his community for Dessau-Törten.
12 See: Gilbert Herbert: „Fabrikgefertigte Häuser oder industrialisierte Massenunterkünfte? – das Gropius Wachsmann Paradox" in: Stiftung Bauhaus Dessau (Hrsg.): *Zukunft aus Amerika* (1995), S. 239.
13 Mies van de Rohe: „Ich mache niemals ein Bild," S. 885, zitiert nach Jean-Louis Cohen: *Ludwig Mies van de Rohe* (Basel, Berlin, Boston: Birkhäuser, 1995), S. 98, transl. into English by author, original German text: „Und ich habe gesagt, Menschenskind, mach doch die Bude gross genug, dann kannst du hin und her drin laufen, nicht nur in einer vorgezeichneten Bewegung, oder was du dir gedacht hast, wie es benutzt werden soll. Wir wissen ja gar nicht, ob die Leute es so benutzen, wie wir es gerne möchten. Die Funktionen sind erstmal nicht eindeutig, und dann sind sie nicht beständig. Die wechseln viel schneller als der Bau. Unsere Bauten, die halten für ein paar hundert Jahre."
14 Jean-Louis Cohen, op. cit., p. 99.
15 By 1939 the "New Bauhaus" had merged into the "Institute of Design" which 10 years later became affiliated with the Illinois Institute of Technology.
16 "An Organic Architecture means more or less organic society.... What we call organic architecture is no mere aesthetic nor cult nor fashion but an actual movement based upon a profound idea of a new integrity of human life wherein art, religion and science are one: Form and Function seen as One, of such is Democracy." Frank Lloyd Wright: *The Sir George Watson Lectures of the Sulgrave Manor Board for 1939. An Organic Architecture. The Architecture of Democracy* (London: Bradford, 1970; im Nachdruck London, Lund Humphries, 1939), S. VII und 47.
17 „Weben? Weben hielt ich für zu weibisch. Ich war auf der Suche nach einem richtigen Beruf. Und so fing ich ohne

grosse Begeisterung mit dem Weben an, da ich mit dieser Wahl nun einmal am wenigsten Anstoss erregte." Anni Albers in an interview with Gee Baro, in: "Anni Albers, Gee Baro, and Nicholas Fox Weber" (New York: 1977), cited according to Georg Költzsch (Ed.): *Bauhaus, Dessau, Chicago, New York* (Essen: 2000, Exhibtion Catalogue Museum Folkwang).

18 „Als ich 1924 auf den Rat Moholy-Nagys vom Vorkurs in die Metallwerkstatt hinüberwechselte, hatte man dort eben begonnen, zur Serie geeignete Gegenstände, wenn auch völlig handwerklich, zu produzieren... Zuerst wurde ich nicht eben freudig aufgenommen: Eine Frau gehört nicht in die Metallwerkstatt, war die Meinung. Man gestand mir das später und hat dieser Meinung Ausdruck zu verleihen gewusst, indem man mir vorwiegend langweilig-mühsame Arbeit auftrug. Wie viele kleine Halbkugeln in sprödem Neusilber habe ich mit grösster Ausdauer in der Anke geschlagen, und gedacht, das müsse so sein und ‚aller Anfang ist schwer'! Später haben wir uns dann prächtig arrangiert und aufeinander eingestellt." From: Marianne Brandt „Briefe and die jüngere Generation" in Eckard Neumann (Ed.): *Bauhaus und Bauhäusler* (Köln: DuMont, 1985), S. 157f.

19 See also the big international exhibition „50 Jahre Bauhaus," 1968 in Stuttgart. Instead of a historical representation of the movement, this exhibition celebrated the Bauhaus as the greatest cultural achievement in Germany of the 20th century; and for this reason the exhibition was received very well in the US, where so many former Bauhaus teachers and students had emigrated.

20 A predecessor of the more popular Situationist International Movement.

21 „Ich warne sie davor, den namen ‚bauhaus' für versuche ihrer art zu verwenden, denn dieser name ist geschützt und darf ohne bewilligung nicht verwendet werden. Ich habe die ausdrückliche bewilligung ihn zu verteidigen. Sie werden mit mir in scharfen konflikt kommen, wenn es ihnen einfallen sollte, trotz meiner jetzigen warnung den namen ‚bauhaus' in irgend einer form für ihre zwecke zu missbrauchen. In ulm wird weiter gearbeitet im alten sinne des ‚bauhaus' denn niemand weiss besser als ich, auf welche weise man im sinne von kandinsky, klee, mohogly und albers weiterarbeitet." unpublished letter from Max Bill to Asger Jorn, from 14. 01. 1954, Archive Artmuseum Silkeborg, DK.

22 Jorn: „Ob herr. Gropius ihnen die name ‚bauhaus' verkauft, gegeben oder beauftragt hat, das bleibt doch dasselbe, eine einfache geschäftsfrage. Künstlerisch und moralisch haben sie es nicht bekommen vorher sie dieselbe inspirierende wirkung schaffen, wie das alte ‚Bauhaus.' Denn die bedeutung künstlerische Doktrinen ist ihren vermögen zum schaffende tätigkeit zu inspirieren. Ist das Bauhaus nicht die nahme einer inspiration, dann ist es die nahme einer doktrin ohne inspiration. Ist es das was sie von das neue Bauhaus machen wollen.
Es scheint so... Solsche schöne federn zu nehmen um damit sich zu smücken ist das was mann kultur nennt, und ehrlich gesprochen habe ich mehr lust zu kultivieren als orginal zu sein. Das ist mann oder mann ist es wohl nicht. Ist es nicht so?
... Sie wundern sich warum ich von Bauhaus mich beschäftigen will ohne es zu kennen.
Meine deutsche kammeraden wunderen sich warum ich damit beschäftigen will, wenn sie wissen, dass ich es kenne und es darum entsagen brauchte...
Ich bitte ihnen herzlich nicht als einen idiot zu benehmen. Nach ihren angenehmen briefwechsel werden sie mich mehr und mehr lieb. J'aime les ‚petit suisses.'
Mit freundlichste grüsse Asger Jorn (grand danois)."
Undated, unpublished letter from Asger Jorn to Max Bill, probably from 1954, Archive Artmuseum Silkeborg, DK.

N. AlSayyad: Consuming Heritage or the End of Tradition
pp.179–205

1 N. Gibbs, "Apocalypse Now," *Time*, July 1, 2002.
2 D. Bell: *The End of Ideology* (New York: The Free Press, 1960).
3 D. Bell, op. cit., p. 373.
4 F. Fukuyama: *The End of History and the Last Man* (New York: The Free Press, 1992).
5 F. Fukuyama, op. cit., p. xi.
6 K. Ohmae: *The End of the Nation-State* (New York: The Free Press, 1995).
7 R. Jacoby: *The End of Utopia* (New York: Basic Books, 1999).
8 R. Jacoby, op. cit., p. 48.
9 N. AlSayyad: *The End of Tradition?* (New York: Routledge, 2004), p. 3.
10 K. Ohmae, op. cit.
11 Of course, the First and Third Worlds are not homogeneous entities. The exercise of polarizing them into dualistic categories helps only in fleshing out fundamental differences between the attitudes of the former colonizers and the formerly colonized.
12 B. Barber: *Jiha*; D. Bell, op. cit. *d Vs. McWorld*: (New York: Ballantine Books, 1995).
13 Mitchell, Timothy. "McJihad: Islam in the US Global Order" in: *Social Text* (no. 73, vol. 20, no. 4), Winter 2002, pp. 1–18.
14 There are, of course, many other classifications produced by others that may be helpful in this regard. See, for example, S. S. Fainstein and D. R. Judd, "Cities as Places to Play," in Judd and Fainstein (eds.): *The Tourist City* (New Haven and London: Yale University Press, 1999), pp. 262–267.
15 Gupta and Ferguson, "Beyond Culture: Space, Identity, and the Politics of Difference," *Cultural Anthropology*, February 1992, pp. 6–23.
16 Ibid.
17 E. Gable and R. Handler, "In Colonial Williamsburg, the New History Meets the Old," *Chronicle of Higher Education*, October 30, 1998, pp. B10–B12.
18 Ibid.
19 N. AlSayyad: *Consuming Tradition, Manufacturing Heritage: Global Norms and Urban Forms in the Age of Tourism* (London and New York: Routledge), p. 10.
20 There is a significant anthropological literature on Bali by major scholars. See, for example, C. Geertz: *Person, Time and Conduct in Bali: An Essay in Cultural Analysis* (New Haven: Yale University, Southeast Asia Studies, Cultural Report Series, 1966).
21 D. D. Hall, "Community in the New Urbanism: Design Vision and Symbolic Crusade," *Traditional Dwellings and Settlements Review* (vol. 9, no. 2, spring 1998), pp. 23–36.
22 W. Hoge, "In Stone, a Prince's Vision of Britain," *The New York Times*, June 11, 1998, pp. B1, B6.
23 N. AlSayyad, "From Vernacularism to Globalism: The Temporal Reality of Traditional Settlements," *Traditional Dwellings and Settlements Review*, Vol. 7, No. 1 (Fall 1995), pp. 13–24.
24 K. Robins, "What in the World's Going On?" in P. du Gay (ed.): *Production of Culture / Cultures of Production* (London: Thousand Oaks, and New Delhi: SAGE Publications, 1997), p. 33.
25 J.V. Iovine, "A Tale of Two Main Streets," *The New York Times*, October 15, 1998, pp. B1, B12.
26 Ibid.
27 As presented by a guide provided by Disney as part of a guided tour organized for ACSA Conference participants in April 1993.
28 Biermen, unpublished paper. "Disciplining the Eye: Perceiving Medieval Cairo" in N. AlSayyad, I. Bierman (eds.): *Making Cairo Medieval*, (New York: Lexington, 2005), pp. 1–27.
29 N. AlSayyad, "Cairo Stories." Unpublished paper presented at the conference Cairo, A Medieval City for a Modern World, held at the University of California, Berkeley, April 2004.
30 N. AlSayyad and J. Bourdier (eds.): *Dwellings, Settlements, and Tradition*, (Lanham: University Press of America, 1989), p. 28.
31 D. Upton, "The Tradition of Change," *Traditional Dwellings and Settlements Review*, Vol. 5, No. 1, Fall 1993, p. 14.
32 Nezar AlSayyad, "Hybrid Cutlure / Hypbrid Urbaism" in N. AlSayyad (ed.): *Hybrid Urbanism: On the identity*

Discourse and the Built Environment (Westport: Praeger, 2001), p. 13.

33 J. M. Jacobs, "Tradition is (not) Modern: Deterritorializing Globalization," in N. AlSayyad (ed.): *The End of Tradition?* (New York,: Routledge, 2004), p. 30.

34 G. Mathews: *Global Culture / Individual Identity: Searching for Home in the Cultural Supermarket* (London and New York: Routledge, 2000), p. 1.

35 G. Mathews op. cit., p. 4.

36 D. Gaonkar, "On Alternative Modernities," *Public Culture*, vol. 11, no. 1, 1999, pp. 1–18.

37 Ibid.

38 A. Reichl: *Reconstructing Times Square: Politics and Culture in Urban Development* (Lawrence: University Press of Kansas, 1999); and Todd W. Bressi, "Reveille for Times Square: It's a New Day for Manhattan's Traditional Entertainment District," *Planning*, Vol. 62, No. 9, September 1996, pp. 4–8.

39 J. Baudrillard, *Selected Writings*, edited by M. Poster (Palo Alto: Stanford University Press, 1988), p. 166.

S. Lee:
Architecture Remixed
pp. 214–242

1 In Plato's Republic in Book IV: Wealth, Poverty and Virtue, Socrates states, "Then to sum up: This is the point to which, above all, the attention of our rulers should be directed – that music and gymnastics be preserved in their original form, and no innovation made. They must do their utmost to maintain them intact. And when anyone says that mankind most regard 'The newest song which the singers have,' they will be afraid that he may be praising, not new songs, but a new kind of song; and this ought not to be praised, or conceived to be the meaning of the poet; for any musical innovation is full of danger to the whole State, and ought to be prohibited. So Damon tells me, and I can quite believe him; he says that *when modes of music change, the fundamental laws of the State always change with them.*" In the same discussion Adeimantus subsequently continues, "Why, yes, he said, and there is no harm; were it not that little by little this spirit of license, finding a home, imperceptibly penetrates into manners and customs; whence, issuing with greater force, it invades contracts between man and man, and from contracts goes on to laws and constitutions, in utter recklessness, ending at last, Socrates, by an overthrow of all rights, private as well as public."

2 In this article, I have used the term, "writing" to mean the techniques of producing legible objects by means of characters, diagrams and notations. In this sense, "writing" places the primary emphasis on the relationships and procedures in order to produce certain configurations and compositions between constituents.

3 Russolo, Luigi: *The Art of Noise* (Futurist Manifesto, 1913) (originally published as A Great Bear Pamphlet, Something Else Press, 1967. Reprinted by Ubu Classics), pp. 4–5.

4 Rf. *Collected Works of Velimir Khlebnikov* (Cambridge: Harvard University Press, 1987–97).

5 Rf. *Popular Electronic: Early Dutch Electronic Music from Philips Research Laboratories 1956–1963.* Tazelaar, Kees & Raaijmakers, Dick. Producers. *Aalsmeer*: Basta Music. 2004 (Basta 30.9141.2).

6 Rf. *The Worlds of Nam Jun Paik.* John G. Hanhardt. Curator. New York: Guggenheim Museum Publications. 2000.

7 John Cage: *Silence* (Middletown: Weselyan University Press, 1973), pp. 57–58.

8 Allen Weiss: *Phantasmic Radio* (Duke University Press, 1995), pp. 35–36.

9 Rf. Chapters 4 and 5, Artaud, Antonin: *The Theatre and Its Double*, translated by Mary Caroline Richards (New York: Grove Press, 1958).

10 For reflections on the critical

relationship between music and image, and the politics of mass media, see Hanns Eisler & Theodor Adorno: *Composing for Films*. (London: Athlone Press, 1994).

11 Jacque Attali: *Noise: The Political Economy of Music*, translated by Brian Massumi (Minneapolis: University of Minnesota Press, 1990), p. 5.

D. Barajas:
Notes on Architecture for Globalized Bodies
pp. 243–257

1 According to Beck, "globalization" is commonly confused with "globalism," which he defines as the "neo-liberal dictatorship of the global market that liquidates, particularly in the marginal world, the fundaments of a democratic auto-development." "Globalization" includes political, social and cultural processes and not only the domination of corporate capital or homogenization. Ulrich Beck: *Libertad o Capitalismo. Conversaciones con Johannes Willms*, translated by Bernardo Romero Carillo (Barcelona: Ediciones Paidós, 2002), p. 22.
In a similar direction, Arjun Appadurai, argues the existence of a process of differentiation and resistance within globalization itself, against homogenizing global forces, and presents his notion of "Grass-roots Globalization," or globalization from bellow. He explains the appearance of multiple ways of resistance, new re-conceptualizations of democracy and autonomy in the face of the globalization from above, corporate capital and the nation state. Arjun Appadurai, "Grassroots globalization and the research imagination," in Arjun Appadurai (ed.),: *Globalization* (Durham and London: Duke University Press, 2001), pp. 1–21.

2 Lucas Nieto. *Asi Como la Guerreo Aqui*. Video documentary, Madrid, 2004.

3 "The spatial and material systems of the city constitute not only the domain but foremost the embodiment of their cognitive system." William J. Mitchell: *ME ++: The Cyborg Self and The Networked City* (Cambridge: MIT Press, 2003), p. 19.

4 "The various flows we see – objects, persons, images, and discourses – are not coeval, convergent, isomorphic, or spatially consistent." This is what Appadurai has called disjunctures. Arjun Appadurai: "Disjuncture and Difference in the Global Cultural Economy," *The Globalization Reader* (Malden and Oxford: Blackwell Publishers, 2002).

5 Diego Barajas: *Dispersion. A Study of Global Mobility and the Dynamics of a Fictional Urbanism* (Rotterdam, Episode Publishers, 2003).

6 Ulrich Beck argues that globalization and individualization as he defines them are intimately interrelated concepts, but this relation still remains insufficiently examined. Ulrich Beck, op. cit., p. 82.

7 Marisol Rivas and Diego Barajas. "Ludwig Hilberseimer. Radical Urbanism," in: *Research for Research* (Rotterdam: Berlage Institute, 2001).

8 According to de Oliveira, it was precisely in Lina Bo Bardi's exhibition spaces where "her rupture with both the hegemonic idea of progress and the Western model of an historical linear time, homogenous, irreversible and always directed towards the future was strongest." Olivia de Oliveira. "Concerning Lina Bo Bardi," *2G International Architecture Review*, No. 23–24 monographic issue on Lina Bo Bardi, Barcelona, Editorial Gustavo Gili, 2002, p. 8.

9 For an essay about Habraken's division between infill and support, where the infill was a set of dividing panels, a few windows and doors, from which the user could choose to complete his house, filling a structure of floor slabs and columns which was the support, see Koos Bosma, Dorine van Hoogstraten, Martin Vos: *Housing for the Millions, John Habraken and the SAR (1969–2000)* (Rotterdam, Nai Publishers, 2000), p. 92.

10 Contradicting the idealized definitions of public space, derived from the insistence on unity, that mistake monumental public space for the totality of public space, this essay illustrates the parallel existence of several publics, different from that of the liberal bourgeois sphere. "In the United States, counter-publics of women, workers and immigrants have historically established civil rights but also demanded new rights based on their specific roles in the domestic and economic spheres. Always changing, these demands continually redefine democracy and redraw boundaries between private and public." According to Crawford, the concept developed by Nancy Fraser, in "Rethinking the Public Sphere: A Contribution to the Critique of Actually Existing Democracy," in Bruce Robbins (ed.): *The Phantom Public Sphere* (Minneapolis: University of Minnesota Press, 1993), quoted on p. 24 of "multiple publics, contestation and redefinition of public and private can be extended to the physical realm of public space. First, these ideas suggest that no single physical environment can represent a completely inclusive space for democracy. Like Habermas's idealized Bourgeois public sphere, the physical spaces often idealized by architects, the agora, the forum, the piazza, were constituted by exclusion. Where these single publics are construed as occupying an exemplary public space, the multiple counter-publics that Fraser identifies necessarily require and produce multiple sites and public expression. These spaces are partial and selective in response to the limited segments of the population they serve from among the many public roles that individuals play in urban society." Margaret Crawford, "Blurring the boundaries: Public space and private life," in John Chase, Margaret Crawford, John Kaliski (eds.): *Everyday urbanism* (New York: The Monacelli Press, 1999), p. 23, p. 25.

11 Anthony Vidler: *The Architecture of Uncanny* (Cambridge: MIT Press, 1996), p. 217.

12 For a complete history of the model implemented by Nokia, see Dan Steinbock: *The Nokia Revolution* (New York: Amacon press, 2001).

13 Antonio Negri and Michael Hardt: *Empire* (Cambridge: Harvard University Press, 2001), p. 292.

14 Antonio Negri and Michael Hardt, op. cit., note 9, for more information on Transformation Economy.

15 According to Lucas Bolsuis Alderman for Public Space in Rotterdam, the Belhuis will disappear soon, because the rapid process of the integration of second generation immigrants into Dutch society will loosen their ties and links with their country of origin. This opinion ignores the fact that the dynamics of migration today are very much pushed by the media and that communication technologies are a constantly creating a process of multiple migrations putting into questioin the traditional *on-way* concept of migration. Conversation with Lucas Bolsuis, member of the Rotterdam local government, Alderman for public space (among other responsibilities, affiliated to the CDA, Christian Democrats Political Party. Rotterdam, 31 of October, 2002.

Architecture of Iconography, Representation and Convention. Robert Venturi and Denise Scott Brown
pp.260–275

1 Fukui, Sadako. *Japanese Indigo Design: The Collection of Sadako Fukui.* Kyoto, Japan: Kyoto Shoin Co., Ltd., Mamoru Fujioka, 1991.

2 We described what we believed to be the fallacies of this view and the problems it engendered, in *Learning from Las Vegas*, Part II. Venturi, Robert and Denise Scott Brown with Steven Izenour. *Learning from Las Vegas.* Cambridge, Mass.: MIT Press, 1972, (revised 1977).

3 "Historical Precedents Engaging Architecture as Signs," by Robert Venturi; in Robert Venturi and Denise Scott Brown *Architecture as Signs and Systems, for a Mannerist Time*: Cambridge: The Belknap Press of Harvard University Press, 2004, pp. 24-34.

4 "Activities and Patterns," by Denise Scott Brown; in *Architecture as Signs and Systems for a Mannerist Time*, op. cit. pp 120–141.

5 "Measuring Downtown's Future." *The New York Times.* August 16, 2002.

Contributors

Nezar AlSayyad is currently the Chair of the Center for Middle Eastern Studies, the University of California, Berkeley, and the editor of *Traditional Dwellings and Settlements Review*. He is the principal of Office of Xross-Xultural Architecture, and an architect and planner in the US and Egypt.

Aldo Aymonino is an architect based in Rome and Professor of Architecture at Università IUAV di Venezia. He has collaborated with Aldo Rossi and Carlo Aymonino. Recently with Valerio Paolo Mosco, he has edited *Contemporary Public Space: Un-volumetric Architecture* (2006).

Cecil Balmond is an internationally renowned designer, structural engineer, author and Deputy Chairman of the international, multi-disciplinary engineering firm Arup. He is the author of *Informal* (2002) and *Number Nine: The Search for the Sigma Code* (1998). He is currently Paul Philippe Cret Practice Professor of Architecture, at the School of Design, the University of Pennsylvania.

Diego Barajas studies architecture at Universidad de los Andes in Bogota, Colombia and the Berlage Institute in Rotterdam. In 2003, he published *Dispersion*, a research project on mobility and areas undergoing dispersion. Barajas is a member of Space for Urban Research (SUR).

Ruth Baumeister studied architecture at the TU München and architectural history and theory at ETH Zürich. She is a researcher at the Delft University of Technology (IAAU), and lectures at the Eindhoven University of Technology. Her research topics include the Situationist International and Asger Jorn's concept of 'une architecture sauvage.'

Jordi Bernadó is a professional photographer based in Barcelona, Spain. He studied architecture at the Escola Tècnica Superior d'Arquitectura in Barcelona. He served as an editor of the journal *Quaderns d'Arquitectura I Urbanisme* between 1990 and 1999. In 1993 he co-founded Actar, a publisher of art, architecture, photography and design.

Margit Bosch received her diploma in architecture from the Munich University of Technology. She is a practicing architect and photographer and the principal of the design firm Off-White in Berlin and Munich.

Sylvaine Bulle is a sociologist and historian of urban society in the Middle East and Africa. Her research focuses on contemporary wars and conflicts, ideology and urban planning, as well as post-colonialism and space. Her book *Seeing the Cities* presents a history of Palestinian cities in tension between nationalism and international influences.

Stefanie Bürkle studied scenography at the École Nationale Supérieure des Beaux-Arts in Paris and painting at the Hochschule der Künste in Berlin. Currently she is working on a video project, 'Loi chao tu Hanoi,' on the Vietnamese living in Germany.

David Chipperfield founded his practice in London in 1984, and it currently includes offices in Berlin, Milan and Shanghai. He has won numerous competitions and awards including RIBA and AIA awards for design excellence. In 2004 he was appointed Commander of the Order of the British Empire for his services in architecture.

Paolo Desideri is a practicing architect in Rome and is Associate Professor of Architecture and Urban Design at the Università degli Studi "G. d'Annunzio" in Pescara. He has taught in many schools of architecture, including the University of California, Berkeley, the Technical Universities of Stuttgart and Vienna, and the Bauhaus in Dessau.

Winny Dijkstra is a psychologist and freelance photographer based in Amsterdam. Her photography focuses on everyday life situations and encounters. Her work has been published in numerous magazines.

Arif Dirlik is the Knight Professor of History and Cultural Anthropology and the director of Center for Critical Theory and Transnational Studies at the University of Oregon, Eugene. Dirlik specializes in the history of modern China, with an emphasis on social, political and historical thought. He is the editor of the book series *Pacific Formations*, and is the co-editor of *Postcolonial Explorations*. His current work includes studies of the Chinese revolution of 1960's as well as contemporary cultural criticism.

Jörg H. Gleiter was Professor of Architecture Theory and Design at the Bauhaus University in Weimar, Germany and the director of the MediaCity program. He is also the editor of the book series *Philosophische Diskurse*, and his research interests include architectural theory, new media, critical theory, and Friedrich Nietzsche.

Josef S. Green is a freelance photographer whose work deals primarily with American and Eastern European topics. He characterizes his work as rogue photography. His current project focuses on the representation of social issues in Verdi's operas.

Deborah Hauptmann is Associate Professor of Architectural Theory at the Delft University of Technology. Hauptmann also directs the master curricula for theory and is an assistant nestor for Ph.D. research for the Delft School of Design. Her most recent publication is an edited collection, *The Body in Architecture* (2006). She is currently working on a book entitled *On Bergson's Notion of Space* to be published with a definitive translation (with Patrick Healy) of Bergson's *On Aristotle's Conception of Place* (1889).

Arata Isozaki established Arata Isozaki & Associates in 1963. His work represents his efforts to integrate the spirituality he finds in different cultures with Japanese tradition; and he attempts to achieve this through his use of forms and materials, which he considers to be the primary means of creating a poetics of architecture.

Fredric Jameson is William A. Lane Professor of Comparative Literature and Romance Studies at Duke University. A seminal figure in philosophy and literary studies, Jameson has published numerous books on political and social thought and the interpretation of modernist and postmodernist assumptions. His best known books include *The Political Unconscious* (1981), *Postmodernism*, or, *The Cultural Logic of Late Capitalism* (1991), and *The Cultural Turn* (1998).

Rem Koolhaas founded the Office for Metropolitan Architecture (OMA) in 1975 together with Elia and Zoe Zenghelis and Madelon Vriesendorp, and he currently directs the work of OMA as well as of AMO - the conceptual branch of OMA.

Sang Lee is an architect based in Rotterdam and an adjunct professor of architecture at the Delft University of Technology. He is currently engaged in numerous experimental projects including improvisation and architectonics, language poetry and Asger Jorn's ideas on architecture.

Gordon Mathews is Associate Professor of Anthropology at the Chinese University of Hong Kong. His research encompasses culture, identity, global culture and anthropological theory. He has written and edited several volumes including *Global Culture/Individual Identity: Searching for Home in the Cultural Supermarket* (2000), *Consuming Hong Kong* (2001) and *Japan's Changing Generations: Are Young People Creating a New Society?* (2004).

Valerio Paolo Mosco received his diploma in architecture from the Università degli Studi 'La Sapienza' in Rome in 1992 and received his doctorate in 1998 with the thesis, 'Temi del Modernismo Contemporaneo.' He has edited, with Aldo Aymonino, *Contemporary Public Space: Un-volumetric Architecture* (2006).

George Ritzer is Distinguished University Professor at the University of Maryland and the author of *The McDonaldization of Society* (1993). His writings apply social theory to the everyday realms of the economy and consumption. He is the editor of the two-volume *Encyclopedia of Social Theory* and the eight-volume *Encyclopedia of Sociology*.

Frederic Schwartz is an architect based in New York. His designs include the new Staten Island Ferry Terminal at the tip of Manhattan; and most recently the master plans for Singapore Harbor and the Shanghai World Expo 2010. Schwartz founded the THINK team, whose master plan for the new World Trade Center in New York received international recognition.

Ettore Sottsass is an architect and one of the most prominent Italian designers of the twentieth century. His Memphis group, founded in 1981, became a symbol for Italian 'nuovo' design, and his works gained worldwide recognition not only for their functionality and decorative qualities but also as projections and realizations of human life and emotions.

Varakan Tipparapa is an architect and a photographer based in Bangkok. In addition to architecture, he also pursued his photography work at the Bauhaus University in Weimar, Germany, at John Sexton's workshop and at Arnold Newman's workshop in Maine. He practiced architecture and photography for several years in Chicago.

Robert Venturi and **Denise Scott Brown** are the principals of Venturi Scott Brown and Associates in Philadelphia. Venturi is principal in charge of architectural design and Scott Brown is principal in charge of urban and campus planning and design.

Hajime Yatsuka studied architecture at Tokyo University under Kenzo Tange and Sachio Otani. In 1984 he established his own practice in Tokyo. He is the president of the Urban Project Machine Co. Ltd. in Tokyo. His research interests are focused on contemporary French philosophy and postcolonial studies in architecture.

Credits

The publication of this book has been funded by the FIPSE, the US Department of Education, Washington D.C., and the Directorate General of Education and Culture, the European Commission, Brussels.

Editors Sang Lee and Ruth Baumeister
Copy Editor Harvey Mendelsohn
Book Design by Piet Gerards
and Ralf de Jong
Printed by Die Keure, Brugge

ISBN 978-90-6450-566-9